STATES *of* NATURE

The Nature | History | Society series is devoted to the publication of high-quality scholarship in environmental history and allied fields. Its broad compass is signalled by its title: nature because it takes the natural world seriously; history because it aims to foster work that has temporal depth; and society because its essential concern is with the interface between nature and society, broadly conceived. The series is avowedly interdisciplinary and is open to the work of anthropologists, ecologists, historians, geographers, literary scholars, political scientists, sociologists, and others whose interests resonate with its mandate. It offers a timely outlet for lively, innovative, and well-written work on the interaction of people and nature through time in North America.

States of Nature is the second volume in the series. The first was *Shaped by the West Wind: Nature and History in Georgian Bay,* by Claire Elizabeth Campbell.

General Editor: Graeme Wynn, University of British Columbia

NATURE|HISTORY|SOCIETY

STATES *of* NATURE

CONSERVING CANADA'S WILDLIFE IN
THE TWENTIETH CENTURY

◆

TINA LOO

FOREWORD BY GRAEME WYNN

UBC Press Vancouver and Toronto
University of Washington Press Seattle

15 14 13 12 11 10 09 08 07 06   5 4 3 2 1

Printed in Canada on ancient-forest-free paper (100% post-consumer recycled) that is processed chlorine- and acid-free, with vegetable-based inks.

Library and Archives Canada Cataloguing in Publication

Loo, Tina, 1962–
    States of nature : conserving Canada's wildlife in the twentieth century / Tina Loo.

(Nature, history, society ; 1713-6687)
Includes bibliographical references and index.
ISBN-13: 978-0-7748-1289-4 (bound); 978-0-7748-1290-0 (pbk.)
ISBN-10: 0-7748-1289-3 (bound); 0-7748-1290-7 (pbk.)

    I. Wildlife conservation – Canada – History. 2. Wildlife conservation – Government policy – Canada – History. 3. Wildlife conservation – Canada – Citizen participation – History. 4. Wildlife management – Canada – History. I. Title. II. Series.

QL84.24.L66 2006   333.95'416'0971   C2006-900044-1

Canadä

UBC Press gratefully acknowledges the financial support for our publishing program of the Government of Canada through the Book Publishing Industry Development Program (BPIDP), and of the Canada Council for the Arts, and the British Columbia Arts Council.

This book has been published with the help of a grant from the Canadian Federation for the Humanities and Social Sciences, through the Aid to Scholarly Publications Programme, using funds provided by the Social Sciences and Humanities Research Council of Canada, and with the help of the K.D. Srivastava Fund.

Printed and bound in Canada by Friesens
Set in Monotype Bembo by George Kirkpatrick
Copy editor: Deborah Kerr
Indexer: David Luljak
Proofreader: Jillian Shoichet

Moose image overleaf: Glenbow Archives, NA-843-22

UBC Press   University of Washington Press
The University of British Columbia   PO Box 50096
2029 West Mall   Seattle, WA
Vancouver, BC V6T 1Z2   98145-5096, USA
604-822-5959 / Fax: 604-822-6083

www.ubcpress.ca   www.washington.edu/uwpress

For my parents

CONTENTS

ILLUSTRATIONS

◆

FIGURES

PHOTO ESSAY
(following page 136)

FOREWORD BY GRAEME WYNN

◆

Troubles with Nature

A FEW WEEKS BEFORE I began this essay, a friend told me about a coyote seen loping, in the middle of the day, through an old established residential area in Vancouver. Those who lived in the neighbourhood found several things wrong with this. In their minds, the animal was an intruder, a wild thing that did not belong on the genteel streets of the inner city. *Its* place was far away, beyond the farthest suburbs, in "the country." This coyote, and others like it, constituted a threat. Given half a chance – or less – some thought, it would steal food from bowls left out for family pets, prey on domestic cats, attack young children, and knock over elderly citizens. *It* had no right to terrorize small well-loved animals or to instill fear in the minds of toddlers' parents. Indeed, this coyote seemed particularly brazen: was it not supposed to be a nocturnal animal? What was *it* doing swaggering – not even skulking, but strutting as though it had every right to be there – through human space in broad daylight? This was haughty behaviour indeed in a creature that, for all its dog-like appearance, was a bother, a nuisance, a pest, and a trespasser.

The good, comfortable middle-class citizens who reacted in this way were hardly the first to express such views. Coyote sightings have been fairly common in the city of Vancouver since the 1980s.[1] Various reports place *Canis latrans* "smack in the middle" of the city, lurking in various recreational areas, following joggers on their morning runs, plucking a terrier from the front steps of a dwelling, and even taking refuge behind the snack counter of a busy gas station. "They're all over the place," an exercised city councillor told a local news reporter. One was spotted "sitting and watching a wedding [of all things!] in the rose garden" of the city's most famous park. Biologists suggest that there may be three hundred or more coyotes in Vancouver, and their presence clearly disconcerts many residents.

Bears sometimes wander from the forests of the North Shore mountains into the wealthy hill-slope suburbs of West Vancouver, but their intrusion into city space is simultaneously somehow more frightening and less challenging than that of the coyotes. Black bears may be more dangerous to humans, but their assaults on backyard garbage cans are generally detected, reported, and acted upon quickly. Wildlife officials move in, trap or tranquilize errant members of the species *Ursus americanus,* and relocate them in the wilderness, "where they belong." Coyotes defy such decisive action (and the order on which it is predicated). They slip into and out of view; they are not easily poisoned, shot, or detained by leg-hold traps because these strategies would endanger humans and their pets; and they are generally cunning enough to avoid live traps.

Most city dwellers may believe that coyotes belong "in the boonies" but, unlike bears, these creatures have found amenable habitat in urban areas. Once confined to the open grasslands of the North American west, they expanded their range as wolf populations declined and have adapted effectively to new settings. Urban forests, ravines, golf courses, vacant lots overgrown with vegetation, thickets of brush, even abandoned houses and dark areas under porches have provided foraging and denning sites for urban coyotes. "It was amazing how comfortable the animal was in the city" reflected one Vancouverite who gave chase to a coyote after it snatched his poodle. In the eyes of many, these opportunistic predators have claimed space beyond their entitlement. They have made themselves at home in "our" space. By doing so, they have forced many of "us," their neighbours, to reshape our behaviour in immediate and practical ways. Vancouver pet owners have been warned to confine their animals or risk losing them to predation.

It has become fashionable of late to attribute such challenges as coyotes pose to urban dwellers to the ways in which we think about the world, and the labels that we ascribe to things within it.[2] Simply put, this is to say that we find it hard to accept bears and coyotes in the city because we call them wild animals and cling to our convictions that the wild and the civilized are distinct realms, that the urban and the rural are separate spheres, and that culture is human and nature is, well, natural. There is a deal of useful truth in this line of argument. Wild and tame are ideas. Like "Nature," in this view, they are not simply physical entities that are "out there" or given: they are ideas that take on "different meanings in different cultural contexts." Just as "Nature" is "a social construction that directs us to see mountains, rivers, trees, and deserts in particular ways," so wild and tame are concepts that help us make sense of a complex world by sorting things into classes or kinds.[3] All such classifications order and simplify. In doing so, they frame the ways in which we expect things to be. When behavioural categories such as wild and tame parallel spatial expressions such as country and city, they define where certain things belong. Our views impose an ideological order on the world, but this is neither obvious to, nor observed by, all creatures within it. Ultimately, then, urbanites' problems with coyotes in the city stem from the persistent human desire to categorize and classify, and they reflect the particular ways in which Vancouverites (and most other urban North Americans) think about wildlife. In this view, the anguish that coyotes cause citizens is socially constructed. Here the trouble with nature is at least as much a product of human attitudes as it is a consequence of the behaviour of non-human creatures. If we thought about the world differently, let us say more ecologically, we might be less exercised about urban coyotes.

The work of American science writer David Quammen helps point us in this direction by insistently excavating the variety of human-environment relations. In *Monster of God,* for example, Quammen sets out to show how humanity lives with large predators, and writes, "Great and terrible flesh-eating beasts have always shared landscape with humans. They were part of the ecological matrix within which *Homo sapiens* evolved. They were part of the psychological context in which our sense of identity as a species arose. They were part of the spiritual systems we invented for coping." Humanity's extraordinary capacity to modify the world has also been central to Quammen's concerns, and he has argued, powerfully, that anthropogenic transformations of the planet favour weedy species, humans, animals, and other organisms that are able to flourish in disturbed environments. By this reckoning, coyotes and humans are both adaptive generalists.

Like raccoons, squirrels, black rats, pigeons, sparrows, and houseflies, as well as dandelions and other plants that we commonly know as "weeds," they are ready to travel, able to adapt to disturbance, to switch food sources, and to breed prolifically; thus equipped, they thrive almost anywhere. They belong together, in disturbed and degraded (or "unnatural") environments such as cities.[4]

Yet this takes us only so far. Acknowledging that domesticated landscapes are not necessarily the exclusive domain of humans may lead us to reconsider the categories by which we define the world, and prompt us to redraw conceptual boundaries long taken for granted. It may help us to think differently, in the abstract, about coyotes in particular and nature in general. *Canis latrans* may not warrant reclassification as "man's best friend," but perhaps the cunning and resilience of members of this species might be acknowledged, as it is accepted that humans are a part of (rather than apart from) the howling, buzzing world of nature. None of this will save Fifi and Fido from predation, however. Nor will it stop the raccoons (that are far more common in most suburban areas than they are in the neighbouring countryside) from fishing in our garden ponds and spilling carefully packaged household garbage on the sidewalks. Moreover, even ecologically minded urbanites are likely to be distressed by the losses and messes that result from such animal acts. To point out that bird populations tend to increase as cat numbers fall is unlikely to assuage the grief felt by the owners of felines that have fallen victim to prowling coyotes, and the raccoons' offence in disturbing the garbage is only compounded by the fact that it is likely to attract rats, flies, and other potentially harmful (revealing terms) *vermin* and *bugs*. Human relations with nature are immensely complicated, and they cannot easily escape the web of words (and the attitudes and convictions embedded in them) by which people navigate the world. They have a history, a rich and deep foundation of mutually constituted experience and engagement, and this history is not easily ignored, summarized, or remade.[5] It does, though, need to be understood, in order to grapple meaningfully and effectively with the sorts of challenges – the troubles with nature – that the brazen coyote presented to the group of Vancouverites with whom this foreword began.

This is where *States of Nature* makes its contribution. In the pages that follow, Tina Loo explores the "complex, contradictory, and conflict-laden" but hitherto largely unexamined history of Canadians' efforts "to conserve and manage wildlife" in the first three-quarters of the twentieth century. The story she tells ranges widely over space, as well as time, and examines the actions and ideas of a remarkably diverse group of persons who (and organizations that) shaped Canadian attitudes towards wildlife and its management, and more generally towards the natural world, between 1900 and 1970. In sum, Loo's account limns three noteworthy arguments. First, and least unexpectedly, she points to the increasing effectiveness of "state" intervention in the conservation of wildlife, and notes the marginalizing impact of this trend upon local and customary attitudes (and associated behaviours) towards wild animals. Second, and somewhat surprisingly in view of the first argument, she insists that private individuals and organizations, many of whom were closely associated with the very groups that the state held responsible for wildlife decline, were at least as important as state functionaries in conserving certain species and habitats. And third, she argues that wildlife management and conservation efforts, in all their varied forms and whether driven by the state or not, were basically about "the values that should govern humans' relationships with nature." Diverse though they were, in other words, twentieth-century wildlife conservation efforts contributed to the colonization of rural Canada and advanced a normative agenda of social, economic, and political change, the legacies of which Canadians live with to this day.

Each of these arguments warrants careful attention. The first is broadly familiar: several American scholars have written at length about the ways in which eighteenth- and early-nineteenth-century rural dwellers developed practices to regulate the use of common resources, and others have charted the rise of the Progressive conservation movement, the development of centralized and increasingly efficient bureaucracies designed to manage nature, and the growing authority of trained and certified specialists in resource management and other spheres, associated with the expanding privilege afforded professional (and often scientific) expertise. Nonetheless, Loo's argument is also significantly different, in distinctly Canadian ways.[6] Here is a case in which that old saw of Canadian historical scholarship, that in the final analysis everything comes down to the question of federal-provincial relations, has some relevance. The division of powers between political jurisdictions in the Confederation gave substantial responsibility for wildlife to provincial governments, and created

a far more intricate patchwork of regulations – and thus a more complex history of wildlife management – than prevailed to the south
and especially across the vast federal domain of the American west.
This has several consequences for the story told here.

Wisely, Loo eschews the challenge of detailing the plethora of
provincial legislative, regulatory, and administrative arrangements
that were put in place to govern game, limit predation, and control
vermin in the years after 1867 (and indeed earlier, in the various colonies of British North America). Instead, she deals with these matters
allusively, emphasizing the influences of English tradition, American
Progressivism, and anti-modernist sentiment in shaping the variety of
game laws implemented across the country. She also recognizes that
these initiatives created both conflicts and opportunities. Parks and
game reserves excluded Native peoples from traditional hunting areas
in Canada as they did in the United States. Rural dwellers, especially those on the pioneer fringes of settlement, and Native peoples,
both of whom typically hunted for subsistence, were disadvantaged
and distressed by new regulations that privileged the sport hunting
of "game" over the killing of wild animals for consumption.[7] Yet
regulations were often honoured in the breach. Many held a strong
sense of entitlement to the resources of the country, and exploited
them in defiance of the law, with insouciant bravado or stealthy cunning. Enforcement of the regulations was inevitably erratic as widely
scattered populations took their chances to hunt and fish, aware that
the relatively small numbers of game wardens were unable to mount
effective surveillance or convincingly pretend their omnipotence.
Trying to cope, wardens resorted to forms of what we might today
describe as group profiling, identifying Native people, foreigners, and
the poor as particularly likely to offend against the law, and subject-
ing them to hefty fines if their transgressions were detected. For all
of this, a number of Native people were able to respond positively to
changing circumstances by selling their local knowledge as woodcraft and serving as hunting guides for those whose pursuit of fish and
game was sanctioned by law.

The second of Loo's main arguments, emphasizing the role of private individuals and local organizations in the work of conservation in
Canada, is eye-catching because it runs counter both to well-known
regulatory trends of the twentieth century and to common convictions about some facets of the Canadian conservation movement. In

an area in which there has been too little scholarship, understanding has been framed by Janet Foster's claim, in *Working for Wildlife: The Beginning of Preservation in Canada,* that a group of "dedicated civil servants" (including the superintendent of Rocky Mountain [Banff] Park, Howard Douglas; the director of the federal Forestry Branch, Robert Campbell; Parks Commissioner James Harkin; and Dominion Entomologist Gordon Hewitt) laid the foundations for Canadian wildlife policy and brought about a dramatic change in national attitudes in the four decades spanning the turn of the twentieth century.[8] According to this account, they achieved these goals by securing effective protection for "game" within national parks and forest reserves, by setting up sanctuaries for pronghorn antelope, wood bison, and St. Lawrence seabirds, and by negotiating international protection for migratory birds.[9] Published in 1978, Foster's book was, at least in part, a refutation of Roderick Nash's comment, made ten years earlier at a conference in Calgary, that Canadians lagged two generations behind Americans in wilderness appreciation.[10] By insisting that James Harkin and others were "fifty years ahead" of their time, Foster polished Canadian pride, even as she acknowledged American influences, particularly through Gifford Pinchot and John Muir, upon many of those who worked for parks and wildlife protection in Canada. Yet by celebrating these "far-sighted, resourceful" civil servants who "moved a conservationist agenda forward, winning over politicians and the public to the cause" by developing "strong conservationist philosophies based on their own experiences in nature, an on-the-job understanding of how wildlife populations were under threat by modern civilization, and the influence of American thinkers coming to the same conclusions," Foster, perhaps inadvertently, gave credence to what Alan MacEachern has called "a distinctly Canadian tale" featuring the "bureaucrat as hero."[11]

By extending the scope of her analysis beyond the early 1920s, and by broadening her focus to include "non-Ottawa men," Tina Loo carries understanding of Canadian attitudes towards wildlife well beyond the beachheads established by Nash and Foster and shows that various types of "grassroots environmentalism" *were* in evidence before 1970.[12] From individuals as various as Jack Miner, the unschooled yet charismatic bird man of Essex County, Ontario; Charles Elton, a scholarly, pragmatic scientist from Oxford University who spent years studying the population dynamics of Canadian snowshoe rabbits and Arctic wildlife; Farley Mowat, trenchant critic of wildlife science and *homo bureaucratis,* "that aberrant product of our times who, cocooned in convention, witlessly wedded to the picayune, obsessed with obscurantism, and foundering in footling facts, nevertheless considers himself the only legitimate possessor of revealed truth and, consequently, the self-appointed arbiter of human affairs"; and Andy Russell, the high-school dropout become hunting guide whose later career as writer, filmmaker, and public speaker led some to describe him as "a living icon of Canada's conservation movement," Loo assembles a fascinating parade of characters whose far-from-uniform and far-from-simple views of wildlife, and humanity's relationships to it, both charted and changed Canadians' attitudes towards nature in the twentieth century.[13]

There is no easy way to summarize the always complex, sometimes contradictory, and frequently shifting values that underlay the ways in which these individuals (and members of Canadian society at large) regarded wildlife and conceived of human-animal relationships through these years. Jack Miner may have been "Canada's famous naturalist," but he had no doubt that "God put birds and animals here for man's use and ... control." Elton sought to "apply the scientific method to living animals," but Mowat, hired by the Canadian Wildlife Service to study barren ground caribou, came to see a pair of northern wolves, which he called "George" and "Angeline," in very human terms – they were, he said, "as devoted a married pair as one could hope to find." He wrote the widely read (and controversial) *Never Cry Wolf* to pour scorn on the scientific conviction that they and others of their kind were savage marauders. So too Andy Russell sought to "rehabilitate" an animal deeply misunderstood by the public, with his film and 1967 book *Grizzly Country,* though he continued to defend hunters' rights to pursue the bears.[14]

Yet Loo finds a way through this maze of ambiguity in her quest to discern the values that have shaped Canadian attitudes to nature. In broad terms, government officials (bureaucrats and scientists) pursued an increasingly interventionist approach to wildlife management through the late nineteenth and early twentieth centuries. Beginning with efforts to limit the destruction of certain species (by restricting hunting through licensing and regulation), they moved on to govern animal numbers, through efforts at predator control and habitat management, in ways that rendered wildlife work increasingly scientific, rational, systematic, reductionist, and abstract. All of this served to reconstitute space (as wilderness parks or backcountry preserves), to devalue the local knowledge of rural peoples (from indigenous hunters to homespun philosophers such as Jack Miner), and to convert animals into "populations." At the same time, it broke decisively with the earlier and immensely popular Canadian tradition of nature writing (as practised in particular by Ernest Thompson Seton and Charles G.D. Roberts), in which life stories of animals were told from the animals' points of view.[15] It also took the sting out of "Wilderness Man" Grey Owl's nostalgic anti-modernist rhetoric proclaiming that wildlife had been "made a burnt offering on the altar of the God of Mammon."[16]

In the 1960s, however, new social and environmental movements began to challenge the scientific, bureaucratic, and commercial hegemony that had come to dominate many facets of life in Western societies through the previous century. In years marked by growing student unrest, the emergence of the counterculture (so-called) and back-to-the-land movements, the rise of popular ecology, and the birth of radical new forms of environmentalism, prevailing attitudes towards wildlife were also brought into question.[17] In Canada, Farley Mowat and filmmaker Bill Mason (whose two feature-length documentaries *Death of a Legend* and *Cry of the Wild* were immensely popular in the early 1970s) found responsive audiences for their portrayals of wolves as moral creatures and their efforts to bridge the divide between humans and nature. In stressing the decency, playfulness, and responsibility of wild animals, both Mowat and Mason spoke (as Joy Adamson had a few years earlier in the book and subsequent film *Born Free*) to questions on the minds of many contemporaries, about the importance of gratification and the nature of freedom.[18] If their answers (and the convictions that underpinned them) differed in detail, this was of little consequence to those disaffected with their lives and times. For Mowat and Mason, the war on wolves was a synecdoche for modernity's assault on the quality of life, and their meditations on human alienation from nature turned on the conviction that there existed (in Mowat's words) a "lost world that was ours before we chose the alien role."[19] Emotion, rather than ecology, underpinned these arguments, and others would reassert the importance of ecological science to the work of conservation, the preservation of wild places, and the development of new ways for humans to live in and with nature, but the fundamental proposition at the heart of these claims – that wildness held intrinsic value and was not something to be possessed and manipulated by humans – encouraged people to think differently about the environment, and about the roles of humans and wild creatures within it.

Still, the change in attitudes was far from pervasive. If Mowat's anthropomorphic account of "George" and "Angeline," Mason's emotional entanglements with his tamed wolf cubs, and Russell's portrayal of the grizzly bear as "an important and highly desirable link in the ecological life chain" led many late-twentieth-century Canadians to feel differently about wolves and bears and (to paraphrase the title of Ernest Thompson Seton's most famous book) other wild animals they had known vicariously, deep down they clung to the conviction, encapsulated by chance in another of Seton's titles, that such creatures had their place and that it was separate and apart from the everyday habitat of humans. In *Wild Animals at Home,* published in 1913, Seton argued that the establishment of Yellowstone Park had provided a sanctuary for "fourfoots," where the "excessive shyness and wariness" that they exhibited in the face of lawless, rifle-toting skin hunters was replaced by "their traditional Garden-of-Eden attitude toward Man." In this safe haven, wild animals could be themselves and nature-lovers and camera hunters who travelled to "the Wonderland of the West" could encounter exemplary beasts. At the beginning and the end of the twentieth century, in Seton's words and the minds of many an urban Canadian, separation seemed to serve both humans and animals well.[20]

To be sure, all of this gets very complicated at times. To the delight of camera-toting tourists, deer wander the streets of Banff (a small town within a national park) at certain times of the year, raising questions, for those who stop to consider such things, about whose space this rightly is. But generally, coyotes, bears, and other (potentially dangerous) wild creatures that invade "indubitably" human spaces such as the inner suburbs of large cities are regarded as out-of-place and unwelcome. Concerns about self- and pet-preservation no doubt account for some of this, and neither ecological logic (humans, coyotes, and bears are links in the same life chain) nor social constructionist argument (that our notions of wild nature are human creations) is likely to allay these entirely. The more we grapple with these matters, the more intractable they seem. Are humans parts of nature, or is nature nothing more than a human invention? Though scientists may insist on their capacity to understand ecosystem relations and to document the workings of "nature" through careful observation, the developments traced in this book make it clear that emotion and sentiment have often exercised enormous influence upon conceptions (and thus constructions) of nature and wildlife. Yet this is not to say that the physical world is a product of the human imagination or that there is no such thing as reality. Neither Farley Mowat nor any of the others who appear in these pages doubted for a minute that the birds and beasts with which they were concerned were corporeal entities, although they variously endowed these creatures with particular characters and attributed meaning to their actions. The trouble with nature stems from its omniscience and its complexity, as well as from the ways in which it has been represented. But history can carry us forward here. Years ago, Charles G.D. Roberts claimed that "the animal story ... is a potent emancipator ... It leads us back to the old kinship of earth, without asking us to relinquish by way of toll any part of the wisdom of the ages."[21] By reflecting, as Tina Loo encourages us to do, on another set of stories about animals and humans, detailing various facets of wildlife conservation in Canada, we are encouraged to both humility and a sense of connectedness with nature, as we are forced to acknowledge the many ways in which the non-human world has been conceived and to respect its distinctiveness. Thus may the past guide us (as all good humanist scholarship should) in formulating our own answers to the questions with which most of those who appear in these pages struggled, in one way or another: how do we want to live in the world and what kind of people do we want to be?

ACKNOWLEDGMENTS

◆

IT IS A GREAT PLEASURE to thank the many people who made this book possible. Chief among them are the archivists and librarians at institutions across Canada who helped track down obscure references, gain access to closed collections, acquire copies, and haul heavy boxes in and out of storage. For this, I would like to thank Mac Culham and David Mattison at the British Columbia Archives; Diane Rogers at the Jewish Historical Society of British Columbia; Jim Bowman at the Glenbow Museum and Archives; Don Bourdon, Lena Goon, and Elizabeth Kundert-Cameron at the Whyte Museum of the Canadian Rockies; Judith Hudson Beattie at the Hudson's Bay Company Archives; Sandra Ferguson at the Archives of Ontario; Chantal Dussault at the Canadian Museum of Nature; Shiri Alon and Victoria Dickinson at the McCord Museum of Canadian History; Jo-Anne Colby at the Canadian Pacific Railway Archives; and the reference staff at the Vancouver Public Library, the Courtenay and District Museum, Library and Archives Canada, the Nova Scotia Archives and Records Management, and the Provincial Archives of Newfoundland and Labrador.

Michael Egan, Susan Johnston, Allan Robertson, Susan Roy, and Shirlee Anne Smith did stellar research on my behalf. Conversations with them helped to clarify my thoughts and arguments, as did the opportunities to present my work to different audiences. In particular, I would like to thank Peter Gossage and Wendy Mitchinson, former editors of the *Canadian Historical Review,* who pushed me to elaborate some of the central ideas in the book in a piece for the journal's "Forum"; Green College at the University of British Columbia; and the Departments of History at the University of Alberta, Concordia University, and Dalhousie University.

I am grateful to the Social Sciences and Humanities Research Council of Canada and the Dean of Arts at the University of British Columbia for grants which partly financed this work. I am equally indebted to my colleagues in the History Departments at Simon Fraser University and the University of British Columbia, and especially two Chairs, William Cleveland and David Breen, for supporting my work and creating a wonderful environment in which to carry it out.

Notably heroic were the friends and colleagues who found time over the years to read the manuscript in whole or in part. Their helpful comments improved the contents, while their supportive silences improved my mood. Thanks to Ted Chamberlin, John Jennings, Bob McDonald, Suzanne Morton, Meg Stanley, John Stubbs, Graeme Wynn, and the two anonymous reviewers for UBC Press and the Aid to Scholarly Publishing Programme.

Without exception, the people at UBC Press have been terrific to work with. Thanks particularly to Peter Milroy, the Director, Jean Wilson, my editor and ski pal, Ann Macklem, the project coordinator, and Deborah Kerr, who did an amazing job copy-editing.

This book grew from a love of "wild" places, from the woods behind the Ontario house where I grew up to the mountains in the part of the world I now live. For their companionship and counsel while sharing them – and for the rides there and back! – I thank Karen Ferguson, Gerry Hallowell, Paige Raibmon, Meg Stanley, Carolyn Strange, and John Stubbs. For all of this, and for his inspiration, four-boot enthusiasm, and bowls of latte, my thanks and love to Ed Johnston.

INTRODUCTION

◆

I LIVE SURROUNDED BY tall buildings. As I write, the local news-
papers are full of stories about the newest addition to the skyline, the
Shangri-La, which at sixty storeys and 642 feet will be the tallest in
the city – a "signature building" for Vancouver.

Despite the promoters' aspirations, it is not likely that the Shangri-
La will be featured on the postcards on offer in the gift shops on
neighbouring Robson Street, souvenirs of the city sold to the tourist throng. Instead of buildings, most feature the word "Vancouver"
or "Canada" emblazoned over photographs of Stanley Park and the
North Shore mountains, and more incongruously, over portraits of
moose, marmot, and beaver – creatures which, despite the city's considerable diversity, are hardly common sights on its streets, to say the
least.

My experience of looking at the postcards on Robson Street
could, I suspect, be repeated in every city in Canada. Wildlife has
been emblematic of the country from the days of the fur trade, when
beaver pelts were a medium of exchange, to the present, when the
"proud and noble creature" sells Molson Canadian beer, emblazons
Roots clothing, and can be found burrowed in every pocket and
change purse, adorning the country's coins, along with the caribou,
loon, and polar bear.

The extent to which wildlife is common currency in Canada is
one manifestation of the central place that nature, and particularly
wilderness, holds in defining national identity. Canada's cultural producers literally "naturalized the nation" by rendering certain landscapes iconic.[1] The Canadian Shield of the Group of Seven, Emily
Carr's rainforests, and William Kurelek's sky and grass are celebrated
for capturing both the essence of the place and people's relationship
to it. Canadians, for all their differences, are said to be products of
their environment: a "northern" people whose character was forged
by a particular encounter with nature, and whose history and political
culture are defined by the country's geography and the serial exploitation of natural resources – cod, beaver, trees, wheat, minerals.

But as cultural critics have pointed out, these national icons also
do other kinds of ideological work. The product of "imperial eyes,"

the emptiness of these vast landscapes perpetuates an angle of vision that overlooks the history of indigenous use as well as the conflict, disease, and dispossession that emptied them of people.[2]

Representations of Canada's wilderness are not limited to canvases. Thanks to environmental action, art has become life. Activists have persuaded governments to establish wilderness areas, large tracts of land protected from human settlement and development, for purposes other than recreation and tourism. As some historians have observed, insofar as North American environmentalism has been preoccupied with wilderness preservation, it too is a colonialist enterprise.[3] But according to historian William Cronon, the trouble with wilderness is both broader and deeper. While people have invested it with both negative and positive qualities over time, their concepts of wilderness have consistently placed it outside history. This duality between nature and culture characterizes North American environmental thought and action and, in his view, is harmful to both. By embracing wilderness as "other," we locate ourselves outside the natural. In so doing, we cultivate a way of seeing and being that precludes forging a truly sustainable relationship with the environment, one that has a place for people, and more importantly, one that does not equate using nature with abusing it:[4]

As much as its geography, Canada's wildlife has also been saddled with the burden of national identity, not so much through the work of its painters as its writers. "One of the most important developments of nature writing in the late-nineteenth century," the realistic wild animal story was pioneered by Canadians at the turn of the twentieth century – in particular by Ernest Thompson Seton and Charles G.D. Roberts – and carried on by postwar authors such as Fred Bodsworth, Roderick Haig-Brown, Farley Mowat, Marion Engel, and R.D. Lawrence, among others.[5] According to literary critic James Polk, the "lives of the hunted" rendered by Seton and Roberts are statements of Canadian identity. Designed to elicit sympathy for their animal victims, these tales can be read as allegories for Canada's precarious position in the world, particularly vis-à-vis the United States. According to Polk, "as Canada's perennial questioning of its own national identity is increasingly coupled with a suspicion that a fanged America lurks in the bushes, poised for the kill, it is not surprising that Canadian writers should retain their interest in persecution and survival."[6] Margaret Atwood makes a similar point, arguing that these stories "provide the key to an important facet of the Canadian psyche."[7] The four-legged protagonists of British animal stories are, in her view, really "Englishmen in furry zippered suits," a commentary on that country's class system. American animal stories do not turn on social relations but conquest. These triumphal hunting tales reveal the "general imperialism of the American cast of mind."[8] The Canadian ones, however, differ significantly from both. They are "about animals *being* killed, as felt emotionally from inside the fur and feathers." To Atwood, Canadians' identification with these animal-victims is "the expression of a deep-seated cultural fear" of being overwhelmed – made extinct – by the United States.[9] The creatures who inhabit the Canadian realistic wild animal story, she concludes, "are us."[10]

But if wilderness has a human history that makes it a problematic national symbol, so too do wild animals. Take the beaver, for instance. The rodent is Canada's national animal not because of its earnest industry, but because its pelt was a valuable commodity. When Canadians celebrate the beaver then, they are celebrating the fur trade – and its mass slaughter of wildlife in the name of fashion. Or take the coyote. First Nations storytellers like Thomas King have taught Canadians to see the animal as a trickster. A figure that can turn the world upside down, Coyote is capable of bringing a better order through chaos. His actions remind us that humans don't rule the world. But try telling that to urbanites who discover their treasured pets missing and their children threatened when they reach out to pet the new "doggie" that appears in their backyards or the local park.

For humans, the trouble with wildlife is that flesh and blood creatures do not always live up to their representations. When that happens, the gap between animal and "manimal" often proves fatal – sometimes to people, but more frequently to the wild creatures who can find themselves staring down the barrel of a weapon wielded by the local conservation officer.

As these examples illustrate, the history of humans' relationship with wildlife is complex, contradictory, and conflict-laden. This book details just one aspect of that history, the efforts of Canadians to conserve and manage wildlife over the twentieth century to about 1970. I chose 1970 as the end point because that year marked the beginnings of a shift in the nature and tactics of the debate over how to treat wildlife – something associated with the establishment of Greenpeace. More broadly, I use wildlife conservation as a way of understanding the shifting and conflicting attitudes toward the natural world. In that sense, this history of wildlife conservation provides a particular perspective on the history of environmentalism in Canada (defined broadly as a concern for the natural world), and specifically on the attitudes and roles of the state, urban sportsmen, and rural peoples, from resource workers to First Nations.

Both "wildlife" and "conservation" are words that need some explanation. For much of the period under study, "wildlife" did not exist. People occasionally used the phrase "wild life," but referred far more often to "game" and "vermin." The former were animals or birds that were hunted, worthy objects of pursuit that gave pleasure in the chase. The latter were a motley assortment of creatures that preyed on game or otherwise compromised human interests. Provincial governments across the country had game wardens and game departments which were charged with framing and implementing the provisions of the game act, a piece of legislation that protected valuable animals and birds and put a price on the heads of those that threatened them. It was not until the mid-twentieth century that the "wildlife service" emerged as a branch of the federal and provincial governments, staffed by "conservation" officers. Interestingly, fish were not usually included in wildlife, and I have maintained that convention. The book does not deal with fisheries management.

Although "conservation" and "preservation" were often used interchangeably, it is useful to distinguish between them. Except within the boundaries of provincial or federally administered parks where harvesting wildlife was prohibited or restricted only to First Nations, wildlife management policy was directed largely toward the conservation of species, that is, toward initiatives designed to safeguard the long-term survival and health of animals in order to ensure their continued use by humans. Conservation strategies might involve preservationist measures like barring the harvesting of certain species altogether, but these restrictions were temporary, and were meant to allow numbers to recover to levels that would sustain a return to hunting or trapping.

While we know pieces of the conservation story, a larger narrative has yet to emerge. Despite the acknowledged contribution of the wild animal story to the development of nature writing, the role of wildlife in articulating national identity, the prominence of the fur trade in Canadian history, and the central role Canadian activists played in campaigns against sealing and whaling in the 1970s and '80s, environmental history is an emerging field, and only a handful of works deal with the history of wildlife conservation in Canada. Most examine a particular region, individual, organization or level of government, a single species, or policy.[11] Although the subject is not dealt with directly here, the literature on fishing has been particularly useful in informing my thinking, as has the work that explores various government management schemes for the fisheries and the conflict among interest groups.[12]

I have drawn on these scholars' insights to present a picture of wildlife conservation from a broader national perspective. It is one that inevitably loses some of the subtlety and in-depth coverage of more closely focused works. For instance, while Aboriginal peoples are a significant part of the story, the book does not examine indigenous beliefs and management practices (nor those of other rural people) systematically or in any detail, except to the extent that they came into focus and conflict with government conservation regimes. I hope, however, that these losses are compensated somewhat by the arguments the book offers about change over time, the range of actors and their roles, and the impacts and meanings of various conservation initiatives. They are meant to act as a framework within which to locate and understand the more specific episodes in the history of wildlife conservation that people have written about and will continue to explore.

The American literature on environmental history and the history of wildlife conservation is substantial. My thinking about the subject has benefited in particular from examples of writing that is critical in its focus, highlighting the normative nature of environmentalism.[13] This work draws attention to the class and race dimensions of environmental action, whether in the form of pollution control, the creation of national parks, or wildlife conservation.[14] Of course, American historians are not the only scholars to frame environmentalism in terms of power. Researchers focusing on the South rather than the North have done some of the most interesting work of this kind. Historians like Ramachandra Guha have revealed the connections between ecological questions and social equity in fights over resource use in India, Peru, Thailand, and Brazil. These episodes

5

in the "environmentalism of the poor" raise fundamental questions about the nature of development, as well as the conservation models used to counter it.[15] Thinking about environmentalism in terms of values, judgements, and power has led me to frame wildlife conservation as a normative project of social, economic, and political change.

With all this in mind, the book offers three main arguments. The first is about change over time. Until the late nineteenth century, wildlife management, as we would call it now, was a highly localized, fragmented, and loose set of customary, informal, and private practices carried out by a diverse range of individuals and groups, from First Nations to the Hudson's Bay Company (HBC) and local white sportsmen through rod and gun clubs. Their efforts were aimed at conserving the resource for subsistence, commercial return, or recreation. The state's involvement in conservation was limited: local assize courts set seasons, bag limits, and bounties, and prosecuted offenders brought before them.

At the turn of the twentieth century, however, the state began to take a more active role, setting in place the structures that would allow for a more coordinated, encompassing, systematic, and ultimately more scientific approach to wildlife conservation. Statute law remained a key management tool for the state but eventually ceded its central place to science. Influenced by developments in ecology and the new discipline of game management in the 1920s and '30s, state conservation strategy slowly shifted from simply limiting predation to increasing wildlife numbers though intense intervention. From almost its beginnings in the early twentieth century, conservation policy had the effect of marginalizing local customary uses of wildlife, and in that sense was part of the colonization of rural Canada.

The second argument is about the key actors. Despite the growth of government conservation over the twentieth century and the hegemony of scientific management, private individuals and organizations carried out some of the most important wildlife work in Canada. The very kinds of people who were targeted by state management regimes as responsible for the decline in wildlife – rural people who hunted for their own tables and for money to supplement their incomes or who made their livings in the bush – did as much if not more to further the general cause of environmentalism and in many cases to conserve particular species and habitats as those who were employed by the state.

Finally, whether it was carried out by the government or not, wildlife conservation was about the values that should govern humans' relationships with nature (e.g., Christianity, private property, nonconsumptive use, efficiency, biodiversity) *and* the values that would come from conserving it; chief among them was the capacity for people to connect meaningfully – emotionally – with their own natures and with other people. Learning to live with wildlife was, for many who worked on its behalf, about creating ethical human communities. The normative nature of wildlife conservation meant that it invited commentary from a diversity of people – management was not solely the purview of government bureaucrats or experts. Over the twentieth century, sentiment, as much as science, shaped the content and trajectory of wildlife work.

The book is organized chronologically and thematically. Chapter 1 examines the legal regime that was created to regulate wildlife in the twentieth century, exploring its English antecedents as well as the twin influences of Progressivism and anti-modernism. Laws regulating wildlife stretched back to the medieval period, but at the turn of the twentieth century, provinces across Canada as well as the federal government created new bureaucracies and regulatory frameworks that centralized control over the resource and administered their provisions over broad geographic areas. Wildlife conservation was largely a matter of controlling predation through restrictions on hunting. More broadly, however, conservation policy sanctioned the non-consumptive use of wildlife, promoting sports hunting rather than hunting for the table, and through it a particular relationship between humans and the natural world. By centralizing control and privileging one kind of use of wildlife and relationship to it over others, government conservation policies created the context for conflict.

That conflict is the focus of Chapter 2, which makes the point that rural people were the targets of the game laws and investigates how they responded. It argues that wildlife conservation deepened the divisions of class and race. Moreover, in extending state control over the countryside and marginalizing the consumption of wildlife, as well as the local knowledges and practices that underlay it, conservation was an instrument of colonization. That said, however, even as some individuals were marginalized by the game laws, a handful were also able to profit from the new opportunities made available by the emphasis on the non-consumptive use of wildlife in state conservation policy. They did so by commercializing their knowledge of the natural world, transforming and redeploying it as guides and outfitters or as rural entertainers. In selling local knowledge as woodcraft, rural people became implicated in the creation of a new set of relationships with nature that highlighted their skills and knowledge even as it marginalized them.

In examining the changing organization, substance, aims, and impacts of wildlife conservation, the first two chapters differ from the ones that follow, which are more closely focused case studies. Rendering these broad brush portraits presented certain methodological challenges. Anyone who writes about resource management in Canada must come to grips with multiple jurisdictions and different government departments. The division of powers in the British North America Act placed wildlife under the jurisdiction of the provinces. The exceptions to this were migratory birds and wildlife in the national parks and the Northwest Territories, all of which fell under federal jurisdiction. Rather than present an exhaustive recounting of the provisions of the game laws and policies of each province and the federal government, in the first two chapters I have chosen instead to identify the salient interpretive issues and to illustrate them with examples drawn from all over.

Chapters 1 and 2 make reference to the knowledge about the natural world that rural people possessed and the important role it and they played in shaping state conservation policy and practice. In Chapter 3, I deal more fully with the substance of that local knowledge, examining the career of Jack Miner, an Ontario farmer and brick maker who in the 1920s became Canada's first celebrity conservationist. Miner's career, a case study in rural ecological knowledge, provides an opportunity to understand its formation and characteristics. His ideas about conservation were an outgrowth of the Christian idea that man should have dominion over all the creatures of the earth, and were shaped by his experience of trying to make a living from the land. Despite "Uncle Jack's" great popularity and his contribution to the cause of conservation and research on migratory birds, his relationship with government wildlife workers and formally trained scientists was a difficult one that highlights the differences between two ways of knowing the natural world.

Finding common ground between scientific and local knowledge on which to build conservation initiatives was not easy, but as Chapter 4 discusses, the Hudson's Bay Company managed to do so. Not only did it support the early research of Charles Elton – a man who would go on to become one of the founders of the "new ecology" – but it also developed a program of beaver conservation in northern Quebec in the 1930s and '40s based on ecological principles. While the federal government was showcasing Grey Owl and his trained beaver to promote the cause of conservation, the HBC was assisting researchers from Elton's Oxford Bureau of Animal Population and implementing measures aimed at increasing the beaver "crop" through the application of scientific knowledge. Although their management was informed by ecology and directed by scientists, the success of the preserves was ultimately due to the knowledge and cooperation of the Cree who worked in them.

The conservation measures implemented on the company's beaver preserves anticipated the shape of wildlife management in the postwar period. As Chapter 5 shows, after 1945 wildlife conservation became a much more proactive project aimed at actively managing animal populations. Biologists joined the ranks of wildlife workers at both the federal and provincial levels, conducting basic research into species, often with the cooperation of universities as well as the warden service, whose members were expected to have more formal training than before 1945. As wildlife work became more scientific and professional, it became more national and international, further distancing conservation from its local roots. Wildlife conservation also became concerned with increasing animal numbers through intensive management, as the federal government's management of the barren ground caribou and bison shows. In many ways it was not until after 1945 that the turn-of-the-century rhetoric of Progressive conservation, with its emphasis on efficiency and productivity, was fully manifested.

Despite their authority, however, scientists and science did not have an uncontested place in formulating public policy relating to wildlife. Focusing on the treatment of predators, Chapter 6 complicates the story of postwar conservation, arguing that when it came to dealing with this particular class of animals, scientists had to share that role with a vocal and insistent group of park wardens, cattlemen, farmers, trappers, and outfitters whose views were shaped by their experience and economic interest. Scientists had been making the case for predators since the 1920s, but rural sentiments and practices persisted. Their strength was evidenced by the bounty, an important local institution that persisted into the 1950s, and in some jurisdictions like Ontario, into the 1970s. Even within the ranks of the government service, there were inconsistencies. While predators continued to be killed out of curiosity, fear, and greed into the 1960s, attitudes began shifting in the early years of that decade. By the 1970s, the new "values for varmints" that had been articulated a generation earlier by scientists had taken hold because popular writers like Farley Mowat and filmmakers like Bill Mason had managed to crystallize an emerging urban sentimentality about predators.

Mowat's *Never Cry Wolf* and Mason's *Death of a Legend* and *Cry of the Wild* spoke to a growing disquiet about the modern world; for both these men, wolves represented a wild that was fast disappearing. Save the wolf and the wild would be saved along with it – or so they implied. Whatever their disagreements with Mowat and Mason, government biologists largely shared the two men's singular focus on the animal. While scientists appreciated the importance of habitat in determining the health of wildlife populations, habitat preservation did not become part of conservation policy until the late 1960s.

As Chapter 7 argues, by that time, groups like Ducks Unlimited Canada (DUC) had thirty years of experience working with prairie residents to save wetlands, and outfitters like British Columbia's Tommy Walker and Alberta's Andy Russell had established themselves as vocal defenders of mountain habitats. Whereas the urban-based leadership of DUC was motivated to save habitats in order to preserve opportunities for recreational hunting, Walker and Russell were moved to save wild places in order to promote a certain kind of community, a way of life in which physical nature and human culture were more integrated. A lifetime in the mountains had taught Walker and Russell that there was a connection between environmental integrity and social cohesion. Their "land ethic" was very much a social ethic.

CHAPTER ONE

◆

Wild by Law: Animals, People, and the State to 1945

> The people of the United States now mourn the loss of their
> wild life and are endeavouring to rescue the remnant from
> complete extermination, realizing what a great asset it is ... A
> young country [like Canada] enjoys the advantage of being able
> to profit by the mistakes of older countries ... It rests with us
> to prove that the advance of civilization ... does not imply the
> total destruction of the wild life but that civilization in its true
> sense signifies the elimination of the spirit of barbarism and the
> introduction of an enlightened attitude.
>   – C. Gordon Hewitt, *The Conservation of the Wild Life*
>   *of Canada* (1921)

AS WITH MUCH in Canadian history, the story of saving Canada's
wildlife can be framed, as the country's first consulting zoologist
did, with reference to the United States. By the time Hewitt wrote,
bison had been virtually eliminated from the North American plains
and the passenger pigeon was extinct. These losses were regrettable,
but where the United States had failed, the young dominion might
triumph, preventing the extermination of wildlife and in so doing
demonstrating Canada's superiority.

For Hewitt, "civilization in its true sense" had a place for both
people and animals. The existence of wildness was not a sign of back-
wardness or barbarity, but evidence of an "enlightened attitude" that
was at the core of civility. Such sentiments were thoroughly modern,

emerging from a fundamental shift in Western attitudes about the wilderness that began in the eighteenth century. Initially synonymous with barren desolation, by the end of the nineteenth century wilderness came to symbolize the opposite qualities, becoming for many the embodiment of Eden.[1]

If Hewitt's sentiments about wildness were distinctly modern, so too were the methods he outlined for preserving it. People could save what they had destroyed. Indeed, by the time he wrote in 1921 the rescue project was well under way, as the main substance and strategies of wildlife conservation that would prevail until midcentury were well developed. His book outlined the conservation efforts undertaken by all levels of government as well as individual Canadians, highlighting federal and provincial game acts, the creation of game reserves and parks, and the work of fish and game protective associations. For Hewitt, a scientist, regulation was the key to making a place for people and animals. While the country's "impenetrable forests, trackless wilderness, and mountains ... [had] retarded settlement," and thus saved its wildlife from complete destruction, Canada would remain wild only by law.[2]

This chapter examines the substance, strategies, and aims of wildlife conservation in Canada to 1945. It argues that there was a fundamental change in its organization and aims at the turn of the twentieth century. At that time, federal and provincial governments began to involve themselves in the enterprise more actively. Influenced by American Progressivist thinking, which conceptualized trees, fish, and wildlife as "resources" to be scientifically managed, Canadian governments began to reconfigure conservation. Although technocrats did not dominate wildlife work in the first half of the twentieth century as they did in the United States and in the management of other resources, it was nonetheless transformed from a number of fragmentary localized practices concerned with controlling the kinds and numbers of animals killed to a centralized and bureaucratized set of policies aimed at promoting a particular relationship with wildlife. Indeed, in a process broadly similar to that described by Louis S. Warren for the United States, the involvement of both levels of government in conservation work altered the nature of wildlife as common property.[3]

COMMON PROPERTY AND LOCAL CONTROL:
THE NINETEENTH-CENTURY CONTEXT

While informal measures controlling resource use, like the taboos about hunting possessed by indigenous peoples, are of ancient lineage, in the English common law tradition statutes regulating the use and consumption of wildlife date back to the medieval period. In medieval England, hunting had evolved into a class privilege. The great English estates had their own gamekeepers who patrolled borders against poachers and husbanded the wildlife within them, killing predators, restocking grounds with valued birds like grouse or pheasant, and maintaining habitats conducive to game by, for instance, burning heather. These birds and animals were reserved for the sporting pleasure of the estate's owner and his guests, and their exclusive ownership was backed by the criminal law. Wildlife conservation and management were thus highly localistic, both in terms of the class interests they served and the area covered.

The injustice of the game laws and class-based nature of conservation became a target of criticism. In his celebrated *Commentaries* (1765-69), William Blackstone made the case that his country's game laws were a vestige of the "Norman yoke" and a subversion of English liberties.[4] His attack was grounded in two key observations. Wild animals were common property, and moreover, hunting was a natural right, one possessed by "every man from prince to peasant," subject only to such restraints as served the public interest.[5] Although his fellow jurists took issue with his arguments, Blackstone's position was embraced wholeheartedly in Britain's North American colonies.

North America's demography made Blackstone's views on the game laws seem like common sense.[6] Frontier conditions, which made hunting a necessity, combined with the sheer abundance of animals (and a scarcity of gentry) only reinforced the idea that wildlife belonged to everyone, and rendered class-based prohibitions on taking it irrelevant and even dangerous. Indeed, in the Thirteen Colonies particularly, any controls that limited free taking were considered unduly restrictive. According to historian James A. Tober, wildlife became a point of "articulation [for] deeply held beliefs about New World freedoms."[7]

Colonists in the non-rebelling colonies did not seem to consider state regulation of wildlife – which was fairly modest in any case – as corrosive of the liberties they enjoyed. Indeed, over the eighteenth and nineteenth centuries they actively pressed for it. Across British North America, individuals acting alone or through the auspices of local fish and game associations petitioned governments to pass or amend laws relating to wildlife and contributed to both their substance and enforcement.[8] Perhaps the best example of this comes from Nova Scotia, where, led by officers of the Halifax garrison, a group of urban sportsmen established the Game and Inland Fishery Protection Society in 1852.[9] So effective – and well connected – was the organization that the government turned over much of the enforcement of its wildlife legislation to it in 1884.[10]

Colonial governments across British North America responded to similar pressures by passing legislation regulating wildlife. While these statutes announced government jurisdiction over the entire resource, in practice state conservation and management remained narrowly focused on particular kinds of wild things. Until the mid-twentieth century, the law's bestiary contained references to "game" and "vermin" only.

"Game" was an ever-shifting, diverse assortment of creatures, some of which were not even native to the region, but were introduced by local sportsmen as "exotics." If Nova Scotia's statute books are any indication, snipe and woodcock were the only game in that colony in 1816. Moose became game in 1843, followed by pheasants and robins in 1856, caribou in 1862, non-indigenous American elk in 1894, and "animals valuable only for their fur" in 1896.[11]

"Vermin" were a smaller and somewhat more constant collection of predators, consisting most commonly of wolves, bears, coyotes, and cougars. Their undiscerning carnivorous palates, which favoured wild game as well as domestic livestock, literally earned them a price on their heads and the undying animosity of lawmakers. "Whereas great damage hath been done to the farmers of this Province by wolves, bears, loup-cerviers [lynx], and wildcats," Nova Scotia's first bounty law made provision for rewards to be given for their killing.[12]

If colonial governments were concerned only with husbanding certain kinds of wildlife, then the tactics they used to do so were equally narrow. As the bounty law suggests, the main conservation strategy they pursued centred on controlling predation. Laws encouraged the destruction of some animals and limited or prohibited killing of others by setting seasons and bag limits. In that sense, the wildlife management practised by the state was much more limited than that carried out privately and locally, whether by indigenous peoples or fish and game associations, both of whom were interested in limiting demand as well as increasing the local supply of game. Certainly it paled in comparison to the measures undertaken by the HBC in the nineteenth century. The company had a direct interest in maintaining adequate stocks of beaver and to that end initiated a series of conservation measures in the territories under its control. These were premised on a sophisticated and precocious understanding of the relationship between habitat and population, and included measures to shift hunting pressure to other species and establishing a beaver sanctuary.

Not only was early government wildlife conservation more limited than that practised privately, but its substance also reflected local knowledge and interests. In mid-nineteenth-century Nova Scotia, for instance, the colonial government empowered local justices of the peace to make provisions regarding the preservation of moose for their districts and to set rules and establish rewards for killing vermin.[13] By 1872, local control over wildlife regulation increased when the provincial legislature empowered "the General Sessions of the Peace in every county and district ... to make all such rules and regulations as to them shall seem necessary" to carry out the provisions of the act.[14] New Brunswick's game laws suggested just how particularistic colonial wildlife conservation could be. In 1810 the colony prohibited moose hunting in a particular place – Grand Manan Island – but exempted a particular individual. As the original importer of moose to the island, Moses Gerritson was allowed to reap what he had, literally, sowed, despite the act's preamble, which noted that the preservation of moose would be "beneficial to ... the whole of the Province."[15]

Until the end of the nineteenth century then, conservation, whether carried out privately or publicly, under state sanction, was a fragmentary and uncoordinated set of practices concerned mainly with controlling the kinds and numbers of animals killed. Despite various colonial governments' assertion of jurisdiction, wildlife, in Louis S. Warren's term, largely remained a "local commons" – a resource regulated by local users in response to local conditions and according to practices that had emerged through a long history of indigenous use.

CHANGES

In response to concerns over the decline of animal and bird populations, the organization, substance, and aims of wildlife conservation
changed, as did the status of wildlife as common property. Inspired
by American Progressivist thinking, federal and provincial governments centralized control over wildlife in the early twentieth century,
creating new bureaucracies dedicated to conservation. While these
changes eroded local participation to a certain degree, in Canada
wildlife was not transformed from a "local commons" to a "national"
one as it was in the United States. Federal and provincial governments certainly consolidated their control over wildlife, but rather
than creating one national commons, their involvement in conservation produced several centralized ones whose regulation was not
entirely "delocalized." Thus, there were some important continuities
with nineteenth-century practice.

More substantive changes occurred in the tactics and aims of wildlife conservation. At the turn of the century, conservation strategy
shifted from simply being a matter of numbers to include promoting a particular relationship between people and wildlife. Premised
on an ethic of exploitation that endorsed non-commercial and non-
consumptive use, this new relationship was the basis of a different
kind of environmental citizenship, one that its supporters believed
was the real key to conservation.

To observers in the late nineteenth and early twentieth centuries,
there was little doubt that wildlife populations were declining. Nor
was there much question about the reasons for that decline. Extinction was a by-product of expansion. Opening the western and northern reaches of North America to European settlement and urban
and industrial development involved the purposeful and inadvertent
destruction of wildlife habitat. The axe, the ox, and the plough turned
forests into farmland, marshes into meadows. Railways disrupted the
migration routes of the bison on the prairies and caribou in Newfoundland and were the cause of serious and uncontrollable fires that
had both immediate and long-term impacts on populations and their
food supply. Railway construction crews, as well as the men who
laboured in mining and forestry camps, also took their toll, entertain-
ing themselves by throwing the occasional stick of dynamite in a lake
or testing their marksmanship on anything with feathers or hooves.

Piles of bison skulls, like this one by a railway siding near Saskatoon, Saskatchewan, were a common sight on the Canadian prairies in the late nineteenth century, testimony to the environmental costs of settlement (1890). Glenbow Museum and Archives, NA 354-29

Not only was wildlife pushed, parched, burned, starved, and blasted out by European settlement, but it was also in danger of being gunned down and served up to meat-hungry settlers. Colonization was famishing business, and wildlife came under increased pressure from hunters who sought to feed themselves and their families or to earn a living supplying a growing urban market with fresh animal protein. Well after the frontier period, wild meat remained a significant part of the diet of rural people and was a feature of urban tables well into the twentieth century.

The scale and extent of the destruction elicited a response from the state. From about 1897 to 1917, the structure of wildlife management in Canada was substantially remade. Provincial governments across the country, as well as the Yukon's territorial government, consolidated their game laws and created new bureaucracies – offices of the game warden or game guardian – that centralized policy making and enforcement under one roof.[16]

The federal government followed suit in the few areas over which it had jurisdiction, mainly the national parks and the Northwest Territories. In 1909, it passed an Order-in-Council making provision for the hiring of game wardens in all of the country's national parks. Two years later, in 1911, it created a Dominion Parks Branch charged with coordinating wildlife policy for the areas under its control, among other things.[17] As well, under Gordon Hewitt's direction, Ottawa undertook a major revision of the Northwest Territories' game act. Passed in 1917, the revised act put new species under protection, required non-Aboriginals to take out licences to kill musk-ox and to export caribou skins, and placed responsibility for its administration and enforcement in the hands of the dominion parks commissioner, who already had responsibility for protecting game, and a corps of "competent game wardens" who would relieve the overworked Mounties.[18]

The trend toward bureaucratization deepened and took on new dimensions when Canada signed the Migratory Birds Convention Act with the United States in 1916 and the federal government assumed responsibility for enforcing its provisions. The process of negotiating this treaty made bureaucrats aware of the need for interdepartmental coordination and cooperation in setting wildlife policy, and to that end, the federal government created an Advisory Board on Wild Life Protection in 1916. Bringing together representatives from the National Parks Branch, the National Museum, the Commission of Conservation, and the Department of Indian Affairs (DIA), the Advisory Board dealt with the international administration of the Migratory Birds Convention, as well as with the management of wildlife in the Northwest Territories.[19]

Canada's push to systematize, centralize, and bureaucratize wildlife conservation was influenced by developments in the United States. Inspired by American president Theodore Roosevelt's National Conservation Commission, formed just the year before, the Liberal government of Wilfrid Laurier established a Canadian Commission of Conservation in 1909 to investigate the state of the country's natural resources. Although applied scientists did not dominate its membership as they did on the American body and in the American movement in general, Canada's Commission of Conservation nonetheless shared similar Progressivist views.[20]

For Progressives, conservation was the "wise use" of resources; it was exploitation carried on in a manner that we would now term "sustainable." According to environmental historian Samuel P. Hays, Progressive conservationists believed that "foresight and restraint in the exploitation of the physical sources of wealth" would guarantee "the perpetuity of civilization, and the welfare of present and future generations."[21] "Scientific management" was the key. Not only did it entail changes to the organization of conservation – the rationalization of the game acts and the centralization of policy making – but it also involved turning over the responsibility for the substance of those policies to experts who would formulate ways to alleviate the pressure on wildlife resources. To that end, Canada's Commission of Conservation directed over two hundred scientific studies in the twelve years of its existence. Dealing with subjects ranging from oysters to air pollution, each was a chapter in the "doctrine of usefulness" that was the bedrock on which North American conservation rested.[22]

Technocrats did not dominate wildlife work in Canada at either the provincial or federal level as they did in the management of other resources. Indeed, in 1919 the Commission of Conservation urged provincial governments to encourage the formation of local fish and game protective organizations.[23] In the first half of the twentieth century, wildlife management was distinguished from other management regimes by the role it gave to the amateur and the lack of resources committed to scientific research. In part, this reflected the state of wildlife science at the time.

Unlike forestry and fisheries management, wildlife management only emerged as a formal discipline in the first half of the twentieth century. Animal ecology, the discipline on which it was partially built, was just being established as a result of the work of Charles Elton (1900-91), an Oxford University zoologist who had connections with Canada. Elton's book *Animal Ecology* (1927) helped lay the foundation for modern ecosystem ecology, outlining many of its key concepts, including food chains, niches, and community.[24] Despite his institutional affiliation, Elton was committed to developing a discipline that had practical applications. To that end, in the 1930s he began to write about the need for a "conservation ethic," motivated in part by meeting Aldo Leopold (1887-1947) at the Matamek Conference on Biological Cycles, an international meeting of scientists held in Labrador, Canada, to discuss fluctuations in wildlife populations.[25]

A hunter and Yale-trained forester who had conducted game surveys for American sporting groups, Leopold went on to teach at the University of Wisconsin and was working on what would become the bible of the new discipline of game management when he encountered Elton at Matamek. If meeting Leopold introduced Elton to conservation issues, meeting Elton convinced Leopold that ecological principles had to inform game management. Published in 1933, *Game Management* bore the imprint of Leopold's Progressivist conservation training at Yale. For Leopold, game management was "the art of making land produce sustained annual crops of wild game for recreational use."[26] Limiting predation would always be important, but Leopold devoted much of his book to outlining the biological factors that influenced wildlife populations, making the case that conservation had to take into account the relationship of animals to their environment. Game managers had to shift their focus from "controlling guns alone" to manipulating food, water, cover, and disease, and they had to learn how to conduct proper population surveys.[27] Like ecology, game management was for Leopold a quantitative and experimental discipline devoted to the study of organisms in relation to their environment.

Despite the importance of Elton and Leopold in the development of their respective disciplines, their ideas did not influence wildlife management practice until after 1945. Until then, conservation remained the purview of practical men rather than experts. That said, there could be significant differences in the skills they possessed. At one end of the spectrum stood men such as Percy Taverner; at the other, Nathan Sabean. Taverner, a taxidermist and draftsman by training, was a self-taught naturalist. His skills earned him the position of staff ornithologist at the National Museum in 1911, a position he occupied for more than thirty years. According to his biographer, Taverner laid the foundations for scientific ornithology in Canada, and was a leading advocate for wild bird protection, involved as he was in the negotiations for the Migratory Birds Convention and the establishment of several national bird sanctuaries. Taverner wrote 299 scientific papers, comments, and reviews, but his greatest contribution were his bird identification handbooks, used by scientists and amateur bird watchers alike.[28] Nathan Sabean, on the other hand, authored no scientific papers, but certainly saw himself as possessing all the qualifications to be a game warden. "I know all about the woods here, every hole and corner," the Nova Scotia man wrote in 1921. "And," he added, "I try to keep the law."[29]

Men like Nathan Sabean dominated the membership of the warden service, which was drawn from local populations.[30] Any man handy with an axe and who knew his way around the woods seemed to meet the qualifications for employment.[31] In 1921 New Brunswick made such skills an absolute requirement, insisting that each prospective deputy game warden pass an examination "as to his knowledge of woodcraft, habits and resorts of game and fur-bearing animals, the game, fishery, and fire laws of the Province ... and other matters as may be required."[32] These skills would be brought to bear in enforcing the law and reporting on wildlife conditions in their districts, information that would be forwarded to the chief game warden or guardian and used to frame policy. So, while Canada's wildlife commons was being centralized, the preponderance of "practical men" in the ranks of conservation during the first half of the twentieth century meant that localism continued to inform it.

Local fish and game associations also influenced government conservation policy. In western Canada, the perspectives they offered were, as historian George Colpitts points out, shaped by their social location as much as by their geographic one. Although the men who belonged to these organizations certainly spent time in the woods, they were not working-class woodsmen like Nathan Sabean. Instead, they tended to be middle-class urban dwellers – drawn from cities like Calgary and Vancouver, and towns like Red Deer and Fernie. Not only did they carry on the nineteenth-century tradition of doing conservation work themselves, but like the men in the warden service they also reported on wildlife conditions and offered advice on seasons and bag limits.[33]

Important as it was, the local advice offered by wardens and fish and game associations was just that: advice. With the expansion of the state into conservation work, local people – whatever their class position – no longer regulated the resource directly. The information and recommendations they provided about one particular locale were weighed against those provided by others and shaped in accordance with the conservation priorities of an entire province that had been set by outsiders. Local influences continued to shape government conservation but were channelled through a centralized bureaucracy.

Despite the continuing but reconfigured influence of the local, the techniques that characterized the wildlife work undertaken by both levels of government certainly reflected Progressivists' activist approach to conservation. Concerned with regulating demand by imposing bag limits and seasons and by creating parks and game preserves, governments also worked to increase the supply of game birds and animals by restocking depleted areas. The best-known example of this occurred in 1907 when the federal government purchased Michel Pablo's herd of bison and relocated it to Buffalo National Park, as a sanctuary for what Parks Commissioner Howard Douglas called the "relics of the countless monarchs of the plains."[34] Building on the work of individuals and local fish and game associations, provincial governments made similar efforts, often with game birds that they raised on state farms.[35] While they usually confined their propagation efforts to indigenous species, sometimes they attempted to introduce "exotics" – including beaver and red deer to the Queen Charlottes and moose to Newfoundland – to provide sport for local and non-resident hunters.[36]

It was only a short step from reintroducing species to producing them. In the 1920s both levels of government began to promote fur farming. As human settlement encroached on their habitats, there were fewer fur-bearers to keep up with the growing demand. In this context, domesticating threatened species like beaver and fox seemed to offer an effective way of conserving wild stocks while meeting market needs – but only if it were conducted along "scientific" lines.[37] To that end, the federal Department of the Interior disseminated information to prospective farmers on the scientific production of furs, and along with the provincial governments of Quebec, Ontario, and Manitoba, established model farms and experimental stations. Spurred on by rising prices, fur farming boomed, particularly in Atlantic Canada, until the Second World War, when falling prices and a shift in taste toward wild fur brought it to an end.[38]

Wildlife conservation in Canada also bore the imprint of Progressivists' commitment to rationalizing use. While federal and provincial game laws limiting the numbers and kinds of wildlife that could be killed remained a key management tool, their substance was the product of much more systematic efforts to understand game conditions. At the turn of the twentieth century, both levels of government began to collect information from field officers on a regular basis. Local input from individuals or fish and game associations continued, but was channelled through a bureaucracy that fashioned it into a single set of regulations whose application was standardized across political jurisdictions. These could be quite large, ranging from a single national park to a province, a territory, or in the case of the Migratory Birds Convention Act, the entire country – areas that could encompass considerable social as well as biological diversity.

In addition, both levels of government imposed a licensing system to rationalize and regulate use. While visitors might have been asked to take out a hunting licence in the nineteenth century, locals had largely been exempt. That changed in the twentieth century: game laws across Canada required both resident and non-resident hunters to be licensed, a provision that not only brought game departments much-needed revenue, but also allowed them to keep track of and regulate the kill.[39] In British Columbia the licensing requirement was extended in 1913 to include firearms as well.[40]

Aboriginal peoples were exempt from these licensing provisions. Indeed, the Department of Indian Affairs as well as many First Nations contended that Aboriginal peoples were not bound by any provincial game act by virtue of the treaties they had signed which guaranteed their hunting and fishing rights. The provinces, not surprisingly, had another view, and their attempts to impose the law on First Nations were a frequent cause of conflict, as will be discussed in Chapter 2. Despite Indian Affairs' position, the Parks Branch insisted that everyone was bound by the laws that forbade hunting in the national parks. Those prohibitions were contested, evaded, and ignored by First Nations, and in the case of Wood Buffalo National Park, they were modified. The Parks Branch allowed the Chipewyan to continue to hunt all animals except the endangered bison within the boundaries of the park. The federal government agreed to this modification not because it recognized the Aboriginal right to hunt, but in order to avoid the potential cost of supporting a group of Aboriginal people who could no longer feed themselves through customary means.[41]

Because of its jurisdiction over Aboriginal peoples, the federal government was somewhat more attentive to the social and economic impacts of wildlife policy than was its American counterpart or its provincial ones. National parks policy in the United States prohibited all hunting except that carried out by parks personnel to eliminate predators.[42] The federal government's sensitivity, born of paternalism, explains the one exception to Aboriginal peoples' general exemption from the provincial game acts, namely, the requirement for all trappers to register their lines. Pioneered by British Columbia in 1925, the trapline registration system developed in response to increased pressure on fur resources brought about by the influx of white trappers drawn north by rising fur prices and the prospect of easy money in the 1920s. The Great Depression of the 1930s drew more people to the backcountry. For the government of British Columbia, trapline registration was a way to rationalize resource use and to limit conflict between Aboriginal and non-Aboriginal trappers. Once registered, trapline holders had an exclusive right to take animals in specified areas. Although the DIA had argued that Aboriginal peoples were generally exempt from the provincial game acts, it considered trapline registration to be in their best interests and agreed to bind them to this particular provision. Other provinces followed British Columbia's lead and established their own registration systems: Ontario in 1935, Alberta in 1937, Manitoba in 1940, Quebec in 1945, Saskatchewan in 1946, and the Yukon in 1950. The federal government passed similar legislation for the Northwest Territories in 1949.[43]

The same awareness of the connection between conservation and social welfare also explains the federal government's best-known wildlife conservation initiative, namely, the establishment of Reindeer Station in the Northwest Territories. Concerned about the incidence of starvation among the Inuit and desiring to relieve hunting pressure on the caribou, the federal government plunged into the reindeer business, hoping that the skin and meat provided by these animals would serve as a substitute. In 1929 it hired Sami herders to drive the three thousand animals it had purchased from Alaska to the Mackenzie Delta, and then to school the Inuit of the western Arctic in the pastoral arts, thus reducing their dependence on hunting. After a drive that lasted six long years, the herd arrived and transformed the region's economy and ecology.

THE ETHICS OF EXPLOITATION

To Progressives, wildlife management was largely a numbers game. Conservation involved managing the pressure on the resource by regulating demand and supply. But the ideology of wise use does not entirely explain the character of Canada's turn-of-the-century game laws, namely, the restrictions on how animals could be killed and what could be done with their remains. For instance, in Ontario it was illegal to hunt deer in water or waterfowl from a "sail-boat, yacht, or launch propelled by steam or other power"; in Nova Scotia to snare moose, trap them in pits, or run them with dogs; and in Saskatchewan to hunt at night or to use "poison, opium, or other narcotic" to bait and kill game birds.[44] The only legitimate way to hunt game animals and birds was to shoot them – as long as the weapon was not automatic.[45]

Having bagged their quarry at the right time and place, and by proper means, hunters were not entirely free to dispose of it as they might like. The federal and provincial game laws limited the commercial sale of wild meat. These restrictions, which evolved into prohibitions in some places, were designed to get at what many conservationists at the time – and many environmental historians now – considered the root cause of wildlife decline, namely, the commodification of game and fur-bearing animals. "It is a widely accepted principle of conservation that no wild species can long withstand commercial exploitation," American conservationist William Hornaday told his Canadian counterparts in 1919. "If any principles in wild life protection can be regarded as settled for all time, it is the [necessity of] the ban on the sale of game and on the sale of the plumage of wild birds."[46] The delegates at Canada's first National Conference on Conservation of Game, Fur-Bearing Animals and Other Wild Life agreed, passing a resolution asserting that "the sale of protected game for food ... is positively inimical to the conservation of our game resources."[47]

The conference resolution reflected a growing consensus about the destructive effects of the market for wild meat. At the turn of the twentieth century, almost all provincial game laws as well as the Yukon Game Ordinance of 1900 and the federal Northwest Game Act of 1917 prohibited the sale of game except during open season, and required buyers and sellers of game meat to take out a licence.[48]

In some jurisdictions, such as Nova Scotia, moose hunters planning to sell their kills had first to submit the carcasses for inspection to ensure that the animal had not been taken by illegal methods.[49] When wartime shortages of meat sent opportunistic market hunters to the woods, some provinces imposed further strictures, banning the sale of game outright.[50]

The operative idea behind these restrictions seemed to be that Canada had reached a stage in its development where it was no longer necessary to consume wild meat; to do so signalled one's primitiveness and geographic and social marginality. In this respect, it is significant that the only people exempted from the provisions of Canada's game laws were those living in remote districts or who were Aboriginal, and the only exception to the general trend of restricting market hunting and the sale of game meat was the Yukon.[51] Although the 1920 revision of the Territory's game ordinance required market hunters and game dealers to be licensed, no bag limit or seasonal restrictions applied to those holding a commercial hunting licence.[52]

The restrictions on how animals could be killed and the limits on the commercial use of wildlife point to the existence of an ethic of exploitation rooted not in the doctrine of wise use, but in a different set of ideas. As much as it was a numbers game, wildlife management was also a matter of morality, of creating a principled relationship between human beings and the natural world. The injunctions against wasting meat, killing animals during breeding season, and killing females and their young drew upon the moral authority of biology, while the prohibitions against taking animals by means that were too easy or effective were rooted in some general sense of justice and fair play. Bag limits and the restrictions on the sale of game meat were premised on a particular understanding of human nature, namely, that people were fundamentally greedy and motivated by the market, and that in the absence of state regulation, they would exhaust their resources. Taken together, these strictures pushed subsistence and commercial hunters to the moral margins. The only legitimate reason to kill game was for sport, that is, for non-consumptive purposes. Indeed, as Leopold pointed out, the aim of game management was to produce "wildlife crops" for "recreational use."

As much as they exemplified Progressive conservation's doctrine of wise use, Canada's game laws were also the embodiment of the principles that comprised the "sportsman's creed." Reproduced in everything from conservation tracts to tourist brochures, the sportsman's creed was nothing less than a set of rules for ethical hunting that was meant to serve as the basis for environmental citizenship.[53] Gordon Hewitt believed that living by the code would "secure ... the conservation of our unsurpassed game resources," as did a number of fish and game associations across Canada and North America.[54] Among other things, the sportsman's creed declared that "no man can be a good citizen and also a slaughterer of game"; "a market-hunter is an undesirable citizen and should be treated as such"; "the best hunter is the man who finds the most game, kills the least, and leaves behind him no wounded animals"; and that "the killing of an animal means the end of its most interesting period."[55]

At its core, the creed asserted that wildlife was simply too important to be eaten. It was meant to serve a larger purpose, namely, elevating the human condition by providing sport and diversion for modern men. "In the settled and civilized regions of North America there is no real *necessity* for the consumption of wild game for food purposes," it read. "The highest purpose which the killing of wild game and game fishes can hereafter be made to serve is in furnishing objects to overworked men for tramping and camping trips in the wilds."[56]

As the game laws and the sportsman's creed suggest, an ethical relationship with nature was one based on the non-consumptive use of wildlife. Hunting for sport was one such non-consumptive use; wildlife appreciation in the national parks was another. Managing wildlife in the parks was not simply about protection: it also involved deploying wild animals to enhance and indeed create a generalized wilderness experience for tourists – even if that meant sacrificing the animals' lives or, in other cases, their wildness.

At Rocky Mountain Park, federal officials hoped that visitors would come away with a new or deepened appreciation for wild nature. But just in case the hot springs and mountains were not enough to instill the desired awareness, superintendents and wardens made animals part of the park's pedagogy. Instructing tourists in wilderness appreciation was so much easier if a bison or elk got their attention first. British Columbia's chief game warden argued that "scenery attracts all classes, but where one person would go to see scenery or big timber there are hundreds who would go long distances out of their way to see them in combination with the wild life indigenous to the mountains and forests. Eliminate the wild life from a park or forest reserve and its greatest charm is gone."[57]

More charismatic than trees and certainly than the uniformed wardens, wild animals were, however, singularly unreliable teaching assistants, often failing to show up for their classes. To address this problem, the park's management had some of Rocky Mountain's larger mammals killed, stuffed, and mounted as exhibits in the Banff museum as a way of "fostering interest in wildlife conservation."[58] As the exhibits were assembled, Howard Douglas, Rocky Mountain's second superintendent, ordered an animal paddock built in 1898. The five-hundred-acre enclosure housed elk, moose, deer, antelope, and bison, including "Sir Donald" (after his donor, Lord Strathcona), patriarch of the Banff bison herd until he was gored to death in 1909, when his head was stuffed and mounted in the parks commissioner's office.[59]

The success of the paddock encouraged Douglas to add more animals. These were chosen not because they represented the park's fauna, or even that of the region or province, but because they represented some of the country's main species or, in the case of exotic species like the Persian sheep, because he found them interesting.[60] Soon plans were under way for the construction of a full-fledged zoo, which at its opening in 1911 contained cages housing several foxes, cougars, a marmot, and a porcupine. In 1912, the park traded two moose from its paddock for a polar bear, which remained "an outstanding favourite" with visitors until 1937, when the zoo finally closed.[61] For the purposes of teaching wilderness appreciation and non-consumptive use of nature, it was more important, it seemed, that park visitors see wildlife – any wildlife, even if it was dead, caged, or exotic – rather than learn anything specific about the place itself or the relationship between its indigenous species and the Bow Valley's ecosystem.

Animals outside the paddock and zoo were also subject to management designed to "embellish the tourist's wilderness experience."[62] For instance, in 1921 Jasper's superintendent reported that he had been working hard to acclimatize the elk that had been imported from Yellowstone, getting them used to people so they would become a draw for tourists. In congratulating the wardens at Buffalo National Park for taming "Granny" (a bison) and "Maud" (an elk), Commissioner J.B. Harkin suggested that similar efforts might be undertaken

One of the more unusual experiments with introducing exotic species in Canada was this attempt to transplant yaks to Buffalo National Park, outside Wainwright, Alberta (ca. 1920s). Adapted to high altitude habitats (13,450 to 20,000 feet), these creatures must have found life at approximately 2200 feet uncomfortable. Glenbow Museum and Archives, NA-5413-2

in other parks. While they did not quite become wild animal tamers, the wardens at Banff did install salt licks along the Banff-Windermere road in 1922 so that game would be drawn there in full view of the motoring public. The possibility that they might be luring the animals to their deaths was not, it seems, discussed.[63]

The ethical relationship between people and the natural world that was embodied in the sportsman's creed and other forms of wildlife appreciation gained much of its purchase on public policy not so much from the Progressivist ideology, but from a concurrent social and intellectual movement, namely, anti-modernism. For anti-modernists, growth and the very "gospel of efficiency" so embraced by the Progressives was socially and spiritually debilitating.[64] Modern life, for all its comforts, was empty and sterile, lacking in meaning. The middle class particularly may have benefited from the fruits of human ingenuity, but had become incapable of enjoying them. In

29

Visitors to Canada's national parks were often encouraged to feed animals like these antelope as a way of cultivating an appreciation for wildlife (ca. 1920s). Glenbow Museum and Archives, NA-5413-3

fact, it seemed incapable of feeling anything but boredom or emotional exhaustion. Such was the price it paid for living in an "electrical age." "We moderns ... are keyed up to a concert pitch," observed one anonymous writer who called himself "The Doctor" in 1908. "The demands upon us are urgent and nerve-prostrating ... There is no tyranny like twentieth-century civilization."[65] As a result, these people sought what they called "authentic" experiences – experiences that would alleviate their boredom and above all, teach them to feel the full range of emotions again, to achieve a balance between reason and passion. It was this bourgeois reaction against the "over-civilizing" effects of modernity and the search for the real that lay at the core of anti-modernism.

For many bourgeois people, authenticity meant an encounter with the primitive, whether in the form of Eastern mysticism, medieval society with its warrior-knights, or folklore.[66] But for many more, the

Warden Davison with his pet elk Maud at Buffalo National Park outside Wainwright Alberta (ca. 1920s). Glenbow Museum and Archives, NA-5413-4

path to the primitive led outdoors.[67] Camping, canoeing, and simply tramping around in the woods "getting aboriginal," as one enthusiast put it, were all the rage, just the thing for the growing numbers of enervated brainworkers populating Canada's cities.[68] While the monotony of modern life led many to consume "strong stimulants in tea and coffee," or to pursue "wrong-headed amusement" in the form of "strong drink, tobacco, and cards," and "horse-racing, stock-gambling, and lower grades of sport," the true cure was to be found "in the woods and waters, in which the artificial life is cast off for a natural one."[69] As an Ontario author calling herself "Wahnipitae" put it, "What a delightful feeling it is to sit out in the open around the big camp fire, and feel we cannot be disturbed by any trolley cars, trains, or other signs of civilization. How much at home a fire makes us feel in a very few minutes! How little we miss the daily papers! Surely some of us are inoculated with the 'call of the wild' and are happy in getting back to our original way of living!"[70]

Mr. Campbell McNab and his hunting trophies, fetishes of bourgeois masculinity (1873). Notman Photographic Archives, McCord Museum of Canadian History, I81218

Though modernity's middle-class victims looked to the outdoors to cure what ailed them, the recommended dosage differed. Whereas organized camping and canoeing were often enough to cure the modern woman of what ailed her, men seemed to require a different encounter to achieve the same ends. In many ways, modernity had taken a greater toll on middle-class men, rendering them overly rational, soft, a breed prone to nervous exhaustion and incapable of being men; that is, they were incapable of acting decisively and aggressively, of doing the kinds of things that had made civilization possible in the first place.[71] A weekend by the lake in a cabin might alleviate some of the stresses of modern life, but really countering its effects required a much closer and more intense engagement with the *wild,* and not just the outdoors.

Short of war, hunting was the most effective way to restore bourgeois masculinity to its former strength and glory. As one writer in *Rod and Gun in Canada* noted, "if ... men whose brains are kept in a continual state of excitement, whose stomachs are ruined by artificial tonics, [or] ... who are cooped up at their desks the year round would try a little *play* and take a holiday in a duck marsh, they will find ... an antidote that will drive the cobwebs and aches from their brains, and their digestions will knock dyspepsia endways."[72] Echoing these thoughts, Quebec's Saguenay Club told its prospective members that "with the severe demands of modern business life on the nervous and physical energy of its devotees, it is most important that a way be opened up so that the businessman may get into God's great out-of-doors for at least some time each year. Such a holiday provides the greatest nerve tonic ever known."[73] The transformation was remarkable: men who went on big game hunting holidays "go into the woods with delicate white hands and soft bodies and come out again in a fortnight brown, hale, and hearty, able to eat like a horse and work like a Trojan."[74] "Breathing the purest of air, with the blood tingling under the stimulus of sport," Quebec's Triton Club members, who in 1908 included Theodore Roosevelt, felt they were "laying a reserve force of vitality that will not only lengthen [their] days but will enable [them] to present a steady front to the duties of life to which [they] have to return."[75]

Heeding the "Red Gods" – the "primitive instinct" to hunt – did not, however, mean surrendering to the passions completely and engaging in indiscriminate and savage bloodlust. Instead, the value of hunting for middle-class moderns was the premium it put on feeling *and* thinking. As American sharpshooter Annie Oakley told *Rod and Gun,* hunting was not about killing. "It is not a desire to kill that makes this [hunting] a pleasure, but something totally different. I suppose it might be called the pleasure of conscious superiority over that which is shot at."[76] Bird hunter A.L. Phelps agreed. "The killing isn't everything. To me the roaring rise of the partridge is almost ... as pleasurable as bringing one to bag."[77] For Franklin Hawley, the joy of hunting was "following the deer, and gaining a vantage point from which you MIGHT SLAY but DO NOT. The real sport lies in the conquest, not in the killing."[78]

While anti-modern social criticism was generated in elite circles, its central ideas about the degenerative effects of modernization and the regenerative power of wilderness had broad popular cultural appeal, in large part because of the reach and influence of a number of specialized magazines. At least ten emerged in the late nineteenth and early twentieth centuries to meet the growing interest in the outdoors, including *Canadian Athletic* (Toronto, 1892), *Rod and Gun in Canada* (Montreal, 1899), *Western Canadian Sportsman* (Winnipeg, 1904), *Outdoor Canada* (Toronto, 1905), *Canadian Alpine Journal* (Banff, 1907), and *Sports* (Halifax, 1908).[79] Of these, *Rod and Gun* was by far the most popular, with a circulation of some eighteen thousand in 1913.[80] Other important vehicles for popularizing anti-modern ideas included pulp fiction, juvenile literature, sporting goods companies, arms manufacturers, and – in Canada particularly – railways who advertised the country's sport and scenery to prospective tourists.[81] Organizations like Teddy Roosevelt's Boone and Crockett Club, Baden-Powell's Boy Scouts, and Seton's Woodcraft Indians also prescribed the "strenuous life" of the outdoorsman as a preventive cure for the malaise of modernity. Circulated through these media, these ideas gave rise to a multi-million dollar industry designed to cater to the sporting tourist.[82]

As much as they considered wildlife an economic resource, government conservationists also recognized its therapeutic power, and shaped management policy accordingly. The influence of Progressive conservation was apparent in the bureaucratic structure of management and the initiatives aimed at regulating and rationalizing the exploitation of wildlife. The scope of anti-modernism's influence on conservation, on the other hand, can be measured by the extent to which management policy encouraged the non-consumptive use of wildlife, whether by making animals into tourist attractions, promoting sports hunting, restricting hunting for the market, or protecting and propagating certain species because of their recreational value. It is also reflected directly in the sentiments of Fred Bradshaw, Saskatchewan's chief game guardian. Commenting on the importance of wildlife, Bradshaw observed that its value "is not so much as an article of food, although that is considerable in itself ... but as an inducement that attracts farmers from the monotony of their daily work, and clerks, tradesmen and merchants of the cities to the prairie and the woods."[83] Even conservation bureaucrats like Gordon Hewitt embraced anti-modernism's arguments about the value of the wild. "What man is there," he asked, "who, after months of unremitting toil, takes down his gun, rod, or camera, and seeking the silence of the open air for a week or two, does not come back physically and mentally refreshed and remade?" For this hard-headed scientist, "nothing calls for resourcefulness so much as the quest for wild life, when the beaten tracks of a more civilized life ... are left and one has to return to the primal competitive habits."[84] Provided such encounters with nature followed particular rules of engagement – the sportsman's creed – they reinvigorated the body and spirit. In placing a premium on reason and passion, they restored the balance of human nature.

In promoting the therapeutic power of recreational encounters with wilderness and wildlife, government conservationists were not offering a fundamental critique of the conditions of modernity. They were not calling for an end to its "unremitting toil" or the "high pressure of city conditions,"[85] nor were they arguing for a permanent return to the primitive. Instead, engaging with the wild was meant to allow people to go back to the city renewed and ready to do battle in jungles of a different kind. Conserving wildlife as "objects for over-worked men" was framed as a way of "increasing human efficiency."[86] It was thus a way to treat the symptoms of modernity without getting at their root causes.

Although Progressivism and anti-modernism pulled wildlife conservation in different directions, they did not, in the end, produce a set of management practices that were inconsistent or fundamentally at odds. Insofar as anti-modernism shaped a wildlife management policy concerned with efficiency and with reducing the frictions of modern life, its contribution was completely consistent with and indeed reinforced the general purpose and direction of Progressive conservation. Regulations and policies for the wise use of one resource – wildlife – made for the more effective development of another, namely, people. Hunted with a gun or camera, wildlife could cure nervous exhaustion and early-twentieth-century ennui and thus make men fit for the marketplace. When domesticated by Aboriginals, it could civilize savages, turning nomadic hunters into settled farmers who would be less of a drain on the state. Managed properly, wildlife was a corrective to over-civilization and barbarity.

Wildlife conservation in Canada was a modernist project aimed at controlling nature and human nature, designed to temper the effects of modernity systematically by making a place for wildlife along Progressivist and anti-modernist lines.[87] Both these ideologies were responses to the effects of industrialization and both shaped the fundamental changes in wildlife conservation that began to unfold at the turn of the twentieth century.

As federal and provincial governments centralized control over wildlife in the early twentieth century, creating new bureaucracies dedicated to conservation, local participation in management was reconfigured. The game laws of the eighteenth and nineteenth centuries had left the details of policy to the representatives of local government – to justices of the peace and grand juries – and placed enforcement in the hands of private citizens. Twentieth-century game laws contained different provisions, placing the responsibility for the substance and enforcement of the laws in the hands of government-appointed game wardens and ultimately the civil servant who headed the provincial office of that name. Local input from individuals or fish and game associations continued, but was funnelled through a bureaucracy that established regulations for an entire province rather than particular areas.

These changes in the organization of conservation altered the nature of wildlife as a common property resource. As both levels of government involved themselves in conservation, Canada's wildlife shifted from being a "local commons" – a resource defined and regulated informally by resident users – to a more centralized one controlled increasingly by outsiders. While the trajectory of change it followed was broadly similar to that which occurred in the United States, Canadian wildlife did not become a "national commons," its regulation completely "delocalized." The division of powers in Canada meant that its wildlife could not be "federalized" to the extent that it was south of the border, particularly in the American west. Its regulation would always be somewhat fragmented. In Canada, government involvement in wildlife conservation resulted in the creation of not one, but several centralized commons controlled by the provinces and, in the first half of the twentieth century, administered by "practical men" often drawn from the very kinds of communities they policed. Thus, although it was rationalized at the turn of the twentieth century, the Canadian wildlife commons remained informed by localism.

This did not lessen the potential for conflict. The implementation of these conservation policies met with opposition. While local users took issue with the specific limits on killing and using wildlife, the root of the conflict lay elsewhere. As much as it was about limits and numbers, the program of wildlife conservation pursued by governments across Canada also aimed to promote a particular ethical relationship with nature that could be the basis for an environmental citizenship. Like all definitions of citizenship, the one embedded in Canada's game laws reflected certain views. Government wildlife conservation might have become less localistic in the first half of the twentieth century, but it remained firmly grounded in particular interests defined by class and race.

An Alberta game warden nabs a poacher near Hardisty (ca. 1912). Glenbow Museum and Archives, NA-2284-13

CHAPTER TWO

◆

Make Way for Wildlife: Colonization, Resistance, and Transformation

IN THE SPRING of 1913, Albert J. Wilson wrote a letter to British Columbia's provincial game warden asking him to clarify a recent amendment to the game act. Lest Bryan Williams think his concerns were those of a crank, Wilson insisted that his questions were "vital to hundreds of us pre-emptors who are trying to make a living off the land. Many of us are heavily in debt and half starved having to live for weeks on rabbits and such," he noted. "If there are laws forbidding us to kill deer for food all I can say is that the men that made them could never have known the hardships we have to suffer when trying to open up this country and live."[1]

Although the rhetoric of conservation stressed that wildlife protection was in the public interest, Wilson's letter suggests otherwise. While it was difficult to gauge the success of management initiatives in the short term – to know, for instance, if wild stocks had increased or if enervated city folk had been regenerated through their encounters with wildlife – there was little doubt that they had a significant and immediate impact on the lives of ordinary people in Canada's countryside.

The changes in the organization, substance, and aims of wildlife conservation that began at the turn of the twentieth century had been justified as a safeguard against the privatization of an increasingly scarce resource, something that was viewed as the real threat to access. "God forbid that the old country systems should ever prevail," Ontario's chief game warden told an American audience in 1906. "If we desire to increase anarchy and dissatisfaction we will allow the rich men to acquire all the best hunting and fishing grounds in our countries, fence them from the roads, and stick up trespass notices ... It is a safe policy for all Governments to legislate for the masses. The classes will look after themselves."[2]

The emphasis on wildlife as common property deflected attention away from the interests that were served by government conservation. The management regimes that emerged across the country promoted the non-consumptive use of wildlife, conserving it for the sporting and viewing pleasure of middle-class Canadians. Their implementation marginalized certain groups even as they facilitated particular kinds of relationships with wild animals. Members of the rural working class – many of them non-British immigrants – and Aboriginal peoples found themselves prosecuted for doing what they had always done, wresting a subsistence and a living from the woods. Despite the biological, social, and cultural diversity encompassed within their jurisdiction, and the slight modifications to their content over time, the game laws were instruments of colonization, imposing an urban and bourgeois sensibility about wildlife on rural Canada.

Making a place for wildlife involved pushing some people out of the way. Sometimes they pushed back. This chapter tells that story. While it is one that has yet to be told for Canada as a whole, the plot line is familiar, having been played out around the world. There is, however, another part to it – and one that ties the story of conservation and colonization to another narrative, that of rural transformation. Resistance was not the only response to the imposition of government conservation initiatives. Some individuals marginalized by the game laws profited from the new opportunities made available by conservation's emphasis on the non-consumptive use of wildlife. The desire for a wilderness experience created a market for people with the skills to facilitate it. The game laws may have proscribed "the liberty of the woods" they had previously enjoyed, but some men from rural areas were able to redeploy their local knowledge, finding jobs as hunting guides.[3] In selling their knowledge as woodcraft, rural people became implicated in the creation of a new set of commercial relationships with nature that simultaneously highlighted their skills and marginalized them. The transformation of local knowledge was a part of the transformation of the countryside, a process that saw it integrated into a system of power that defined rural areas as urban playgrounds.

CONSERVATION AND COLONIZATION

After just three years in office as British Columbia's first chief game warden, Bryan Williams took some pride in reporting that "respect for the Game Laws is infinitely greater than it was, both by the Indians and the Whites." Unfortunately, the outlook for wildlife conservation in the province was not entirely promising, largely because of the presence of "foreigners." In his view, the "Asiatics" were the most dangerous offenders, taking animals and birds with reckless abandon. "All game is alike to them, whether pheasants sitting on eggs, or grouse with young broods, or does with fawns." Despite their improved attitude, Aboriginal people were just as undiscerning, but "luckily they are generally wretched hunters and the poorest of shots, or the game would suffer more than it does."[4]

, As Williams' comments suggest, those who worked for wildlife considered certain groups more prone to commit crimes against nature than others, and directed their energies accordingly. Fur, feather, and scale may have been under general assault by the forces of progress and development, but in Canada, as elsewhere, the battle to save animals, birds, and fish amounted at times to class and race warfare, with farmers, resource workers, and Aboriginal peoples shouldering the burden of making a place for wildlife.

In surveying the state of wildlife affairs in its first year of operation, Ontario's Fish and Game Commission singled out the province's farmers as among the groups most likely to disregard closed seasons and to use illegal methods to kill animals.[5] Its assessment was broadly shared. Canadian farmers often found themselves at odds with the game acts, which, much to their chagrin, made them criminals for protecting their interests. While any wolf, coyote, or lynx could be shot on sight, farmers were constrained from killing game animals that treated their fields and kitchen gardens as salad bars – unless, of course, the animals made the mistake of doing so during open season. "This year I set out 220 young apple trees," complained Nova Scotia farmer William Rourke in 1925, "and the deer have destroyed

41

nearly one-third of these ... [T]his fall it is even worse as they are now beginning to eat the bark off the larger bearing trees ... This is a very serious matter for me, as unless I have some protection, I will have to give up farming."[6] Similarly, on the other side of the country, an orchardist outside Nelson, British Columbia, complained that bears had taken a hundred boxes of McIntosh apples and four hundred pounds of grapes from two different orchards, the wily beasts "having been able probably by instinct to know the exact time when these were ripe and ready for consumption."[7]

Although most game acts in Canada allowed a farmer to kill animals out of season if they were "depasturing" his fields, the onus was on him to prove that his actions were the equivalent of justifiable homicide. Farmers had to swear affidavits detailing the circumstances of the shooting, and could expect to be visited and interrogated by the local game warden to confirm them. "We were defending our beans," explained Russell Cross, outlining how a deer came to be lying dead of a gunshot wound in his Lunenburg garden. Given that a drought had claimed most of his crops, Cross asked if he might keep the venison: "If I could use the deer it would at least recompense me for the loss of the vegetables." Not wanting to encourage trigger-happy farmers, the Nova Scotia game act required that they give up the dead animal so as not to profit from their actions – but in this case Chief Game Warden F.A. Harrison agreed to Cross's request.[8] While the law acknowledged that people killed game animals for reasons other than sport, by calling people like Russell Cross to account, it simultaneously deemed their relationships with wildlife exceptional, outside the norm of non-consumptive use.

The exemptions for needy settlers living in remote districts also worked to acknowledge and marginalize the consumptive use of wildlife. Almost all provincial game acts allowed individuals who had limited access to sources of domesticated protein to kill protected animals and birds at any time. However, they had to prove their need, and were permitted to kill only for their own and their families' consumption. While these conditions were meant to prevent over-killing and market hunting, they also placed individuals at the mercy of local wardens whose assessment of need could often shade into one of character.

However two-edged, the exemptions offered by the provincial game acts to the residents of remote districts were not extended to

Canada's resource workers, whose logging, mining, and construction camps were often on the frontiers of settlement. Employers were expected to provision them properly, eliminating the need for workers to go "pot-hunting." Some provinces, including New Brunswick, entrenched this expectation in law, holding the "heads of lumbering establishments, foremen, contractors and subcontractors engaged in lumbering or railway building" liable for any violations of the game act by the men under their employ.[9] But given the savings to be had by living off the land, many companies probably preferred to take their chances. In any case, whether they were adequately supplied by their employers or not, some workers may have welcomed the opportunity to go hunting – a needed break from the monotony of work.

In many places their depredations were an open secret. "There has been hundreds of Quebec frenchmen [sic] for two years or more cutting pulpwood," complained Bruce Jackson from Mooseland, Nova Scotia, in 1930, "and in the summer they set up snares to catch moose to get meat for their camp."[10] According to Bryan Williams, almost all of British Columbia's logging camps "buy game meat or allow men to go out hunting and pay them for their time just as if they were working," thus spreading the cost and risk to those who were most vulnerable.

Although logging foremen like Noah Adams and K. Tahara, the chief of a Japanese crew, were prosecuted for feeding their men entirely on British Columbia venison, more often than not it was the workers themselves who were punished most severely.[11] Adams and Tahara were fined $75 each for possessing deer out of season, but a Japanese man convicted of throwing dynamite into the Capilano River a year earlier was fined $300.[12] Frustrated by the difficulties of convicting railway workers in 1914, Sault Ste. Marie, Ontario, overseer Charles Fitzsimmons decided to take preventive action, "taking away all weapons in possession of foreigners, to render them incapable of doing damage."[13]

In the cities, the marginal also figured prominently among those prosecuted successfully for violations of the game act. Although C.A. Harrison, the proprietor of the Hotel Driard claimed that grouse and pheasant were "being served in the public eating houses in Victoria," few hoteliers were prosecuted.[14] Instead, it was easier to go after the suppliers, people like "Lee, a Chinaman" who had twenty-nine grouse, five hen pheasants, and four cocks for sale at Vancouver's

City Meat Market in 1908; or an unnamed "Oriental" who sold unborn fawns preserved in alcohol as a folk remedy to the residents of Nanaimo's Chinatown in 1910; or Stephen Maloney, a Mi'kmaq from Nova Scotia's Shubenacadie reserve, who was caught selling venison in Halifax's city market in 1934.[15]

Many conservationists believed that Aboriginal people like Stephen Maloney, more than farmers or resource workers, were the real threat to wildlife populations. Not only did they provision Canada's logging, mining, and construction camps with wild meat and supply game animals and birds for urban tables, but they also engaged in the profligate destruction of wildlife in the pursuit of their own subsistence. Although in many places in Canada their right to fish and hunt was guaranteed by treaty, Aboriginal peoples were targets of condemnation by sportsmen, fish and game clubs, and provincial authorities.

For instance, rod and gun club members in Calgary, Lethbridge, Edmonton, Red Deer, McLeod, and Moose Jaw petitioned the minister of the interior in 1893, complaining that Aboriginal people took "innumberable [sic] eggs" and "slaughter thousands of young birds before they are able to fly." In their view, conservation required that "the Indians be strictly confined to their several reservations during the breeding season for chicken and wildfowl, say from June 1st to Sept 1st."[16] Similarly, James Brewster, the well-known Banff outfitter, complained about the depredations of the Stoney Indians on the area's valuable mountain sheep. "There is no discrimination in their shooting," he wrote in 1905, "rams, ewes, and lambs all look alike to the Indian and if a whole herd is cornered up they are all exterminated."[17] Knowing that confinement on their reserves was impossible, he asked that the band be moved to the eastern prairies, away from the mountains. Brewster's colleague Philip Moore agreed and painted this picture of the Stoney with grudging brushstrokes: "an Indian of the Stoney tribe is an incomparable hunter, patient & tireless & they seldom miss a shot. A track never escapes them & they can follow a trail over the bare rock. Many of them will surround a mountain & driving everything to the top kill it there ... No animal escapes. They clean the country like a rake."[18]

Accusations like these got a sympathetic hearing from provincial game authorities, whose comments underscored their bias toward the non-consumptive use of wildlife. Calling attention to Aboriginal peoples' illegal hunting of moose and elk, Fred Bradshaw, Saskatchewan's chief game guardian, framed his concerns in terms of the impact it had on the province's reputation as a big game hunting destination. Sportsmen coming to Saskatchewan went to "considerable expense and trouble preparing for their annual big game hunting trip, only to find, on arriving at their camp, unquestionable evidence that the Indians have preceded them." Worst of all, Bradshaw continued, "some of the finest heads, that would be considered almost priceless, are slaughtered and left in the woods to rot."[19] His concern over the impact that Aboriginal hunting might have on the sports hunting economy was echoed by his Quebec counterpart, who noted that in his jurisdiction, the "Indians were slaughtering the animals, taking away the meat for food and leaving the heads to rot in the bush."[20] With the recreational use of wildlife established as normative, wise use and waste were defined in different terms, ones that marginalized those who hunted to eat rather than those who hunted for trophies. Ironically, when Aboriginals did attach value to trophy heads they were criticized as well. Beginning in the late 1880s and well into the twentieth century, the Stoneys at Exshaw and Morley, Alberta, engaged in a lively tourist trade in trophy heads, selling some directly to CPR passengers and others to Norman Luxton, supplying the taxidermist's Sign of the Goat curio shop in Banff.[21]

Much to their frustration, provincial authorities discovered that the weapons at their disposal were not as effective when levelled against Aboriginal peoples. Although wildlife came under provincial jurisdiction, Aboriginal peoples were wards of the federal government. Their wildlife use was regulated by the federal laws, including the Indian Act, the Migratory Birds Convention Act, the National Parks Act, and the Northwest Game Act, and, where applicable, by treaties, which in many cases granted Aboriginal peoples the right to hunt and fish over the lands reserved for them and over unoccupied crown lands. However, the situation on the ground was not nearly so clear. Confusion reigned, and clarity came only slowly and in piecemeal fashion as cases involving Aboriginal hunting rights were litigated. Generally, Aboriginal people were prosecuted for violations of the game act first, and questions about jurisdiction came later.

Even before the first charge was laid against them, however, Aboriginal peoples were alive to the potential impact of the provincial game acts on their livelihood and existence, and they made their concerns known. As British Columbia reorganized its game department and appointed a salaried chief game warden, the chiefs of the Lillooet First Nation articulated their anxiety. "This new game act as a whole is hurting us altogether. Should it be put in execution it would mean our entire destruction. Hunting and fishing is our living. It is our daily bread for which we have a right and which no law can take away from us," they wrote in 1905. "We have a right to live."[22] Similarly, the Cowichan took the opportunity provided by the visit of British Columbia's Royal Commission on Indian Affairs in 1914 to ask that they be given permission to kill "siwash ducks" for food, especially as their white neighbours did not consider them fit for consumption. Chief Joe Eukahalt thought it wise to ask, since "white men are making laws that are getting our people in trouble. The way they are now, our people cannot ... get their grub anywhere without being guilty of violating some law."[23]

It was all too clear to both Aboriginal peoples and the Indian agents who oversaw their affairs that the game acts were aimed at restricting, if not eliminating, the use of wildlife as food. Benjamin Lawton, Alberta's chief game guardian, observed that the law was not designed for individuals who depended on hunting for their subsistence. "It is a well known fact that an Indian and his family cannot exist on one deer [per season]," he wrote his superiors in 1908, "this being the limit allowed under the game act."[24] However, neither Alberta's game law nor the others in Canada recognized "the extensive demands generated by a kin-based subsistence economy."[25]

Concerned about the impact that hunting restrictions would have on their expenditures for welfare, the Department of Indian Affairs convinced provincial governments to allow Indian agents to issue special permits to needy Aboriginals to hunt for food. Not wanting to leave any more to the agents' discretion than was necessary, British Columbia's chief game warden sent a circular outlining the game department's criteria for awarding such permits. "In considering such applications I should require to know, as near as possible, the age of the Indian, the number of his family," he wrote in 1914. "Young Indians who are capable of work are certainly not entitled to them, it is for the more older class of Indians who have been in the habit of hunting all their lives and feel more severely the enforcement of the present game laws."[26] As was the case with other exemptions to the game act, this one also served a normative and disciplinary function, in this instance strengthening the link between consuming wild meat and primitiveness.

Wildlife was not just the basis of Aboriginals' subsistence; it was also their point of intersection with the capitalist economy. In proscribing the killing of animals and the sale of wild meat, the game laws limited Native peoples' participation in the commercial economy, often leaving them without money to buy provisions. For the Natives of Stuart Lake, British Columbia's ban on beaver hunting in 1905 not only "annihilated rights of immemorial date," but confronted them with the possibility of "complete starvation."[27] According to Robert McCandless, Aboriginal men derived a good income from supplying meat to Yukoners in the period before the Second World War. In Dawson alone, wild protein accounted for a third of all meat consumption. But when the territorial government required market hunters be licensed in 1920, it put an end to the occupation. By the 1940s only ten to fifteen market hunting licences were issued per year. The costs of licensing outweighed the benefits to be derived from selling meat.[28]

While the consequences of adhering to the game laws were dire, the penalties for violating them were equally grim. Not only did Aboriginal people face heavy fines – or jail time if they found themselves unable to pay – but they also stood to lose their property and what economic independence they had. When Chilcotin George Achow was caught with a red fox out of season in 1917, he was sentenced to three months in prison and lost the valuable fox fur. Reduced to destitution, his family was completely dependent on support from relatives, who were themselves with few means, and the Department of Indian Affairs.[29] While the lost revenue from a seized pelt was serious enough, when Aboriginal people had their traps or firearms confiscated they stood to lose their ability to make a living. Commenting on the sentences given to two Shuswap in 1921 for having deer in their possession out of season, Indian Agent J.F. Smith took issue with the court's decision to impound one man's gun. "As it is not easy to estimate what an Indian's gun means to him, being practically a part of his being, the extreme hardship inflicted in the loss of this main food getter can hardly be exaggerated," he wrote.[30]

The loss of pelts, guns, and traps was only part of a larger pattern of dispossession experienced by Aboriginal peoples as a result of state conservation practices. Like the provincial game acts, game preserves and national parks dislocated Aboriginal peoples in Canada, as they did in the United States.[31] According to Duncan Campbell Scott, superintendent of Indian Affairs, although game sanctuaries and national parks were "praiseworthy innovations necessary in the public interest," they nevertheless aggravated "the difficulties of the Indians."[32] The Chipewyan of northern Alberta could testify to how aggravating the public interest could be. When a North West Mounted Police investigation of the wood buffalo population in the Northwest Territories revealed that the herds, though protected by law, were being decimated by the Chipewyan around Fort Smith, Maxwell Graham of the Parks Branch argued that stronger steps were necessary to preserve the animals and recommended that a game preserve be established and the Chipewyan relocated. Graham got his preserve: Wood Buffalo National Park was established after the First World War – in an area that encompassed the hunting territory of the Chipewyan. Although they were not forced to move, and in fact were allowed to hunt within the park's boundaries, the Chipewyan were prohibited from killing the animal that was their most important source of protein: the buffalo.[33]

Confronted with growing competition from white trappers in the 1920s, the Chipewyan found it increasingly difficult to make a living, even with the limited hunting rights they had in the park. They asked that the government set aside a hunting preserve for their exclusive use. What they got instead was an extension of the existing park's boundaries. Although their hunting rights were coterminous with the enlarged park, its boundaries had been extended not to provide more hunting territory for the Chipewyan, but to provide sufficient rangeland for the growing herd, which flourished at their expense. To the Chipewyan it seemed "the Government were taking up more of their hunting grounds to feed more buffalo being brought into their Country without their permission."[34] Addressing his letter to "the Chief of the Indian Department," Chief Jonas LaViolette summarized what for him was an impossible situation. "No one seems to care what happens to us," he wrote in 1927. "There are lots of men here looking after Buffalo, but no one looking after us."[35]

To make matters worse, the men looking after the buffalo were not, in some Aboriginal peoples' opinion, doing a very good job. Some, like Blackwater Johnnie, argued that the local warden was targeting the wrong people: "the whites are killing all the year

48

round," he insisted, "and he pays no attention to them whatever."[36] The Indian agent at Fisher River, Manitoba, agreed, finding fault with the game acts themselves, rather than those who enforced them. "The Game Authorities also argue that the application of their game laws to Indians is for the protection and preservation of game," he wrote in 1917. "But when the Provincial Authorities issue licenses by the thousand to men of means who are well able to buy beef, giving them the power to kill the game they profess to protect, their argument appears most ridiculous."[37]

Some Aboriginal people offered critiques that were even more fundamental, raising questions about whether management policy rested on a sound biological basis. In 1919, for instance, Natives around Stuart Lake petitioned the government of British Columbia, taking issue with a game act provision that required them to trap every year or risk losing their claim. While compliance might make sense from an administrative standpoint, it did not from an ecological one. "It is sometimes necessary to have a trapline vacant for two or three years to allow the animals to increase," they noted, "but by the act we are compelled to trap every line by November 14 in each year or run the risk of having our line occupied by some other person when [sic, then] it is lost to us for all time."[38]

Beyond questioning the bias of regulation and whether it actually served the purposes it purported to, some Native people insisted that they needed no instruction in conservation. Since "time immemorial" they had rationalized and regulated the use of wildlife, in a way that sustained both human and animal populations. British Columbia's 1905 ban on beaver hunting might be the key to preserving the animal in other parts of the province, but in the North such measures were unnecessary. "We have laws of our own which we may call natural by which Beaver is protected," the residents of Stuart Lake wrote. "For instance every group of families have a certain special circuit where they do their hunting and they understand that it is their interest to see that the game is not destroyed, to that effect we never hunt two years in succession on the same streams."[39]

To the extent that wildlife conservation marginalized, dispossessed, and displaced rural people by imposing and legitimating one kind of relationship with nature over others, it was an instrument of colonization. But conservation was not just a way of managing the marginal, disciplining them to use resources properly: it was also an attack on local knowledge. In taking issue with the prohibition on trapping beaver, the people of Stuart Lake made the case that they could govern their own affairs; that they had developed strategies of wildlife conservation based on their experience hunting the region for generations. From their perspective, the fundamental problem with state regulation was that it overlooked the existence of informal systems of management like theirs, or discounted their efficacy and the validity of the local knowledge on which they were based.

Aboriginal peoples were not alone in experiencing wildlife conservation as a challenge to local knowledge. Much to their frustration, those who counted themselves among the strongest supporters of state wildlife management found that their interests were not always served by the very processes they had helped to put in place. Members of Canada's numerous fish and game associations and rod and gun clubs had been instrumental in lobbying for better laws and stronger enforcement. Gordon Hewitt considered them of "incalculable" benefit to conservation and called for more such organizations to be created. As "trustees" for the wildlife in their particular district, these sportsmen acted as extra eyes and ears for the government warden service, propagated wild birds for restocking purposes, reported on fluctuations in wildlife populations, and consulted on seasons and bag limits.[40]

Their direct involvement – in many cases invited by provincial governments – created an expectation that management initiatives would reflect local perceptions of the distribution of wildlife and serve their interests. This was particularly the case in Nova Scotia, whose fish and game associations had for more than twenty years been mandated by legislation to both frame and enforce the game act. The history of their involvement had created a political culture of entitlement that shaped their engagement with the provincial game bureaucracy long after their formal role had disappeared. They firmly believed that their views should be taken seriously. For instance, members of the West Pictou Rod and Gun Club felt that Nova Scotia's game act went too far in protecting birds. As law-abiding sportsmen, they had done their bit for conservation, obeying the closed season and allowing the game bird populations to rebound. By 1929 it had, and they were unwilling to make "unnecessary sacrifices" and deprive themselves of shooting. "We do not consider it necessary to have birds as plentiful and as tame as barnyard fowl."[41] Similarly, C.H. Brown of Windsor, Nova Scotia, wrote to complain about the short season for partridge, noting that the birds were plentiful in Hants County. In reply, Chief Game Warden Otto Schierbeck noted that though Hants might enjoy a healthy population of partridge, other parts of the province did not. "It is impossible to have an open season in one part of the province and a close season in another ... It would certainly cause trouble."[42]

The clash of local and provincial perspectives came to the fore again in locating Nova Scotia's first game sanctuary in the late 1920s. The fish and game associations in western Nova Scotia had lobbied hard for the Boundary Rock area in Annapolis County and were angry when Otto Schierbeck rejected their advice. In their view, Schierbeck's decision amounted to a rejection of their local knowledge. In particular, they took exception to being told by an outsider that they did not understand the ecological qualities and environmental limits of the place in which they lived. "I ... cannot see why it is necessary to import a man from Denmark to make a report upon a subject upon which he has no personal knowledge," wrote E.R. Clarke on their behalf, especially "when we have men of native talent who could have supplied the information." Not only was Schierbeck ignorant, but he was also insulting, "intimat[ing] that we were a lot of lack-wits and incompetents, and so far foolish as to not know what we were talking about when he says that the country around Boundary Rock is without a food supply, and lacks shelter," he continued. "There were about sixty sportsmen who attended this convention in Annapolis, and among them you could find men of really first class ability and intelligence, and I doubt if you could find one of the perfect fools that Mr. Schierbeck esteemed us to be."[43]

Frustrated by what they perceived to be Schierbeck's failure to appreciate and act on local expertise, the members of the province's fish and game associations went on the offensive and organized to make their voices heard in framing wildlife policy. Thus when Otto Schierbeck arrived for a meeting with them in 1928 to discuss amendments to the game act, he was made to wait for an hour on the staircase outside the conference room. When he was finally ushered in, he discovered, much to his annoyance, that "all discussion of moose law had been done, resolutions adopted, and that all gov't officials had been debarred." Instead of engaging in a consultative process, Schierbeck was simply presented with the fish and game associations' consensus position on the game act and sent off to implement it. He was appalled, his modern sensibilities as a scientist offended at the triumph of the local – and in his view, the irrational. "The whole question of game conservation has become ... political," he complained.[44]

The marginalization of local knowledge was not specific to Nova Scotia or simply the result of one bureaucrat's insensitivity. Instead, it was inherent in the centralized structure of state regulation. Wildlife management depended on local input but for administrative reasons was framed in general terms. While not specific to wildlife conservation, the problem of scale – of framing provincial policies that would be sensitive to local conditions – was exacerbated by the fugitive nature of the resource. The fact that wildlife moved made the politics of regulation all the more complicated and contentious.

Otto Schierbeck's experience suggests that ordinary people could be openly critical of the game laws and defy both their substance and the authority that underlay them. But resistance to wildlife conservation was not limited to Aboriginals and sportsmen, nor to petitioning and mockery, but instead encompassed a diversity of individuals and tactics, ranging from simple non-compliance to murder.

Rural people everywhere resented the incursions of game wardens; they bent and flouted the laws – often with impunity and no small amount of pride. Throughout the 1920s and '30s, there was a series of letters, many of them anonymous, in the Department of Lands and Forests records for Nova Scotia informing the chief commissioner of violations of the game act that give some sense of the terms of their compliance and, more frequently, the ease with which people could poach. Some Nova Scotians thought they should have to pay for a hunting licence only if they were actually successful in bagging an animal; after all, why pay for a failed enterprise?[45]

Others preferred not to bother with the law at all. For instance, John Adams from Hants County told the chief commissioner that "there is an ever increasing number of people here who treat the game law as a joke and its officers with contempt ... I heard of one man who makes his brags that he killed seven cow moose in one year and he also declares that he will continue to kill any game at any time in spite of all law or law officers."[46] An anonymous Cumberland County writer told the chief commissioner that "the game warden

COLONIZATION, RESISTANCE, AND TRANSFORMATION

here has in the past has [sic] not fulfilled his duty as it is a known fact among the people of this place that one man shot three moose in one day not five miles from the game warden's Home. Last winter there was six or eight moose in about the same place shot. I am not a crank or anything of the kind but why not protect the game?"[47]

When threatened with prosecution, some people engaged in threats and violence in return. Nova Scotia warden W.W. Osborne reported that poacher Alex McIntosh walked into a New Glasgow store "with a Bag of [game] meat on his back" and boasted publicly about his illegal hunting, making it known "that he would fill anybody with led [sic] if they attempted to get after him."[48] Demonstrations like these were what led informers like Hugh Smith to be wary. "Now whatever you do don't give me away," he wrote the local warden in 1925, after informing him of a gang of moose poachers operating nearby. "I can find out what they are doing right along if they don't suspect me, and besides I have my woodlot where they sometimes hunt, and they'd think nothing of putting it up in smoke."[49]

It was all too much for some men to bear. "I find on this job of Game Warden," Sub-Ranger J.D. Lockwood wrote his boss, "that I am losing a great many friends and I get lots of hard knocks. People are not hospitable to me when they know my duties. It is mighty hard to get along on $50.00 and loose [sic] all your friends besides."[50] His colleague George Goudey agreed. "Don't be surprised if I throw this affair up," he wrote to the chief game warden. "It is entirely unsatisfactory to me in many ways. First there is nothing in it and one makes a lot of enemies and public sentiment seems to be against the way some of the laws are carried out."[51]

On rare occasions, wardens lost more than their friends and their jobs: they lost their lives – victims of those they prosecuted for violations of the game act. During the Depression, two British Columbia game wardens were killed in separate incidents. In 1930, Dennis Greenwood was shot and killed on the main street of Canal Flats by a man he had charged with poaching deer the previous winter. Two years later, Albert Farey was killed by a man he had stopped to question about a deer hide in his possession. When Farey turned away momentarily, the suspect raised his rifle to his waist and shot the game warden twice in the back. While both these incidents probably speak to the desperation of the Depression years as much as they do to opposition to wildlife management, they do suggest the level of tension and fear that could surround the enforcement of its provisions.

Game wardens were not the only targets of those disaffected with wildlife conservation. Some rural people vandalized the cabins and camps used by tourist-hunters; Aboriginal people "shot out" prime game areas before tourists could reach them; and members of rod and gun clubs openly criticized wealthy outsiders who sought government concessions to establish their own private hunting and fishing preserves.[52] These targets suggest that ordinary people were well aware of whose interests were served by wildlife management practices. The wardens, however despised, were simply the instruments of their dispossession; the real sources of their marginalization were the urban outsiders who treated the woods as their playground and had managed to get the law on their side.

CONSERVATION AND THE TRANSFORMATION OF LOCAL KNOWLEDGE

Unfortunately, threats, assaults, arsons, and shootings were far more common than words explaining them. When rural people did provide explanations, they made reference to customary "rights" (especially in the case of Aboriginal people) or to defending a "way of life." In other words, in registering their opposition to conservation, rural people employed a language of history and authenticity. Rhetorically powerful, this language suggests that ordinary people's response to wildlife management was fundamentally reactive and conservative; that, when confronted with change, the only thing they could do was oppose it, invoking past practice. Such was not the case.

Rural people were not simply acted upon but were implicated in the very changes they experienced.[53] For as much as conservation marginalized customary uses of wildlife, it also created new opportunities for some rural people. Anti-modernist nostalgia led many well-off urbanites to believe that there was no better guarantee of a "real" backwoods experience than to go with a "real" woodsman. Many of them envied their guides' way of life, whose seemingly rustic simplicity and independence stood in marked contrast to their own. "You chaps don't know your luck," the fictionalized big shot Augustus Hoskin told his guide. "I'd give all I own for such a carefree existence. It's ... It's ... incredible. You have meat at your hand – everywhere. No work, no worry, no responsibility. Positively, I envy you. When our short holiday is over, we must go back to the grind." But while Hoskin might have coveted his guide's freedom, there was no question in his mind about who was superior. "Ah," he concluded, "Wealth brings its responsibilities, my boy! Many responsibilities."[54] The same mix of envy and condescension that coloured these remarks was even more visible in the case of Aboriginal guides. If anything, they were even more admirable because, being "closer to nature," they had an almost mystical understanding of the ways of wildlife. But the same qualities that made guides valuable in the woods rendered them socially and culturally inferior to their clients.[55]

Despite the inequality between clients and guides – and between urban and rural – that these remarks suggest, some rural men were in a position to take advantage of these stereotypes, to capitalize on the authenticity that had been claimed for them. Whereas young men might once have used their skills and knowledge to fill their own larders or meet the commercial demand for wild meat, the new desire for wilderness experiences created a market for their know-how itself. As hunting guides, rural men got paid to lead their urban counterparts through the woods and mountains that were once their own domain, helping them to kill the animals they once stalked. They thus benefited from the new economy of non-consumptive wildlife use even as their neighbours suffered.

By trading on their local knowledge, the guides transformed it from something whose value lay in its use to something that also had exchange value. Commodified, local knowledge became "woodcraft," a body of skills and knowledge that could guarantee their clients a comfortable and successful hunt, and, in Johnnie Johns' case, earn them an income and a valuable international reputation in the process.

Born in 1898 in the southeastern part of the Yukon, Johnnie Johns was one of a handful of entrepreneurs who capitalized successfully on the Territory's emerging reputation as a sportsmen's paradise. In the first two decades of the twentieth century, the Yukon became renowned in sporting circles for its big game thanks to the work of F.C. Selous, an Englishman who had made a career of chronicling his hunting exploits in the far corners of the Empire, and his American counterparts Charles Sheldon and Thomas Martindale. Their books

An Aboriginal hunting guide with his kill. Jewish Historical Society of British Columbia, LF.1A.262.P9

drew like-minded sportsmen with deep pockets to the region and created a demand for guide-outfitters, men who could act as midwives for these sportsmen's wilderness rebirth: men like Johnnie Johns.

Unlike the other guide-outfitters of the period, Johns was Aboriginal, part of a Tagish and Inland Tlingit family, and probably grew up hunting and trapping. His introduction to hunting as a business came in 1917, and in 1923 he was hired as a camp helper with A.R. "Shorty" Auston, a white guide-outfitter working out of Carcross, south of Whitehorse. After reading an outdoors magazine discarded by a wealthy trophy hunter and seeing all the advertisements for guide-outfitters, Johns realized he could strike out on his own. With the money he had made working for Auston and others, he accumulated a substantial "outfit" consisting of "16 horses, 20 saddles, 6 tents, 6 chairs and tables, 4 stoves, and 6 axes." This was enough to qualify him for a chief guide's licence, which he was granted in 1927.[56]

Over the next forty years, Johns became one of North America's pre-eminent hunting guides, and could list many of the continent's rich and famous among his clientele.[57] He knew very well what they wanted. "Your success is our success," he told them. "There is no particular problem obtaining trophy size animals of any of our species, providing you give yourself enough time." While hunters would be treated to spectacular wilderness, Johns realized they could get too much of a good thing. "All of our hunting is done by horseback," he wrote. "Walking is kept at a minimum. The hunter being required to walk only for a final stalk." But just to make sure his clients knew that his outfit was for serious hunters only, Johns made a point of adding this warning in his pamphlet: "We do not furnish women or liquor! (Bring your own.)"[58] Credited with bringing millions of dollars into the Territory, Johnnie Johns had clearly benefited from commodifying his local knowledge. His success was all the more notable because it was achieved at a time when the Yukon's indigenous peoples were being pushed to the margins, displaced and dispossessed by development, particularly after the 1940s and the building of the Alaska Highway.

But Johns' achievements belie the complexity of his engagement with the new economy of non-consumptive wildlife use. Selling his woodcraft was not simply a matter of entrepreneurship, of seeing an opportunity and exploiting it. For Johns local knowledge was not so easily separated from his own culture. Its commodification forced him to confront complex and difficult questions about identity, and to alter who he was.

To retain (and perhaps to attain) his status as chief guide, Johns gave up his legal status as an Indian. He was enfranchised in 1927, a decision probably made in response to the growing antipathy toward Aboriginal people in the industry. White guide-outfitters did not welcome Native competition and probably pressured local government agents not to issue licences to men like Johns. Regardless of whether or not they spoke out against Johns' application directly, immediately after Johns received his licence in 1927 the territorial agent in White-horse wrote the Yukon commissioner asking that he not grant chief guide licences to Aboriginal people. "It really means taking away the livelihood of guiding from the white man if any more Indians are granted the privilege of acting as Chief Guides," he argued.[59] His advice was followed, for a few years later, in 1933, the Yukon com-missioner informed a prospective tourist that "every non-resident hunter must be accompanied by a licensed White Chief Guide."[60] Applications from other Aboriginal men – even well-known ones like Tlingit photographer George Johnston – were rejected. Native peoples could work as wage-earning camp helpers or assistant guides, but they could not establish themselves as independent operators.

If becoming a chief guide required Johns to give up his legal status as an Indian, working as one entailed confronting certain cultural proscriptions about the use and treatment of animals. According to anthropologist Catharine McClellan, the Tagish and Inland Tlin-git believe in an "animal mother" who set out rules for the proper treatment of animals: "she is emphatic that no game animals are to be hunted just for their skins, for if their meat is not also used her children will 'suffer.'"[61] While there are specific rules for particular animals, the ones dealing with moose and bears are most interesting in terms of Tagish and Inland Tlingit involvement in big game hunt-ing. Moose heads were to be treated carefully, the skulls placed high in trees to prevent dogs from chewing them. Bear heads were never to be brought into camp; instead, they were to be burned or placed in trees. Failure to abide by these rules of the hunt would constitute an insult to the animal and result in a lack of success in the future.

One can only imagine what Johnnie Johns and other Tagish and Inland Tlingit thought of men who paid thousands of dollars to hunt for trophy heads, or of their own role in facilitating this insult to the animals. Johns' forty years in the guiding business indicates that he managed to reconcile these issues of culture and identity at least to some degree, and that he was changed in the process: he lost his status, accommodated his peoples' beliefs to new economic opportu-nities, and became rich and famous.

While Johnnie Johns' career illustrates how wildlife conservation facilitated the transformation of local knowledge and identity, the story of Nova Scotia's guides reveals how it was implicated in the larger shift in power from country to city. Like Johnnie Johns, Nova Scotia's guides established an international reputation in the first half of the twentieth century. However, they achieved it not so much by selling their skills to prospective big game hunters, but by marketing them as entertainment. Repackaged and displayed at "guides' meets," rather than deployed in the pursuit of a trophy animal, their woodcraft had mass appeal. While these competitions promoted the province as a sporting destination and showcased the skills of the men who would make the experience memorable, the long-term benefits were less certain. Although the guides' meets began as celebrations of working-class rural culture, over the long term the transformation of local knowledge into entertainment was a manifestation of the disempowerment of rural societies that came in part as a result of wildlife conservation.

Required by law to be licensed, Nova Scotia's guides rapidly developed a professional identity centred on the skills they had honed working in the woods as loggers, farmers, or trappers. In 1909 licensed guides mainly from the province's western counties came together to form the Nova Scotia Guides' Association, an organization dedicated to both conserving game resources and securing "the greatest benefits possible from the pursuit of their business."[62] While the association offered advice to the government on fish and wildlife management, it was best known for the guides' meets it held in conjunction with its annual meetings. Designed to showcase members' woodcraft, these meets began in 1909 as modest affairs consisting of just a handful of events over a day, with token prizes – like a plug of tobacco – being awarded to the winners. By the 1930s and '40s, however, the meets had grown into week-long spectacles drawing tens of thousands of spectators and supported in part by corporate sponsors like the CPR, the Chestnut Canoe Company, and Montreal's Dominion Cartridge Company. In 1937, the event received national coverage on CBC radio, which introduced the country to the unparalleled talents of Nova Scotia's guides.

Although the scale and frequency of guides' meets grew over the twentieth century, the skills showcased remained relatively constant. Local guides along with others from Quebec, New Brunswick, and Maine, competed in dry land and water sports, including trap shooting, moose calling, and kettle boiling contests, as well as fly-tying, log rolling, and canoe racing. Although these events were dominated by men, women did compete in shooting, swimming, and log roll-ing, as well as in something called the "rolling pin contest" (where the implements were thrown for distance, not accuracy).

The popularity and renown of the association's meets earned it an invitation to the New England Sportsmen's Show in the mid-1930s. Sponsored in part by the provincial government, twenty-eight Nova Scotia guides travelled to Boston in 1934 to sell their talents and the province's outdoor recreational opportunities. Loaded down with travel literature, maps, and motion pictures, as well as a family of moose and aquariums of trout and salmon, they set up an elaborate display in the Boston Gardens. Joined by Mi'kmaq demonstrating their "crafts," for twelve days they staffed their booths and competed in the usual events, with the quieter waters of the Gardens' artifi-cial lake substituting for those of Lake William, where they usually competed. Creighton Balcomb, one of the guides in the 1934 show, recalled the scene this way: "Right out in front of our tent was a big cage with seven or eight racoons in it. Over in the corner on our right were eight or nine Virginia deer. Right out in front of them was a bear chained to a big iron bolt on the floor. On our left was a big cage with three or four alligators in it, ten foot long."[63] To publi-cize the show, the guides paraded up to the Boston Commons, with "packs on their backs, canoes and paddles, cross-cut saws, anything that went with the meet."[64] Although the New England Sportsmen's Show folded after only two years, Nova Scotia's guides were impres-sive enough to become regulars on the American sportsmen's show circuit from the mid-1930s to the 1960s, performing as the "North Country Guides," the "Huskies," and the "He-Woodsmen."

For the participants, the guides' meets were occasions to socialize, especially with members of the opposite sex. According to Watson Peck, a competitor from Bear River, the yearly contest at Lake Wil-liam was an occasion for "sporting and courting and many a maid met her man."[65] During the darkest days of the Depression, however, the meets were also a way to make some money or to win useful prizes like hunting knives, sweaters, and rubber boots. Although the competition was friendly, that did not mean the participants took the events lightly. Many of them, like champion pistol shot Laura Wam-boldt, entered to win. Deadly serious, she and her husband "were there for the money. I was never to a dance while I was there, or in the dining room ... I didn't go there for fun," she recalled.[66]

Laura Wamboldt may not have gone for the fun, but most of the people who watched her did. What for the Guides' Association was a salute to their profession and a test of skills was for the audience a pleasant diversion. Although they began as grassroots celebrations of rural working-class life, the guides' meets abstracted woodcraft from the social and economic context that created it and sold it as entertainment. As the meets grew in size, drawing participants and spectators internationally, the shooting, moose calling, canoeing, por-taging, chopping wood, and boiling water became abstract sporting events: entertainment severed from the social and economic context that had created it. If their woodcraft was increasingly unrecogniz-able as work, so too were the guides increasingly unrecognizable as workers. Indeed, by the 1930s many of the competitors had no con-nection to guiding at all, but took out a guide's licence just so they could compete. "I don't know if they ever guided anybody in their lives," recalled Laura Wamboldt. "There were quite a few who didn't know what [it] was."[67]

In showcasing their members' professional skills, the Nova Scotia Guides' Association transformed and reduced them into spectacles that were consumed as recreation rather than recognized as labour. The conversion of woodcraft into entertainment was a small part of a larger and fundamental transformation of Canadian society, from rural to urban. While the transition is usually measured in terms of the shifting location of demographic and economic power, from the country to the city, it also manifested itself culturally, in the com-modification of rural life for urban consumption. The guides' meets and particularly the international sportsmen's shows in which Nova Scotia's guides participated were artefacts of urban power, created by conservation's new economy of non-consumptive use.

Pushed aside to make a place for wildlife, farmers, resource work-ers, and Aboriginals mounted a challenge of their own, ignoring the law when they could and wielding petitions, threats, assault, and arson when they could not. But their response to conservation was not limited to resistance. Some rural men were able to exploit the oppor-tunities provided by conservation's emphasis on non-consumptive wildlife use to their advantage, making a living as hunting guides, camp helpers, packers, and cooks. They benefited from conservation and reinforced its assumptions, even as their neighbours contested and were marginalized by them.

While some individuals may have profited in the short term, in the long term conservation helped position rural life as something urban people could consume as recreation. In that sense, wildlife conservation was implicated in one of the key social transformations in twentieth-century North American society.

As will be discussed, the very kinds of people who were identified as threats to wildlife also did some of the most important conservation work in Canada. Jack Miner, the subject of Chapter 3, was the country's first celebrity environmentalist. A humble farmer and brick and tile maker, Miner did not so much commodify his hunting and guiding skills as he did conservation itself. The story of "Jack Miner and the Birds" was one he packaged and performed, selling his gospel of conservation as entertainment.

CHAPTER THREE

◆

The Dominion of Father Goose:
Local Knowledge and Wildlife Conservation

ACCORDING TO HISTORIAN Janet Foster, the Canadian conservation movement lacked visionaries like John Muir and Theodore Roosevelt, charismatic leaders whose work inspired millions and led to the emergence of a modern environmental consciousness. Instead, the job of saving Canada's wildlife was left to a handful of virtually anonymous and farsighted Ottawa men. Their legacy is largely forgotten, their voices muffled by the thick walls of bureaucracy.[1] While Foster is right to highlight state involvement, the division of powers meant that the bulk of government wildlife work in Canada was done at the provincial level with important input from local fish and game associations.

That said, the emphasis on the government, whether federal or provincial, completely misses the fact that some of the most influential conservation work in Canada before the Second World War was carried out by a private individual, and one who was every bit as charismatic and, at the time, as well known as Muir or Roosevelt, namely, Jack Miner. While his popularity alone demands analysis, Jack Miner's career illuminates the formation and characteristics of local ecological knowledge.

Born in 1865 in Dover Center, Ohio, this poor and unlettered son of the soil was possessed of an inveterate curiosity about the outdoors, and established a bird sanctuary outside his family's Kingsville,

Ontario, farm and brickworks in 1904. The ducks and geese that took up residence by the thousands in the Miner ponds piqued his interest. Were the same birds coming back to him every year? To find out, he began banding birds in 1909, one of the first people to do so in North America. By the time he died in 1944, over fifty thousand ducks and forty thousand geese had carried a thin aluminum band on their legs stamped "Write Box 48, Kingsville, Ontario."[2] He sent his early findings to the federal government, hoping to assist it in its negotiations with the United States for the Migratory Birds Convention.[3]

But Miner's impact lay more in shaping public opinion about conservation than in influencing government policy or ornithology. Even before he banded his first bird, a Minneapolis newspaper had dubbed him the "founder of the Conservation movement."[4]

His Kingsville sanctuary became a tourist attraction, drawing as many as fifteen thousand people in one day.[5] While thousands came to visit "Uncle Jack" and his birds, still more learned of his work through his books, lectures, radio broadcasts, and films – all tremendously popular. The four thousand copies of his first book, privately published in 1923 and distributed by his son, sold out in nine months. It is still in print.[6] Promoting it in Winnipeg, he drew nearly double the audience – thirteen thousand people – that David Lloyd George did, despite the fact that the former British prime minister and international statesman lectured for free and Miner charged admission.[7] One radio broadcast in the 1920s elicited over eight thousand letters to the station.[8] In 1926 alone, he received over a thousand invitations to speak from all over North America.[9] Summarizing his career, H.R. Wade estimated that between 1910 and 1940, Miner "had spoken to more people than any other individual."[10] His message was simple: what was good for the goose in Jack Miner's sanctuary was good for Canada.

Known for his homespun wisdom and his impatience with "arm chair theorists" and government experts, Miner was the darling of the rich and powerful. He had the patronage of American industrialist Henry Ford and was a frequent visitor of Prime Minister Mackenzie King. During his life, he was likened to St. Francis of Assisi and his

(Facing page and page 67) "Jack Miner: The Pioneer Naturalist," comic strip (n.d.). Reprinted with permission from Walt McDayter.

JACK MINER
THE PIONEER NATURALIST

IT IS 1877, AND OUTSIDE A LITTLE SCHOOLHOUSE NEAR DOVER CENTRE, OHIO...

JACK MINER, STOP YOUR SQUIRMING! YOU'RE 12 YEARS OLD, AND IT'S *HIGH TIME* YOU GOT SOME BOOK-LEARNIN'!

WALT McDAYTER
NORMAN DREW

BUT JACK TAKES TO SCHOOL MUCH LIKE A CAT TAKES TO WATER. FOR THREE WHOLE MONTHS HE SUFFERS THE *HUMILIATION* OF BEING A SCHOLAR...

ONE DAY, HOWEVER, ON HIS WAY TO SCHOOL...

A SKUNK! I'M GOING TO *CATCH* ME THAT POLECAT!

1-17

...AND ALTHOUGH HE DOESN'T KNOW IT, THAT SKUNK IS GOING TO PLAY A LARGE PART IN *ALTERING* THE COURSE OF HIS LIFE!

ONE DAY IN 1877, EN ROUTE TO SCHOOL, JACK MINER CORNERS A SKUNK... WITH *PREDICTABLE* CONSEQUENCES!

PHEW!

SPRAYED WITH SKUNK SCENT, YOUNG JACK MISCHIEVOUSLY ENTERS THE *SCHOOLHOUSE.*

GET OUT! GET OUT *AT ONCE!* 1-18

WALT McDAYTER
NORMAN DREW

NOW HE COULD GO HOME AND HONESTLY SAY HE HAD BEEN *CHASED OUT* OF SCHOOL. HE WOULD NEVER RETURN!

I'LL GET MY *LEARNIN'* FROM THE FORESTS AND LAKES, NOT FROM...

...BOOKS!

SAVED FROM SCHOOLWORK BY AN EXPERIENCE WITH A SKUNK, JACK MINER GETS HIS EDUCATION DIRECTLY FROM *NATURE.*

THAT BOY KNOWS MORE ABOUT WOODLORE AND WILDLIFE THAN EVEN THE REDSKINS!

HIS MOTHER COULD OFFER LITTLE OBJECTION, SINCE THE REWARDS OF HIS HUNTING ARE *NEEDED* TO FEED THE 10 CHILDREN IN THE FAMILY.

THESE TWO MALLARDS WILL MAKE A NICE *DUCK DINNER,* MOTHER.

1-19

BUT LIFE IN OHIO IS *HARD,* AND IN 1878, WHEN JACK IS 13, HE HEARS HIS FATHER SAY:

PACK UP! WE'RE *MOVING* TO CANADA!

WALT McDAYTER
NORMAN DREW

JACK MINER MOVES TO KINGSTON WITH HIS FAMILY... AND AS A *YOUNG MAN* FINDS A GOOD LIVING IN HUNTING, OFTEN SELLING HIS GAME TO MARKETS IN WINDSOR...

THESE ARE PLUMP PHEASANTS. YOU SHOULD RE-SELL THEM AT A HIGH PRICE!

WALT McDAYTER
NORMAN DREW

THOUGH HE'S A HUNTER, JACK HAS A TRUE LOVE FOR NATURE, AND HE AND OTHER SPORTSMEN FORM ONE OF ONTARIO'S FIRST *GAME PROTECTIVE ASSOCIATIONS!*

OUR AIM IS TO *SPREAD KNOWLEDGE* OF CONSERVATION OF WILDLIFE TO OTHER SPORTSMEN THROUGHOUT THIS PROVINCE!

FOUR YEARS LATER, A TRAGEDY BOTHERS HIM...

COULDN'T I EVER BEEN ABLE TO *MAKE FRIENDS* WITH CANADA GEESE?

1-20

BUT MAYBE HE HAS *TRIED* HARD ENOUGH!

IN 1904, JACK MINER HOPES TO *ATTRACT* GEESE AND DUCKS TO HIS *POND* BY SPREADING CORN ALONG THE SHORES.

AND THESE HALF DOZEN TAME GEESE WITH CLIPPED WINGS MAY HELP THE WILD ONES *FORGET* THEIR SHYNESS

WALT McDAYTER
NORMAN DREW

FOR FOUR YEARS HE PERSISTS *WITHOUT* SUCCESS, AND CHILDREN FROM KINGSVILLE, ONT., *TAUNT* HIM...

MR. QUACK, MR. QUACK, HE TALKS TO DUCKS, AND THEY QUACK BACK!

1-21

BUT ONE APRIL DAY, 1908, HIS NEIGHBORS ARE SURPRISED TO LEARN:

DAD, JACK MINER'S DONE IT! ELEVEN GEESE HAVE *LANDED* ON HIS POND!

GOOD! SON, GRAB ME MY GUN! I'M GOING TO VISIT OLD JACK MINER, AND DO A BIT OF *GOOSE-HUNTING!*

IN THE SPRING OF 1908, 11 GEESE LAND AT JACK MINER'S SANCTUARY... BUT *THRILL-SEEKING* NEIGHBORS SHOOT AND KILL FIVE!

SAY, THIS IS LIKE SHOOTING DUCKS IN A *BARREL...* ONLY EASIER!

BUT EACH YEAR MINER CONTINUES TO ENTICE THE BIRDS TO HIS POND WITH CORN, AND BY MARCH OF 1910 MORE THAN *400 GEESE* SETTLE.

BUT THERE IS *NO SAFETY* HERE FOR THE GEESE! EVEN JACK MINER, AN AVID HUNTER, OCCASIONALLY SHOOTS DOWN A CANADA GOOSE FOR THE SPORT...

1-22

WALT McDAYTER
NORMAN DREW

...UNTIL KILL, WHEN HE SHOOTS DOWN A VERY SPECIAL GANDER, ONE WHICH WILL DRAMATICALLY TEACH HIM THAT THE SHOOTING HAS TO *STOP!*

NEXT WEEK: A LESSON IN LOYALTY!

65

philosophy favourably compared to that of Aristotle.[11] *Outdoor Life,* a major American periodical, awarded him its gold medal "for greatest achievement in wild life conservation on the continent for 1929," the first time a Canadian was recognized in the US for conservation work.[12] In 1943 he was named to the Order of the British Empire.[13] After his death, he was added to the *Book of Knowledge* as one of the fifteen great men of the world.[14] The Canadian Parliament followed with its own recognition in 1947, creating National Wildlife Week in his honour. Forty years after "Wild Goose Jack" banded his last bird, Sir Peter Scott, chair of the World Wildlife Fund, considered him "an outstanding champion of conservation issues and a leader in the raising of public awareness of wildlife conservation."[15]

Unlike the wildlife workers employed by the state, Miner did not think of conservation as a matter of systematic regulation through the law. In fact, in a period when the formal apparatus of wildlife management was being established, elaborated, and contested, the state hardly figured at all in his vision of conservation. Instead, wildlife conservation was a question of how people positioned themselves in relation to nature.

Miner's experience of working and living in the woods in combination with his Methodist faith led him to frame the relationship between people and animals as one of "dominion," and to take a pragmatic rather than romantic view of wildlife management. Armed with a knowledge about wild things garnered through a childhood spent playing in the woods and an adult career as a market hunter and guide, Miner established his dominion by altering nature – improving it – to his advantage.

Dominion was different from thoughtless exploitation. Humans may have been superior to God's other creatures, but their dominion was made manifest by knowing and caring for nature as well as using it. Moreover, dominion did not preclude a sentimental attachment to nature. Indeed, much of the power of Miner's message lay in its appeal to the emotions. His success was as much evidence of his own tremendous charisma as that of the feathered allies he marshalled to his cause. While Progressivism and anti-modernism may have been key ideological influences, the popularity of Jack Miner speaks to the power of sentiment in shaping public opinion about wildlife and its conservation.

IN 1911, JACK MINER AIMS HIS GUN AT ONE OF THE CANADA GEESE THAT HAS SOUGHT SAFETY AT HIS SANCTUARY NEAR KINGSVILLE, ONT..

GOT IT... HIT ITS WING!

WALT McDAYTER NORMAN DREW

BUT WHEN MINER TRIES TO PICK UP THIS GROUNDED BIRD, TO HIS ASTONISHMENT ANOTHER GANDER LANDS IN HIS PATH, READY TO FIGHT FOR AND PROTECT ITS FALLEN COMRADE.

WELL, I'LL BE...!

SO MOVED IS HE BY THIS DISPLAY OF LOYALTY IN THE GEESE, HE COMES TO A DECISION...

YOU CAN READ! FROM NOW ON THERE'LL BE NO SHOOTING AT BIRDS ON MY SANCTUARY!

HUNTING ABSOLUTELY PROHIBITED

1-24

INSTEAD OF SHOOTING AT THE THOUSANDS OF DUCKS AND GEESE THAT TAKE REFUGE AT HIS KINGSVILLE, ONT. SANCTUARY, JACK MINER PLANS TO STUDY THEM.

WE HAVE A WONDERFUL CHANCE TO LEARN THE MIGRATION PATHS OF ALL THESE BIRDS!

HE BECOMES A PIONEER IN ATTACHING BANDS TO BIRDS' LEGS, TO IDENTIFY THEM...

EACH BAND WILL CONTAIN THE DATE, AS WELL AS MY NAME AND ADDRESS.

AFTER THOUSANDS OF BIRDS HAVE BEEN BANDED, HE ERECTS A HUGE MAP OF NORTH AMERICA OUTSIDE HIS HOME...

1-25

WHENEVER A HUNTER SHOOTS DOWN ONE OF OUR BIRDS, HE'LL RETURN THE BAND TO US. BY LOOKING AT WHERE THE BAND WAS MAILED FROM, WE CAN TRACE THE ROUTE THE BIRD FLEW.

WALT McDAYTER NORMAN DREW

THROUGH THE YEARS, JACK MINER RECEIVES HUNDREDS OF BANDS BACK FROM NORTH AMERICAN HUNTERS, WHO FIND THEM ON THE LEGS OF DUCKS AND GEESE THEY HAD SHOT DOWN.

A GRIM HARVEST... YET IT WILL PROVIDE US WITH ESSENTIAL KNOWLEDGE OF BIRDLIFE.

1-26

THESE BANDS ENABLE NATURALISTS FOR THE FIRST TIME TO LEARN THE FLIGHT PATHS OF CANADA GEESE AND OF DUCKS!

THEIR MIGRATION ROUTES ARE BORDERED NORTH BY HUDSON BAY, DOWN SOUTH AS FAR AS LOUISIANA, OUT WEST TO SASKATCHEWAN AND AS FAR EAST AS NEW YORK STATE!

WALT McDAYTER NORMAN DREW

IN LATER YEARS, MINER INCLUDES A SCRIPTURE FROM THE BIBLE ON EACH LEG BAND, MUCH TO THE ASTONISHMENT OF MANY A SUPERSTITIOUS ESKIMO!

AND ARCTIC MISSIONARIES HAVE KNOWN ESKIMOS TO BE CONVERTED TO CHRISTIANITY BECAUSE OF THE BIBLICAL VERSES CARRIED TO THEM ON THE WINGS OF A BIRD!

JACK MINER'S SANCTUARY AT KINGSVILLE, ONT., BECOMES TOO POPULAR WITH BIRDS. HE'S THREATENED IN 1915 WITH BANKRUPTCY...

WE JUST CAN'T FEED ALL THESE BIRDS. EACH YEAR THEY'RE EATING UP $6000 WORTH OF CORN!

MINER TRIES TO ALLEVIATE THE SITUATION BY GROWING AND HARVESTING CORN ON HIS FAMILY'S LAND.

THIS ISN'T THE ANSWER. WE JUST CAN'T GROW ENOUGH TO FEED ALL THOSE GEESE AND DUCKS!

WALT McDAYTER NORMAN DREW

1-27

THERE'S ONLY ONE SOLUTION.

I'M GOING TO HAVE TO TALK MY WAY OUT OF THIS MESS...

TO EARN MONEY FOR THE UPKEEP OF HIS SANCTUARY AT KINGSVILLE, ONT., JACK MINER GOES ON A TOUR OF CANADA AND THE U.S., LECTURING ON BIRDLIFE CONSERVATION.

1-28

JACK MINER GUEST SPEAKER TONIGHT

MASSEY HALL

THOUGH HIS LANGUAGE IS COARSE, AND HIS KNOWLEDGE "UNSCIENTIFIC" HIS DOWN-TO-EARTH HUMOR DELIGHTS AUDIENCES OF THAT DAY!

WHY, I CAME FROM A FAMILY SO POOR THAT WE WERE ALL BORN BAREFOOT!

WALT McDAYTER NORMAN DREW

BOOKS -- WHICH HE ONCE LOATHED AS A YOUTH -- PROVIDE ANOTHER SOURCE OF REVENUE!

JACK MINER AND THE BIRDS

JACK MINER ON CURRENT TOPICS

SO FAMOUS DOES HIS SANCTUARY BECOME THAT EVEN THE ONTARIO AND FEDERAL GOVERNMENTS OFFER TO SHARE THE EXPENSES!

ONTARIO GOVERNMENT

THROUGHOUT THE YEARS, THOUSANDS OF PEOPLE ARE ATTRACTED TO JACK MINER'S KINGSVILLE SANCTUARY TO CATCH A VIEW OF THE BIRDLIFE PROTECTED HERE. IN 1931 A FOUNDATION IS STARTED TO ADMINISTER THE PRESERVE.

WALT McDAYTER NORMAN DREW

Toronto Telegram News Service

ON THIS SITE, IN HIS LIFETIME, MINER BANDS THE LEGS OF 50,000 DUCKS AND 26,000 GEESE...AND FEEDS COUNTLESS MORE!

1-29

JACK MINER DIES IN 1944, BUT THE WORK HE STARTED IS CARRIED ON BY HIS THREE SONS.

MINER WAS NOT THE FIRST TO BAND BIRDS IN NORTH AMERICA, NOR THE FIRST TO FOUND A SANCTUARY. BUT IT WAS HE WHO POPULARIZED BOTH, AND CAUSED THEIR SPREAD THROUGHOUT OUR CONTINENT!

THE DOMINION OF FATHER GOOSE

Explaining his perspective on conservation, Jack Miner began by noting that he was "a firm believer in the teachings of scripture and base[d his] reasonings in the field of nature management and control as outlined in Genesis."[16] The passage to which Miner referred – in which God gave "man ... dominion over the fish of the sea, and over the birds of the sky ... and over all the earth, and over every creeping thing that creeps on the earth" – appears in almost every publication dealing with Miner or written by him.[17] For good reason: it was central to his work. "Now, dear reader," he wrote in 1923, "lest I forget I want you to know His promise in this verse is the foundation of a great percentage of my success in taming and controlling these so-called wild creatures during the last twenty years."[18]

Although the importance of his faith cannot be ignored, Miner's own account of how he came to be more interested in the "living thrills" of conservation than in the "dead thrills" of hunting suggests that religion did not so much motivate him as provide him with a language to explain his actions and understand their success. It may have been God's will that Jack Miner have dominion over the birds of the sky, but his own material circumstances shaped his need to do so and influenced the content of his environmentalism.

Miner was born one of ten children of a poor family and forced to eke out a living in the Ohio and Ontario woods; given this, it is hardly surprising that he believed that wildlife and nature in general were "for man's use and for man to control."[19] Although his parents might have worried about his lack of interest in school, the family came to rely on the income Jack brought in with their six traps. He sold his first pelt (a skunk) at age eight, and by age eleven he was bringing in as much as five dollars a week. Despite his financial contributions, the Miners barely scraped by, moving six times between 1870 and 1878.

The last move, which took them to Ontario, finally brought them some economic stability, though it rested once again on their ability to wrest a living from the earth. Taking advantage of low land prices outside Kingsville, the Miners bought a hundred acres "in the heart of a settlement of colored people."[20] When Jack's sister contracted malaria shortly after the family settled in, they discovered the real reason for their bargain: the land they had just purchased was in the middle of a swamp. Unable to move on and start over, Jack, his father, and his elder brother began the laborious job of ditching and draining their property to make it habitable.[21] In the process, they discovered deposits of the same kind of clay that the senior Miner had used in his former occupation as a brick maker. "J.T. Miner and Sons, Farmers and Drain Tile Manufacturers" was born.

The process of establishing the farm and making the brickworks pay was a protracted one, and the family found itself relying again on Jack Miner's proficiency with the gun. "As quail and grouse were so very plentiful and good warm clothes were scarce, the second fall we were here my brother and I started to hunt for the market," he recalled.[22] Jack and Ted were not alone. In the late nineteenth century, the Ontario Fish and Game Commission complained that boys like the Miners were regularly "hired by state-drivers, train hands, commission merchants, and others, to bring in as large a supply [of game birds] as possible" for the nearby American market.[23] The "slaughter" was incredible. Jack was particularly proficient, teaching himself to mimic a bob-white call and examining the crops of the grouse he shot to see what they fed on so he could position himself to kill even more.[24] Practice in the field made perfect. In short order he and Ted "soon became expert shots and the result was we left a bloody trail behind us."[25]

Word of the Miner boys' skills spread, and in 1882 they were hired by some of Kingsville's most prominent citizens as hunting guides. Jack had been hunting deer since he was a child and had even melted down one of his mother's pewter spoons to make shot; over the ensuing years, he had honed his tracking and butchering skills. The results were impressive. "Young man, who taught you to disembowel a deer?" inquired one admiring client. "Jack just likes to do that," replied Ted. Grateful for a successful expedition, the men invited their "dear Gorilla Chief," as they dubbed Jack, and Ted to join the elite Kingsville Gun Club, thus beginning their transition from market hunters to sportsmen.[26] When Ted was accidentally killed during one of their hunting expeditions in 1898, Jack vowed never to return to the woods — but several months later he found himself back in the Quebec bush. Jack's deadeye aim and his unquenchable desire to hunt led him to kill far more than his family needed. But rather than forego a hunt, he kept the local cemetery society supplied with moose meat for its charity dinners — and kept up his reputation in the process.

In 1902 a stranger appeared at the brickyard, looking, Miner recalled, for "the greatest hunter in Canada": him. The man was the passenger agent for the Canadian Pacific Railway, and he was there to hire Miner to take a railway car of hunters to northern Ontario and lead them on a hunt. Miner accepted, and by 1904 was taking 180 armed and anxious tourists up to bag their moose.

Out of sheer necessity, Jack Miner learned much about the natural world. Whether it was turning swampland into farmland, trapping skunks, shooting birds, or disembowelling the deer shot by his clients, he came "to know nature through labor," to use Richard White's phrase.[27] While White makes a distinction between knowledge about the natural world that came through work and that which came through play – a more discretionary and episodic engagement with the environment – the boundary was blurred among rural working-class people like Jack Miner.

For Miner and other rural people who made a living from the land, play blended into work and vice versa. As a child, he spent his days "roamin' the country round for miles till I knew every tree, every ditch an' pond, every trail, every stream."[28] His first pet was a blue jay, and he entertained himself for hours climbing trees to get at birds' nests, watching polliwogs transform themselves into frogs, and testing snapping turtles' ability to find their way to water after he removed them from their ponds.[29] Although he spent a grand total of three months in school, he and his friends "learned Nature's secrets, the ways and habits of the wild things in the forest an' the open – to talk with the rabbits and the squirrels an' the foxes an' the wild ducks an' the robins."[30] This childhood play and the understanding he gained of "Nature's secrets" flowed seamlessly into his adult work; and his adult work, whether as a market hunter or guide, was both an occupation and a form of recreation. Indeed, Miner so enjoyed what he did that by his definition ("work consists of what you are compelled – and don't want – to do") much of his work was play, and the knowledge he gained from both was indistinguishable due to its transferability.[31]

His decision to establish a bird sanctuary came from the observations he made while hunting. During the 1903 hunting season, he waited, hidden in the reeds, for the flocks of Canada geese to come into shooting range. As he watched, the birds flew over two men coming out to ditch on the next farm, apparently taking no notice of them, though they were in full sight. However, just as the flock came into Miner's range, the big gander leading them honked loudly and veered away sharply, taking the birds – and Miner's dinner – with him. "I felt like a one-cent piece coming home from Klondyke!" he wrote. "Why did he [the gander] pass right over, within shooting range of these two men, and then shy before he got that close to me?" Having "studied wild geese until [he] felt like flying," Miner concluded that because the geese returned to the area year after year, the gander recognized his red hair. "'That's our deadly enemy! Everybody get, for your lives!' were the cries he uttered."[32]

Fear had no place in Jack Miner's dominion. Disturbed by the idea that useful animals like ducks and geese identified him as their enemy, Miner had a change of heart. According to one of the many chroniclers of his conversion, "it became the ambition of Jack Miner's life to be known among the birds themselves, as the friend of the birds."[33]

Having made a machine in the garden – having built a brick and tile works out of the Essex County forest – Miner proceeded to reverse the process, turning one of his clay pits into a pond in the spring of 1904. He then convinced his neighbours to refrain from shooting any more wild geese, promising them "I would bring some right to that place and we would shoot a limited number when the opportunity was right." After acquiring seven Canada geese from a man who had trapped them illegally, Miner clipped their wings and ensconced them in his "mud-hole." Then he waited.[34] After enduring four years of derisive comments, Miner was rewarded in April 1908 when eleven geese settled on his pond. He allowed his patient neighbours to kill five. The next year thirty-two returned, and ten were taken. The year 1910 proved to be the turning point. With over four hundred geese on his property, Miner was hard pressed to buy enough corn to feed them. He sold part of his large collection of big game trophy heads to the CPR to finance his experiment, and went on the road, literally lecturing for birdseed.[35] The legendary "Father Goose" was born.

Wearing what would become his trademark red and black plaid mackinaw jacket and matching trousers, Miner enthralled audiences with his tales of "taming" wild ducks and geese, and of the importance of conservation – occasionally breaking into song to keep things light. A few years later, in between choruses of "Pack Up Your

Troubles in Your Old Kit Bag," he could also tell them about the migration habits of ducks and geese, knowledge he had gained from his bird–banding experiments.

Interested in the movements of animals since his childhood, Miner banded his first duck in 1909 and his first goose in 1915. He used simple homemade aluminum bands stamped with his address on one side and, following a directive he received on "God's radio," a scriptural passage chosen from a Salvation Army calendar on the other.[36] Miner did not consider his banded birds martyrs to science, but to religion. When one of them was killed, its death spread the good news. Bands reading "Have Faith in God" or "Watch and Pray" were apparently received as "benedictions" – particularly by the disadvantaged and the Aboriginal peoples of the North. For example, a cartoon in the Salvation Army's *War Cry* depicted an Inuit man shooting a goose. When he read the scriptural message on its leg, he immediately went to the mission to pray – the implication being that he was converted to Christianity by the experience. According to the cartoon's text, "The Esquimaux said 'JACK MINER HIM GREAT MAN, HIM SEND FOOD FOR TUMMY AND FOR SOUL. JACK MINER HIM GOD'S MAN.'"[37]

Whatever one thought of his methods or his message, there was little doubt that "Uncle Jack" was an effective communicator and the best thing that could happen to the conservation movement. "Jack Miner was here to the protection meeting and lectured on his geese," Percy Taverner, the Canadian Museum of Nature's chief ornithologist wrote to a friend in 1919. "He certainly is a genius. Though his grammar is a minus quantity his religious interpolations boresome and his humor unsophisticated[,] his enthusiasm, sincerity and lack of self consciousness are such that his audience go crazy over him and every one that hears him loves him and takes his lesson to heart ... He ... can do more for protection than any other agency I know of."[38]

"Let man have dominion over all" was Jack Miner's constant refrain. Establishing dominion meant exerting control over nature, something that was justified by scripture but necessitated by circumstance. Although Jack Miner's experience in the woods had revealed the wonders of God's works to him, he was singularly unromantic about nature and had little compunction about altering it to meet his own needs and desires, and to satisfy his curiosity. When a malarial swamp threatened the family's survival, it was drained – even though it was home to many of the small creatures he professed to love.

When he found clay on his property, he excavated it, removing the top three feet of soil in the process. When he had cleared the native forest to establish his farm and brickworks, he planted exotic trees and flowers and eventually built birdhouses out of his own drain tile to attract the species that had been displaced by settlement. And when he discovered that the wild geese were afraid of him, he lured them to his artificial ponds with corn, taming them – so "hunters could knock them off as easy as chickens." One critic estimated that between 1915 and 1925, Miner's "sanctuary" was responsible for "the death of more geese than it saved."[39]

For Jack Miner, there was nothing wrong with changing nature. Change was inevitable, and in his opinion it was a good thing. The difference between dominion and exploitation lay not in how much one altered the earth, but in how one addressed the collateral damage. To have dominion over nature was to exert control and take responsibility, mostly individually, by doing things like creating a bird sanctuary, but collectively as well, by establishing national parks. Elaborating on his father's perspective in 1948, Manly Miner argued that

> ever since Columbus discovered America man has had to interfere with Nature to make North America what it is today.
>
> Only 100 years ago, buffalo ... controlled. Man came in, turned the sod upside down, and made it the greatest wheatfield in the world ... But this could not have been had man not interfered with Nature. No, man did not exterminate the buffalo. He placed them in a park. Or as my late father would say, they became man-controlled. "What would you rather see," he challenged his readers, "the Canadian northwest as it is today, or as it was 100 years ago?"[40]

The pressure of circumstance may have made him unromantic about untouched nature, but it certainly did not preclude Miner from developing a deep knowledge of animals and birds and strong feelings for particular species. Jack Miner backed his views on animal behaviour with the authority of experience and conveyed them with the certainty and fervour of a Methodist camp preacher. For him, the natural world was a moral universe, and its salvation depended on marshalling as many converts as he could to the cause.

UNCLE JACK'S GOSPEL OF BIOLOGY

Cognitive scientists argue that people have always classified and reasoned about the organic world; that they put organisms together into like groups to understand their behaviour and the relationships among them. This everyday understanding of nature is "folk biology." Scholars of folk biology examine how people name and categorize the organisms that occupy the world they live in, arguing, among other things, that how they see the natural world shapes how they act in it.[41] This is certainly borne out by Jack Miner's example. His folk biology as well as his theories about extinction and evolution were shaped by a Christian morality that led him to love and protect certain animals and to despise and exterminate others.

Miner's folk taxonomic system included a number of different species ranging from robins to moose, all of which fell into two main genera: good and bad. The category of "good" creatures embraced a small but wide-ranging group of birds; these included insectivorous ones like robins, as well as ducks and, of course, Miner's beloved honkers, the Canada geese. Their goodness was defined by their usefulness to people. Quail were "the farmer's friend" because their diet consisted mainly of weed seed; woodpeckers were "God-given forest-protectors" whose taste for wood grubs saved the life of many a tree.[42] "Through their help a hundred years before I was born," Miner wrote, "I am able to have a nice quarter cut oak in my home to-day."[43] Ducks and geese made for good hunting – and eating.

As important as these birds' utility was to defining their goodness, Miner also valued their aesthetic qualities. Insectivorous birds did good works keeping pests at bay, but Miner reminded his readers not to forget "the song service" they performed. He waxed lyrical about "the cheerful clear note of such as the bobolink as he flutters across the meadow, singing 'Johnny why don't you mend your britches?' or of the cat-bird, who is perfectly willing to come sing in your back yard if you will plant just a little shrubbery."[44]

While the tin-eared might differ, no one who was the least bit observant could deny the quality and strength of these birds' moral character as was evidenced in their behaviour. Robins earned their place among good animals due to their industry. "Long before the average farmer is out of bed," Miner wrote, "he [the robin] is in the field, hopping from one plant to another in search of these worms;

and when he gets two or three in his throat he flies across to his family, and in less than three minutes he is back again."[45]

As his comment about the robin suggests, however, industry was not the only aspect of the birds' moral character that Miner admired. Their parental responsibility, loyalty, and restraint did not just distinguish them from other animals; they made them models for humanity – and objects for conservation. If robin fathers won their place in Miner's taxonomy by being good providers, ducks did so by being stay-at-home mothers. "Faithful and true," ducks stayed with their clutch of eggs and brood of ducklings, protecting them from harm – all without the assistance of the drakes, "lazy drones" who abandoned their mates as soon as the eggs were laid. While he compared a mother duck to "a kind washerwoman who is compelled to bring her nursing baby with her while she scrubs the morning away," he had less kind words for the drake. While the duck was being both mother and father to her brood, Miner imagined "the lazy, good for nothing father is loafing around the smoky end of nowhere, swapping garbage stories and remarking about some lady who is passing the dirty window that is corroded with smut."[46]

If ducks were the paragons of parental responsibility, geese were the epitome of fidelity and restraint. Miner's parable of "David" and "Jonathan" was framed as a tale of brotherly devotion, perhaps reflecting his own relationship with his brother Ted. David and Jonathan were part of a group of five geese headed for the Kingsville sanctuary when two of their number were killed by hunters. David had his wing shattered by a shell and was delivered to Miner by his chagrined neighbours for repair work. After reconstructing the wing as best he could, Miner released David among the pinioned and tame geese in his ponds. Shortly after, with thousands of geese in the sky, David gave a big honk and two geese – the other survivors of the original group of five – descended. The three stayed together for weeks until one – a goose – flew off, continuing her migration northward. But "Jonathan," as Miner dubbed him, did not. "Really," wrote Miner, "it was one of the most self-sacrificing sights of my life to see this big gander give up all his liberties ... and voluntarily live in captivity with his brother." At least "twenty times a day," Jonathan would try to get his "brother" David to fly, "but when he saw his brother ... was not coming he would alight and swim back to him." It was a sight that convinced those who saw it never to shoot another goose.

Only death could part the two. Seven years later, the "noble" Jonathan was killed by a great horned owl as he defended David and the pinioned geese who could not fly from the predator.[47]

Goose devotion was paternal as well as fraternal, and also characterized relationships between mates. When one "old mother goose" nearly expired from sunstroke because she refused to leave her unprotected nest, Miner took the eggs and placed them under a domestic hen, where they hatched. After seeing his goslings' devotion to their "step-mother," their father, "Jack Johnson," took responsibility for his blended family, "guarding" the hen as one of his own. Nonetheless, he never forgot about his old mate, and when she died, he called plaintively for her for over two years. Miner found this touching – but only to a certain point. Jack Johnson's "sad honking ... became so dreadfully mournful to one and all that I finally got rid of him."[48]

While Jack Miner could not stand the "deep mournful cries" of a bereaved gander because they "make the whole place gloomy," he did celebrate the monogamy that prompted them.[49] Unlike drakes, who after mating "live the life of a Brigham Young for the rest of the season," ganders were one-goose men.[50] "I have heard good honest men say that their wild ganders when turned with a flock of tame geese will mate with more than one," Miner wrote. "But here at my home everything is as near the natural state as I can possibly make it, and I haven't seen these geese show any inclination toward acting that way."[51]

The capacity for geese to exercise restraint was not limited to their monogamy. Not only would ganders not mate with more than one goose, but they also observed the bounds of genetic propriety and did not engage in incest. Miner came to this conclusion not by simply observing the birds on his ponds, but scientifically. Discussing "our model Canada Goose," Miner described how he "went so far as to keep four full brothers and sisters in an enclosure by themselves for nearly three years." During that time, and despite whatever urges they may have had, "they lived together as brothers and sisters only." Lest some of his readers think the birds were sexually dysfunctional, he was quick to add that once released, the penned birds swiftly paired off with non-relatives.[52]

Despite Miner's tendency to anthropomorphize and judge animal behaviour using particular human standards, his understanding of duck and goose biology was accurate. According to one standard scientific text dealing with North American waterfowl, "male mallards desert their incubating females at various times, from as early as the start of incubation."[53] Indeed, male mallards were observed "joining other females after the original mate had begun nesting activities."[54] Compared to them, Canada geese were the paragons of virtue Miner depicted them as being. They were "monogamous," mating for life and "exhibit[ing] strong pair and family bonds."[55] If the family – the "basic social unit in Canada geese" – was inadvertently separated over the course of a year, they "always reassembled."[56] Such closeness did not, however, ever edge over to the inappropriate. Writing in 1967, more than forty years after Miner and with somewhat less verve, biologist G.A. Sherwood "found no polygamy, promiscuity, or pairing between brood mates."[57]

For Jack Miner, birds were not just an interesting study in themselves, but, as the tale of "old Tom Johnson" shows, they were models for human relations, both familial and international. Like other ganders, Tom Johnson and his friends took their role as protectors seriously, keeping a watchful eye on Miner's group of defenceless pinioned geese. When two eagles began harassing the flock, they took action. So did Miner, once again putting words to the birds' behaviour: "it was a great sight to see these faithful, self sacrificing old ganders at the head of their little bunch with their wings up, ready to strike, saying by their actions, 'You must cut us down before you can have one of our loved ones,'" he wrote. Watching the staring contest between the ganders and the eagles, Miner got ready to step in and assert dominion with his rifle. But, he wrote, "good things come to those who wait." Just as he thought they would go at it, the eagles calmly flew off. Once again the birds taught him a lesson – not only about the virtues of patience, but also about how to resolve differences. "Yes," he wrote, "they apparently settled by arbitration. When I saw how it turned out my heart bubbled over with more love than ever for these two beautiful birds, and as I started for the house I couldn't help but thank Almighty God for the Canada Goose and the American eagle, and ask Him to hasten the day when this whole world mass of humanity will settle their differences as these lovely birds did on this occasion."[58] It was an example that ditch diggers and diplomats alike could learn from.

Given what good birds stood for, it is not surprising that Miner considered any animal that preyed upon them as bad. Although he devoted three chapters of his book to "the natural enemies of our birds," he had very little to say about their habits and behaviour beyond what he considered their propensity for destruction. Instead, he devoted most of his authorial energies to demonizing them and describing ways to kill them. Owls and hawks were cats with wings, their "cruel, blood thirsty and murderous depredations" on insectivorous birds, ducks, and geese more than outweighing their utility in keeping mice down.[59] For their sins, Miner caught them in a "pole trap," a device hidden in a tree and designed to catch them by one leg, making them easy prey for other raptors.

As rapacious as owls and hawks were, however, nothing, in his opinion, matched the brutality of a murder of crows. They, along with grackles and English sparrows, were among the "worst nest robbers in America." "I am sure that fifty per cent of the eggs and young of our song, insectivorous, and game birds in Ontario are devoured by these cold-blooded ... cannibals," he insisted. "The quail, killdeer, and dozens of other such beautiful mothers are perfectly helpless and can no more keep [the 'cannibal' birds] off than a human mother's naked hands could keep a vicious lion from tearing her baby into fragments."[60] To make sure that his readers appreciated the viciousness of the English sparrow, Miner took the five featherless bodies of bluebird nestlings who had been victims of a sparrow's attack, pinned them to a piece of cardboard, and took their picture, which he included in his book.[61]

Animals that "murdered babies" deserved to be struck down. But the way Miner suggested they be dealt with underscored the merciful dimensions of human dominion. The crows were live trapped in a cage of Miner's own design and given to the local gun club for target practice. The clubs would release the birds at set locations and club members would shoot them as they would clay pigeons. In this way, Miner wrote, "what is now the crow nuisance will be turned into sport." He even had the details of the scheme worked out: "the shooter will not be charged for the crows he kills but will be fined for every one he allows to escape," he elaborated. "These fines will be used for buying up old, faithful horses which will be humanely destroyed and used for bait to decoy more of these old, black Pharaohs to their just doom."[62]

Jack Miner's biological insights were not limited to taxonomy, but included theories about extinction and evolution that again were the combination of close observation and faith. Apart from the bison, no animal symbolized the impact of humans on nature more than the passenger pigeon, a bird that once made up between 25 and 40 percent of all birds in North America and which was slaughtered by the millions in the nineteenth century.[63] The last bird died in captivity in 1914, just as Jack Miner was beginning his transformation into Canada's first celebrity conservationist.

Yet for Miner, there were no conservation lessons to be drawn from the extinction of a species that had once been so numerous it darkened the skies of North America. Arguments that pointed to over-hunting as the reason for the passenger pigeon's disappearance were, in his opinion, "laughable." Indeed, in his view, humans had nothing to do with its extinction. That was simply impossible. "Do not entertain, for one second, the thought that they were exterminated by mankind," he wrote. "If there is any one thing on earth that I know a little about, it is hunting, trapping and netting birds; and speaking from observation and experience, I am here to state that if all the people on the North American continent had concentrated with one single aim upon the extermination of the passenger pigeon in order to save our own lives, I know we could not have done it in such a short time."[64]

Instead, extinction was God's will. Observing the cycle of population boom and bust in the animal world – something about which ecologists like Charles Elton were just beginning to theorize in the 1920s – Miner postulated that there was "a system of providential control" at work. The only force that could make numbers fluctuate as they did had to be divine. If humans did not kill animals in sufficient numbers, God would, he argued. "And sometimes He not only reduces to a limited number, but He exterminates altogether."[65] If the passenger pigeon taught humans anything, it was to trust in the wisdom and power of God.

If God's wisdom and will were apparent in the appearance and extinction of certain species, they were also evident in their evolution. For Miner, moose antlers were a case in point. In the process of "securing a private collection of the heads and antlers of these lordly monarchs of the solitudes," Miner came to his own conclusions about why bull moose sported such large head ornaments.[66] Antlers were not, as some argued, used as snow shovels, allowing the moose to forage in the winter.[67] Instead, they were God's way of limiting the bulls' sex drive. Miner did not know of an animal as over-sexed as the bull moose.[68] In the fall, cows fled from these "infuriated beasts," taking refuge in the deep bush, where the bulls, burdened with their broad antlers, could not follow. By putting horns on the bull moose, the "Managing Power," as Miner referred to God, protected the vulnerable cows from being "ravished." "Take the antlers off the bull moose and these noble animals would become extinct in twenty-five years."[69]

Preaching his own gospel of biology in his books and on the lecture circuit, Jack Miner became a larger-than-life public personality. While his charisma drew people to him, his authority rested on his own "personal experience and observation." Having learned "Nature's secrets" first-hand, Miner was uniquely positioned to offer insights about the workings of the natural world. "I assure you that these views are not second hand," he wrote in the preface to *Jack Miner and the Birds,* "as I am a very poor reader and have never read a book through in my entire life."[70]

Miner may have been a unique individual, but his views were not entirely his own. In attributing human qualities to animals and emphasizing the ordering hand of God in nature, Jack Miner's accounts shared many of the characteristics of the realistic animal story, a new genre of nature writing that emerged in the late nineteenth and early twentieth centuries. A "counterforce to the intellectual currents generated by nineteenth century science," and particularly Darwinism, the wild animal story rejected the idea that the natural world was cruel and amoral, inhabited by organisms engaged in a ruthless and unrelenting struggle for survival.[71]

Writers like Charles G.D. Roberts and Ernest Thompson Seton, two of the genre's most important and prolific authors, offered their readers a world of "animal heroes," noble creatures whose individuality was as remarkable as their intelligence, and who worked cooperatively, helping each other in times of need. Theirs was an orderly world, not the least bit like the bleak and chaotic one governed by the survival of the fittest. Like other nature writers of the time, Jack Miner lent his animals human qualities and gave them distinct personalities. His insistence that birds had their own language and were expert at setting their own broken legs was consistent with the genre's emphasis on the reasoning beast.[72] Despite his disgust with much that was written about the animal world, he surely would have agreed with Roberts's 1925 characterization of the gander as "a gentleman in feathers," or with other authors' discussions of "animal marriage," "animal chivalry," and "wild adoption."[73]

In revealing the moral order of the natural world, Miner joined his fellow nature writers in the "revolt against instinct," challenging the central arguments of Darwinism.[74] But he differed from them in three fundamental ways that reflected his faith and his class. While writers like Seton painted a world in which order and reason were generated by the animals themselves, Miner insisted their source was divine. In discussing the migration and nesting habits of geese, Miner acknowledged there was an intelligence at work. But it was that of God, not the goose. "I have heard such a variety of names for this goose-knowledge that I don't try to look up the meaning of these artificial words," he wrote. "I am sure if all their meanings were boiled down, and all the man-made, artificial names were skimmed off, the real interpretation would be – 'G O D.'"[75] He could not understand how anyone – especially those who claimed to spend time outdoors like Roberts and Seton – could not come to the same conclusion. "How can men who study God's great out of doors, and the multitudes of creatures that occupy it, be intelligent and yet say there is no God?" he asked. "I am even told they write Nature books and ignore this great, loving power."[76]

Moreover, for Miner, order and reason were limited to the world of good animals. The nobility and self-sacrifice of Seton's wolf "Lobo" or the wit of "Silverspot" the crow would not have resonated with him at all, for Miner's predators were degraded brutes, motivated by their base appetites.

Finally, he was close enough to his rural working-class origins that he could not embrace sentimental renderings of animals that could harm his livestock and threaten his livelihood. Nor could he argue against hunting, as the middle-class Seton and Roberts did. Even though his "shooting desire relaxed" by the 1920s, Miner admitted that he still loved "to see wild ducks, both on the table and in the air."[77] Moreover, while migratory birds and moose may have been safe from Jack Miner, predators continued to find themselves caught in the crosshairs of his rifle sights. The "father of Conservation" could still take "great satisfaction" in watching as a "two-hundred-grain bullet blew [a wolf's] heart into fragments."[78] In his view, hunting made men "better sons, husbands, and fathers in our homes, and better citizens of the neighborhood and township, county and country in which we live."[79]

While the wild animal story was tremendously popular, its premises proved quite controversial and were publicly debated in what became known as the "nature faker" debate. The critics, who included American president Theodore Roosevelt, raised questions about the veracity of these stories and suggested that Seton's best-selling book might better be titled *Wild Animals I Alone Have Known*. At the centre of the controversy was the issue of whether animals were capable of reason.[80]

Although no one accused Jack Miner of being a nature faker, he was a controversial figure.[81] Writing to a friend after hearing of Miner's death in 1944, the Canadian Museum of Nature's chief ornithologist observed, "I see they are making quite a splash over Jack Minor [sic] again. It is quite a joke, isn't it – 'Canada's famous naturalist.' One would think him the only man who ever banded a bird."[82] While Percy Taverner's comments might be dismissed as professional jealousy, his criticism stemmed in no small part from Miner's controversial views about nature and the practices that arose from them.

"Canada's famous naturalist" often found himself at odds with the small community of scientific men like Taverner who began to be employed by the federal government in the 1920s. These conflicts shed more light on Miner's brand of conservation and point to different ways of knowing the natural world.

"THE 'EXPERTS' ARE GETTING IN MY HAIR"

When Manly Miner wrote in 1948 that the "experts" were getting in his hair, he was reflecting on both his father's and his own dealings with the university-trained men who, in their view, had lots of education but no learning, and Jack Miner's belief that game management should be left in local hands, not in those of "someone three or four thousand miles away."[83] For the Miners, the clash between education and learning was nowhere more sharply drawn than in the debate carried out in the pages of the *Canadian Field-Naturalist* in the 1920s over their treatment of predators. It began politely enough – after all, it was hard to take on a legend. "To find fault with Jack Miner ... is rather like complaining about the sun because of the sun-spots," observed one *Canadian Field-Naturalist* writer. "But," he continued, "one could wish for a little more tolerance for predatory birds and mammals."[84]

The *Canadian Field-Naturalist* began by raising questions about the distinction that lay at the heart of Miner's taxonomy, that between good or useful animals and bad ones, or vermin. Any species of bird was useful insofar as it could be the source of satisfaction for people. "For many people there is quite as much satisfaction to be derived from seeing and being acquainted with a Great Horned Owl as from seeing and being acquainted with a Ruffed Grouse," the editor argued in 1923. "And a great deal more satisfaction than could be obtained by killing and eating the Grouse."[85] Commenting favourably on the journal's position, the eminent anthropologist Frank Speck insisted that vermin – if native – were "as interesting as many of the preferred life forms" that enjoyed their status only because of "animal propaganda evoked by sentiment or fancy for this songster or that insectivorous bird."[86]

In addition to making the case that all birds were useful, the *Canadian Field-Naturalist* went a step further and criticized the anthropocentrism that underpinned the very definition of a bird's "usefulness." Not only were owls and grouse "useful to mankind," but they also performed other functions: they were useful to other creatures and to their "native haunts." "Each species of bird is of service ... to other forms of life beside man," the editorial continued, "and there seems to be no reason why such usefulness should not be taken into account."[87]

Taking a less anthropocentric view would mean establishing sanctuaries for the benefit of all birds that lived within their bounds. Proper management of these places would consist of interfering only to the extent necessary to maintain the "balance of nature." Indeed, some who wrote letters to the journal, like Charles Townsend, made the case that there should be no human interference whatsoever. "Bird sanctuaries will best fulfil their purpose if the evil effects of man and his works, together with his domestic cat, are excluded," he insisted.[88] In the journal editor's view, "passive protection" was best.[89] Too much human interference would turn sanctuaries into game farms. "Bird sanctuaries and game farms are not one, neither can one take the place of the other, and there is no reason why they should be confused."[90]

Miner did not respond directly to the *Canadian Field-Naturalist*, probably because he did not read it. But he made his position clear in his books and in the magazine articles Manly wrote to elaborate on his father's ideas. Working from Genesis, Miner saw predators as robbing humans of what was rightfully theirs. "We feel when man came to North America and took over, the deer should have been preserved for man's food and use, and not for the sport of a horde of rapacious wild beasts," argued Manly.[91] Since the wolves did not see things in the same way, local farmers pressured the government to place a bounty on their heads. Similarly, the Miners did "not believe in protecting certain kinds of hawks which steal chickens, partridge, pheasants and grouse," wrote Manly, "especially when we so quickly clap a man in jail for doing what the hawk does."[92] Theft was theft, whether it was committed by a hawk or a human. It deserved punishment.

Fundamentally, however, Miner's position on predators was shaped less by his Christianity and more by his belief that there was no such thing as a balance of nature – at least not one that existed independent of human intervention. "The minute man put foot on American soil, discharged a gun and shot a bird, he interfered with Nature," he argued.[93] It was now up to humans to re-create a balance that took into account their own consumption. According to Miner, thinking in terms of "'Nature's balance,' ... 'upsetting Nature,'" and "'Nature's own'" or "some pretty theory out of a textbook" would do much more harm than good.[94] If people did not "reduce" the predator population in the same proportion as they killed game, the latter would soon disappear.[95]

Miner was not alone in raising doubts about whether the natural world was self-regulating. He had a number of allies in his attack on the balance of nature, some of them from the ranks of the "back-to-nature theorists" he so derided. Noted Canadian wildlife painter and naturalist Allan Brooks labelled the "Balance of Nature" an "ancient phantasy" used by "fanatics" who probably would speak out against weed control because they took "esthetic pleasure in a thistle or cockle-burr."[96] William Rowan, professor of zoology at the University of Alberta, agreed. If crows, owls, and hawks could be shot for bounty outside a sanctuary because of their destructive habits, it made no sense to protect them inside its boundaries. Without an adequate system of predator control, bird sanctuaries would become nothing more than "vermin farms." In his view, only the "unreasoning sentimentalist" would argue otherwise. Making the case that owls were as useful as grouse was "entirely fallacious," he continued. "It would be just as sound to argue that because the village idiot is somebody's darling and has to buy food and clothing from the village store ... he is as beneficial to the village community as the local schoolmaster."[97]

Government wildlife managers also shared Miner's views on predators and their control. As will be discussed in Chapter 6, despite growing dissent within the scientific community about the efficacy of the bounty as a conservation measure, there was a good deal of public support for it and it remained a part of federal and provincial wildlife management policy.

But attitudes were shifting, particularly among those who dealt with birds at the federal level of government. Jack Miner's practices with respect to both predators and banding came under increased scrutiny in the mid-1920s, in part because of the organization of bird conservation. Although all wildlife was a "fugitive resource," birds were particularly so. Attempts to manage them exposed the shortcomings of local and even national measures and the benefits of international cooperation. Symbolized by the Migratory Birds Convention, the internationalization of bird conservation forced a new level of system and rationality on management practices – or at least an awareness of their necessity among bureaucrats. As a result of the shift in the scale of the conservation project, local initiatives, like Jack Miner's sanctuary, took on a different cast and came under new critical scrutiny.

MANAGING THE MINERS

As chief ornithologist at the Canadian Museum of Nature, Percy Taverner was in the unenviable position of managing the Miners. Self-taught as well, Taverner probably had a good deal of respect for what Jack and Manly Miner had accomplished at Kingsville. He had little desire to alienate "amateurs" like them, not the least because the museum was still trying to complete its collection of bird specimens and, like other North American institutions of its kind, depended on the cooperation of naturalists like the Miners to do so.[98] Nonetheless, his position as the head of the country's community of scientific ornithologists, as well as his role as federal civil servant, meant that it was his job to make the Miners conform to shifting sensibilities and practices regarding predators and banding. Taverner and his superiors were well aware of the Miners' power in shaping public opinion and they hoped by their interventions to harness it to further a larger conservation agenda. Their efforts to manage the Miners reveal both the points of divergence as well as the intersections between local and scientific environmental knowledges.

Although he was aware of the growing reaction among Canadian naturalists against the "callous pain" inflicted by Jack and Manly Miner on predators, Taverner did not attempt to engage them on the subject directly, but first tried to convince them to work with the museum by playing on their sensibilities. "I notice from a number of sources that you are killing quite a number of hawks and owls at your place this winter. I do not want to take up the subject of the advisability of killing all these birds for the sake of a few admittedly bad ones but I would like to ask you when they are killed if you would not send them to the Canadian National Museum here at Ottawa," he wrote in 1926. "Why not let them do as much good here as specimens to balance a little of the evil they may have done in life?"[99] The Miners, only too happy to comply, sent the grim and well-frozen harvest of their pole traps to its redemption in Ottawa by express post on a regular basis.

The relationship established, Taverner was in a position to moderate the Miners' provocative rhetoric as well as their actions. Reading Jack's diatribes against raptors, the ornithologist noted "a common reference to 'Cannible [sic] Birds'" and took the opportunity to set Miner straight. "A bird must eat its own species to be a 'cannible.' An Owl that eats quail is no more a cannible or even if it eats another owl than we are cannibles when we eat cows or even monkeys," he wrote.[100] Taverner's gentle admonitions soon gave way to more frank exchanges. "Calling the Crow an Arch-fiend is absurd. He eats what there is to hand as it is necessary to his existence – just as we do," he told Manly in 1926. "I suppose that some may say that you and your father are quite devilish because you prevent honest Hawks, Owls, and weasels from making a living the way the Lord intended they should."[101]

But when it came to correcting their actions, the ornithologist was more circumspect, gently reminding them, for instance, that if they were going to "send hawks or other such stuff to get it off early in the week rather than late, as if they remain in the express office ... over a weekend it is apt to be bad for them."[102] When the Miners reported that a number of red-tailed and red-shouldered hawks had been accidentally killed in their pole traps, Taverner did not take them to task, but instead simply suggested they consider padding the jaws of the traps to make it difficult for these raptors to be caught inadvertently.

While he may have found the cruelty distasteful, what bothered Taverner most about Miner's approach to the study of birds and conservation was its highly localized and unsystematic nature. The chief ornithologist had no doubt that the crows were as "thick as clouds" near Kingsville and that they had committed the depredations Jack had written so powerfully about. But he was unconvinced that they had no redeeming features. The evidence was simply lacking. "The trouble is that the Crow has not been seriously investigated in Canada," he wrote to Manly. "One man says one thing, another the next ... We all see things we look for and largely disregard everything else. Isolated, accidental and occasional occurrences are thus magnified. Such evidence has little weight and convinces only the man who is already convinced."[103]

Although Manly mocked Taverner's call for a crow census, the ornithologist advised the Miners that their cause — not to mention their reputation — would be better served if they undertook a study of the bird rather than by marketing Jack's crow trap.[104] In urging them to contribute to ornithology rather than their pockets, Taverner tried to school the Miners in the principles of scientific inquiry and rhetoric, revealing in the process the core of the differences between them. "I think you want to work for a thorough investigation of the Crow ... If you have a good case there is no reason to fear [it]," he insisted. "Don't ever over state your case. You have good arguments without that and it only gives the other side valid grounds of criticism," he continued. "Admit the good arguments on the other side – and find a way to answer them – keep to cold facts and steer clear of sentimentality ... and calling names may be satisfying but it 'butters no parsnips' – anyone can do that."[105] For the chief ornithologist, environmental knowledge came through methodical and dispassionate investigation, and a respect for all the evidence.

The Miners did listen, not the least because they were sensitive to the need to protect their reputation.[106] Insisting that he was "very careful about condemning a bird till I have the facts to back me up,"

Manly reported that they would begin banding crows.[107] They also took to heart Taverner's advice about the need for scientific investigation. To that end, Jack Miner dispatched sixty hawks to the Royal Ontario Museum (ROM) in 1930, hoping that an analysis of their stomach contents by its zoologists would provide the evidence for his long-standing views about the raptors' destructive habits and convince the provincial government to legalize their killing. It did, and – ever aware of the value of public opinion – Miner proudly displayed the results in a news release. What "Facts on Hawks by Jack Miner" did not reveal, however, was the assistance he apparently rendered the ROM's scientists in their investigations. Unprepared to put his reputation entirely in their hands, Miner "jammed a meadowlark down the throat of one of his specimens" to make the relationship between predatory hawks and useful songbirds clear.[108] QED – or so he thought. Unfortunately for Miner, the "young whippersnappers" at the ROM had benefited from their "book lerning [sic]" and knew that hawks had better manners than he had given them credit for. Rather than swallowing their prey whole, they tore it to pieces first.[109]

While the Miners were willing to bend slightly in their attitudes toward predators, the chief ornithologist was singularly unsuccessful in convincing them to change their banding practices. Contrary to popular belief, the Miners were not the first in North America to band birds. The practice of marking birds with bands that would identify their sex, age, location, and date of banding began in Europe in the 1890s and spread to North America at the beginning of the twentieth century. Percy Taverner pioneered the practice in Canada, working with J.H. Fleming of Toronto to record the first systematic banding and return of a robin in 1905. With the practice growing in popularity, in 1909 – the same year that Jack Miner banded his first duck – the American Bird Banding Association was formed to standardize practices. After the signing of the Migratory Birds Convention, the US government took over banding in 1920, with the Canadian government following suit in 1922. To avoid confusion, both governments agreed to use a single, standard, serially numbered US Biological Survey band for all marking and to limit the practice to authorized or licensed personnel.[110]

The Miners did not use numbered bands, nor did they record the sex and age of the birds they banded. They were able to identify the date a bird was banded due to the scriptural passage they stamped on each band. For instance, geese banded in 1915 – the first year in which Miner used scriptural bands – bore the message "Have Faith in God" on their legs.[111] Although the Miners enjoyed great success in having their bands returned, Taverner, along with other federal wildlife bureaucrats, believed that their efforts would be even more useful if they used the standard-issue bands. Hoyes Lloyd, the federal government's superintendent of wildlife protection, asked Taverner to "coach" the Miners on "ornithological subjects," reminding the chief ornithologist that what they were doing was, strictly speaking, illegal. "The Miners do not hold any Permit allowing them to band birds for scientific purposes," he wrote in 1926, "and of course no such Permit can be issued unless they use authorized official bands."[112] Taverner agreed and once again emphasized the importance of standardization as the basis of systematic scientific investigation. "We do wish you could be induced to use the standard bird bands," he wrote to Manly. "You people are the only exceptions in North America and while you are technically violating the law that has and will be overlooked ... but should many others attempt to do the same and get out their own bands and keep their own system, chaos would result."[113]

The Miners remained unmoved. In Jack's opinion, the scriptural messages were the reason their banding experiment was such a success. By using them, the Miners had succeeded in branding bird banding as their own. Jack Miner claimed he received as many US Biological Survey bands at his Kingsville post office box as he did his own, evidence that the public associated the Miners with the banding project.[114] Manly argued that the Biological Survey, rather than the Miners, should change its practices.[115]

Indeed, the battles between the Miners and the federal government did not end in a standoff so much as they did in a Miner victory. While the Miners did not succeed in changing the Biological Survey's banding practices, neither were they forced to change their own, largely because of their public standing. Admitting defeat, Hoyes Lloyd noted that "the Miners' work has been of such a calibre that from this point on banding has not been raised officially and personally will not be raised officially so long as Jack Miner lives."[116] Not until 1946, two years after Jack Miner died, did the Jack Miner Migratory Bird Foundation, the institution set up to carry on his work, begin to use serially numbered tags.[117]

Percy Taverner found Jack Miner's unconventional approach to conservation maddening and his stubborn refusal to change his ways frustrating, but the two were not as far apart as one might have guessed from their exchanges on predators and bird banding. In part, this was due to the organization of ornithology, which despite its increasing professionalization in the 1920s and '30s still had room for the self-taught. Amateurs like Taverner could rise to the position of chief ornithologist, and men like Miner could give papers alongside academics at international gatherings such as the North American Wildlife Conference because the nature of ornithology was such that research was focused on collection and close observation, and hence remained accessible to a wide range of practitioners. In her survey of the main ornithological journals of the twentieth century, Marianne Ainley observed that, in 1925, 63 percent of the articles in the *Auk,* 91 percent in the *Wilson Bulletin,* and 67 percent in the *Condor* were contributed by authors with no institutional affiliation and who received no financial compensation for their research.[118] In her view, unlike other sciences, twentieth-century ornithology was an inclusive pursuit. While Taverner faulted Miner for his lack of scientific rigour, the two still broadly shared a methodology of careful observation and record keeping that bound amateur and professional together in a close, if sometimes uneasy, relationship.

JACK MINER'S THEORY OF GAME MANAGEMENT

1. Nature is wonderful; man is more wonderful; God is most wonderful.
2. God put birds and animals here for man's use and for man to control ...
3. Man is nature's first assistant, or God's viceroy. What is man without God? What is God without man? They are, or should be, working partners.

> – Manly F. Miner, "The 'Experts' Are Getting in My Hair," *Forest and Outdoors,* November 1948, 30

As exceptional an individual as he was, Jack Miner's life with birds offers historians insight into the formation and characteristics of working-class rural environmentalism in the first third of the twentieth century. While religion gave him a language to situate people between God and nature, the substance of his understanding of the environment came from his childhood and adult experience wresting a living from the land. For Miner and his family, knowing nature – knowing the haunts and habits of the animals they shared the woods with – was crucial to survival. The sentiment that came to characterize Miner's folk taxonomy – one that distinguished "good" animals from "bad" – was born of necessity, but it took on a life of its own. Thanks in no small part to Jack's – and Manly's – savvy self-promotion, people who had never lived as close to the economic margins as the Miners had came to embrace his anthropocentric and anthropomorphic gospel of biology, flocking by the thousands to hear him speak or to visit his Kingsville sanctuary.

Though the geese feeding from Jack's hand and the robins perched calmly on Manly's tousled head projected the image of the harmony that could exist between animals and people, the Miners did not believe there was a balance of nature that needed to be preserved, or even that nature itself had to be preserved. Having dominion meant using nature: "God put birds and animals here for man's use and for man to control." But it also meant transforming it, "assisting" and, by implication, improving nature, whether by carving artificial ponds out of the Essex County clay bed or annihilating predators.

Popular though they were, the Miners' ideas and practices frustrated government scientists like Percy Taverner, who tried to make the Miners conform to scientific convention. Taverner's attempts revealed just how blurred the boundary was between amateur and scientist. For despite their differences, Taverner and Miner shared a good deal of common ground – common ground provided by ornithology, whose methodologies of collection and observation made it accessible to a broad range of practitioners in the 1920s and '30s.

Building on that common ground was no easy task. Jack Miner had turned conservation into entertainment, and though doing so had heightened people's awareness about the need to work for wildlife, it also limited the extent to which he could modify his message – even if he was inclined to. Miner's ideas might not have been sound biology and the practices that stemmed from them might have had questionable conservation value, but they diverted and delighted his audiences consistently. Having built a public career on them, he was probably loath to jettison his script. The limelight had made it hard to see the difference between promoting conservation and promoting himself. But, out of the glare of publicity, it was easier to find a way between local knowledge and scientific conservation. As will be discussed in the next chapter, the Hudson's Bay Company was able to do just that.

CHAPTER FOUR

♦

The Hudson's Bay Company and Scientific Conservation

IN 1942 THE CLARENDON Press in Oxford published a hefty tome with the rather unpromising title of *Voles, Mice, and Lemmings,* five hundred carefully reasoned pages outlining "problems in population dynamics."[1] Charles Sutherland Elton's monograph was just the sort of work many imagined would be produced by the university, a testament to a scholarly single-mindedness powerful enough to overcome the distractions and disruptions of the real world and particularly the war.

Only the frontispiece and dedication suggested that the author was no insular academic, but one who embraced connections to the world outside the library and laboratory. Elton included a full-page portrait of a man on snowshoes, with a dog cavorting at his side. This, the caption read, was "Captain George Cartwright visiting his fox traps in the eighteenth century, south of Hamilton Harbour, Labrador." Cartwright was a British half-pay officer turned entrepreneur who established and operated a fish and fur trade business on the Labrador shore from 1770 to 1786, eventually selling out to the Hudson's Bay Company. Despite the curious prominence the scientist gave to this eighteenth-century adventurer, Elton dedicated his book to someone else: Mr. Charles V. Sale. Sale was not, as might be expected, a fellow scientist, nor a particularly influential teacher. Instead, he had been a governor of the Hudson's Bay Company.

The portrait of the fur trader and dedication to one of the company's governors acknowledged the Bay's corporate sponsorship of Elton's work. *Voles, Mice, and Lemmings* represented the culmination of his relationship with the Hudson's Bay Company, which had supported the young ecologist's work beginning in the late 1920s. Sale might not have been particularly knowledgeable about ecology, but he knew a good investment when he saw one. Thanks to the HBC's financial and research support, Charles Elton was able to lay the foundation for the work on biological cycles that would make him a "father of ecology."

The HBC's sponsorship of Elton was not just an incidental act of good corporate citizenship, born out of Oxford's clubby confines. Instead, it was part of the company's long-standing commitment to scientific research and conservation. While federal and provincial governments in Canada were only just beginning to hire scientists and conduct systematic field research in the first half of the twentieth century, the HBC had a long history of international collaboration with scientific researchers and research institutions.[2] In the 1930s, '40s, and '50s, the company supported and funded a number of Canadian-based projects carried out by Elton's Oxford-based Bureau of Animal Population. At the same time, it established a number of beaver and muskrat preserves in northern Quebec, Ontario, Manitoba, and Saskatchewan, operating them according to the principles of scientific game management, and with the help of a university zoologist. These were models for the government programs in fur conservation undertaken by the Department of Indian Affairs and various provinces.

If a private individual was Canada's best-known conservationist, then the private sector represented the cutting edge of scientific conservation in the years before the Second World War. Influenced by Progressivist thinking, the Hudson's Bay Company's corporate conservation initiatives represented the shape of things to come in wildlife management, namely, the key role of science. But the success of the HBC's preserves was not just due to the guiding role it gave science in shaping its conservation efforts. For, unlike the wildlife management initiatives undertaken by the federal and provincial governments up to this time, the conservation projects of the Hudson's Bay Company also effectively and substantively integrated local people. For the fur trade company, wildlife conservation was as much a social issue as an economic and biological one.

HBC: HERE BEFORE CONSERVATION

According to the historical geographer Arthur J. Ray, the Hudson's Bay Company was a pioneer in conservation in North America, initiating "what must have been one of the earliest attempts ... to put a primary resource industry on a sustained-yield basis."[3] Given the myriad of conservation measures that characterized indigenous communities, it is probably more accurate to recognize the HBC as the first European concern to implement a systematic policy of wildlife management in North America.[4]

Like the Progressive conservationists who would follow them a century later, the Hudson's Bay Company considered wildlife an economic resource that had fallen victim to thoughtless exploitation. Years of intense rivalry with the North West and XY Companies at the end of the eighteenth and the beginning of the nineteenth centuries had decimated both big game and fur resources in the company's "Northern Department," particularly in the area south of the Churchill River and east of Lake Winnipeg and Red River. With whole territories emptied of animals, the subsistence of both Aboriginal peoples and traders was threatened, as were the profits of the Hudson's Bay Company. Aboriginal peoples responded to this resource depletion as they always had, by moving on.[5] Doubly threatened – by both the decline of fur-bearing animals and the hunters to supply them – the company had no prior experience upon which it could draw to address the problem. It was forced to innovate. In conservation, as in so many other areas, George Simpson, the HBC's governor, proved equal to the task.[6]

Appointed to reorganize the HBC following its merger with the North West Company in 1821, Simpson turned his attention to "nursing" the Northern Department's trade back to health.[7] It was not a straightforward task. The regulatory environment confronting the company was complex. Not only was the territory it administered huge, but the HBC also lacked much in the way of coercive powers to change people's – especially Aboriginal people's – behaviour. Given this, the company did not attempt to restrict Aboriginal hunting directly, but shaped its own policies in ways that it hoped would influence Aboriginal behaviour.

Under Simpson, the HBC implemented a conservation policy in the 1820s and '30s that consisted of moderating its own demand for beaver and shifting hunting pressure. The company refused to take in summer pelts, which were inferior in quality anyway, and imposed quotas on each of its Northern Department posts, limiting chief factors and traders in what they could take in. When it became apparent to Simpson that his quotas were being ignored by the company's officers, who, after all, were paid in shares and had an interest in amassing as many pelts as possible, the governor imposed a system of stiff penalties to secure compliance.

The HBC's efforts to shift hunting pressure consisted of banning the further distribution of steel traps, which were more lethal than traditional Aboriginal methods of taking beaver, and refocusing hunting activity on new areas and new species. As Arthur J. Ray argues, the HBC pursued a policy of "curtailment and expansion" under Simpson, closing posts in trapped-out areas and opening others in new areas.[8] By changing post locations, the HBC hoped to draw Aboriginal peoples away from areas with diminished beaver resources to new hunting grounds. Curtailment and expansion also allowed the company to practise conservation without, it hoped, any diminishment in its fur returns. Similarly, the HBC also began to encourage Aboriginal peoples to trap different species, especially muskrat, to relieve the pressure on the beaver. Recognizing that these "small furs" were less valuable, the company offered a premium on them, hoping it would be a sufficient incentive for Aboriginal people to leave the beaver alone.

In the James Bay region, the Hudson's Bay Company went a bit further in its conservation efforts, establishing a beaver sanctuary on Charlton Island in 1836. At the suggestion of Chief Trader Robert Seaborn Miles, the company sent fourteen pairs of beaver to Charlton, rid the island of predators, including lynx and otter, and forbade Aboriginal peoples to trap the animals.[9] By 1845 the HBC estimated there were at least forty lodges on the island, and in 1846 Aboriginal people reported they had counted sixty. By 1851, the beaver were so numerous that Simpson ordered five thousand trapped.[10]

The HBC's commitment to sustainability in the Northern Department was rooted in its desire to ensure profits over the long term. But in areas where the company did not have a continuing interest, it pursued a rather different and contrary set of policies. As Simpson attempted to nurse the Northern Department back to health, he was busily exterminating the beaver in the neighbouring Columbia

Department to the west. Although he acknowledged that the area south of the Columbia River was a "rich Beaver preserve" that "if properly managed ... would yield handsome profits," he also recognized that it would probably be annexed by the United States.[11]

Rather than conserve the beaver for the Americans, Simpson hired former North West Company trader Peter Skene Ogden to trap the country bare from 1824 to 1830. Not only would the company reap immediate profits from Ogden's "Snake River Expeditions," but by creating "a fur desert" Simpson also hoped to deter the Americans from moving north and making inroads into the HBC's territory. "The greatest and best protection we can have from opposition is keeping the country closely hunted," he wrote to Fort Vancouver chief factor John MacLoughlin in 1827. "The first step that the American Government will take towards Colonization is through their Indian Traders and if the country becomes exhausted in Fur bearing animals they can have no inducement to proceed thither."[12]

Whether the goal was conservation or extermination, the HBC's policies regarding resource use rested on its understanding of the natural world. Traders knew that it was best to kill beaver in the winter – unless your purpose was to wipe out the population; in that case a spring hunt, like those pursued by Ogden's expeditions, was most effective because it disrupted the animals' breeding season. The company's most sophisticated use of ecological knowledge in the pursuit of profit came, however, in its attempt to employ wildlife demography to shape its conservation initiatives and the market for furs in the 1820s and '30s.

In encouraging Aboriginal peoples to trap species other than beaver, the Hudson's Bay Company relied on its knowledge of wildlife demography to ensure that supplies of muskrat would be sufficient to warrant a shift in hunting pressure without a loss in fur returns and profits. Its experience in the field had taught it that water levels played a particularly important role in determining population in the short term. Put roughly, high water from rainfall and runoff in the spring usually meant muskrat numbers would be high and a profitable hunt could be had. Low water levels limited the growth of the aquatic plants the animals fed on and fostered disease, putting a dent in the overall population. After a two-year drought in eastern Saskatchewan and western Manitoba ended in 1825, George Simpson predicted muskrat numbers would rebound quickly, but waited a year before advising his officers in the area to encourage Aboriginal people to trap the animals. His prediction proved so accurate that by 1827 he could report that Aboriginal people in the Swan River area had enjoyed "ample employment in rat hunting." So good were the returns that the chief factor had no difficulties in convincing them to leave the beaver to recover.[13]

If the company used fluctuations in water levels to predict the yearly return of the muskrat, it deployed its knowledge of longer-term oscillations in animal populations to play the London fur market. In 1820, HBC surveyor Peter Fidler was the first to recognize the existence of "wildlife cycles," that is, the ten-year population booms and busts that occur in some fur-bearing species irrespective of hunting pressure.[14] Their dynamics are still not completely understood, and were certainly not in the nineteenth century. But as Lorne Hammond observes, while wildlife cycles threatened the stability of the fur market, participants in the fur trade business also recognized they were opportunities for speculation.[15]

The Hudson's Bay Company took advantage of that opportunity, using its ecological knowledge to protect profits. For instance, Simpson knew that if the company put the one million muskrat skins it had taken in the boom year of 1829 on the market, prices would plummet. Storing that many skins meant gambling on prices increasing sufficiently to recoup the costs of warehousing. If 1830 were another boom year, prices would fall even further, eroding profits even more. But Simpson had the equivalent of insider information: HBC fur returns indicated that the boom had started in 1824 and that the muskrat population was beginning its downturn. "It is evident that the importation of next year will be small compared with that of the present," he wrote to the London Committee of the HBC. "We beg leave to suggest that a part only be exposed to sale this year, and the remainder held until the following, when 'tis probable they will command better prices."[16] He recommended the same course of action with respect to the glut of lynx pelts in 1839, noting that the height of the boom rarely lasted more than three years.[17]

Knowing when a population would bust could also be of competitive advantage. Hoping to cash in on a shortage of furs, companies like the Astors' American Fur Company would often buy up excess pelts or hang on to ones they otherwise might have sold cheaply as inferior. Again, warehousing costs made this a gamble, but one that could pay off handsomely for those whose predictions were accurate.[18]

The economic potential of unlocking the wildlife cycles of fur-bearing animals was still clear a century later, when in 1924 another Hudson's Bay Company governor received a young man who had come down from Oxford with a letter of introduction in one hand and a copy of a recent scientific paper he had written in the other. The young man was called Elton, and the paper "Periodic Fluctuations in the Number of Animals: Their Causes and Effects."[19] With a recently completed MA in zoology and several arctic expeditions under his belt, Charles Elton had become intrigued by animal population dynamics. He had read with great interest Gordon Hewitt's 1921 work relating the fluctuations in the numbers of snowshoe rabbits to corresponding changes in the numbers of Canadian lynx and fox.[20] While Elton incorporated these findings in his article, Hewitt's work was less important for its conclusions, which linked the wildlife cycles of different species to food supply, than it was for introducing him to the records of the Hudson's Bay Company.

Although fur traders had long been aware of the cyclical nature of some animal populations, the absence of sufficient consistent information meant these cycles had never been charted with any precision, nor were their dynamics understood. Hewitt's great contribution was locating a data series that would allow him to plot the demographic cycles of a variety of species over a period of time long enough to allow patterns to emerge.[21] While the fur returns suggested that the numbers of lynx and marten rose and fell regularly and in relation to the prey available to them, neither the company nor Gordon Hewitt explained what might have caused the fluctuations in the food supply that were responsible for the shifts in the prey population in the first place. No one had – which was why Elton's article stood out. Synthesizing the literature on everything from rodents to insects, the young zoologist offered an answer that was as simple as it was speculative: wildlife cycles everywhere were caused by the climatic changes precipitated by periodic solar activity: sunspots, to be precise.[22]

Elton's piece brought the wildlife cycle to the attention of biologists and set a research agenda that is still being played out more than two generations later. Which species experienced cyclical fluctuations in population? What accounted for those cycles? Writing forty years after Elton, scientist Lloyd B. Keith insisted that the importance of these questions to animal conservation could not be overstated. "As a phase of animal conservation, there is probably no single aspect of greater importance on the North American continent than the solution of the ten-year cycle."[23] Elton's own explanation dominated the literature for a decade, and though it was subsequently attacked, it has never been fully discounted. Meteorological explanations for wildlife cycles remain both popular and prominent.[24]

The sheer audacity of Elton's scientific reasoning might have escaped HBC governor Robert Kindersley, but the economic impact of his findings did not. The pragmatic Elton was careful to point out the commercial applications of his research. "In the fur industry," he wrote, "efficient prediction of the number of skins which will be obtained is of the utmost importance."[25] The governor agreed. Not only did Kindersley and his successor, Charles Sale, grant Elton access to the company's records in 1925 – some six years before the HBC had even established an archives and opened it to the public – but he also agreed to distribute his questionnaire asking traders in the field to comment on the scarcity or abundance of particular species. Moreover, the company also gave him a grant-in-aid of his research, referring to Elton from time to time as its "Biological Consultant" or, suggesting its interest in his work, its "Fur Consultant."[26]

The company's support of Elton was a manifestation of its long-standing interest in and commitment to scientific research. From its establishment in 1670, the HBC had made its records available to the Royal Society, a gesture that reflected the fact that five of the company's founders, including Prince Rupert, were members of it.[27] It also facilitated research by funnelling requests from the Royal Society for assistance in collecting specimens as well as observations about meteorology and natural history to its chief factors and traders. Indeed, as Houston, Ball, and Houston argue, these interventions on the part of the company placed Canada – and the HBC – at the centre of natural history research in Europe.[28] Although some of its employees were "reluctant conscripts to science," many of the company's officers were enthusiastic participants, and some went on to establish impressive scientific publication records of their own.[29] In the eighteenth and nineteenth centuries, Hudson's Bay Company men were responsible for helping to amass some of the most important natural history collections in Europe and the United States. Moreover, the company's records were crucial to unlocking "one of the most perplexing problems in biology": the wildlife cycle.[30]

Elton had benefited from access to those records, and thanks in part to the company's ongoing support, he was able to continue his work on wildlife cycles at Oxford, where he established the Bureau of Animal Population in 1931.[31] With the HBC's cooperation and in many cases, its funding, he and his colleagues undertook two long-term studies aimed at mapping the geographical distribution and nature of the cycles of a number of Canadian species, including snowshoe rabbits, arctic foxes, lemmings, and snowy owls. The "Canadian Snowshoe Rabbit Enquiry" ran from 1931 to 1948, while the "Canadian Arctic Wild Life Enquiry" ran from 1935 to 1949. These projects covered over a hundred years (thanks to the HBC's records) and a geographic area of millions of square miles, but their ambitiousness was belied by the simplicity of their purpose: to find out how animal populations varied over time and space and in relation to each other. It was basic science that embodied Elton's commitment to understanding living animals in their own environments, a commitment he developed in opposition to mainstream zoology's emphasis on laboratory-based work on embryonic development and evolution.[32]

Elton's concern was to "apply the scientific method to living animals," but he did not believe that science was wholly the realm of the university scientist.[33] Although his world was international and professional, he recognized that the observations of ordinary people were crucial to furthering the understanding of animal ecology. "It is worth while bearing in mind that the ecologist can frequently get ... facts which he would otherwise never come across himself, and he should make every effort to enlist the help of other people to cooperate," he advised his fellow zoologists in 1927.[34] He followed his own advice, working with Hudson's Bay Company traders, Royal Canadian Mounted Police constables, and game wardens from Aklavic to Ungava and Victoria to St. John's.

The success of his Canadian studies rested on getting reliable information, something that required knowing how to work with ordinary people. For Dennis Chitty, one of Elton's collaborators, this involved acknowledging their informants' strengths and weaknesses. "Satisfactory help can only be expected if ... the animals are well known ... and the observations required are simple," Chitty observed.[35] If the number of yearly responses Elton and his colleagues received is any indication, their questionnaire was effective.[36]

The importance of the HBC's support of scientific research was recognized early on, at the Matamek Conference on Biological Cycles in 1931. Sponsored by wealthy American Copley Amory and motivated by the research done under the HBC's auspices, thirty scientists from around the globe as well as Canadian federal and provincial authorities convened at Amory's summer home in Labrador to discuss "the problem" of fluctuations in wildlife populations.[37] Present as the HBC's "scientific representative," Elton discussed his work, illustrating some of his findings with a poster prepared by the company.[38] "Scientific research conducted by the Company with the aid of records and observations at their fur trade posts suggests that the scarcity or abundance of fur bearing animals is governed by climatic factors which move in definite cycles," it read.[39] Understanding these cycles was not simply an intellectual exercise with an economic payoff, but was work that had a larger social significance as well. Not only did wildlife cycles influence the "quantity of fine furs for sale," but they also affected Canada's indigenous peoples. From the company's perspective, "the abundance or scarcity of fur bearing animals turns the scale of health and prosperity among the Indians of the Canadian forest [and] the Eskimos of the Canadian Arctic."[40]

At the time of the Matamek Conference, the health and prosperity of Canada's Aboriginal population were declining, particularly in the North, in direct relation to the decline in the beaver population. In response, the HBC instituted a program of beaver conservation in northern Quebec. Although the company hired a University of Toronto zoologist as a consultant, the program's success, like that of Elton's work, rested on the effective integration of local knowledge and expertise, and more broadly on thinking of conservation as a social as well as an economic issue.

THE COMPANY, THE CREE, AND CONSERVATION

Despite the company's hopes, scientific research subsequently revealed that, unlike other northern fur-bearers, beaver do not go through a cycle of abundance and scarcity. While disease can decimate populations, over-hunting was generally acknowledged as the cause of the decline of the animal populations in northern Canada in the late 1920s. Drawn by high fur prices at the end of the First World War, large numbers of white trappers had made their way north, thanks in large part to the airplane. As prices rose still more, both foreign and indigenous hunters put increasing pressure on the resource, so that by the early 1930s the animal had virtually disappeared in many regions, including James Bay.[41] By 1936 Chief Trader J.W. Anderson reported that most of the Aboriginals at Attiwapiskat Post on the western shore of the bay had "actually never seen a live beaver in their lives."[42] Anderson's observation was confirmed by a survey of the area that revealed the existence of only one lodge in the fifteen thousand square miles surrounding the post.[43]

For the Cree these changes in the land brought widespread poverty and privation. Although they had faced lean times before, they had frequently been able to rely on company credit to get them through. But not in the 1930s. Confronted with the economic realities of the Great Depression, the Hudson's Bay Company severely curtailed the amount of debt it allowed Aboriginal peoples to carry.[44] The results were devastating for both the region's wildlife and its human residents.

The disappearance of the beaver meant other fur-bearers like the muskrat, as well as big game, became increasingly important sources of food. In this context, the HBC's decision to curtail credit only increased pressure on a resource that was already being severely taxed.[45] In very short order, a whole range of wildlife was decimated. "I was very much impressed by the scarcity of mammalian life," wrote a scientist with the Carnegie Museum's expedition to James Bay in the mid-1930s. "Never before have I seen so vast a region with so little animal life in it."[46]

The curtailment of credit and the disappearance of wildlife took its toll on the human population of northern Quebec. Ralph Parsons, the HBC's fur trade commissioner, reported that "a score" of people died of starvation at Great Whale River in 1931.[47] A diet of roots, tree bark, and water could not support many for very long – particularly the young. Maud Watt, the wife of the manager of Rupert's House Post, recalled how Cree children were especially vulnerable to malnutrition. One family lost all thirteen of their children; another lost ten of their twelve. The starvation she witnessed "was like a slow creeping mold that brought paralysis and the hush of death along the shores and into the forest."[48]

Provincial governments across Canada responded to the disappearance of the beaver across the North by prohibiting trapping altogether and, in British Columbia, instituting a system of trapline registration (see Chapter 1). Neither of the initiatives addressed what contemporaries in eastern James Bay saw as the fundamental cause of the crisis, namely, the breakdown of "traditional" forms of land tenure.[49] According to Reverend John Cooper, who made a study of Aboriginal landholding systems in 1933, the James Bay Cree had hereditary individual or family hunting territories: "every foot of land," he wrote, "is owned by somebody." Although owners did not object to others fishing or picking berries on their land, or even shooting a moose or caribou for food, hunting fur-bearers without permission was considered to be an infringement of their rights.[50]

Ownership brought particular forms of stewardship. According to Cooper, the Cree always left behind at least one breeding pair of beaver in each lodge they trapped, and rotated the portions of their territory in which they hunted for migratory animals. Both practices were carried out "for the express[ed] purpose of conserving the game supply," Cooper insisted. "The Indians are thoroughly conscious of this."[51] The Hudson's Bay Company's officers on the ground agreed. "In the olden days," James Bay Cree families each "had proprietary rights in a certain section of trapping lands," wrote J.W. Anderson. As a result, "the primitive Indian family took a vital interest in the beaver colonies ... [I]t was natural and easy for them as well as very beneficial, to conserve the supply so as to furnish a regular income and regular food supply over the years."[52]

With the influx of outsiders and the increased competition for fur resources in the North, these conservation practices began to break down. Outsiders had no compunctions about trapping wherever they found animals, and were either unaware of or ignored Cree territorial boundaries. Even where whites were thin on the ground, Aboriginal people were not confident that the government would recognize or protect their family hunting territories in cases of conflict. According to Cooper, whether the Cree encountered actual competition or merely the threat of it, many chose to reap the immediate profits from trapping out their land rather than leave it to the depredations of others. The HBC agreed. "As the old tribal laws lost their effectiveness and the Indian gradually lost control of his tribal lands, he naturally tended, like the white trapper, to kill everything in sight," echoed the HBC's J.W. Anderson, "because if he did not, some other trapper would."[53]

While government prohibitions on trapping and trapline registration systems might stop over-hunting in the short term, in Cooper's opinion, effective conservation would come only by restoring what he considered to be the traditional system of tenure and the care of the land that flowed from it. His case for government recognition of Aboriginal landholding as a form of conservation anticipated Garrett Hardin's "tragedy of the commons" argument and revealed Cooper's ideological bias.[54] "The Indians in the area of which we are speaking (James Bay) have been drifting rapidly from private ownership of real property to a system of communism in property holding," he wrote. "The chief remedy seems to be a reversion from the present drift towards communism back to private land ownership."[55]

While the HBC stopped short of advocating "private land ownership" for the Cree, it did develop a conservation scheme that was premised on a similar understanding of their land tenure system. Unlike the initiatives developed after the merger in 1821, this one was not developed by the company's governor, but by one of its post managers. Local knowledge shaped James Watt's understanding of the problem and helped him frame a solution. Stationed at Rupert's House, Watt had seen first-hand the starvation that resulted from the disappearance of the beaver and was moved to act. In 1929 he began thinking about creating a sanctuary, motivated in part by his discovery of an old letterbook that detailed the Charlton Island experiment of a century earlier.

For Watt, restoring the Cree system of "private property" was the key to conservation. "Were it possible for a hunter to uphold his right to certain hunting lands it would do more to conserve beaver than any close season," he argued to his district manager in 1929. To that end, he proposed that Aboriginal people be allowed to stake out specific lakes and creeks for their exclusive use, registering them with the HBC. Although they would not be allowed to trap the beaver immediately – in order to allow the population to grow – in a few years time they would be given an exclusive right to harvest a certain number. Watt made it clear that the HBC would report those who broke the sanctuary's rules to the RCMP as well as "arrange a black list and refuse advances to those who infringed the law," but his conservation scheme did not so much turn on coercion as it did the

James Watt, the local Factor responsible for initiating the Hudson's Bay Company's beaver conservation program, oversees the live trapping and transfer of beaver at the Charlton Island Preserve in 1939. Hudson's Bay Company Archives, 1981/28/70

Crees' historical recognition of and respect for hunting territories.[56] In 1932, after Watt secured a lease from the provincial government of Quebec to over seven thousand acres of land surrounding Rupert's House and overcame the company's reluctance to involve itself in "doubtful zoological experiments," his idea began to take concrete form.[57] The Rupert's House Beaver Preserve operated on the basis of Cree local knowledge and company paternalism. In compliance with Quebec's game law, the HBC was obliged to survey its leasehold and to hire game guardians to police it. It did this in 1933, choosing a number of local Aboriginal men to locate all the beaver lodges on the concession, mark them "with tree blazes or posts with the letters HBC," and conduct a census.[58] The information was mapped and details regarding the condition of the habitat recorded. In all, the first

The Hudson's Bay Company hired young Aboriginal men like these at its Attiwapis-kat Preserve to carry out its conservation program (ca. 1948). Hudson's Bay Company Archives, 1987/363-B-20.2/2

survey revealed only thirty-eight lodges containing just 162 beaver.[59] The counts were repeated yearly by the guardians, whose wages were meant, in part, to compensate them for not being able to trap beaver (although they were allowed to take other animals). As permanent employees of the company, they were given uniforms as well as "a badge of office and an impressive document with a seal." This was a practice that originated in the eighteenth-century fur trade, and was aimed at underlining "the importance of the beaver sanctuary and the authority of the game guardians" to other Native people.[60] Recognizing that the sanctuary rested on the cooperation of these other Native people, Watt also made efforts to explain its workings to them, designing a poster illustrating how beaver would increase if left to their own devices and publishing a booklet in English and Cree syllabic to explain the rate of increase.[61]

According to the company's in-house magazine, the first five years of the sanctuary were the hardest, "but when they [the Cree] saw how the beaver were increasing they agreed to hang on." By 1940 the yearly lodge tally revealed that the population had rebounded sufficiently to allow controlled trapping to begin. Twelve families chosen by Watt took 450 beaver. By 1943, when eighteen hundred were trapped, the experiment was considered a resounding success. Not only were there approximately thirteen thousand animals on the preserve, but "every Indian at Rupert's House has a credit balance with the Company," the magazine reported. It was "an unprecedented state of affairs."[62] As Rupert's House had witnessed the birth of the Hudson's Bay Company's trade in Canada, it seemed only fitting to some in its employ that it was also the site of the first scientifically managed beaver preserve. As *The Beaver* put it, "the Governor and the Company of Adventurers trading into Hudson's Bay are again pioneering in the North."[63] The success of Watt's Rupert's House preserve was enough to inspire the company to undertake other beaver conservation efforts in the James Bay region, on Charlton (1934) and Agamiski Islands (1935) in James Bay itself, at Attiwapiskat (1936) and Kapisko (1940) in Ontario, and Fort George (1940) in Quebec. It also established muskrat preserves at Steeprock (1934) in Manitoba and at Cumberland House (1936) in northern Saskatchewan.[64] All of them were managed with the same combination of local knowledge, paternalism, and the emerging principles of scientific game management. As was the case at Rupert's House, Aboriginal people carried

Three kids and three kits at Rupert's House. Beaver had become so scarce that some children like these had never seen one (ca. 1942). Hudson's Bay Company Archives, 1987/363-B-20.1/I

out annual censuses under the direction of an HBC manager, the results of which were used to determine whether animals would be trapped and in what numbers. The preserve manager then allocated quotas to individual families based on his assessment of their need.[65]

In light of its "rapidly expanding conservation work," the company felt local knowledge was not sufficient to operate its preserves, and that it needed "technical assistance in the study of disease, food supply, density of population and related matters."[66] To that end, in 1938 it made a five-year grant of $250 per year for scientific research and hired Dr. Leonard Butler, a University of Toronto–trained zoologist.[67] Butler worked with the HBC until at least 1950, regularly monitoring the pH of the water on the preserves, sampling aquatic plants, and experimenting with ways of increasing the oxygen content of lakes in the winter.[68]

At the muskrat preserves, the company added habitat modification to its repertoire of scientific management techniques in the late 1930s and early 1940s. At Steeprock and Cumberland House, it experimented with increasing production by building dams to raise the water levels in the marshes and planting wild rice to supplement the natural food supply.[69] These could be large-scale, labour-intensive projects involving, as the one at Cumberland House did, more than fifty men pulling a dragline to dredge canals. Again, however, projects like these also relied on local, as well as scientific, knowledge. The HBC manager at Pukatawagan Post consulted with the chief of the local band on the best location for such dams.[70]

Through its beaver and muskrat preserves, the HBC established a reputation in the North American management community for its innovative work. In the late 1940s and early 1950s, provincial governments across the country regularly approached the company for advice. "Your Company has had a lot to do with beavers," wrote the supervisor of Alberta's Department of Public Works in 1949, "and it may be that you can give me reference to certain records which may be available."[71] James Hatter, a biologist with British Columbia's provincial game department, considered the HBC a practitioner of "intelligent beaver management" and asked for its tables of beaver increase as well as information about beaver habitat and trapping practice.[72] The company's efforts were also known in the United States, and it fielded similar requests from state governments and the US Fish and Wildlife Service, as well as American academics like Paul Errington of Iowa State, who considered the HBC's management "highly creditable from the technical standpoint."[73]

For the Hudson's Bay Company, conservation was an economic necessity, but it also realized that effective management rested on decentralized control and understanding resource use in its social and cultural context. In essence, what the company did on its preserves was re-create a local commons – one that was of its making and under its oversight, but a local commons nonetheless, where a community of users was actively involved in regulating wildlife. According to the HBC's Donald Denmark, one of the strengths of his company's conservation program was that it "places local control in the hands of its post managers, who, by reason of their training, experience and knowledge of each native's capabilities, are in an excellent position to administer their areas."[74] But the long-term success of the preserves was rooted in the company's approach to conservation, which recognized that regulating resource use required an understanding of the community of users as well as of the resource itself. The beaver and muskrat conservation initiatives the HBC began in the 1930s not only relied on the labour and cooperation of the local indigenous population, but they also built on existing Aboriginal norms and practices, creating a conservation program that gave the beaver, the Cree, and the company a future.

"A SINGLE GREEN LEAF": GREY OWL AND THE BEAVER

Despite the success and influence of the HBC's conservation initiatives, they were practically unknown to those outside the world of the fur trade and scientific conservation. If the public thought at all about beaver conservation in the 1930s, '40s, and '50s, the name that would invariably have come to mind was not the Hudson's Bay Company, but that of another English adventurer who found his way to northern Ontario and Quebec: Archibald Stansted Belaney, the man from Hastings, England, who became known as Grey Owl.

While the Cree were busy rebuilding beaver stocks with the Hudson's Bay Company in northern Quebec, the federal government chose to hire an Indian (one who later turned out to be a fake) and his pet beaver in 1931 to further the cause of conservation. From his specially built cabins-cum-beaver-lodges in Riding Mountain and Prince Albert National Parks, and through his writing and speaking tours across the country and around the world, Belaney made his plea for the beaver, framing conservation as a kind of nostalgia, a way to preserve a remnant of a lost world.

He was enormously popular – more so than his contemporary, Jack Miner, who had a much longer career. Grey Owl was a public figure for less than a decade, but in that time he galvanized audiences like no other Canadian. He got his start writing magazine articles for *Canadian Forest and Outdoors,* penning twenty-five between 1930 and 1935.[75] But it was his first book, *Pilgrims of the Wild,* which established him as an international celebrity. Published in January 1935, it was reprinted five times in nine months, and then monthly,

The pile of sticks in the corner isn't kindling, it's a beaver lodge. Grey Owl's Lake Ajawaan cabin was a duplex, housing him and his wife Anahareo, and his pet beavers (ca. 1933-34). Glenbow Museum and Archives, NA-4868-206

from November to February, when he was on his first book tour in England. *Pilgrims* flew off the shelves at a rate of five thousand per month.[76] His children's book, *Sajo and the Beaver People,* sold equally well and contributed to drawing over half a million people to the two hundred appearances he made.[77] At the peak of his influence, he was earning $30,000 year, an incredible sum in the middle of the Great Depression.[78] Even after he died in 1938 and was exposed as an impostor, he continued to generate revenue. All 100,000 copies of a hundred-page tribute to him disappeared in two days.[79] According to the London *Times,* Archie Belaney's "death has done as much for the renown of Hastings as ever did the death of HAROLD."[80]

His message was simple: civilization, and more specifically, the commodification of living things was responsible for the destruction of the beaver. Wildlife had been "made a burnt offering on the altar of the God of Mammon," he wrote.[81] In his view, effective conservation was hampered by seeing nature as a basket of resources that could return an income if properly managed. "Surely it ought not to be necessary, amongst an enlightened people, to stress the commercial aspect of game preservation," he wrote.[82] But enlightenment would come only with a change in attitude, when human beings discarded the concept that lay at the heart of Jack Miner's conservation. "'Man shall have dominion over all' ... but with what result?" he asked.[83] "He has dominioned it by bossing, ill-treating, betraying and exterminating the creatures placed in his charge – yes, devastating three quarters of our God-given forests."[84]

To move beyond the concept of dominion, humans had to position themselves differently in relationship to the environment. "Remember," Grey Owl told his readers, "that you belong to Nature, and not it to you." Moreover, people had to see animals as "fellow dwellers on this earth."[85] His approach did not preclude hunting or, more generally, using nature's resources for subsistence, but it did require adopting an attitude of respect when doing so.

The content of Belaney's anthropocentric and anti-modern conservation message was inseparable from the way in which he conveyed it. It was no accident that the man London's *Times* called "the Indian Thoreau" chose the beaver to be his "furry retainer."[86] The animal's familiarity to Canadians made it a "powerful weapon," he wrote in *Tales of an Empty Cabin*. "Placed in the vanguard [of his conservation movement], the beaver constituted the thin edge of the wedge," making the argument for saving all wildlife and wilderness.[87]

Belaney was keen to share "facts about their life habits and mannerisms which have never before been tabulated."[88] In his view, the beaver's value lay in its human qualities rather than in any biological role it might have played in an ecosystem. His beaver each had names – McGinnis, McGinty, Jelly Roll, Rawhide – and his writing highlighted their characters, an emphasis which revealed his interest in individual animals rather than the species as a whole.[89] At his public performances, the audience was invited to "chuckle at Jelly Roll's comic turns and [be] ... equally amused at Rawhide's solemn dignity."[90] Grey Owl portrayed the beaver with the same kind of sentimentality that characterized the tales of Father Goose.

Each beaver had "the calculated and serious intentness at his work that a man has, and, like man, [the beaver] is not infallible, making occasional mistakes which ... he corrects," he noted. They could be almost child-like in their emotions and attachments, apparently coming to him "in some small sorrow ... and burying their heads in my arms, or climbing on my knee and clutching my clothes tightly while they push their wet noses against my neck."[91] His life with the beaver taught him that "these beasts had feelings and could express them very well ... they knew what it was to be happy, to be lonely ... [and that] they were little people!"[92] No one who came to that realization could ever trap again. As the anthropomorphism that animated his characterizations of the beaver suggests, Grey Owl believed that the key to wildlife conservation was to see animals as human.

As much as he wanted to reveal the habits of a remarkable animal to an ignorant public, he was even more committed to showcasing his relationship with the beaver – something he considered a model for the kind that humans could have with nature.[93] That relationship was a curious one. In spite of his insistence that humans and other animals were "co-dwellers," the relationship he had with the beaver of Riding Mountain and Prince Albert National Parks was not one of equals.[94]

While he took issue with Jack Miner's idea of dominion and insisted that the beaver he wrote about and travelled with performed their "interesting manoeuvres" willingly and were "in no way ... dependent on [him] for anything," the language he used to describe the animals and his treatment of them suggested otherwise. He referred to "his" beaver – so much for humans not owning nature – and described his work with the animals as "bringing them to a state of domesticity," not with cages or chains, but with chocolate bars.[95] As well, in Grey Owl's opinion, the beaver's potential could be realized only by people. "There are unsuspected possibilities lying dormant in the natures of our Little Brethren of the Wilderness," he wrote. All that it would take to realize them was "but a little interest and kindly understanding" on people's part. This might not have been a "domineering" attitude, but it was an anthropocentric one. For Grey Owl seemed to believe that in order to be saved, the beaver had to change its behaviour, accommodating itself to people.[96]

The anthropocentrism of Archie Belaney's conservation message was matched by its anti-modernism. Just as he had explicitly chosen

Why wear faux fur when you can have the real (live) thing? Grey Owl models the latest in outdoors fashion: the Saskatchewan beaver stole (ca.1933-34). Glenbow Museum and Archives, NA-4868-213

the beaver to carry his message, he also made a self-conscious decision to adopt a particular persona to communicate his ideas, the persona of what historian Shepard Krech III calls the "ecological Indian."[97] According to his biographer and friend Lovat Dickson, Belaney knew that "if he was to draw attention to the approaching extinction of Canada's national animal ... he could do this better if he spoke as an Indian"; if, in other words, he used aboriginality as a source of authority. "Indians and beavers, they shared the same plight," Dickson observed. "The civilization of machines was overwhelming them."[98] But of the two, only the Indian could speak to the effects of progress and point the way forward.

Just as the beaver had to become human to be saved, Grey Owl argued that humans had to become Aboriginal in order to be conservationists. Whereas "civilized people try to impose themselves on their surroundings, to dominate everything," Aboriginal peoples had a very different way of being in nature that everyone could learn from. "The Indian's part of the background," Grey Owl argued. "He lets himself – not just drift – but go with Nature."[99] Those who lived in the bush saw every part of it as a "living, breathing realit[y]" with "a Personality – a Soul."[100] When Aboriginal people killed wildlife, they did so "with apologies to [the] victim." They "respected the plan of Nature" and "put adult vanity on the shelf."[101] If only everyone would do the same, the world would be a better place.

For Grey Owl, conservation meant a return to simpler times, a return to the past. His was a nostalgic message, something that appealed in the tumultuous 1930s, an era of economic depression and looming war. He was not an ecologist or even an amateur naturalist, but rather, as Lovat Dickson recalled, "a poet, recreating for us dreams of innocence[,] ... when the earth was untrammelled by the yokes by which men in search of wealth enslave their weaker kind and hold them captive to their jobs in cities."[102] Addressing his English audiences, Grey Owl himself put it this way: "You are tired with years of civilization. I come to offer you – what? A single green leaf."[103] It was a green leaf of new beginnings, ones that were found, ironically, in days gone past, in "a cool quiet place where men and animals lived in love and trust together" and "where the screams of demented dictators could not reach, where the air was fresh and not stagnant with the fumes of industry."[104]

Like Jack Miner, Grey Owl harnessed the power of popular entertainment to spread his message. Indeed, even more than his counterpart, he literally embodied conservation, performing it before millions. The man might have been a fraud but his message rang true. Yet unlike Miner, there was a fundamental tension in Grey Owl between the medium and the message. He had railed against commodification yet had commodified himself and his message. The same capitalist economy that had nearly wiped out the beaver could also save them – and him.

None of those contradictions seemed to matter at the time. The appeal of Archie Belaney's message was a reflection of the angst of the 1930s, but however much it resonated it was not, in the end, really a plan to move forward. Grey Owl himself recognized as much. In an interview with journalist Matthew Halton, he revealed that his objective in "sav[ing] as much as possible of the wilds" was to provide modern people with a sense of history. "When people want to know what the past was like, they go to museums or books," he observed. "I want Canadians of future generations to be able to get in their cars and drive into wilderness preserves where animals and men live as they lived in earlier times."[105] Nothing was said about changing people's behaviour, nor was there any awareness that cars and driving were a part of a culture that had destroyed the nature he wanted to preserve.

BACK TO THE FUTURE: GOVERNMENT FUR PRESERVES

Preserving remnants of a world that was largely lost might have satisfied the state's conservation objectives were it not for the economic crisis of the 1930s. The Great Depression forced the federal government and its provincial counterparts to take a more comprehensive and systematic approach to wildlife conservation. The beaver and muskrat preserves they established in the 1930s and '40s in Quebec, Ontario, Manitoba, and Saskatchewan were developed primarily as unemployment relief and were aimed particularly at addressing the rising costs of Aboriginal welfare.

If people – particularly Aboriginals – could make a living from the land by trapping, they would, the thinking went, be less of a drain on government coffers. But in order for that to be possible, there had to be enough beaver and muskrat. Hence the interest on the part of

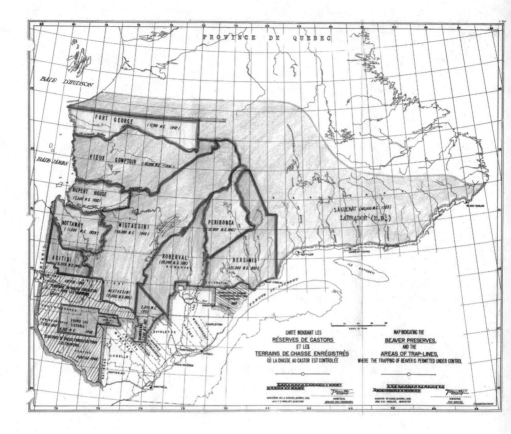

Map of beaver preserves in northern Quebec (n.d.). Hudson's Bay Company
Archives, E.149/1

both the federal and provincial governments in fur preserves. Their
management was on the HBC model: it was informed by science and
involved different levels and branches of government. In that sense it
anticipated the shape of wildlife conservation in the postwar period.
But the most remarkable aspect of these preserves was unique to the
conservation of fur-bearers, namely, the integration of local knowledge and local people in management.

   Given the HBC's early efforts, it is perhaps not surprising that the
Quebec government was one of the first to establish beaver preserves.
Concerned that the company was locking up large tracts of land
and establishing a de facto and lucrative monopoly on beaver pelts
through its preserve system, Quebec worked with Indian Affairs to

create a number of preserves in the late 1940s and early 1950s, sometimes with the administrative and technical assistance of the HBC.[106]
By 1951, some thirty million acres of the province were being managed as part of its fur conservation program, "using the Indian system
of land tenure as the basis of organization."[107]

Similar conservation measures were instituted on the prairies.
With federal funding, in 1936 the Manitoba government initiated
the first large-scale attempt to increase the number of fur-bearers by
modifying habitat.[108] The Summerberry Game Preserve was aimed at
controlling the water levels in part of the Saskatchewan River delta
to increase the muskrat population. After a closed season lasting four
years, the seed population of 5000 animals had increased to more than
200,000, and trapping began. From 1940 to 1944, over half a million
muskrat pelts valued at more than $1 million were harvested. The
success of the Summerberry project inspired joint initiatives with
Indian Affairs in Manitoba, Saskatchewan, and Ontario in the 1940s,
all of which were administered scientifically, with attention to population numbers and dynamics, water levels, and fire control, as well as
more effective means of transplantation and restocking.[109]

As innovative as the habitat modification undertaken at Summerberry was, the most inventive aspect of prairie fur conservation was its
management structure. In the mid-1940s, Manitoba developed a system of co-management that involved representatives from the province, the Indian Affairs Branch, and the trappers themselves.[110] The
province was first divided into conservation blocks, with watersheds
or other topographical features as boundaries, and then subdivided
into community trapping districts. Each of these elected a council
of five to work with provincial and federal authorities to oversee the
allocation and administration of traplines in the community, as well
as conduct a census of fur-bearers. More importantly, the council
represented local trappers' interests to a Fur Advisory Committee
that oversaw fur resource management for the province.

This structure facilitated a new level of understanding between
provincial game officials and the field personnel of Indian Affairs,
two groups that were often at odds over wildlife conservation. More
importantly, however, it also allowed for local perspectives to inform
management. "Too often in the past trapping seasons and quotas
were changed without any knowledge of animal populations or local
conditions," recalled Hugh Conn of Indian Affairs. Under the new

system of co-management, "each field officer attends trappers' meetings and conventions as well as the conferences held in conjunction with meetings of the Fur Advisory Committee. He has the opportunity of expressing his views, of listening to men in charge of other districts, and of discussing his problems with the administrative officers who form the Committee." The result was a conservation regime that worked to everyone's satisfaction. "Out of these free and sometimes very frank discussions have come policies based on adequate field information which are acceptable to the administration, the field service, and the trappers alike," Conn concluded.[111]

This "revolutionary" system, characterized by "the admission of the trappers themselves into partnership," was adopted in Saskatchewan in 1946 and Ontario in 1950, and anticipated the co-management boards that would be developed as part of Aboriginal self-government and wildlife policy in the late twentieth century.[112] Yet it could be tracked back to a "doubtful zoological experiment" undertaken by the Cree and "Jimmy" Watt in the 1930s that blended local and scientific knowledge together in a way that reconverted wildlife into a local commons, a resource regulated to a great extent by the people who depended on it and used it. Insofar as these measures were successful, it was because they framed conservation in both social and economic terms, as locally sustainable community development. This was not, as will be discussed in the next chapter, a way of thinking that characterized the conservation initiatives undertaken by government in the postwar period.

CHAPTER FIVE

◆

Buffalo Burgers and Reindeer Steak: Government Wildlife Conservation in Postwar Canada

IN 1962 WALTER DINSDALE, minister of Northern Affairs and National Resources, announced that "250,000 pounds of top quality meat from Wood Buffalo National Park [will] go on sale from Jan. 17 ... Everything from streamlined hindquarters to packaged buffalo burgers has been prepared to give jaded Christmas appetites a lift."[1]

Thinking of places like Wood Buffalo as ranches is jarring to present sensibilities, but thanks to the efforts of government wildlife workers in various branches of the federal government, by the 1960s some parks in Canada were almost indistinguishable from the agricultural operations that surrounded them. Wood Buffalo, Buffalo National Park, and Elk Island National Park all had corrals, chutes, squeezes, and abattoirs. Roundups and slaughters were a regular part of their operations, as they were in the parks at Prince Albert and Riding Mountain.[2] The boundaries of Elk Island had been expanded twice – in 1922 and 1947 – to accommodate increasing animal numbers, but not in the way one might have expected. Instead of being used as range, the land was used to grow hay, oats, and greenfeed for the bison herd, which the Parks Branch had been providing for since its arrival in 1907. In the 1940s, Elk Island's managers estimated that feed requirements – amounting at that point to some fifteen hundred tons – would only increase given the rising pressure on the park's natural grasslands. They were right. By 1956 more than a section (640 acres) of the park was under cultivation, but still it was not enough.[3] The following year, Ottawa expanded Elk Island again by purchasing a six-hundred-acre neighbouring farm. The produce from its operations not only fed the bison within the park but was shipped out to feed animals at other parks.[4]

By the time Wood Buffalo burgers were being served up at Expo '67 in celebration of Canada's centennial year, some of the country's "animal parks" had become stockyards producing "choice cuts for choice people."[5] Wardens worked as cowboys and the Canadian Wildlife Service managed a reindeer ranching operation in the Mackenzie Delta. Moreover, the bison – iconic species of the North American conservation movement, an animal that symbolized the disappearing wild – had come to be treated as "meat" by the very institutions that had been instrumental in its rescue and preservation at the beginning of the century.[6]

Writ large, the story of these transformations is the story of postwar wildlife conservation in Canada. In the years after 1945, the gap between Progressivist rhetoric and conservation practice closed. Rationalized in the first decades of the twentieth century, government wildlife work became a much more coordinated and research-based enterprise directed by scientists and formally trained personnel. As well, rather than being primarily focused on conserving existing stocks by controlling their harvest, conservation policy in the postwar period was more proactive, aimed at increasing the production of certain species through intensive scientific management.

This chapter parallels the first, examining the changing organization, substance, and aims of wildlife conservation in the postwar period. Although the trajectory of these changes was evident across Canada, nowhere was it exemplified more clearly than in the North, a region whose development was considered crucial to the country's political and economic future in the second half of the twentieth century. Unencumbered by conflicting provincial jurisdictions, the federal government was able to impose a comprehensive vision of economic development on the North, transforming its resources into a national commons for the benefit of all Canadians.

SCIENCE AND THE PROFESSIONALIZATION OF
WILDLIFE CONSERVATION

With the end of the Great Depression and the war, Canada's wildlife resources were under increasing pressure from economic development – particularly in the North, an area that the federal government was trying to open up – and from the expanded leisure time that characterized postwar North America. With greater disposable income and greater amounts of time to devote to recreation, Canadians and Americans headed to the countryside in ever-increasing numbers. Attendance at Canada's national parks skyrocketed from approximately 500,000 in 1940 to nearly 2 million in 1950, and 5.5 million in 1960. Provincial governments across the country created their own parks, particularly in Ontario and Quebec, and issued ever-increasing numbers of hunting licences. In New Brunswick, for instance, approximately forty thousand residents took out licences in 1950, double the number who did so just a decade before.[7] The rush outdoors put pressure on fish and wildlife as well as their habitats. In a policy that reflected the current expansion of the state, governments directed more and different resources toward wildlife conservation.

While postwar game legislation remained concerned almost exclusively with controlling the harvest of wildlife, government conservation practices broadened and became much more scientific and professional, a shift reflected in personnel, emphasis on research, and organization.[8] In 1947, the federal government created the Dominion Wildlife Service (soon renamed the Canadian Wildlife Service or CWS), an organization charged with the management of Canada's wildlife in the Northwest Territories and the national parks. Although it employed just under thirty people, many of them were drawn from the ranks of a new "rising generation" of university-trained biologists, whose presence quickly grew.[9] Just four years later, in 1951, the CWS had twenty-one full-time biologists, as well as technicians and other staff.[10] In 1959, the number had almost doubled to forty.[11] There was a similar, albeit slower, expansion of scientific personnel at the provincial level, a recognition that, as one of Nova Scotia's first wildlife scientists put it, "past policy relying on protection through statutes, enforcement and sanctuaries was inadequate for the future."[12]

What was needed was research, scientific work that could be applied directly in formulating management policies. CWS biologists were mandated to carry out investigations "relating to numbers, food, shelter, migrations, reproduction, diseases, parasites, predators, competitors, and uses of the wild creatures ... being managed."[13] It was a tall order for a small, if growing, staff. Nonetheless, in the first year of its operation, the CWS began what would become a multi-year study of the barren ground caribou, examined the biological and economic significance of muskrat in the Northwest Territories, and reported on the region's other fur-bearers. In addition, it studied snow geese on Hudson Bay, woodcock and snipe in Ontario, sandhill cranes on the prairies, and waterfowl across the country.[14] Indeed, as zoologist Ian McTaggart-Cowan noted, waterfowl were the most studied of species.[15]

Their provincial counterparts carried out similar kinds of research. In Newfoundland, for instance, biologists in the 1950s examined moose and ptarmigan range and investigated the age distribution of snowshoe rabbits, all with an eye to protecting the health and population of these species.[16] At the same time, Quebec biologists focused their efforts on deer, collecting information on reproduction, mortality, and predation, while their counterparts in Alberta devoted part of their time in the late 1940s to banding pheasants to determine their range.[17] According to Nova Scotia wildlife scientist Donald Dodds, the 1950s were the first time that the government applied ecological principles to wildlife conditions. "We read about population 'densities,' wildlife 'habitats' and 'ecological studies,'" he recalled. It was a sign of the growing acknowledgement of "the need for a carefully planned game policy based upon scientific principles."[18]

The scope and intensity of government wildlife research was increased through liaisons with Canadian universities, many of which began offering programs in wildlife management in the 1940s. In addition to training future generations of wildlife scientists, university faculty also did contract research for both levels of government in their departments and through more specialized research institutes.[19] On the west coast, University of British Columbia zoologist Ian McTaggart-Cowan served as a scientific advisor to the province's Game Commission and surveyed big game populations in the mountain national parks, and in Ontario Wesley H. Curran of Queen's University conducted studies of the coyote at Point Pelee National Park.[20]

The scientization of wildlife conservation in the 1940s was not limited to employing staff biologists, but extended into the ranks of the warden service. Not only were wardens the keys to implementing the wildlife policies designed in Ottawa and the provincial capitals, but they were also essential to carrying out much of the scientific research that informed them. This was particularly the case in the national parks. Wardens there had long kept diaries recording sightings of various flora and fauna, but the rigour and regularity of their observations varied greatly. Shortly after the creation of the CWS, a set of wildlife observation cards was instituted to systematize this work. The cards directed wardens to note the species, age, sex, and condition of the birds or animals sighted, as well as their location, age and sex ratios, and the state of their feed. Completed at the end of each day, these cards formed the analytical grist for wildlife biologists' reports like those completed in the early 1950s by CWS mammalogist A.W.F. Banfield on the fauna of Prince Albert and Fundy National Parks.[21] Not only did wardens do basic data collection for CWS biologists, but in some cases they also conducted their own scientific studies. For instance, Banff's wardens tagged mountain sheep in 1957 so they could monitor their movements.[22]

Along with the expectation that wardens participate actively in research came the expectation that they should possess a certain level of formal training. Gone were the days when a strong back and good aim were sufficient job qualifications for the federal and provincial warden service. As W.J.K. Harkness, chief of Ontario's Fish and Wildlife Division, argued, "two essential features of satisfactory fish and wildlife administration are realistic, practical plans and a competent trained staff to carry them out."[23] In his view, those plans had to include a rigorous training program for wardens. The professionalization of the warden service was thus a by-product of the scientization of wildlife conservation.

In the decade after the Second World War, the Ontario government instituted and refined a program for its wardens that centred on attending "ranger school," a thirty-three-week program of study designed, in part, "to indoctrinate them in the principles of wildlife management."[24] Special short courses on new methodologies or technologies, like conducting a browse survey (a census technique for ungulates) or animal inventory, were offered as the need arose, as were refreshers on "deer aging" and determining the species, sex, and age of waterfowl – necessary instruction for wardens who worked in the province's deer-checking stations, or who patrolled its marshes during hunting season. For a time, the government required wardens in southwestern Ontario to undertake wildlife investigations of their own. Those studies, which included an analysis of beaver damage to a watershed, Hungarian partridge population fluctuations, and highway deer kill, were meant to cultivate the kinds of analytical skills and research habits required for effective wildlife management. As Harkness observed, when a warden "has to collect and analyse his own data and come to some conclusion, he realizes the need for care with all the details associated with the collection of information."[25]

The professionalization of Canadian wildlife management entailed more than the desire to improve practitioners' qualifications. It manifested itself in a manner similar to that of other specialized vocations: in contributions to specialized journals, the appearance of in-house publications, and attendance at conferences, all of which created a growing intellectual community around the enterprise and a shared identity for its practitioners. In outlining Ontario's training program for wardens, Harkness noted that the division encouraged its members to subscribe to "at least one professional periodical" and "to attend conferences of a provincial, national, or international nature ... to take advantage of the information given in lectures, and to meet and discuss the work with men from other areas."[26]

Meetings like the North American Wildlife Conference and the Federal-Provincial Wildlife Conference, both of which began in the mid-1930s, were evidence not just of the professionalization of wildlife management, but also of a growing recognition that wildlife was a fugitive resource that crossed geographic and jurisdictional boundaries and as such called for different kinds of governance. While effective management required scientific research – often aided by new technologies – it also called for new bureaucratic structures. The Migratory Birds Convention (1916) was an early example of international cooperation in wildlife management that resulted in new governance structures, but other initiatives also forced different levels of government as well as different government departments to work together. For instance, trapline registration in British Columbia and the establishment of beaver preserves in Quebec brought officials from the federal Indian Affairs Branch together with representatives from provincial game departments.

The combined influence of science, professionalization, and the integration of conservation across jurisdictional lines meant that management was distanced even more from its local roots and became an enterprise shaped increasingly by agendas and attitudes set elsewhere. This was particularly the case in Canada's North, where the shifting substance and aims of postwar wildlife work were especially apparent. There the conservation agenda was set outside the Wildlife Service, by the federal government's new interest in exploiting the economic potential of northern Canada.

After years of neglect, politicians and bureaucrats discovered the North, led there in part by the expanding apparatus of the new welfare state, which was charged with guaranteeing a social minimum to all Canadians, and by the needs of the Cold War.[27] While northern development was a matter of concern for successive federal governments in the postwar period, it was a particular priority for the one headed by Conservative prime minister John G. Diefenbaker (1957-63). Earlier regimes had framed northern development in pragmatic and instrumentalist terms. In contrast, Diefenbaker's view of it was, in his own words, suffused with "an Elizabethan sense of grand design."[28] As his biographer observed, "Diefenbaker promised not material prosperity alone, but a vision of northern development which would make the community morally and politically whole."[29] Developed in the mid-1950s and announced in 1958, his "Northern Vision" was a "new national development programme" focused on opening the northlands. While the country's first prime minister and nation-builder, John A. Macdonald, had envisaged a Canada that ran east-west, Diefenbaker dreamed of "a new Canada – a Canada of the North." Fulfilling his Northern Vision would not only bring prosperity and independence from the United States, but would give the country "new hope" and "a new soul."[30] With Diefenbaker's election, a region that had been marginal to the country's economy, society, politics, and imagination was transformed into the keystone of Canada's survival, development, and identity.

Although Diefenbaker's Northern Vision was especially electrifying, people from across the ideological spectrum shared its imperialist assumptions about the nature of northern resources. The North was empty: as Canada's commons, its riches would benefit all Canadians. To facilitate the exploitation of northern resources, in the 1940s and '50s both Liberal and Conservative governments established and expanded a bureaucratic apparatus to direct northern development along scientific lines.

Scientists were assigned leading roles in the unfolding of this national and nationalist agenda of postwar northern development.[31] The federal government centralized research in the area, offered grants for work on northern resource development, and established links with the country's universities to assist in policy making. While it would be an exaggeration to say the federal government considered wildlife the most important of the region's resources to be exploited, it did establish the Canadian Wildlife Service, whose subsequent conservation work was certainly cast in terms of economic development, particularly in the areas of caribou and bison management.

HARNESSING THE HERD:
BARREN GROUND CARIBOU MANAGEMENT

The evolution of barren ground caribou management illustrates the transition to a more scientific and professional form of wildlife conservation, and highlights the postwar emphasis on management for production. While management strategy over the twentieth century remained focused on the control of human predation, the techniques used and the overall objectives of caribou conservation shifted significantly after 1945. Concerned about declining numbers in the 1920s, government wildlife workers first tried to protect the animals by creating sanctuaries and then introducing exotic species to lower the hunting pressure. In the 1950s and '60s, they embarked on a program of systematic research to determine caribou numbers, using new technology and methods. The result was a management program aimed at removing indigenous predators – both four- and two-legged.

Unlike earlier initiatives that framed wildlife management in the North largely as a form of Aboriginal welfare, caribou conservation in the 1950s and '60s was a way of underwriting economic development. In the view of postwar wildlife managers, caribou were unique and efficient productive units that converted the vast and useless tundra into marketable protein for local and external consumption. Without these animals, Canada's North would remain a wasteland. Management thus focused on harnessing these arctic alchemists, putting them on a sustained-yield basis for economic benefit.

Indigenous to arctic and sub-arctic environments, the barren ground caribou is a migratory animal occupying a range that in Canada stretches from Hudson Bay in the east to the Mackenzie River in the west, an area of approximately 750,000 square miles or some 20 percent of Canada's land mass. The place the animal occupies in the human imagination, as well as in human society, is equally grand.[32] Like those featuring the bison, early accounts of the barren ground caribou emphasize their great numbers, the awesome sight of hundreds of thousands of animals thundering across the tundra "with the wind blowing through their whiskers," as naturalist Ernest Thompson Seton wrote.[33]

The animal was and remains a central part of the economy and society of the North, a source of subsistence for indigenous peoples and outsiders who ventured there over the twentieth century to make a living as whalers, trappers, and miners. Indeed, the barren ground caribou had been so important that CWS biologist John Kelsall argued that "the success or failure of many human enterprises in the north has depended absolutely on whether or not caribou could be secured for food and other necessities."[34] In his view, any economic development program would have to take caribou conservation seriously.

While the Unorganized Territories Game Preservation Act (1894) gave it jurisdiction over wildlife in the Northwest Territories, the federal government's interest in the barren ground caribou grew from its increasing involvement in the Arctic, as an extension of its responsibility for Aboriginal affairs and, particularly after 1945, its pursuit of northern development. When the herds failed to appear in the western Arctic with the usual regularity and in the usual numbers in the 1920s, the federal government undertook the first of three broad initiatives – each encompassing different parts of the barren ground caribou range – to address the decline.[35]

As Clarence Mason, an important figure in the early history of Nova Scotia's wildlife management, observed, one of the most obvious ways to protect valuable resources was to lock them up.[36] In the case of wildlife, that meant creating sanctuaries. A staple technique of wildlife management in the early twentieth century, it was used for barren ground caribou conservation. In 1927, the federal government set aside approximately twenty-five thousand square miles of the central barren lands in what is now Nunavut as the Thelon Game Sanctuary. In an effort to protect the resident populations of musk-ox and barren ground caribou, the federal government prohibited both Aboriginals and non-Aboriginals from hunting the animals within its boundaries, and then enlarged those boundaries in 1956 to comprise an area larger than Mason's home province, some thirty-five thousand square miles.[37] At roughly the same time, it also established a number of other game preserves in the Far North, areas strictly for the use of Aboriginal peoples. While hunting was allowed, wildlife managers hoped that these preserves, along with the Thelon Sanctuary, would reduce the hunting pressure on the barren ground caribou and thus allow their numbers to rebound.

Neither the sanctuary nor the preserves affected caribou numbers significantly.[38] Migratory animals, the barren ground caribou remained vulnerable to hunters on their journey both to and from these protected areas. As large as the areas set aside were, caribou biologist John Kelsall estimated that nothing less than a reserve of 100,000 square miles would have been effective.[39] The nature of the beast meant that other, more aggressive and innovative management measures were called for.

They were not long in coming and took the form of the well-known reindeer experiment that began in the 1930s. Not usually recognized as a caribou conservation initiative, it represented another management technique common to the first half of the twentieth century. The idea was to reduce hunting pressure on the threatened species by deflecting human consumption to another source – often an exotic species. In Newfoundland and Nova Scotia, moose and white-tailed deer were introduced at the turn of the twentieth century as a way of reducing pressure on woodland caribou, and in the western Arctic, the federal government imported reindeer, hoping they would act as a substitute for barren ground caribou. In the Mackenzie Delta, the animals had all but disappeared in the early part of the twentieth century, victims of over-hunting to supply American whaling crews as well as local needs.[40] After a Royal Commission recommended that small experimental herds of reindeer be established in the North to provide the Inuit with an alternative source of protein, the federal government signed a contract with the Lomen Reindeer Company of Alaska in 1929 for delivery of three thousand animals and established two interdepartmental committees to oversee the experiment. Six years later, in 1935, the herd arrived, settling on the 6,600-square-mile Mackenzie Reindeer Grazing Reserve.[41]

The reindeer project was not just meant to save the caribou: it was also designed to be the salvation of the Inuit, most immediately by providing them with sustenance, but over the longer term by teaching them to be civilized. Domesticating reindeer would transform nomadic hunters into more sedentary herders like the Sami in Finland, and render them less dependent on country food and the vagaries of the commercial fur trade. As the government-owned herd of three thousand grew, individual Inuit were given animals to establish their own independent herds, which, it was hoped, would eventually become self-sustaining. Although the goals of the project were never fully realized, the reindeer experiment attests to the ongoing faith of wildlife workers in the transformative power of animals, and the often-intertwined goals of wildlife conservation and social engineering. Just as the conservation initiatives discussed in Chapter 1 were ways to regenerate middle-class masculinity, the reindeer experiment was designed to give both the caribou and the Inuit a future.

Although the story of the herd's epic journey from Alaska to Reindeer Station is well known, the details of its impact on caribou conservation are not. Despite the commencement of reindeer herding operations, the caribou population in the delta did not increase but instead fluctuated greatly in the 1940s and '50s. While surveys suggested that barren ground caribou in the region of Great Bear Lake near the grazing reserve were being "under-utilized," it is unclear whether that was due to the success of the reindeer experiment or because of other postwar economic opportunities available to the Inuit which may also have worked to reduce the hunt.[42] Indeed, there is some suggestion that by competing for the same food, the reindeer may have prevented the caribou from recovering as fully as they might have.[43]

With the renewed interest in northern development after the war, there was renewed concern over the decline of the migratory barren ground caribou. At the Federal-Provincial Wildlife Conference in 1947, delegates from both levels of government committed themselves to working together on the first systematic long-term study of the animal. Wildlife science and management technology would, it was hoped, allow biologists to ascertain accurate population numbers and the extent of the caribou's range. These migratory animals had largely remained invisible to researchers because of their mobility, but the bush plane allowed biologists to reach every corner of their habitat rather than just the "one or two localities" that had formed the basis of earlier estimates.[44] Using aerial survey techniques perfected after the war, A.W.F. Banfield and his research team made a number of reconnaissance flights over the tundra in 1948 and 1949, looking for caribou. Once a herd was spotted and its direction of travel determined, an estimate of the ground it would cover could be made. Part of that range was divided into transects that were half a mile wide. Flying over each transect at an altitude of five hundred feet, spotters counted the animals from the air. The total herd population was then estimated on the basis of the number seen in the sample strips and cross-checked against counts made at ground stations throughout the caribou range.[45]

Basing his conclusions on these aerial surveys, Banfield shocked his colleagues with population estimates not in the millions, but in the hundreds of thousands. From a pre-European contact population of anywhere from 3 to 30 million, the numbers of barren ground caribou had dropped precipitously, to 668,000 in 1949. Subsequent surveys were equally shocking, revealing a decline of more than 50 percent in the six years after Banfield's initial survey, to 278,900 in 1955.[46] Losses of this magnitude constituted a "crisis," one that required the joint efforts of federal and provincial wildlife workers to address. In October 1955, CWS scientists as well as officials from Indian Affairs and the Ministry of Northern Affairs and National Resources joined game officers from Manitoba, Saskatchewan, and the Northwest Territories on two Barren Ground Caribou Preservation Committees, one "Technical," which oversaw scientific research into the causes of population decline and recommended management initiatives, and the other "Administrative," which dealt with issues of policy and jurisdiction.[47]

The "caribou crisis," as Banfield called it, was given public form by reports of a "slaughter" at Duck Lake, Manitoba, in the fall of 1955. According to Manitoba game warden J.D. Robertson, sixteen Sayisi Dene hunters killed 750 caribou for their hides, leaving the meat to rot.[48] "The sight that greeted us was something I do not believe could be seen at any other place in the world," wrote the shocked officer. Caribou were "floating and lying on the shores of Duck Lake," some "bloated and [so] raven damaged [as] to be useless."[49] In Kelsall's opinion, a kill of that size "could easily have fed the Duck Lake Indians through the winter if properly handled." But as a result of their apparent improvidence, four months later the same community was "starving, and requesting relief supplies by air."[50]

The photograph that triggered the "caribou crisis" in Canada's North (1955).
Canada's National History Society

Duck Lake pointed to both the causes of the decline and the solution. Despite the fires that had compromised the herd's range, and suggestions that the caribou population experienced boom and bust cycles
similar to those of the fur-bearers studied by Charles Elton, Banfield
and Kelsall identified predation as the primary cause and ongoing
threat to the animal's long-term survival. As a result, an "intensive,
'all-out' effort" at wolf eradication began in the early 1950s. Discussed
in greater detail in Chapter 6, the program eliminated approximately
eleven thousand wolves over a decade in the Northwest Territories.
Given that a single wolf was estimated to kill between eleven and
fourteen caribou annually, predator control on this scale certainly
appeared to save a significant number of animals.[51]

However, the wolf hunt did not address the main threat to the
barren ground caribou: human predation. As Kelsall noted, the loss

inflicted by wolves rarely exceeded 5 percent of the total herd per year, and in any case, "a caribou temporarily saved from wolves does not mean a permanent addition to the population."[52] While biologists estimated the average yearly kill by humans to be 7.8 percent of the total herd in the 1950s and early 1960s, it ranged widely from year to year and from community to community. For instance, Banfield estimated that Aboriginal people harvested 13 to 15 percent of the herd, or anywhere from 86,000 to 100,000 animals in the winter of 1948-49. In his 1955 resurvey, Kelsall put human predation at 20 percent, an unsustainable level.[53]

While the commissioner of the Northwest Territories argued "Education Can Help Save the Caribou," government wildlife workers also took more immediate and sometimes more coercive steps to curtail the human kill.[54] Indian Affairs offered "to station a man at Duck Lake to supervise the local Indian population in all its endeavours."[55] More generally, on the recommendation of the Technical Barren Ground Caribou Preservation Committee, Indian Affairs limited access to ammunition and attempted to curtail the use of .22 rifles. Unless the hunter using one was particularly skilled, the .22 tended to wound rather than kill caribou, and as a result, conservationists believed it was responsible for the "crippling loss" of a great number of animals and the wastage of their meat.[56] In addition, government officials insisted on accompanying some Aboriginal hunting parties to ensure there was no over-killing. "For several years [after 1955] almost every major hunt was accompanied by an officer of one agency or another," Kelsall recalled.[57] An RCMP officer, provincial game warden, or Indian Affairs agent oversaw "organized" or "conducted" hunts. After the animals were located, sometimes with the assistance of a snowmobile or aircraft, government officials took small groups of hunters out on the land. They were permitted to take a certain number of caribou, some of which were distributed for immediate use while the rest were transported to refrigerator facilities (constructed at the expense of Indian Affairs) where they were stored and released during the summer months.[58] These organized hunts were costly and labour-intensive affairs: in 1956 one bombardier trip to spot caribou cost $96, eight times the daily wage of the supervising official. Using an Otter aircraft to do the same thing required an even greater expenditure – $135 – and transporting the meat to refrigeration facilities was equally expensive.[59] The willingness of penny-pinching federal officials to undertake such expenditures speaks to the seriousness with which the caribou crisis was viewed and more broadly to the power of scientific men to make their case about the necessity of wildlife conservation.

As well as controlling the hunt, federal and provincial officials provided an alternative protein supply for Aboriginal people. Along with bison meat from the annual slaughter at Wood Buffalo National Park and canned pork, they also received lectures about not feeding their dogs caribou.[60] When the lectures proved ineffective, Indian Affairs organized "fall fishing programmes" and supplied bands with nets, jiggers, and chisels so they could put up enough fish for their dog teams.[61] In some cases, government officials even went so far as to make aircraft available to Aboriginal people so they would not have to use their dogs to get to their hunting and fishing grounds.[62] When these measures did not entirely eliminate the use of caribou as dog food, the Technical and Administrative Committees toyed with the idea of licensing dogs in an attempt to reduce their number.[63]

Federal and provincial bureaucrats did recognize that their success depended on the active cooperation of Aboriginal peoples. To that end, both the Technical and Administrative Committees recommended "the appointment of an Eskimo and an Indian" to their ranks, "in order that there be a better understanding of the Indian and Eskimo point of view, and in order that these people may have a feeling of participation in the decisions regarding ... conservation."[64] However, the recommendation was not implemented at the time, and the paternal, top-down approach to caribou conservation remained. Insofar as Aboriginal people were involved in the government's caribou conservation initiatives, it was as agents for management directives developed in Ottawa. For instance, in the region of Brochet and Misty and Maria Lakes in northern Manitoba, Indian Affairs paid Chief Pat Hyslop six dollars per day for two weeks in the fall of 1961 to ensure "every family or person owning any dogs put an effort into hanging sufficient fish for their winter feed supply."[65]

Although the caribou population continued to drop in the second half of the 1950s, the decline was not as precipitous, and it appeared as if numbers might stabilize. By 1960, the population was an estimated 200,000.[66] Biologists believed that this was testimony to the efficacy of their conservation measures, as well as the fact that "many native people withdrew from a life on the land ... to enter wage

employment."[67] In the Yellowknife Agency, for instance, the superintendent insisted that "there can be no doubt that the road projects
carried out by the ... Agency ... [,] employing 200 potential hunters, had a very desirable conservation effect. Without it, herds ...
would have been located and utilized much earlier and to a greater
degree."[68] But as important as wage labour was in pulling Aboriginal
people into a new economy and away from their traditional hunting
one, Kelsall also noted that some withdrew from the land "because
they could no longer support themselves in isolation on [the declining numbers of] caribou."[69]

As his observation suggests, leaving a life on the land was not
always entirely voluntary. Indeed, in at least two cases, Aboriginal
people appear to have been forcibly relocated away from the caribou
as a conservation measure. In his 1968 monograph, Kelsall noted that
"many of the caribou-hunting Eskimos of Keewatin moved, *or were
moved*" to other communities.[70] This was perhaps an oblique reference
to the relocation of the Sayisi Dene – the alleged perpetrators of the
1955 Duck Lake caribou "massacre" – from their traditional lands to
Churchill in 1956.[71] Three years later, Alex Stevenson of the Department of Northern Affairs and National Resources told his colleagues
on the Technical Committee that "they had moved more Eskimos
to the east coast," where they subsisted on seal meat and fish. "These
Eskimos are getting along fine on this diet," he reported. "Thus the
pressure is off the caribou ... which in turn are now increasing."[72]
Given the fact that many Aboriginal villages were located in the path
of major caribou migrations and the perceived effectiveness of relocation as a conservation measure, Kelsall suggested that "voluntary and
government-aided withdrawal of substantial portions of the human
population" continue.[73]

The measures undertaken by state wildlife workers to conserve
the barren ground caribou in the years after the Second World War
are remarkable for their scale and invasiveness. To save the caribou,
government officials were prepared to station themselves in some of
the more remote corners of the Canadian tundra and boreal forest
– sometimes for weeks on end – to oversee the actions of groups of six
to ten hunters or fishers, and then to chaperone their harvest back to
purpose-built refrigeration facilities that could be hundreds of miles
away. But if saving the caribou meant expending civil servants' time
and public money, it also meant sacrificing Aboriginal autonomy, and

PHOTO ESSAY

◆

Men posing with dead deer outside the Clinton Hotel (n.d.). Jewish Historical Society of British Columbia, LF 29859B

"Men Posing with Dead Deer at Clinton Hotel." "Man with dead cougars." "Man with rifle beside two dead bears." The headings in the card catalogue went on. "Roy's first grizzly." "Hunters with game birds and guns – possibly Cranbrook." "Engineers with dead moose." And incongruously, "Really Big Dead Fish." ("Isn't that what it is?" asked the concerned staffer on the reference desk when I explained my burst of laughter.)

I was looking for images for this book, and in archive after archive, my search led to titles like these. Somehow, hunting for photos relating to wildlife conservation led to pictures of dead animals. "We've got lots of those," remarked one archivist when I shared my observation with her. "Proud people with weapons – that's what I call them."

Moose hunting near St. Michel des Saints in the Laurentians (n.d.). Canadian Pacific Railway Archives, NS20255

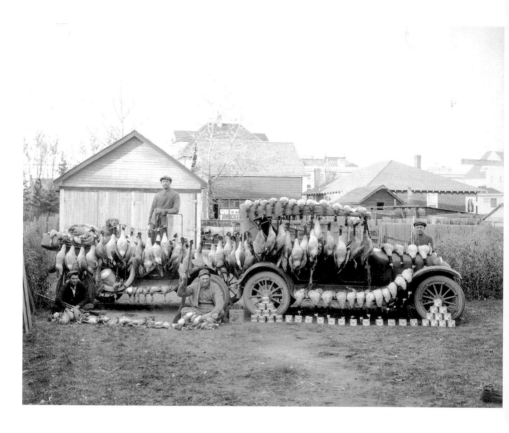

Automobiles covered with geese during hunt, Calgary, Alberta (n.d.). Glenbow Museum and Archives, NA-3884-24

The human faces staring out from these photographs did have a certain grim pleasure about them. These men – and they were almost always men – were well pleased with what they'd done, especially if it was their first time.

Some chose to heighten their accomplishment for the camera by displaying the furry corpse in ways that called attention to the animal's fierceness and size. Teeth were bared and claws splayed, or the body was simply laid out so that its sheer bulk filled the frame. More than one hunter punctuated his deed by placing one foot on the prone beast so as to leave no doubt about who was on top of the food chain. Sometimes only pieces of an animal appeared: in these photos the hunters looked like the window dressers of the wild, carrying severed heads, antlers, freshly scraped skins – mannequin parts in a macabre display of beauty and violence.

Day's shooting, Cardston, Alberta (12 November 1928). Glenbow Museum and Archives, ND-27-36

Bird hunters were equally artful when they had their pictures taken, compensating for the size of their quarry. Their prey might not have been as massive as a bull moose, but their kills were. Dead ducks were draped over horses and cars, piled up around hunters' feet, and strung up against the broad side of a barn.

So powerfully do the photos in this album of achievement communicate control and dominance that it's hard to see that they say anything else about people's — man's — place and relationship to the natural world. Man against nature. Man over nature — literally. How was it that hunters like these could be the mainstays of the wildlife conservation movement for much of the twentieth century?

The animals provide the beginnings of an answer. Not all of them look ferocious in death. In the most arresting photos — and the most disquieting ones — they're at peace: grizzlies seem to sleep at the

Hunters with ducks in front of car (ca. 1928). Glenbow Museum and Archives, ND-27-35

hunter's feet or sit beside him like a best buddy; deer recline in a canoe, apparently content to be paddled across the lake by an accommodating man with a gun.

In these deathly still lifes, the lion has lain down with the lamb. As much as they speak of dominance, they also acknowledge a kind of fellowship between man and beast.

Framing brutality and gentleness, these photos capture one of the central messages of twentieth-century conservationists: we are connected. However, the ties that bind us are built on violence as much as on cooperation. In our rush to embrace ecology's message of interdependence, we sometimes forget that living things eat and are eaten; they kill and are killed.

Perhaps that's why hunter-conservationists like Jack Miner, Aldo Leopold, Tommy Walker, and Andy Russell never called for an end to hunting. They criticized wasteful practices but never regretted the days when they returned home from the hill "covered in blood, hair, and exhaustion"; they never denounced the violence of hunting. We may recoil: but for them, it was part of the natural order of things.

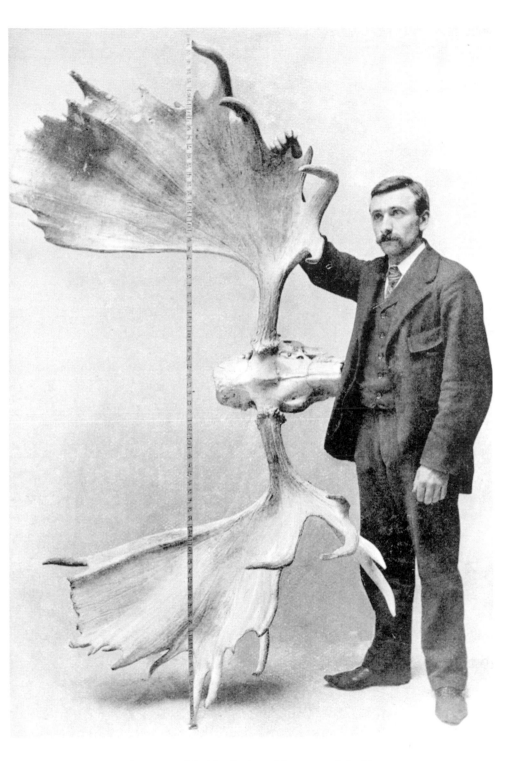

Largest moose antlers on record (n.d.). Glenbow Museum and Archives, NA-3997-1

Moose head (Edmonton, Alberta, 1913). Glenbow Museum and Archives, NC-6-595

Arctic caribou near Fort Churchill, Manitoba (n.d.). Glenbow Museum and Archives, NA-2037-10

Man packing out grizzly (n.d.). British Columbia Archives, G-03680

John Pritchard packing out a blacktail deer (13 November 1939). British Columbia Archives, I-51793

Shawnigan Lake hunter (1900). British Columbia Archives, F-02490

Man with binoculars leaning against dead bear (n.d.). Jewish Historical Society of British Columbia, LF 29860

WORLD'S SECOND LARGEST GRIZZLY BEAR, SHOT AT KWATNA, NEAR BELLA COOL MAY, 1954

World's second largest grizzly bear shot at Kwatna, near Bella Coola, May 1954. British Columbia Archives, D-03097

Frank Swannell with dead grizzly held up like trophy (18 June 1924). British Columbia Archives,
I-58955

Moose (Edmonton, Alberta, 1913). Glenbow Museum and Archives, NC-6-596

in the case of treaty Indians, compromising their hunting rights. As the Indian Affairs Branch informed its field officers in 1958, "during the present critical stage in the caribou populations, the question of complete support of … Indian rights is to be secondary to the very real need for conservation of the species."[74]

The nature and extent of the intrusion into Native peoples' lives and livelihoods in the name of conservation is all the more striking given the uncertain nature of the scientific evidence on which caribou management rested. The census figures that fuelled the sense of crisis were based on a survey methodology that many scientists considered problematic.[75] Yet Banfield's numbers and the subsequent figures derived from resurveying the caribou range were accepted – if not as an exact measure of the decline, then certainly as indicative of its scale.

Moreover, even as they framed management initiatives that would infringe on Aboriginal freedoms in the mid-1950s, the members of the Technical Barren Ground Caribou Preservation Committee admitted that they simply did not know whether human use was actually a factor in the decline of the herds. More research would place them "in a better position to blame or absolve hunting as a factor in caribou decline," they noted. But in the meantime, "human utilization … is something we can do something about. But it may be that some less evident factor is the actual cause of the current decline."[76] That the surveillance and regulation of Aboriginal peoples went ahead speaks both to their marginal position in Canadian society and to the power of scientific conservation.

Unlike the game preserves established in the Far North or the reindeer experiment, these conservation measures were meant to do far more than simply preserve the barren ground caribou, or even to provide a guaranteed subsistence for Aboriginal people. The emphasis on addressing the "crisis" obscures the extent to which biologists like Kelsall envisaged herd management as a project aimed at *increasing* the species to the carrying capacity of its range. After it reached the carrying capacity of the range, he argued, "the animals should be managed on a sustained yield basis both for their own well-being and for the national benefit."[77]

Increasing populations was a desirable management goal itself, but wildlife scientists like John Kelsall also saw it as a way of realizing the economic potential of northern lands. In his view, Diefenbaker's

Northern Vision, with its emphasis on building "roads to resources," conceived of economic development and land use far too narrowly, casting them solely in terms of the exploitation of non-renewable resources. While oil, gas, and mineral development would bring immediate returns, the long-term viability of the North depended on renewable resources like caribou. Properly managed, they could constitute an endless supply of protein that could be harvested for export to southern markets as well as for local consumption, fuelling trapping and mining operations. Moreover, caribou harvesting was a much more effective and efficient form of land use. As lucrative as they might be, "mining, agriculture, fishing, and forestry combined" would use only "a fraction" of the tundra and boreal forest.[78] On the other hand, Kelsall argued, caribou made full and efficient use of the area over which they ranged. Exploiting them was thus a way of wringing value out of lands that, as the scientist pointed out, were of limited worth in 1968 and were likely to remain so in the immediate future.

Expanding reindeer ranching operations would also have been a way of deriving value from tundra and boreal forest, but wildlife biologists in the 1960s and early 1970s considered caribou harvesting to be more ecological and economical. Unlike reindeer or other domesticated animals, indigenous wild animals like the barren ground caribou "offer[ed] the best potential for converting vegetation into useable products." Because "under free-ranging conditions, they select the highest quality forage available to them to meet their nutritive requirements," wildlife biologist George Scotter argued, they did not require the "constant attention, skills, and expense" that raising reindeer or cattle did.[79] His colleague John Kelsall estimated that with careful management the available range could support one million of these organic machines and produce a sustainable harvest of 150,000 caribou annually, representing a value of $8.25 million in meat alone.[80]

"THE BUFFALO RANCHING BUSINESS":
CONSERVING CANADA'S BISON

Important as it was, the emphasis on production was not all that distinguished postwar conservation. As management became more scientific and professional, it also became more interventionist. In the years after 1945, wildlife also became the object of extensive and intensive manipulation – and none more so than the bison. Despite Scotter's argument, extracting an economic return from wild animals did require "constant attention, skills, and expense." Whereas plans for caribou ranching never came to fruition, by the 1950s bison meat from Canadian parks was being marketed commercially and the herd subjected to management regimes derived from agricultural science rather than wildlife biology. The scope, intensity, and nature of these interventions blurred the boundary between the wild and the tame – so much so that by the 1960s bison managers and scientists found themselves redrawing it, moving away from the postwar emphasis on production and intervention and toward a policy of non-interference.

Confined to parks (literally so, in the case of Elk Island, which was fenced) and ranging over a smaller geographic area, bison were easier to manipulate than caribou. Their management followed the same trajectory: from the beginning of the century to the Second World War, the focus was on preservation, something that was accomplished by feeding the bison, shooting carnivores that preyed on them, and patrolling for poachers. It also involved relocation and slaughter. The story is well known: In 1907 the Canadian government purchased a remnant herd of 350 plains bison from Michel Pablo and moved it from Montana to preserves outside Wainwright and Edmonton, Alberta, where in the absence of predators it flourished – to the extent that over-population, and hence over-grazing and disease, became problems. Park managers responded by slaughtering excess animals in the 1920s. At Elk Island in the 1930s, wardens also culled other ungulates – deer, moose, elk (after whom the park was named) – in an effort to reduce grazing pressure and hence improve the health of the bison.[81] When bison slaughter proved unpopular with the public, officials arranged to move part of the Wainwright herd north, to Wood Buffalo National Park, which had been established to preserve the endangered wood buffalo. Amid great controversy, more than six thousand plains bison were relocated there between 1925 and 1928, in what was later described as an act of monumental bureaucratic stupidity: the move did not solve the problem at Wainwright (slaughtering continued until the park closed in 1947), and worse, the plains bison proved to be a source of genetic pollution, hybridizing with the wood buffalo and infecting many of them with tuberculosis.[82]

The 1930s marked the beginnings of a shift toward a more production-oriented and intensive phase of management. For instance, when the Department of the Interior sent J. Dewey Soper to conduct a census of the bison at Wood Buffalo in 1931, it reminded the ambitious scientist of where his priorities should lie. Soper's job was to "advance an exact scientific knowledge of park conditions ... as it bears upon the successful administration of the buffalo to profitable ends," and only "secondly as it embraces the subject of all other wildlife within the confines of the park."[83] In particular, he was to determine whether the herds were increasing at a rate sufficient to justify constructing an abattoir to process meat for relief purposes and for sale to white settlers, suggesting the government's awareness of the revenue potential of the herd. At Elk Island, Ottawa's attentiveness to the market was even more apparent. When it denied permission for bison slaughter at Elk Island in the 1930s, it noted that meat prices were low and that the Parks Branch would not get a particularly good return for the animals. Under these conditions, Ottawa argued, it might be just as well to wait another year, especially as the animals had not reached the carrying capacity of their range.[84]

But it was really after 1945 and the increased interest in developing the North that government wildlife workers took the first concrete and sure steps to realize the economic value of the resource they managed. In the expansion of wildlife research that occurred after the Second World War, CWS biologist William Fuller discovered that approximately 25 percent of the Wood Buffalo herd was infected with tuberculosis.[85] Despite that, the scientist did not consider the aesthetic value of the herd to be compromised by the disease, nor did he think the bison were threatened with extinction. Indeed, Fuller speculated that tuberculosis might even have had a positive effect, stabilizing what had been a growing population. His own aerial surveys in 1949 and 1951 confirmed that the herd had not increased in size since at least Soper's day, remaining at between ten to twelve thousand head.[86] "A large essentially stable population within the carrying capacity of the range is in many respects an ideal situation," he observed.[87] In terms of maintaining the health of the herd and its habitat, then, no intervention was called for. But other values shaped bison management. If intervention was not warranted in terms of herd and habitat integrity, it was justified in economic terms. Because tuberculosis "increases the cost of slaughtering for commercial purposes and results in the wastage of a significant amount of meat," Fuller wrote, it compromised the herd's market value and made intensive management necessary.[88]

In a convenient convergence of interests, the ends of disease control and economic exploitation were served by the same strategy: the 1954 management plan called for systematic and regular slaughter.[89] With the proper infrastructure, roundups and slaughter were opportunities to test for disease, engage in prevention, and collect data on bison pathology, as well as to produce meat for commercial sale. Furthermore, culling some of the healthy herd for market prevented overcrowding, itself a threat to herd health. With the prospect of serving a variety of interests and needs, Ottawa funded the construction of portable and then permanent abattoir facilities at Wood Buffalo.[90] Between 1951 and 1967, the park processed more than four thousand animals, making approximately 1.75 million pounds of meat available to northern and southern markets.[91] While park authorities directed a portion of this meat to the churches for relief purposes, they also sold a substantial amount to Indian Affairs, which distributed it to the Aboriginal people in its charge, and to the Hudson's Bay Company for retail sale.[92] The revenue generated went toward offsetting the costs of bison management.

If the commercialization of the bison herd was a manifestation of the productivist emphasis in conservation, the actual process of transforming bison into a marketable product reveals the high level of intervention that was characteristic of postwar management. Producing meat fit for human consumption required a significant investment in infrastructure and expertise. At Hay and Sweetgrass Camps in Wood Buffalo National Park, wardens and hired hands used snowmobiles and airplanes to herd the bison into an extensive corral system.[93] First constructed in the early 1950s, the system consisted of a wing fence leading to two corrals, one to hold the bison for tuberculosis and, later, brucellosis testing, and the other to hold the animals designated for slaughter.[94] A decade later, the system was expanded substantially to include "a main holding corral five miles in circumference; four small corrals to trap and hold animals for seventy-two hours during disease testing; one small holding corral with a chute and twenty individual stalls, at the end of which was a squeeze pen for testing, branding, vaccinating, ear-tagging, and taking blood samples; and one killing corral."[95]

While wardens and local Metis and Aboriginal men provided the labour for the roundup, other experts oversaw the slaughter and the scientific operations. Wood Buffalo's early slaughtering operations

Roundups like these were commonplace at some of Canada's animal parks from the 1930s to the 1960s, particularly at Buffalo National Park in Alberta and Wood Buffalo National Park in the Northwest Territories (ca. 1928-30). Glenbow Museum and Archives, NB-16-335

had been handled internally, by park employees, but it quickly became apparent that producing meat of market quality required the skills and services of qualified butchers and marketers. To that end, department officials negotiated contracts with Burns and Company and Canada Packers to handle the production and distribution, and in the case of the latter company, to train the Aboriginal crew in commercial meat cutting and handling.[96] A veterinarian appointed by the Department of Agriculture watched over the entire operation, which included facilities for killing the animals as well as cooling, boning, and inspecting the meat. If it passed muster it was given a certified food inspection stamp.[97] The prime cuts were then wrapped in waxed paper, packed in boxes, and flown from the Hay Camp airfield to various destinations.[98]

As much as they believed in the quality of their product, department officials knew they would have to cultivate an outside market for it, especially since the cost was beyond the means of most local people.[99] In 1961 they began a major campaign aimed at whetting southern appetites. Using radio and television as well as magazine advertisements, the Department of Northern Affairs and National Resources tried to entice and reassure Canadians. Calling attention to "the exotic nature of Sweetgrass buffalo," the department underscored it further by noting "the limited quantities available [and] the unique opportunity to create a variety of distinctive Canadian foods." At the same time, however, the ad campaign also assured prospective consumers of "the strict management, slaughter, inspection and processing programme" that had brought the meat to their tables.[100]

After 1945, Canada's bison were wild in name only, having become the objects of intensive manipulation. Fed since their arrival in the parks – something that had habituated them to humans – they were subsequently rounded up, corralled, tested, vaccinated, branded, tagged, and their blood sampled. Some were sent back out to roam a range that was partially or wholly fenced, and at Elk Island, was regularly harvested for hay and cultivated for feed. Others were slaughtered, their carcasses inspected by veterinarians and then "turned [in]to a boned meat product" by expert "knife men."[101] As one official from the planning division admitted, by 1968 it seemed that the Parks Branch was in the "Buffalo Ranching Business," an ironic turn in conservation, given its earlier restrictions on the consumption and sale of wild meat.[102] The bison, monarchs of the plains, animals that literally embodied the frontier wilderness, had been reduced to a bunch of cattle, "grazing units" that were monitored for disease and managed according to the "carrying capacity" of their range.

The management of northern wildlife resources was consistent with the wide-sweeping economic development program elaborated after the war. Wildlife scientists imagined animals like caribou and bison as vehicles to exploit the barren lands for national benefit. But these scientists did not just play a role in realizing the substance of the federal government's agenda of economic development: they also reinforced a way of thinking about resources that was embedded in it, one that facilitated the colonization of the North. By conceptualizing wildlife as productive units and the environment as a series of factors to be controlled, conservation scientists downplayed the myriad ways in which wild animals mediated human relations and gave meaning to them. Abstracting wildlife from its immediate social context made it possible to think of it as a national commons, a resource that belonged to no one and so belonged to everyone equally, and which could be exploited for national benefit.

CONSERVATION AND THE "NEW ECOLOGY"

The reductionist tendencies inherent in wildlife science's way of seeing emerged from developments in ecology, changes signalled by concepts like carrying capacity. As Donald Worster argues, beginning in the 1920s, ecologists started to move away from holistic views of the environment that explained changes in terms of an evolution toward a self-regulating "balance of nature." They also rejected conflict, or more precisely, the Darwinian struggle for survival, as the central dynamic of the natural world. Fully emergent by the 1950s, the mechanistic view that ecologists constructed in its place characterized the natural world as a well-running machine that functioned according to the logic of economics. According to the "new ecology," nature was best thought of as a "system" rather than a "community," a word that invited anthropomorphic comparisons. The components of an "ecosystem" were categorized according to their general roles as "producers," "consumers," and "decomposers," each of which had a particular job and occupied a specialized place, or "niche."[103]

While new ecologists were concerned with understanding the relationship among producers, consumers, and decomposers, their research was also influenced by physics, and particularly thermodynamics. Here the influence of economics was equally evident. By tracking the flow of energy through an ecosystem, the new ecologists could calculate its overall "energy budget," as well as assess the "productivity" and "efficiency" of the energy transfer at each of the system's levels.[104] Understanding how ecosystems worked, and especially their "limiting factors," was not just a theoretical exercise. As one prominent ecologist of the time put it pithily, "the goal of studying the factors of productivity is to raise it."[105] Indeed, as Worster argues, the very language of the new ecology embodied an "agronomic attitude" toward nature, seeing its components as "crops" and concerning itself with understanding "yields."[106] In so doing, it provided the theoretical basis and analytical tools that had been missing from the older utilitarian Progressive conservation, and formed the basis for the new applied science of wildlife management.

Perhaps no single idea embodied the tendency of the new ecology to see the natural world in economic and materialist terms more than "carrying capacity," a concept that underpinned the postwar management of caribou and bison.[107] At its most basic, carrying capacity is the idea that, as two Canadian foresters put it in 1955, "it is impossible to crowd more than a finite number of animals into any unit of environment."[108] In other words, the population of any species in any given area is limited by food and water, as well as by environmental factors like temperature and the presence of toxic substances.[109]

Despite the objectivity conveyed in studies of carrying capacity, with their emphasis on hard numbers, it became a normative concept in the postwar period. The idea that if there is "X" amount of space and resources, there could be "Y" number of animals was, in the ideological context of the new ecology, transformed into the idea that if there is "X" amount of space and resources, there *should* be "Y" number of animals. In other words, carrying capacity came to be interpreted in a way that assumed that environments *should* produce a certain amount of biomass. If they did not − if there were too many animals or too few − then something was wrong. Human intervention, either by culling excess animals or increasing their production, was necessary in order to avoid over-exploiting or wasting the range.

The assumptions about how the natural world should work that were embedded in the idea of carrying capacity were drawn from the world of capitalist economics. In the mid-twentieth century, nature's economy was one in which resources were the only limits on growth and where growth that reached the limits of available resources was normal and good. Healthy ecosystems were those that hosted a maximum number of animals "in good flesh" − that is, a number that did not compromise habitat integrity.[110] Ecologists and managers acted on the assumption that "animals should be in such numbers that they only eat the annual interest from food plants and none of the principal."[111] No account was taken of social factors that might limit population size, much less of whether maximum growth was always desirable.

In the area of wildlife, the alliance between new ecology and management for production was exemplified in the work of Aldo Leopold, one of the most important figures in twentieth-century conservation.

In the influential *Game Management* (1933), Leopold applied the insights of the new ecology, and particularly those of Charles Elton, to construct a new set of wildlife management practices. Although his purpose was to outline "the technique of altering range for greater productivity," he insisted that doing so required coming to grips with the basic principles of ecology, and specifically population dynamics, which formed the basis of management theory.[112] "Before the factors of productivity can be economically manipulated," Leopold argued, "they must first be discovered and understood."[113] To that end, he devoted the first part of the book to identifying the factors that influenced population size, like feeding and breeding habits, mobility, and "tolerance" between species, as well as outlining naturally occurring fluctuations in numbers. He then moved on to describing a set of management practices, including the control of predation, but emphasizing particularly the manipulation of food, water, and cover. Although he used specific examples, he considered the principles he set out to be of universal application. "Each species is governed by the same set of factors," he argued. "Each has a fixed wild breeding potential which factors prevent it from attaining [and] each may be subjected to management by the same general mechanism of factor control."[114]

"Factor control" was exactly what lay behind the studies of animal populations conducted by CWS biologists. Kelsall's work on the barren ground caribou followed the structure of Leopold's book: after describing the animal's food habits, migration and movement, population dynamics, and breeding biology, he went on to analyze the factors that limited population size. Moreover, Leopold's interest in increasing production is clear in Kelsall's management recommendations, which in the short term focused on controlling predation, and in the long term centred on increasing herd size and harvesting the caribou on a sustainable-yield basis.

The emphasis on factor control and managing for production was even more apparent in postwar bison management, which was focused almost exclusively on eradicating disease despite the fact there was no evidence that tuberculosis actually threatened herd survival. But because TB limited the herd's commercial viability, it had to be eliminated, whereas disease in wildlife that had no direct commercial value elicited no such response. Indeed, although Leopold recognized it was a limiting factor, he insisted that in wildlife management "disease control is a matter of doctoring the environment, not the animal."[115] Tick-infested moose and worm-infested deer drew scholarly attention and monitoring but not anything more. Both the degree of intervention that characterized bison management as well as its actual form would be familiar to agricultural scientists: the herd was treated as cattle rather than wildlife.

More broadly, the idea that caribou and bison were vehicles for realizing an economic return from northern lands was a manifestation of the promise of the new ecology, namely, to harness biological processes for economic advantage. Although we more commonly associate the genetically modified organisms used by industrial agriculture as examples of how the productive power of biology has been put to work for human benefit, Canadian scientists' plans for caribou and bison emerged from the same way of seeing: whatever else they might be, from a bioeconomic point of view, the animals were organic machines with the unique ability to transfer and transform one form of energy, which was of no direct value to humans – lichen and grass – into another, which was protein.[116]

Not all wildlife workers were comfortable with the emphasis on productivity and managing to maximum carrying capacity. Even as the commercial slaughter of bison occurred in the 1950s and '60s, some wildlife scientists raised questions about the productivist orientation of management practice and whether their interventions were beneficial to the animals and the habitats they occupied. For instance, although bison at Wood Buffalo were supposed to be slaughtered in accordance with particular sex and age ratios designed to maintain herd size, commercial pressures to provide meat for market meant that this did not always happen. In 1952 and again in 1954, hunters killed more adult females and young animals than they should have to make up for a deficit of mature adult males, much to the disapproval of one government mammalogist.[117] "We are taking the most productive elements of the herd," he wrote angrily. "It is obvious that no industry can be sustained on this basis."[118] In 1960 CWS biologist Nick Novakowski argued that the slaughter, combined with the effects of flooding, had decimated the bison at Wood Buffalo and should not continue.[119] The contradictions between management practices aimed at producing a product for market and those aimed at preserving the species were laid bare the following year, when the floods returned to Wood Buffalo and Ottawa asked for a shipment of

50,000 to 100,000 pounds of meat for the southern market. Fulfilling the request "would not be management, or herd reduction, but sheer mass murder," wrote Park Superintendent B.E. Olsen. "We have here a fundamental contradiction between a scientific and a practical management policy."[120]

At Elk Island, there were debates about the wisdom of management practices that had been focused on increasing the park's ungulate population. W.E. Holsworth's 1959 study of range and ungulate food habits suggested that the large numbers of bison in the park had had an unnatural effect on Elk Island's environment, preventing the natural succession to spruce forest.[121] Moreover, he argued, fire suppression and the practice of haying and cultivating part of the park for bison feed had also changed the park's vegetation.[122] In a complete reversal of the park's management policy to that date, Elk Island superintendent H.R. Webster used Holsworth's report to make the case that the bison, which were not native to the park, might be removed.[123]

Although his recommendations were not implemented, park managers did move toward "reducing productivity" by manipulating the ratio of male to female bison.[124] Acting in consistency with that, the park also phased out feeding. Haying ended in 1967, as did the last commercial slaughter of bison in Wood Buffalo National Park.[125] These changes ushered in a new era of management characterized by non-intervention, a policy direction that gained full expression in the 1980s. But the debate and dissent over bison conservation in the 1960s points to the complexity of the transition to scientific management, the focus of Chapter 6.

CHAPTER SIX

◆

Predators and Postwar Conservation

I do not think we need to shoot them but I think it is unrealistic
to say you should not shoot them. I suspect that if I were living
in one of those areas and had a rifle, I would be shooting them.
— W.W. Mair, Head, Canadian Wildlife Service, on
killing predators in national parks, 1956

W.W. MAIR'S CONFUSED position on predator control encapsu-
lates the complex story of wildlife management in postwar Canada.
A biologist, he was certainly familiar with scientific arguments about
the important role predators played in ecosystems and, indeed, had
presided over the end of the bounty system in British Columbia. At
the same time, however, he headed the province's Predator Control
Branch, overseeing the country's first systematic government program of poisoning, snaring, and trapping that resulted in the deaths
of thousands of cougars, wolves, and coyotes.

Mair's ambivalence about killing predators is the starting point for
exploring the place of science in shaping postwar wildlife management. Chapter 5 made the case that science influenced state conservation in the years after 1945, shaping its personnel and techniques,
as well as its emphasis on research and managing for production. In
many ways, wildlife management was part of a larger state-directed
plan for economic development, particularly in Canada's North.

This chapter takes a step back from these generalizations to com-
plicate the picture of postwar wildlife conservation. Science, and specifically ecology, recognized the important role predators played in

Facing page: Killing gophers was a part of everyday life for boys like James Ray Hart-man of Delia, Alberta (ca. 1920). Glenbow Museum and Archives, NA-4344-8

Above: Nine-year-old George Burns and his dog relax after an enjoyable day of coyote killing (Gleichen, Alberta, 1910). Glenbow Museum and Archives, NA-1633-17

ecosystems, but did not authorize one course of action over another when it came to their treatment. Instead, ecological arguments could be marshalled by both the supporters and opponents of killing predators. Moreover, science was not the only influence shaping attitudes and practices regarding these animals. There were contexts that justified killing them – ones created by human sentiments rather than wildlife behaviour. Curiosity, fear, and greed all motivated government wildlife workers to poison, shoot, and trap tens of thousands of wolves, coyotes, and cougars.

In the backcountry, predator control was underwritten by local knowledge and justified by tradition. An important institution of rural culture, the bounty system was an institution impervious to change by scientific opinion. Its longevity speaks to both the strength of rural knowledge and the uneven transformation of wildlife conservation. Over the twentieth century, the property status of most wildlife shifted as government conservation work became more centralized and professional. In the case of predators, however, that shift was far less pronounced. Whereas other kinds of wildlife became the common property of the federal or provincial state, predators remained part of a local commons into the 1960s and '70s, their treatment and regulation shaped by the human communities that occupied their territories.

Nonetheless, by the end of the 1960s, the new "values for varmints" that had been articulated by ecologists a generation earlier had taken hold – not, however, because of a new-found respect for ecological science or scientists, but because popular writers like Farley Mowat and Bill Mason had managed to crystallize and mobilize an emerging urban sentimentality about predators.[1] Before untangling the various positions on predator control in Canada and the contexts that shaped them, however, I begin with a discussion of the debate over animals that killed other animals.

ECOLOGICAL CITIZENS OR NATURAL-BORN KILLERS?

Predators are animals that kill other animals for food. Doing what comes naturally brings them into direct contact and conflict with other predators, most notably humans. In response, people have tried to establish monopoly control over their prey – whether cattle or caribou – expending great amounts of energy and resources to hunt down their four-legged or winged competitors. As discussed in Chapter 1, bounty laws were often among the first pieces of legislation passed in new colonies. Wolves, cougars, and coyotes were common and long-standing targets, but in various places at various times in the history of North America, other creatures, including crows, hawks, and bears, also found themselves on the human hit list. By the 1920s, '30s, and '40s, when the debate over predators and their treatment was at its most heated, three hundred years of experience with "noxious" creatures had accumulated to inform the discussion.

Each wolf skin, pair of coyote ears, or hawk's wing that was submitted to the authorities for cash payment only reinscribed the distinction between good and bad animals that lay at the heart of North Americans' folk taxonomy, and at the same time entrenched predator control as a legitimate pursuit and an integral part of conservation. Bad animals had to be eliminated so that good animals – both domesticated and wild – would be preserved. In the early twentieth century, predator control in the United States was under the jurisdiction of the Bureau of Biological Survey (BBS), a centralized federal body that directed the kill, trained government predator hunters, and conducted research on the animals they pursued, including more efficient ways to exterminate them.[2] In Canada, predator control remained decentralized, undertaken by private citizens and federal and provincial game officers – in many places until midcentury. Bounties, which historically had been set by quarter-sessions courts, townships, or counties, were in the twentieth century established by provincial law and administered by game departments, constituting one of their largest, if not their single largest, yearly expenditures. Despite the different organization of predator control north and south of the forty-ninth parallel, attitudes toward predatory animals and the practices developed to deal with them were broadly similar, and were framed by a scientific debate about the value of vermin.

In a manner consistent with Progressive-era conservation values, predator control and the debate over its effectiveness turned in large part on the efficient use of resources.[3] Advocates of extermination insisted that the toll on domestic stock and wildlife taken by wolves, coyotes, cougars, and raptors was a form of waste and hence had to be eliminated. In destroying animals useful to humans, predators prevented people from deriving full value from them. In response, critics insisted that domestic stock and useful wildlife were not the primary diet of many of the creatures deemed vermin. Instead, scientific studies showed that predators like coyotes and wolves subsisted on a diet of rodents. In consuming mice and rats, they did great service to humans, whose crops would otherwise be damaged by these pests. If anything, maintaining a healthy predator population would prevent waste rather than contribute to it.

In addition, opponents of control evoked Charles Elton's concept of niches and argued that predators played a role in preserving the balance of nature. Nowhere was this lesson clearer than in the Kaibab National Forest in the mid-1920s. In an effort to preserve and increase the deer herd, the Bureau of Biological Survey had directed a sustained campaign against the wolf, eradicating it from the Arizona forest. Kaibab's deer population exploded, rapidly exceeding the available food supply and the ability of human hunters to limit it. As a result, deer died by the thousands from malnutrition, and in so doing called attention to the central role of predators in sustaining healthy ecosystems.[4]

Despite Kaibab's graphic reminder of what a world without wolves would look like, those who supported the continued killing of predators did not abandon their position entirely. Instead, they moderated it, talking about the need for "control" – kills that were more limited and specific – rather than "extermination." Human control of predator populations was necessary, they argued, because there was no longer any natural balance in nature. Centuries of human intervention had seen to that. "The minute man shoots a deer, man upsets Nature's balance," Manly Miner argued, "and it becomes his responsibility to reduce ... the enemies of the deer in the same proportion."[5] Striking a balance would not come naturally, but could only be the outcome of more human manipulation – like killing predators. Moreover, while critics of control might wax wistfully about preserving the balance of nature, they neglected to acknowledge the benefits human society enjoyed by virtue of altering it. "Nature will balance itself if we all hang up our guns and other weapons [and] civilization [is] wiped off the North American continent," opined the redoubtable Manly. "But who would want to live in such a place? As the farmer from north of Calgary said, not irreverently, 'You should have seen my farm when God had it alone.'"[6]

Rather than question the desirability of progress directly – something that was probably far too radical – the opponents of control answered their opponents indirectly, underscoring the poverty of a debate in which the treatment and fate of animals were determined by their material value to people. Wildlife was valuable for other reasons; there was more to life – literally – than its economic worth.

. Supporters of predator control could draw on the economistic aspects of animal ecology discussed in Chapter 5, casting wolves, coyotes, and cougars as "limiting factors" that required human management. Those who opposed killing predators relied on another strain in contemporary ecological thought, namely, the metaphor of the natural world as a "community" of organisms, each with its own role and niche, linked to each other through the food chain. All organisms, including humans, belonged to an integrated and interdependent biological community, and though they might not be equal, they had a right to exist irrespective of what they did to or for their fellow citizens.

These two distinct and contradictory tendencies in conservation were embodied in Aldo Leopold. The "father" of modern game management loved hunting, and in his younger days advocated exterminating wolves. "I thought that because fewer wolves meant more deer, that no wolves would mean hunters' paradise," he recalled ruefully.[7] Deer irruptions at Kaibab in Arizona and Gila in New Mexico convinced him otherwise, revealing the interdependence of organisms. Not only were predators necessary to maintain a healthy prey population, but they were crucial to sustaining the larger ecosystem of which they were only a part. In trying to make sense of what he had observed, Leopold turned first to philosophy, drawing on the "organicism" of P.D. Ouspensky to argue that the earth was greater than the sum of its parts.[8] Not until he met Charles Elton at Matamek in 1931 did Leopold acquire a scientific language and conceptual framework to understand what he had observed.[9] Elton's concept of an ecological "community" in which organisms occupied specialized "niches" and occurred in numbers that were best described as a "pyramid" informed Leopold's *Game Management* (1933), a book that would become the foundational text of the new discipline.[10]

For Leopold, the interdependence of organisms and their environment did not preclude human intervention. He flatly rejected laissez-faire arguments based on the balance of nature, the idea that nature was self-regulating and had only to be left to its own devices to return to a healthy, steady state. Instead, people had to control nature

– including predators. "The central thesis of game management is ... [the idea that] game can be restored by the *creative use* of the same tools which have heretofore destroyed it."[11] For Leopold, as for Jack Miner, there was no point in hearkening back to an arcadian world before the fall: before humans had despoiled the earth. "The hope for the future lies not in curbing the influence of human occupancy – it is already too late for that," he argued. Instead, conservationists had to look forward, working for "a better understanding of that influence and a new ethic for its governance."[12]

Although the focus of *Game Management* was on the scientific techniques that would "produce sustained annual crops of wild game," Leopold's reference to the need for a new ethic to govern the relationship between people and nature signalled a different fate for predators.[13] Although he had been trained as a forester at Yale, and schooled in the Progressivist conservation philosophy of its founder, Gifford Pinchot, Leopold had come to realize that the ethic governing resource use could not be entirely economic. Instead of wise use, ecological values had to have a central place in conservation philosophy. People needed to "think like a mountain" rather than like mountain men; that is, they had to see the world in ecological terms – ones that were alive to the relationships among organisms and between organisms and their environment.

Thinking in ecological terms revealed the poverty of a conservation system "based wholly on economic motives."[14] In Leopold's view, "we abuse the land when we regard it as a commodity belonging to us."[15] Moreover, because "most members of the land community have no economic value," we dismiss their importance, overlooking the role they play in maintaining the stability and integrity of the whole. As "members of the biotic community," each was "entitled to continuance."[16] Although he made wolves the focus of the essay dealing with the evolution of his own ecological consciousness, ending the war on them was merely a vehicle for preserving the integrity of the larger community of which they were a part.

By thinking like a mountain, Leopold was able to see that people were not outside nature, but part of an ecological community. As such, they had to govern their actions accordingly, in a less anthropocentric way, and one that valued the integrity of the whole community over the welfare of any one part. This was the essence of his "land ethic," as he called it, a way of living that recognized "that the individual is a member of a community of interdependent parts."[17]

Whether government wildlife managers thought in terms of wise use and sustained yields or governed their actions according to a "land ethic" depended very much on the institutional context in which predator control was attempted. Between 1920 and 1940, a group of American mammalogists who were closely associated through their graduate training was influential in ending the extermination of predators in the United States and ultimately in ushering in a management regime based on a communitarian understanding of ecosystems. As Thomas Dunlap reveals, they did so from their positions in the newly established Wild Life Division of the National Park Service, a much smaller bureaucracy than the BBS, and one "free of long-established bureaucratic restraints and more conducive to seeing new ideas transformed into policy."[18] Acknowledging that predators "have a real place in nature," the Park Service ended predator killing by the mid-1930s.[19]

In terms of predator policy, developments in Canada's national parks seemed to mirror what was happening in the United States. As was the case south of the border, predators were unwelcome in the national parks from the time they were first established in the late nineteenth century. Just how unwelcome they were was revealed to Commissioner J.B. Harkin in 1924, when he asked the supervisors of each national park to provide him with a list of the animals and birds being destroyed as predators. The range of species was shocking: wardens, it seemed, destroyed everything from magpies to mountain lions. Harkin insisted there be "a strict tightening up in the matter of killing birds and animals."[20] To that end, in 1928 he decreed that only wolves, wolverines, coyotes, and cougars could be eliminated. Destroying other species would require written permission. Just in case that were not enough to limit killing, Harkin added an economic disincentive: predator pelts, which formerly were the property of the warden who snared or trapped the animal, now belonged to the Parks Branch. Instead of supplementing wardens' salaries, the revenue from their sale went to the government.

These initiatives would, he hoped, meet park visitors' expectations of seeing "various forms of wild bird and animal life"; they were also consistent with scientific opinion about the value of vermin. Echoing American biologist Charles C. Adams, whose article he circulated to park supervisors, Harkin argued, "predatory animals are of great scientific, education, recreational and economic value to society ... Scientists are pointing out that much of the antipathy [toward these animals] is not backed up by evidence obtained from a study of food habits."[21] Just in case these measures were not sufficient to limit the kill, in 1933 successive parks commissioners banned the use of traps, insisting that park predators be shot; in 1940 they prohibited predator destruction altogether.

While ecology informed the views of some of Ottawa's top bureaucrats, it did not shape practices, much less influence attitudes, on the ground among government wildlife workers. Parks commissioners might have acknowledged the value of predatory animals, but that did not prevent the poisoning or shooting of predators in places like Wood Buffalo National Park so that bison could, as one CWS biologist recalled, be "converted to Sweetgrass T-Bones."[22] What happened at Wood Buffalo was not an exceptional case. Despite its undeniable influence on wildlife conservation in the postwar period, science was not the primary force shaping predator management.

Instead, other pressures, including a desire on the part of scientists to conduct research, the need to act or be seen to act in response to environmental "crises," and local resistance and opinion, influenced how wolves, coyotes, and cougars fared. Ecology might have deemed that predators should be left in peace, but human sentiments – curiosity, fear, and greed – often proved equally, if not more, powerful in determining their fate.

CONTEXTS FOR KILLING

Killing wolves, coyotes, and cougars in the name of predator control might have been in disfavour among biologists, but killing them for data was not. One of the long-standing critiques of predator control was that it was based on very little if any understanding of predator-prey relationships. What toll did wolves and coyotes, for instance, really take on deer and caribou? Wildlife biologists working in the postwar period wanted to know. But finding out required killing a statistically significant number of animals so that their stomach contents could be analyzed.[23] In addition, since some form of predator control would always be necessary, research on more efficient and humane ways of killing was called for. Predators were trapped or snared, or more controversially, poisoned using strychnine or Compound 1080 (sodium fluoroacetate) planted in carcasses. Although they were effective, poisoned baits were indiscriminate, killing other wildlife and domestic animals like dogs, thus earning the criticism of both defenders of predators and advocates of efficient and selective control.[24] In the late 1940s, wardens in Prince Albert, Riding Mountain, Jasper, and Banff National Parks experimented with the "humane coyote-getter," a gun that shot cyanide into the throat of the unsuspecting animal that bit its baited muzzle. Not only did these experiments allow the gun's efficacy to be assessed, but they also supplied a number of carcasses for researchers interested in various aspects of predator biology, physiology, and parasitology.[25]

If human curiosity killed the coyote (and the wolf and cougar), human fears proved even more lethal, forcing another postwar departure from what ecology deemed to be the proper treatment of predators. When western Alberta was allegedly threatened by a wolf-borne rabies outbreak in the early 1950s, Parks Branch officials blanketed Banff and Jasper with poison, initiating a campaign one historian describes as the "high tide of aggressive predator control in the national parks."[26] Their provincial counterparts were no less forceful. Alberta's Department of Agriculture distributed some 39,960 cyanide guns, 106,100 cyanide cartridges, and 628,000 strychnine pellets; poison bait stations increased from twenty-five in 1951 to eight hundred in 1956. As well, in an effort to establish a *cordon sanitaire,* the province paid trappers "to ring the settled area of the province with 5000 miles of trap lines and poison stations" in 1953 and 1954.[27] While precise figures are impossible to ascertain, it is estimated that the anti-rabies campaign reduced Alberta's lupine population by 90 percent.[28] Wolves in Banff and Jasper were decimated while, as historian Karen Jones points out, in the town sites "their domestic cousins received vaccinations."[29] They need not have. During the entire campaign, only one wolf was found to be rabid.[30]

Canada's "caribou crisis" did not endanger human health in the same way the rabies outbreak threatened to, but it nonetheless jeopardized the welfare of Aboriginal peoples and threatened northern development. As a result, it elicited an equally uncompromising response toward predators. Confronted with a steeply declining population of barren ground caribou in the late 1940s, CWS biologist A.W.F. Banfield recommended that the wolf population in the

Northwest Territories be reduced as a conservation measure. The Technical and Administrative Barren Ground Caribou Preservation Committees agreed, and coordinated a decade-long intensive control program aimed at reducing wolf numbers.

Using a technique developed by the Manitoba game department, wildlife workers prepared poisoned baits using buffalo or, ironically, caribou, killed expressly for the purpose. They planted strychnine or Compound 1080 pellets at several levels in pieces of meat weighing twenty to a hundred pounds, thus rendering the baits effective over several visits by wolves. Once prepared, the baits were flown to various sites in the wintering grounds of the caribou and frozen into lake ice or the ground so they could not be moved. In the spring, predator control officers returned to the bait sites to assess the kill. They either pushed the dead animals and what was left of the baits under the ice or allowed both to melt through, letting the water dissipate any remaining poison.[31] Working in tandem with the poison campaign, Indian Affairs grubstaked Aboriginal hunters, hiring them to conduct den hunts.[32] According to CWS biologist John Kelsall, it was a remarkably successful campaign. Losses of other species were minimal, and the wolf population was reduced markedly.

While writer Barry Lopez agreed with the biologist's characterization of the kill, his opinion of it differed. In his view, the control measures taken in the name of caribou conservation constituted "the final act of the wolf war in North America," claiming between 11,000 and 17,500 wolves between 1951 and 1961 – casualties that amounted to between a third and a half of the population.[33] Like many wars, this one was waged without a full understanding of the crisis, and the fact it was won – the caribou recovered – may have had very little to do with the losses inflicted on the enemy. On the eve of battle, in 1950, A.W.F. Banfield, the scientist who had recommended the wolf kill in the first place, told the North American Wildlife Conference that "critical analysis" had rendered untenable the popular belief that wolf predation was responsible for the decline of the caribou. Instead, he pointed to "changing habitat conditions caused by spreading agriculture, lumber operations, and forest fires" as "major factors."[34] Despite this, the CWS targeted wolves. As biologist Ernie Kuyt admitted, he and his colleagues embarked on their campaign of "destruction" without knowing "the full effects of wolves and lesser predators upon the barren-ground caribou."[35] In fact, no studies of wolf predation were carried out until Kuyt began his work in the early 1960s, something akin to barring the door after the horse had escaped. Ironically, Kuyt's work was made all the harder because he had few animals to study. "One of the biggest mistakes we made in the past was to conduct a pogrom against wolves without collecting all possible information therefrom," recalled fellow biologist W.E. Stevens. "Subsequently when we wanted to get biological data the wolves were all gone, a situation that has plagued Ernie Kuyt ever since."[36]

Years after the kill ended and caribou numbers had rebounded, Kelsall admitted that it was "still questionable whether or not the wolf control program contributed materially to the caribou population."[37] The CWS had embarked on the kill because of the crisis situation, and "not," he recalled, "because we were certain that the effort would produce a benefit."[38]

If predator-prey dynamics were a mystery to scientists in the 1950s, it seemed clear that wolf predation paled in comparison to the toll on caribou taken by humans. Nonetheless, scientists like John Kelsall considered the wolf campaign justified: "if predator control could eliminate even a portion of that five per cent loss [inflicted by wolves] it seemed worth doing."[39]

While biologist Douglas Pimlott also justified the kill, he did so in terms of the effect it would have on efforts to limit the human hunt. "Throughout the world people believe wolves constitute a serious menace to game populations," he wrote in 1961. "The possibility of gaining cooperation by the native people would have been even less if wolf control had not been undertaken."[40] Jules D'Astous, the regional supervisor of Indian Affairs in Manitoba, echoed Pimlott's sentiments. When the Technical Barren Ground Caribou Preservation Committee proposed a reduction in the wolf kill by cancelling the wolf-denning program, D'Astous urged his superiors to reconsider. "It is recognized that this type of program does not contribute to any great extent to controlling wolf populations," he admitted. But "in view of its obvious moral value in securing Indian co-operation with respect to them feeding less caribou meat to their dogs, it appears desirable to continue for the present at least."[41]

According to Pimlott, when it came to wolf control, wildlife managers had to consider "human psychology."[42] In his view, conservation was a matter of managing the two-leggeds as well as the four-leggeds. This was especially true in the case of predators, where entrenched ideas and local practices proved resistant to the inroads of science, and much harder to eradicate than any vermin.

Wardens in the national parks were among the first to experience the effects of the shift in predator policy and they resented it deeply. Commissioner J.B. Harkin's insistence that predator pelts belonged to the department meant that wardens' earnings would be reduced – in some cases significantly. Revenue from the sale of wolf, coyote, and cougar pelts could supplement the skilful warden's yearly income by anywhere from 10 to 50 percent.[43] The loss meant that Ottawa's subsequent directive prohibiting the use of traps and snares in predator control was even less popular. Wardens were still expected to control predatory animals – and, indeed, to make sure that they did, Ottawa also instituted kill quotas – but doing so with a rifle was much more difficult. Speaking on behalf of the men who worked under him, Jasper's superintendent complained in 1938 that the new rules did not "give the Wardens a fair chance," and called for a return to the more efficient method of trapping.[44] When predators increased to the point that they threatened the parks' valued ungulate populations, the Parks Branch relented and reintroduced the use of snares in Prince Albert National Park. As a result, on the eve of the Second World War, predators were being killed as "indiscriminately" as they ever were.[45]

As important as material considerations were, wardens' resistance to Ottawa's new predator policy was also rooted in the culture of work that characterized the warden service. The men who laboured in its ranks did so because they enjoyed and were skilled at outdoors work, demonstrating a particular proficiency at trapping. It was part of their identity as workers and as men, and it was one that their employer had rewarded them for in the past. Jasper warden Frank Camp recalled that "often a warden's ability and effectiveness was measured by the number of pelts he brought to town each month," while Animal Division Chief Maxwell Graham took delight in informing Harkin of the "individual score" of each warden employed in the Rocky Mountain parks, calling attention in 1917 to those men who had been inducted into the division's "order of merit, based on success attained in destroying noxious, predatory and dangerous animals."[46]

To a great extent, wardens saw killing predators as part of their job, and it was an aspect they were reluctant to give up, particularly when the scientific logic for doing so made little sense. "I am sick and disgusted looking at coyote kills, sheep and deer down all over the country," complained one warden in the 1930s. "But they [predators] don't do any harm at least, so they say down in Ottawa."[47] Another wrote scathingly, "ecologists and other 'gists' to the contrary[,] the policy of preventing Wardens from trapping coyotes is causing a most serious, and in my opinion, shameful waste of our wildlife."[48] These attitudes lingered. Even after the war, zoologist Ian McTaggart-Cowan expressed his concern over the persistence of a "gamekeeper attitude of immediate antipathy towards any carnivore" that prevailed in the warden service. The scientist looked forward to the day "when reaction to situations such as these will be 'Here is something that needs study' rather than the current reaction of jumping to immediate conclusions and going for a gun."[49]

If public opinion were any measure, McTaggart-Cowan would have to be patient. Wardens were supported in their views on predators by both their supervisors and many people who lived outside the national parks, particularly those in the Rockies. The new predator policy and talk of allowing nature to keep a balance made no sense to anyone who had to live with the daily threat posed by wolves, coyotes, and cougars. "An official is needed in Ottawa at the head of game conservation who is something besides a dreamer and theorist," complained the editor of Banff's *Crag and Canyon* in 1934. "A man is needed who will make a study of the problem and will listen to the advice from men who have lived in the mountains all their lives and who realize the present policy is entirely wrong."[50] Alberta's fish and game clubs were among the most vocal critics of parks predator policy, seeing places like Banff and Jasper as refuges for vermin. "We have left the matter too late," they complained, "and the Cougars are now coming out from the Park into the Foothills and have driven the game anywhere from twenty to fifty miles East of the Park. Honestly, it is a disgrace."[51] In the Yellowknife region, locals complained in the 1950s that "the government, while it controls the annual 'take' of caribou by humans, seems to be ignoring or taking no action to control the number of caribou killed by wolves."[52]

"THE GREATEST CONSERVATION MONSTROSITY OF OUR TIME"? DEBATING THE BOUNTY

The vehemence that accompanied public commentary on predator policy in the national parks points to the importance of local sentiments in shaping management. Their influence, as well as the disjunction between science and predator control practice, was especially apparent at the provincial level where the debate turned on the more specific issue of the bounty. In the postwar period, scientists and other government wildlife workers began raising questions about its efficacy. The bounty was expensive: For instance, between about 1900 and 1960, Ontario spent $1 million. British Columbia expended the same amount between 1922 and 1956.[53] But exactly what was the public getting for its money?

Defenders of the bounty argued it was the price of protection, and offered stories about the voracious and insatiable appetites of marauding wolves, which if left unchecked would wipe out livestock and game. Game wardens, settlers, and trappers in Ontario regaled the province's Special Committee on Game with lupine horror stories. In one case a single wolf was said to have taken down five deer in fifty yards. Another disposed of fifty in a square mile. On average, a wolf killed twenty-five deer yearly. Or was it one per week? Or two?[54] "Before we can expect an increase in the deer and moose herds, some control must be put into effect to rid the district of this savage killer," insisted northern Ontario resident Anton Swanson. Wolves were like "weeds in a garden. If we expect to harvest a crop we have to clear the weeds out."[55] Worse, wolves seemed to kill more than they consumed. "Where game is plentiful ... the kill for the sheer fun of killing far exceeds the number actually killed for food," wrote I.P. Callison in 1953. "The history of the wolf in North America is a history of wanton waste staggering in its magnitude and unbelievable in the starkness of its cruelty."[56] The rhetoric of destruction suggested that these were "beasts of desolation and waste," as Theodore Roosevelt called them, animals who had to be exterminated.[57]

Increasingly in the 1940s and '50s, however, scientists were not so sure. There was no doubt that wolves, coyotes, and cougars killed animals useful to humans and that they could not be allowed to prey on livestock, but was the bounty the best way to manage these predators and their prey? Despite what had happened at Kaibab in the

1920s, research on predator-prey relationships was still in its infancy, but what little was known suggested it was complex. Some scientists began to argue that in the case of wolves at least, the bounty did not play any role in reducing predator numbers. Surveying the animal populations of the Rocky Mountain national parks, Ian McTaggart-Cowan concluded that the bounty had "accomplished nothing. Populations of predators have increased and decreased with complete disregard for our nibbling at their fringes."[58] E.C. Cross of the Royal Ontario Museum suggested that his province's expenditure of nearly half a million dollars to kill thirty-three thousand wolves over a decade had "utterly failed to reduce the wolf population." More disturbing, culling the population may even have stimulated its growth. "In effect," observed Cross, "what we are doing with our wolf bounties is to kill off the surplus and thus make things easier for those that remain."[59]

If the bounty did not reduce predators, neither did it protect prey. Predation might have been the most "obvious and simplest explanation for losses among big game," but increasingly scientists questioned whether it was always the right one. "Wolf predation on moose has been overrated," argued biologist James Hatter in 1946, "and in some areas [of central British Columbia] where predation is apparent, the moose population is too large for the carrying capacity of the range."[60] McTaggart-Cowan's findings in the Rockies were similar. Wolves, he argued, were "not detrimental to the park game herds and ... their influence is definitely secondary in the survival of game to welfare factors, of which the absence of sufficient suitable forage is the most important."[61] For W.E. Stevens, all that could be said about predator control in the Northwest Territories was that it had been "highly successful in removing wolves." But as the CWS scientist noted wryly, the campaign had "not demonstrated any overwhelming success in increasing the caribou." Nonetheless, the kill continued largely "because administrators could not think of what other blows to strike for the dwindling caribou."[62]

More broadly, the data implied that substantial populations of wolves and deer — predators and prey — could coexist. As D.N. Omand of Ontario's Fish and Wildlife Division observed, "the greatest number of bounty claims originate [sic] in those areas in Ontario where deer are thriving."[63] Indeed, as Kelsall pointed out, in the wake of what happened at Kaibab, some authorities made the case that "a healthy predator population may benefit a prey species through keeping its numbers below the food limit."[64] As to suggestions that wolves could wipe out their prey, researchers working on caribou in Keewatin and the USSR in 1955 maintained that "in cases where prey numbers are declining to the point of extinction, the predators are always the first to go."[65] As John Kelsall put it, "if wolves were capable of eliminating caribou they surely would have aeons ago."[66]

While a clear understanding of predator-prey dynamics was yet to be established, a consensus was emerging among government biologists about the need to eliminate the bounty. There was little evidence that it made any difference at all: it did not reduce predator numbers appreciably or in the trouble spots that needed it, nor did it protect game species. Worse, it obscured the fact that "man himself is the worst predator on the list" and the only one who had hunted other species to extinction.[67] Advocates of the bounty gave "no thought ... to their own abuses of the wilderness or to any arrangement whereby a hunting environment could be retained in a fair state of balance for the good of the whole," wrote naturalist Tony Lascelles. "Neither do they think it is necessary to be properly convinced before fostering a campaign of destruction."[68] For all these reasons, eminent wolf biologist Douglas Pimlott considered the bounty "a crime cloaked under the misnomer of 'conservation,'" and "the greatest conservation monstrosity of our time."[69]

In taking on the bounty, scientists like Pimlott took on a key institution of rural society. The bounty served many purposes – even if reducing predators and protecting game were not among them. It represented a significant injection of money into local economies, and in fact worked as a kind of rural subsidy, "a welcome supplement to the none too ample income of the northern farmer and trapper."[70] For the CWS's F.W. Burton, however, using the bounty as a "disguised form of relief" was a perversion. Regardless of how much needy northerners might benefit, "the bounty should be evaluated solely as an instrument of wildlife management," he insisted in 1952. Calls for increases in bounty payments were not based on a desire to curb wolf depredations but were the self-interested demands of "the lazy settlement bum types who are normally always on relief or in a bad way for food and clothing."[71] Whatever the merits of Burton's point of view, rural people greeted the prospect of the bounty's elimination with the same enthusiasm members of the federal warden service greeted the news that they would no longer be allowed to sell the pelts of predators they had trapped in the national parks.

The bounty was also an institution of local governance, providing some men with a source of social as well as economic power. In the United States, the bounty hunter emerged in the late nineteenth century as a formidable figure of rural culture. The "wolfer" was as multivalent as the animal he stalked: To some he was "a folk hero ... a man of deliverance. Without him, the nation, hungry for beef and in need of wool, could not carry on."[72] But to others, the wolfer was a drifter, a mercenary whose rootless and bloodthirsty nature suggested a disturbing lack of morality. Regardless of whether they were viewed positively or negatively, bounty hunters embodied a set of values that positioned them in a particular way to the state. Their hard work, perseverance, and self-reliance made government intervention seem unnecessary in some cases, and in others undesirable.

Although bounty hunters occupied a less prominent place in Canadian folk culture, they were important figures in some places in British Columbia, where they "were as vital to their rural communities as the doctor, midwife, or blacksmith."[73] On Vancouver Island, the "cougar hunter" was "king," a man of some local notoriety.[74] Skilled trackers and marksmen, they made their living from the bounty that had been offered by the government almost continuously from the 1860s. Ranging from a low of five dollars in the nineteenth century, the cougar bounty brought in as much as forty dollars in the 1920s. By the end of the 1950s, when the bounty was eliminated, the price on the animal's head had levelled off to twenty dollars.[75]

While accounts of wolfers stress that they were common folk, stories about those who hunted cougars stressed the hunters' education. Indeed, many cougar hunters could claim a connection to Britain's professional or land-owning classes and possessed small private incomes that supplemented their rural earnings. In historian Richard Mackie's words, they were "bush gentry," "second growth Englishmen" with one foot firmly planted in Britain and the other in the rainforest.[76] The combination created west coast "characters" like "Cougar" Annie Rae Arthur of Hesquiat, a village on Vancouver Island's west coast. "A crack shot [and] a beautiful woman when younger," Cougar Annie was said to have buried three or four husbands and delivered her youngest child herself, biting through its umbilical cord. The same fortitude and ingenuity allowed her

In British Columbia cougar hunters like these were important members of rural society (n.d.). Jewish Historical Society of British Columbia, LF.1A.207.P66

to bag between sixty and a hundred cougars in her lifetime, luring them into range by tying one of her goats to a post in her garden. When the trussed-up animal bleated, the cougar was close enough to shoot.[77]

From the early twentieth century, bounty hunters worked on call, bringing their skills and those of their dogs to trouble spots whenever they received a request from local people spooked by a cougar sighting. The province's game department was often among the regular callers, turning to the cougar hunters to eliminate particularly problematic beasts. To encourage the most skilful and to capitalize on local knowledge more effectively, in 1951 British Columbia created the category of "bonus hunter." Any individual who turned in five cougars for bounty could register himself and his dogs with the government. In return, these bonus hunters received an additional twenty dollars for every cougar killed (the bounty was then twenty dollars) and were allocated a specific area where they had to attend to "all problem-related requests to hunt cougar there."[78]

When scientists began criticizing the bounty in the 1940s and '50s and calling for its elimination, they not only attacked an important source of revenue and social standing in rural Canada, but they also challenged the local knowledge that underpinned it. Much of the reaction to plans to eliminate bounty hunting stemmed from the insult rural people felt when scientists purported to know more than they did about the wildlife problems they confronted and the best means of addressing them. The idea that predators did not reduce prey populations, or that killing wolves and cougars would not result in greater numbers of game, or that there was some larger "balance of nature" that the bounty disrupted simply did not square with many people's experience of seeing half-eaten deer carcasses or their perception that game had disappeared. "If there is any more effective system for reducing the timber wolf population," wrote Manly Miner in 1949, "then I am for it. But I certainly do not want to be classed with this new university-taught school of thought that believes the more deer the wolves kill, the more deer we shall have."[79]

Rural people like Manly Miner had very little patience with scientific knowledge, which in their view was becoming ever more arcane and irrelevant to wildlife management. In response to a 1957 story in the Toronto *Globe and Mail* about University of Toronto zoologists, including J.R. Dymond, eating butterflies in Convocation Hall in order to make some scientific point, Manly was positively cutting. "I want to emphasize that my father nor I never did subscribe to eating butterflies in private or before an audience of 800," he told his readers, "but ... I do not take the above incidents as a joke because ... Dr. J.R. Dymond has been the Chief Advisor for the Ontario Fish and Game Department for 25 or more years. To me it is no wonder our Fish and Game condition in Ontario is as it is."[80]

Alive to rural sensitivities, but aware of the growing body of scientific evidence criticizing the bounty, provincial governments experimented with a new system of predator control. British Columbia took the lead. There, reform came in the shape of a professional corps of killers on the government payroll. Acknowledging that it was "very difficult to convince those suffering damage to stock that the payment of bounties is not the answer to the problem of predation," the province's game department nonetheless insisted that "the

Vancouver Island's "Cougar" Cecil Smith was, by his own admission, "subject to call at any hour of the day or night, same as a doctor. A summons for me and the dogs means action" (cited in Richard Mackie, "Cougars, Colonists, and the Rural Settlement of Vancouver Island," in *Beyond the City Limits: Rural History in British Columbia*, ed. R. Sandwell, 136 [Vancouver: UBC Press, 1999]) (n.d.). Courtenay and District Museum and Archives, D-620

best method ... is the employment of specially trained and properly equipped predatory animal hunters."[81] Killing wolves, coyotes, and cougars would no longer be indiscriminate, motivated by materialism or local demand based on parochial prejudice regarding predatory animals. Instead, the predatory animal hunters would deploy their skills only where control could be justified by need. Moreover, whereas bounty hunters creamed the crop, government hunters would have to go after the more hard-to-get killers.[82]

In 1947 the province took the first steps in that direction, creating a new government branch to train these predator hitmen under the supervision of James Dewar, one of Vancouver Island's most distinguished cougar hunters. Dewar's department bought dogs, built kennels, and began to school both hounds and humans in the art of predatory animal hunting near Extension, outside Nanaimo.[83] Three years later, in 1950, the province hired wildlife biologist W.W. Mair to head its Predator Control Branch and put its operations on a modern scientific foundation.[84] While the Branch was engaged with hiring and training hunters, the bounty remained in place, so for a period predator control in the province was carried out by both government hunters and private citizens. However, in 1955 British Columbia completed its reform of the predator control, eliminating the bounty on wolves. Two years later it did the same for the cougar. Mair strove to build a rational and efficient system where control was exercised "according to scientifically determined need." In reaction to the indiscriminate killing that had characterized predator control under the bounty system, his department implemented a plan of selective control, taking pains to distinguish between "agricultural and built-up areas," which would receive "complete control"; "game areas," which would get "partial-to-complete control" as determined by research; and "wilderness areas," in which "light control" would protect trappers' interests.[85]

The other western provinces followed suit in the 1950s, implementing government predator control and eliminating bounties. Developments in Ontario and Quebec were different. Ontario did not establish a predator control unit until 1964, and retained its bounty on wolves until 1972.[86] Although Quebec too combined government control with the bounty into the 1960s, the kind of control carried out under the auspices of the state did not seem very different from that which predated it. Instead of instituting a system of specific, local, and temporary control, wardens poisoned wolves on a regular basis, at their own discretion.[87]

While developments in Ontario and especially Quebec seem on the surface to be at odds with those in western Canada, the regional differences in control were not as great as they initially appeared. If British Columbia is any indication, despite the arrival of scientific control, the predatory animal hunting undertaken by civil servants was not all that different in practice from the bounty system. Hunters might be on government payroll and wear uniforms, but many of them had formerly been bounty hunters.

More significantly, despite the scientists' insistence that effective predator control had to be based on biological need or a demonstrated threat to the safety of people or livestock, much of the killing carried out by government hunters was intended to protect specific economic interests. For instance, in the postwar period, when parks officials began to emphasize the commercial value of bison as meat, they intensified their poisoning campaign in Wood Buffalo National Park. Similarly, in response to pressure from trappers and guide-outfitters about the increasing depredations of wolves on moose, the Predator Control Branch instituted an extensive poisoning program in central British Columbia in the early 1950s – without, it seems, doing any studies to test the validity of local claims. In the face of a declining predator population, moose began to increase, so much so that they started to over-browse their range. As early as 1953, game wardens found some dying of malnutrition; by 1958 it was clear that as a result of continuing predator control, most ranges in the Prince George district were "seriously over-browsed," threatening the very population that was to be protected by predator control in the first place. Not until 1969 – after the wolf was declared a game species – did the province begin efforts to research it in northern British Columbia, evaluating its numbers and predation patterns.[88]

In many ways, all that government predator control did was to end another aspect of local control of wildlife, namely, the bounty. In that sense, it extended the reach of government over rural Canada. Like other aspects of wildlife management mentioned earlier, the elimination of the bounty was thus a means by which the state colonized the backcountry. As with all forms of colonization, however, the process was complex, and the distinction between colonized and colonizer was not always clear. The government may have taken over predator hunting in the postwar period, but as discussed, it was still carried out by local people in response to local demands.

But no matter who did the killing – a government employee or a private citizen – the attitudes toward predators that informed calls for control lingered. Despite what the scientists had to say, in the early 1960s the big bad wolf, as well as the cougar and the coyote, was feared and despised by many rural Canadians, who constituted a powerful lobby influencing wildlife management. Their sentiments had shaped predator policy both before and after the end of the bounty system.

But all of that was in the process of changing. Even as cattlemen, sheep ranchers, trappers, and guide-outfitters counted their influence with each poison bait that was laid and with every year the bounty remained in place, opinion was shifting, especially among the growing numbers of urban Canadians. The wolf was about to be rehabilitated – not by any scientific study, but as a result of the efforts of one of wildlife science's most vocal Canadian critics in the 1960s: Farley Mowat. The far-reaching effects of *Never Cry Wolf* (1963) were testimony to the ongoing power of another set of sentiments – urban ones – in shaping attitudes toward wildlife and conservation practices in a manner that anticipated the environmental movement of the 1970s.

"MY NAME IS SHAWN. I LOVE WOLFS": REHABILITATING THE PREDATOR

Mowat's introduction to the world of the wolf came after the Second World War, when he was hired to work on the CWS's long-term study of the barren ground caribou. His experience in Keewatin observing the legendary predator in 1948-49 convinced him that the wolf had been wrongfully convicted of crimes against humanity. *Never Cry Wolf,* an account loosely based on his experience in the field, exonerated *Canis lupus* and simultaneously condemned another species, namely, *"homo bureaucratis* – that aberrant product of our times who, cocooned in convention, witlessly wedded to the picayune, obsessed with obscurantism, and foundering in footling facts, nevertheless considers himself the only legitimate possessor of revealed truth."[89]

Mowat's particular target was the government scientist, a subspecies that had become besotted with the idea that wolves were marauders that could be stopped only by bringing the whole apparatus of state-sponsored science down upon them. His experience in the field taught him otherwise. "On three separate occasions ... I had been completely at the mercy of these 'savage killers,'" he wrote, "but far from attempting to tear me limb from limb, they had displayed a restraint verging on contempt, even when I invaded their home and appeared to be posing a direct threat to the young pups." In the face of these encounters, he "commit[ed] scientific treason," and rejected conventional beliefs about the wolves. "From this hour onward," he vowed, "I would go open-minded into the lupine world and learn to see and know the wolves, not for what they were supposed to be, but for what they actually were."[90]

What they were was exemplary. Mowat followed the exploits of "George," "Angeline," and "Uncle Albert," the pack at Wolf House Bay, demonstrating that their reputation as bloodthirsty killers was wholly undeserved. While wolves certainly ate caribou, Mowat suggested they tended to prey on the old and weak, and in that sense played an important role in maintaining the health of the herd. Moreover, they had broad palates, sustaining themselves on a varied menu that included rodents. Wolves, it seemed, did not live on a diet consisting solely of caribou. But as Mowat's experiments with feeding himself *souris à la crème* were meant to demonstrate, they could subsist on mice alone. The writer's rehabilitation of the wolf extended further than an examination of these predators' diets, however, and into a re-evaluation of their behaviour.

In Mowat's wild animal stories, like those of Charles G.D. Roberts and Ernest Thompson Seton before him, wolves were noble creatures whose commendable conduct highlighted the morality of nature. George and Angeline were "as devoted a married pair as one could hope to find," and like all wolves, "strict monogamists" who had a sense of playful responsibility, especially toward the pups.[91] The fundamental decency of the Wolf House Bay pack served only to underscore the wickedness of the poisoning campaign carried out against them and the corruption of humans who were so alienated from the natural world that they could orchestrate such a thing.

Critics greeted *Never Cry Wolf* favourably as "a splendid and satisfying book." According to the *Toronto Globe and Mail*'s William French, lupine communities everywhere owed Mowat "a debt of gratitude for rescuing their reputation."[92] The reviewer for *Queen's Quarterly* marvelled in the discovery that "wolves are normal animals living normal lives, playing their part in the realm of nature and constituting no danger to man or his living."[93] Not only did the volume sell over a million copies, but it also was translated into more than twenty languages. As a testament to its ongoing popularity, in 1983, twenty years after its publication, Mowat's book was made into a feature film by Disney.

The scientists who worked for the CWS had a different view, and condemned the book for its egregious errors and emotionalism; they were shocked to discover it in the non-fiction shelves of the country's public and university libraries.[94] "Hardly Knowit" was a "not-so-young angry man" whose views on wolves and the Wildlife Service fell wide of the mark.[95] But how, they observed, could it have been otherwise? After all, as Mowat's former boss, A.W.F. Banfield, pointed out in his review in the *Canadian Field-Naturalist,* Farley's career with the CWS "lasted only about six months," during which time the "second year Arts student" spent just ninety hours in the field watching the animals.[96] What little that did ring true in his account was drawn from Adolph Murie's work on the wolves of Mount McKinley.[97] "Any resemblance between *Never Cry Wolf* and that book is *not* coincidental," the scientist alleged.[98] "Mowat's suggestion that he was hired to produce incontrovertible proof to damn the wolf is a woolly fabrication of fact," he continued. "I am sure his disclosure will come as a shock to those few members of the hunting fraternity who have been condemning the same Service for years as apologists for predators and wolf-lovers."[99] In W.A. Fuller's opinion, biologists (like him) were wholehearted supporters of neither extermination nor preservation, but "the first line of defence in the conservation movement."[100] Banfield agreed. "It is certain that not since Little Red Riding Hood has a story been written that will influence the attitude of so many," he observed. "I hope readers of *Never Cry Wolf* will realize that both stories have about the same factual content."[101]

Rearguard actions like the one undertaken by the CWS in response to *Never Cry Wolf* were difficult battles to win. Doing so became all the more difficult when the public joined the assault. While Mowat might have got some of the details wrong, readers judged his story to be true. The CWS received a flood of mail from concerned and in some cases angry people who rallied to the cause of both Mowat and the wolf – two creatures who had been wronged by "biologists" who, according to Edmontonian Eaton McKay, were reluctant "to get off those pedestals!"[102] Some, like Hugh Jenney, saw wolf control as another form of government waste. "Farley Mowat's 'Never Cry Wolf' is a 50¢ pocket book that you should read before wasting any more taxpayer's money," he advised.[103] Others, like Mrs. F.J. Bacher Jr. of Salinas, California, tried to be helpful, sending the government biologists copies of Mowat's book, or references to other literature.[104] Most people, however, simply wrote to convey their outrage and to ask the government to stop what it was doing. Like Shawn. "Dear Citicens [sic]," he began,

My Name is Shawn. I love wolfs. I want to like you but I cannot because I saw one of you kill a wolf [there had been an
NBC television show about predator control]. Are you listening
I hope so. You can stop killing them I know you can for me! So
stop. love, Shawn.[105]

Just how far attitudes had shifted is suggested by one response to
a public appeal issued by the Jack Miner Migratory Bird Foundation
in the late 1960s, exhorting its supporters to lobby the government
for an increase in the wolf bounty. Father Goose might have swayed
millions in his time, but his son had a more difficult task carrying on
ideas that had become anachronistic. "The drivel recently received,
written by Badly informed Manly, serves only to nauseate anyone
who knows more than the old wives tales of half-truths concerning the deer-wolf relationship," insisted Harold Weaver. "Save your
5¢ stamp," he told the foundation. "Use it to start a fund to get
Manly into Grade 3."[106] Or, he might have suggested, to send Manly
to Algonquin Park. In the late 1960s and '70s, thousands of people
flocked from the city to the park to participate in its wolf-howling
nights – an opportunity to connect with a wild that was fast disappearing.

Rather than continue to react to Mowat's book, the CWS, like the
Parks Branch before it, decided to take its own message to the public
directly. Whereas the Parks Branch had hired Grey Owl in the 1930s
to perform its conservation work live and on site, the CWS used the
medium of film. It hoped to convey two connected ideas: first, that
wildlife had been influential in shaping Canada's past and remained
crucial to its present and future; and second, that "research and
management is vital to wildlife's survival because of the change that
man is making to the environment."[107] Working with the National
Film Board of Canada, it approached Farley Mowat, who, despite his
views of the CWS, was interested but too busy to take on the project
immediately. It then tried Disney – who were too expensive – before
hiring Canadian canoeing legend and filmmaker Bill Mason in 1967
to research, write, direct, and produce a documentary.[108]

While the CWS hoped its scientists might share the limelight with
the wolf – if not having starring roles in its documentary – that was
not to be. The wolves and Farley Mowat's book won Mason over,
and he made not one, but two feature-length films, *Death of a Legend*

(1971) and *Cry of the Wild* (1972).[109] Both were enormously successful, garnering a number of international awards.[110] *Cry of the Wild*
was especially popular. When it opened in New York, it outgrossed
*Papillon, The Sting, Magnum Force, American Graffiti, The Way We
Were, The Godfather,* and *The Paper Chase* – every major film of its
time except *The Exorcist.* It remains one of Canada's most successful
feature-length documentaries to date.[111]

Neither scientists nor their research featured prominently in either
documentary, though Mason admitted he had to rely heavily on men
like Douglas Pimlott, Ernie Kuyt, and Donald Flook, all CWS biologists, to make the kind of film he wanted.[112] Insofar as science and
scientists appeared, Mason used them to highlight the noble nature of
wolves rather than the crucial contributions of science. In *Death of a
Legend,* for instance, the segment showing a biologist radio collaring a
wolf underscored the paralysing fear that rendered the trapped animal
passive and not at all the slavering beast one might have expected.
Nothing is said of the purpose of the research or the value of the
results.

Instead, Mason's interest lay almost solely with the wolves, and in
showing viewers the values, rituals, and dynamics of the moral universe they occupied. "Nature's scheme" and "nature's way" may not
have made sense to people, but wolves worked to produce a cohe-
sive, well-functioning society. Like Mowat's Wolf House Bay pack,
Mason's wolves were good and loving parents who got along well
with their neighbours even if they occasionally resorted to eating
them. Everything was fine until the first Europeans turned up. As in
Bambi, the arrival of man in the forest signalled the beginning of the
end. Standing in the way of "progress," the wolf and its neighbours
were doomed.

Mason intended his documentaries to do more than set the record
straight about wolves, however. "My films are ... an attempt to
bridge the gap between ourselves and things natural," he wrote privately. But it would take more than factual information to build such
a bridge. In his view, people also needed to re-establish an emotional
and fundamentally spiritual connection with nature if the world were
to be made whole again.[113]

For Mason, the environmental and social problems confronting
the late-twentieth-century world were due to people's alienation
from God. "Dissociating God from nature" made it possible to think

that the world was "the result of nothing more than the process of natural selection." For Mason that was simply unbelievable. "I just don't buy that," he wrote. "The world around us speaks to me of an incredible mind ... A mind capable of wonder and awe."[114]

Both wolf documentaries were Mason's attempts to convey the wonder and awe that animated the spirit of nature, which for him was God. In that sense, he was part of a long tradition of natural history that in the Canadian context tied him to the "revolt against instinct" staged by nature writers Charles G.D. Roberts, Ernest Thompson Seton, and Jack Miner. But Mason's emphasis on knowing nature and God through the senses – something that stemmed perhaps from his own evangelical upbringing – distinguished him from these other writers. For Mason, thinking distanced people from nature and God: it was impossible to understand using your mind only. Nature and God were, in his words, "beyond our comprehension."[115] Knowing them would come only by experiencing the wild, through the emotions.

To Mason, wolves embodied the freedom that was the essence of nature's spirit – and of God. Although his years filming wolves in the wild had exposed humans' propensity for destruction, they had also revealed the animals' "capacity for expressing their joy of living" – their capacity for freedom. *Cry of the Wild* was Mason's vehicle for answering the question "what is free?"[116] In doing so, he made an argument about the nature of wildlife, the relationship between people and nature, and the possibilities for conservation.

In *Cry of the Wild,* being free and knowing God meant running with the wolves – and away from people. As the documentary's theme song put it, "I'm going to leave my friends in the city; I'm going to leave my family; I'm going to leave my friends in the country; I'm going to look for what is free, I'm going to look for what is free."[117]

While living with lupines taught him what freedom meant, it was not a reciprocal arrangement. For the wolves, living with people meant the loss of life and liberty. Those who were not poisoned by the government's predator control programs or shot by hunters from planes could no longer roam without restraint, terrorized by the mere sight, sound, or smell of people.

Even encountering someone as sympathetic as Bill Mason turned out to be fatal to their freedom. Although he abhorred hunting, Mason's fascination with the wolves turned him into a hunter – one armed with a camera and a tranquilizer gun, but animated by the same desire to possess. He captured a group of wolves and brought them to the Gatineau Hills outside Ottawa, where they lived on his fenced property, somewhat like large unruly pets. Not only did Mason feed the wolves deer carcasses (supplied by the provincial forestry department), but he also tamed two wolf cubs – "Sparky," a submissive, subordinate female, and "Big Charlie," the alpha male – in the hope that they would allow him to get closer to the rest of the wild pack.

Mason got the footage he wanted, including some fascinating sequences of pups being born, but his wolves lost their liberty in the process. Realizing what he had done, Mason flew them to the Northwest Territories and turned them loose. "I was happy for them," he recalled, "for they would now know what it meant to be free." Free they might have been, but it soon became clear that they had lost their capacity for freedom. The Gatineau pack, raised on a diet of white-tailed deer, proved incapable of feeding itself: Big Charlie, whose "greatest joy in life was having his stomach rubbed," could not lead his pack in a kill. Indeed, he could not, it seems, even track the caribou. In one unforgettable scene, Mason found the herd himself and then went off on snowshoes across the darkening tundra to find his pack, calling "Charlie? Here, Charlie!"[118] Not willing to let them starve, Mason rounded up his wolf-pets again and took them home. As Farley Mowat might have observed, it is not known what results were obtained.[119]

Cry of the Wild is a fascinating film because Mason did not hold back in depicting himself as someone who, in his own way, had defiled the wild. By trying to know nature, to bridge the gap between humans and the natural world, he destroyed what he loved. The unity with nature and God for which he sought eluded him, and indeed, Mason ended up alienated from both. His adventure with the wolves taught him that he must be satisfied "just *knowing* wolves roam wild and free"; in other words, that he must have faith that the wolves (and God) are out there.[120]

Although he did not share Mason's spiritual concerns, Farley Mowat also ended *Never Cry Wolf* with a similar meditation on the fundamental separation between humans and nature. When confronted with the possibility of being attacked by wolves, he realized that his long observation of them had not eliminated his deep human prejudice regarding them. Had he had a gun handy, Angeline and her pups would have been dead. Forever after that, the howl of wolves reminded Mowat "of the lost world which once was ours before we chose the alien role; a world which I had glimpsed and almost entered ... only to be excluded, at the end, by my own self."[121]

Cry of the Wild and *Never Cry Wolf* were not just arguments against predator control and hunting, for in addressing people's capacity to destroy what they love, Mowat and Mason made the case for a new understanding of wildlife and conservation. While their depiction of lupine social life suggested otherwise, the qualities Mowat and Mason most admired about the wolf were not entirely human. Earlier nature writers like Roberts and Seton had written in reaction to Darwin, demonstrating the inherent morality of the natural world. But what Mowat and Mason suggest is that instinct also numbered among the wolf's most admirable qualities. The animal's wildness was as admirable as it was alluring – in part because it existed beyond the pale of human understanding. It was a life force that could be felt but not fully comprehended.

For Mowat and Mason, the wildness possessed by these creatures made it impossible for them to be possessed. Neither wolves nor any form of wildlife could rightly be considered property – common or otherwise. Instead, wildlife just was. Different from the definitions of wildlife articulated in the game acts or by earlier environmentalists such as Jack Miner and Grey Owl, the one expressed by Mowat and Mason had implications for the meaning of conservation.

Unlike the opposition to government conservation that had come from the backcountry since the beginning of the twentieth century, theirs was not an argument over who owned wildlife and who had the right to regulate its use. It was not, in other words, an argument about whether wildlife was a local or a national commons. But if wildlife was not a resource, then conservation could not be synonymous with wise use.

Instead of supporting a doctrine of usefulness, Mowat and Mason advocated an ethic of existence and in so doing signalled a new direction for conservation in the late twentieth century. Like Aldo Leopold, they believed that wildlife had a "right to continuance." But whereas Leopold argued that such a right was delegated by the biotic community in acknowledgement of the role organisms played in maintaining ecological integrity, Mowat and Mason contended that it was inherent to individual animals. Their ethic of existence did not acknowledge the biotic community, much less one that included people. From Mason's perspective, people – and even he – could not live with nature without damaging it irreparably. Their estrangement from nature was a manifestation of their fall from grace. As fallen people, they could know nature only from a distance. This was a far cry from Leopold's vision, which sought to find a way to "conserve wild life without evicting ourselves."[122] Mason's documentaries served notice that humans had to go: conservation was folly, and preservation the only hope.

While ecology had acknowledged the importance of predators since the 1920s, sentiment rather than science shaped public opinion regarding these creatures. For much of the twentieth century, scientists had to contend with a vocal rural lobby that argued predation was a status offence. Wolves, coyotes, and cougars were outlaws simply by virtue of who they were, animals that killed other animals for food. In the 1960s those voices from the countryside were drowned out by others from the city, which made the case for Canada's natural born killers. The people who sided with the wolf did not do so because they had been swayed by the insights of wildlife science. Instead, their attitudes had been shaped by larger social changes: urbanization and resource development had made inroads into the wilderness and in so doing raised fundamental questions about the nature of postwar progress, questions that people in the climate of the 1960s, with its culture of challenging authority, were more given to asking.

In that context, Farley Mowat and Bill Mason were able to take scientific arguments for predators – that the wolf was worth saving because of its role in the ecosystem – and fold them into a larger one that raised questions about the morality of a world that would countenance and indeed participate in its disappearance. For both these writers, the poisonous war on wolves was a violent manifestation of the twentieth-century triumph of the technocratic and the modern, a reminder of the uncertain benefits of a progress built on extinguishing the wild.

Although both Mowat and Mason saw saving the wolf as a way of saving the wild, their emphasis was fundamentally on the animal and not the ecological community of which it was a part. The shift from saving wildlife to preserving wild places was slow to develop and first emerged, as many conservation ideas did, from the backcountry, where people lived in and with nature.

In the years after the Second World War, the bush plane, helicopter, and float plane made the wilderness more accessible to armed tourists looking for a sporting holiday. Hunters could fly in, bag their trophy, and fly out again to enjoy a hot shower and meal before heading back to their desk jobs (1950). Canadian Pacific Railway Archives, NS13813

CHAPTER SEVEN

◆

From Wildlife to Wild Places

ALTHOUGH ECOLOGISTS HAD EMPHASIZED the close connections between organisms and their environments, the ecosystem idea did not push public policy in the direction of habitat preservation in the immediate postwar period. Instead, state wildlife work remained largely focused on basic research on species and managing mortality, primarily through controlling predation and disease, particularly in the case of the bison. Government biologists were certainly aware of the importance of habitats as limiting factors in population growth, but it was not until the 1960s that they began to take the first concrete steps toward assessing and protecting them systematically.

The change was spurred by the passage of the federal Agricultural Rehabilitation and Development Act (ARDA) in 1962, which encouraged the consolidation of small farms into larger and more efficient economic units and the reversion of marginal lands to their "natural" state. To comply with ARDA, governments across the country engaged in the first comprehensive assessment of land use. Started in 1965, the Canada Land Inventory classified over a million square miles of rural Canada in terms of its suitability for agriculture and recreation, or as habitat for hoofed mammals or waterfowl, among other things. Even before it was completed in 1969, the inventory was the authoritative source for decision making on land use, a tool employed by state wildlife workers to designate areas – particularly wetlands – as protected habitats.[1]

By the time governments became involved in saving habitat in the 1960s and '70s, they could join their efforts to those of private organizations like Ducks Unlimited Canada (DUC) and outfitters-turned-conservationists Tommy Walker and Andy Russell, important voices arguing for the need to save wild places. The ideas and actions of Ducks Unlimited, Tommy Walker, and Andy Russell reveal the ongoing importance of private grassroots initiatives in saving Canada's wildlife, and their diversity. Concerned with saving wetlands, DUC positioned itself as a conservation "company" which engineered solutions to the habitat problem. It was enormously successful. From its establishment in 1938 to 2004 the organization completed nearly seven thousand wetland projects across Canada encompassing nearly twenty-five million acres of habitat.[2] DUC's modern managerial approach to wildlife conservation was consistent with the initiatives undertaken by the state, and relied on the cooperation and labour of local people.

Its work stood in contrast to that of two men on opposite sides of the Canadian Rockies. Tommy Walker and Andy Russell were also committed to preserving habitats, albeit mountain ones rather than wetlands. However, in the 1950s and '60s each began raising questions about development in a way that neither the government nor DUC did, targeting it as the main threat to wildlife. In addition, and further distinguishing them from other conservationists, Walker and Russell were motivated by more than a concern for the fate of wildlife in the face of economic development. Saving British Columbia's Spatsizi Plateau or Alberta's "Grizzly Country" was as much about promoting a way of life for the human residents of those habitats as it was about saving goats and bears. Neither wise use nor an ethic of existence describes the kind of conservation they advocated. Instead, for Walker and Russell, conservation was a social doctrine, a moral code for how to live as humans – in nature and with nature.

OF DUCKS AND MEN

> 10 little Canvasbacks feeling mighty fine
>   Their home lake dried up ... and then there were 9 ...
> 2 little Canvasbacks – each a husky drake –
>   With their mates flew northward to a D.U. lake.

There, killers, drought and fire
And countless other dangers
Are checked by D.U. engineers
And naturalists and rangers.
So-o-o
2 little Canvasbacks, saved from dangers plenty
With D.U.'s help fly south again as 2 + 2 + 20.
   – Tom Main, "10 Little Canvasbacks Grew to 24" (1945)[3]

Tom Main's poem captures the purpose of the organization for which he worked. He was hired as Ducks Unlimited Canada's first general manager; his job, like that of all the company's employees, was to increase the number of waterfowl, to ensure that "10 Little Canvasbacks Grew to 24." His task had been set in the 1930s by the organization's founders, a group of wealthy and well-connected American sportsmen who had become concerned about the decline of the birds that had provided them with so much shooting pleasure. While lowered bag limits and prohibitions against live decoys and automatic firearms went some distance in protecting migratory birds, these men felt that more active steps were necessary. Restrictive measures might "retard the rate of decrease but *they do not produce birds*," they argued. *"Man must help Nature produce."*[4]

To that end, they formed the More Game Birds in America Foundation in 1930, an organization that eventually became Ducks Unlimited.[5] Their ten-year, continent-wide plan for increasing the game bird population called for the creation of an agency that would oversee the acquisition, restoration, and management of waterfowl breeding grounds, using public funds raised through a special tax as well as private donations.[6] From the outset, the foundation's directors recognized that their efforts would have to be international. "While many former breeding grounds in the United States can be restored and existing areas made more productive, it is to Canada largely that we must turn for more waterfowl," they noted. "About seventy-five per cent of the waterfowl on the North American continent are Canada-bred."[7]

That turned out to be an underestimate. Canada's importance as a duck breeding ground was only reinforced by the foundation's 1935 International Waterfowl Census. Sponsored by American arms and ammunition companies, as well as by Chrysler, which supplied Dodge cars for the US portion of the survey, this was the first attempt to count migratory birds on their breeding grounds.[8] The results were telling. Of the 42.7 million ducks counted, 40.5 million – or nearly 95 percent – were found in Alberta, Saskatchewan, Manitoba, and a portion of the Mackenzie District.[9]

These figures confirmed the foundation's view that Canada was a veritable "duck factory." Expanding production could come only by concentrating their efforts north of the forty-ninth parallel. To those who questioned whether American dollars should be spent restoring Canadian wetlands, the foundation argued that "it would be unreasonable and unjust to expect Canada to carry the load unassisted, particularly in view of the fact that the bulk of the 'crop' is bagged each year in the United States. Therefore it seems eminently fair that the sportsmen of the United States, far outnumbering the Canadians, should largely bear the cost of maintaining waterfowl supply."[10]

To facilitate the flow of American money to Canada for habitat restoration, the directors of More Game Birds set up Ducks Unlimited Canada in 1938, endowing it with an initial annual budget of $100,000 – an incredible sum, particularly given the economic times. DUC's volunteer officers and directors were drawn from the same social class as their American counterparts, and included Saskatchewan lawyer and later judge W.G. Ross, Winnipeg grain magnate and financier James A. Richardson, and newspaper executive O. Leigh Spencer of Calgary.[11]

Who DUC was shaped how it approached the task of making the ducks come back. Like their counterparts in the United States, DUC's Canadian directors believed that effective conservation could come only by applying business principles.[12] The same sound scientific management that had made their own business enterprises grow and prosper would also produce more ducks. To that end, they invested in expertise. Their first act was to hire Tom Main, the Canadian National Railway's (CN) surface water engineer for the three prairie provinces, as general manager. Before he came to DUC, Main's job was locating and developing water sources – albeit for CN's locomotives – something that in the opinion of DUC's directors was a useful and transferable skill. In their view, as well as Main's, the waterfowl problem was a water problem and one for which there were engineering solutions.

Main's expertise in engineering was complemented by B.W. Cartwright's in birds. Hired as DUC's chief naturalist in 1938, Cartwright was joined by other university-trained biologists in the 1940s, '50s, and '60s in DUC's "Production Department," the organization's research division whose name suggested its purpose. Under the scientists' direction, DUC banded birds, carried out censuses, and worked with local fish and game associations as well as the Canadian Wildlife Service and university investigators at places like Manitoba's Delta Marsh Research Institute. Perhaps one of the organization's most significant scientific initiatives was the Wetland Inventory Program it undertook in Saskatchewan. Beginning in 1955, DUC "catalogue[d] the biological and historical aspects of every water area in the southern part of the province over 640 acres in size." In all, an area of over 100,000 square miles was surveyed and mapped, the data used by the provincial government in assessing drainage applications and by the Game Branch in its efforts to preserve waterfowl habitat. In the late 1960s, when the federal government became involved in wetland preservation, the same information was used again.[13] At the same time as it carried out basic data collection, DUC also conducted more applied research, experimenting with cultivating different plants for cover and feed and investigating avian diseases.

Recognizing the importance of making a good first impression on its American funders, DUC outlined an ambitious program of wetland restoration in its first year of operation. The company would restore 100,000 acres of wetland through three major initiatives, one in each prairie province.[14] Manitoba's Big Grass Marsh was "Duck Factory No. 1." It was followed by Many Islands Lake near Medicine Hat in southern Alberta, and Saskatchewan's Waterhen Marsh near Kinistino.[15]

While the company would go on to restore and manage many other wetlands and expand its operations across the country, the techniques it used in its inaugural projects were emblematic of its general approach. For DUC, conservation was a matter of producing "more waterfowl by assisting nature." It was in the business of re-engineering imperfect landscapes – usually ones that had been rendered that way by earlier human attempts to drain them for agricultural use, as was the case at Big Grass and Waterhen Marshes, or ones that had been created that way by the natural cycles of wet and dry that characterized prairie wetland ecology, as was the case at Many Islands Lake. This was accomplished by building dams on the existing drainage channels to prevent water from flowing away, and by constructing dykes along the marsh to prevent flooding of the adjacent cultivated fields. Because small, deep lakes were less prone to dry out because of evaporation, at Many Islands Lake DUC also constructed a restriction dam to reduce the size of the lake so it more closely matched the run-off of the creek that fed it. In addition, the company built nesting islands, planting them with clover or brome grass, and seeded the lakes with bulrushes and sago pondweed, a favourite food of ducks. To protect the waterfowl that landed at the sanctuaries, DUC put up fences to prevent cattle from grazing – and thus reducing the cover that sheltered the birds and their nests – and killed off predators.

Although the company had initially contemplated buying the land that surrounded the wetlands it managed, it soon realized that doing so would be too costly. Instead, it worked out informal agreements and – later – negotiated easements with local landowners and municipal and provincial governments whereby DUC would restore a wetland and manage it if rents and grazing and haying rights were waived, and costs shared. In some cases, as at Big Grass Marsh, DUC reintroduced muskrat, turning the restored wetland into a fur ranch. The revenues from trapping flowed to the municipalities, an incentive to allow the company to continue its operations as well as proof that "intensive management of the marsh was a money-making proposition."[16] In the other prairie provinces, DUC exerted its influence through rural institutions and provincial boards. In Alberta, for instance, the organization worked closely with the irrigation districts, developing wetlands by using irrigation "waste" water, and in Saskatchewan, DUC representatives sat on the province's Water Stabilization Committee beginning in the 1950s, ensuring that wildlife values had a bearing on decisions about drainage.[17]

DUC was helped immeasurably in its negotiations by its well-connected directors, but its success depended on securing the ongoing cooperation of ordinary people. To facilitate that cooperation, it organized a network of volunteers to do its work on the ground. In the 1940s more than three thousand of these "Kee-Men," as they were called, helped coordinate DUC's bird surveys, reported on water conditions in their districts, and made proposals for new restoration projects. In addition, Kee-Men organized their communities to ensure that stubble burning occurred before waterfowl nested, and that sufficient cover was left at the edges of ponds and sloughs. As well, they tried to ensure that haying was delayed until after mid-July, when eggs had hatched and young were able to leave their nests. In the height of summer, when water evaporated from shallow sloughs, Kee-Men engaged in "drought salvage," rescuing thousands of ducks and carrying them to deeper waters elsewhere.[18]

While the Kee-Men gave the organization a local presence, DUC also heightened its profile through an ongoing public relations campaign aimed at promoting its work as well as educating ordinary citizens in the importance of wetlands. Sponsoring prizes in the provincial crow and magpie control program was one strategy DUC employed to build a positive profile for itself locally. In addition, it used the media to spread the word of its good works. "More Water – More Ducks," "Progress of Waterfowl Research," and "Bumper Harvest from Conservation" were heard on radios across the prairies in the 1940s and '50s, while films like *A Dam Site More Ducks* and *Big Marsh Lives Again* informed American audiences in the 1940s of what their money had built.[19] But perhaps the best-known and longest-lasting public relations and education initiative was carried out by Jake the Drake and Mary the Mallard, the cartoon creations of DUC's assistant manager. Their exploits, rendered in line drawings as well as in the following poem, reached tens of thousands of DU's North American membership through the organization's magazine or on the Christmas cards it offered for sale, spreading the news of the company's work and the need for ongoing support.

> The curly-tailed, green-headed Jake
> Led the way over prairie and lake.
> With a quack that was harsh
> He espied Big Grass Marsh –
> And immediately put on the brake.
>
> With Mary, his sweet bride-elect,
> He landed, the dam to inspect.
>   She said: "Jake, forsooth,
>   told me the truth.
> We'll stay here – a home to select."

So Mary got down to her duties;
And waddled around on her tooties.
　With down from her breast
　She lined her grass nest;
And laid fifteen eggs, they were beauties.

The eggs hatched, and the proud parents watched as their flock grew
fat on the feed planted in the marsh by its managers.

Says Jake – to his friends in D.U. –
"We're seventeen ducks, just from two;
　And there's millions of drakes
　(If you restore the lakes)
Who will multiply ducks – all for you!"[20]

As dissonant as the verse and its sentiments might sound to us now,
they were effective. DUC's campaign succeeded in publicizing its
efforts to an audience that might have had only the faintest idea of
where its money was going. The organization capitalized on this success and established a series of "donor projects," encouraging local
American fish and game clubs to sponsor the restoration of specific
wetlands. The results are visible today in the toponymy of the prairies, in Lake San Francisco (sponsored by the Pacific Rod and Gun
Club of that city in 1942), for instance, and in the Louisiana Lakes
and Lake Nebraska (sponsored by the sportsmen of those states in
1943 and 1944). It seems that DUC did not simply re-engineer the
landscape, it also re-colonized it in the name of conservation.

As a result, Ducks Unlimited Canada was not always assured of a
warm welcome. Some local people believed that the organization's
real purpose was to acquire the best shooting areas for Americans or
to control the harvest for the benefit of foreign hunters.[21] As DUC's
first president, Judge W.G. Ross, told the Manitoba Fish and Game
Association, nothing could be further from the truth. Referring to
"the misguided interpretations which seem to be spreading around
the country in regard to the performances and objects of ... Ducks
Unlimited," the judge insisted that it was "not the purpose of [the
company] to create closed private game preserves for American
owners or Canadian owners to enjoy to the exclusion of the public
... [T]he purpose behind this corporation is not selfishness but ...

natural science which holds that ... a marsh without wild fowl and a forest without deer ... are indicative of desolation and a disagreeable barrenness that should not be allowed to exist in this country."[22]

While local suspicions about the real purpose of DUC were eventually put to rest, there were intermittent conflicts between the company and farmers and ranchers over land and water use. For instance, when heavy rains led to floods on Jackknife Lake in 1947, damaging agricultural land, Manitoba farmer Chris Brickman, supported by his neighbours, sued Ducks Unlimited Canada for damages caused by its dam — part of the Big Grass Marsh complex.[23] In the 1950s crop damage caused by the ever-growing numbers of ducks became a concern of farmers whose fields bordered DUC's factories.[24] Alberta ranchers, short of good grazing areas, resented the fences DUC put up around Many Islands Lake to preserve cover areas for waterfowl. As the organization's historian put it, "the better grass inside the fence, particularly in dry years, is almost irresistible to a rancher with hungry cattle and a pair of wire cutters in his pocket."[25] The Alberta Fish and Game League in Edmonton took issue with one of DUC's projects because the ban on hunting ruled out the only place in the area in which it could hunt.[26] When the government cancelled long-term haying and grazing leases near Ministik, another Alberta duck factory, warden Francis Williams had to deal with the ire of the local community, some of whose members began poaching the sanctuary's muskrat and setting fires in the early 1940s as a protest.[27]

The tensions between DUC and its rural neighbours speak to both the possibilities and the limits of the company's form of conservation. To a great extent, the organization's success in saving wetlands was attributable to the influence of its wealthy and well-connected leadership and the dollars it could bring to bear on the task. DUC's officers and directors were certainly well positioned to open the doors of various government ministries, but they often found those doors were already wide open. In the 1940s particularly, cash-strapped governments were more than happy to do what they could to accommodate an organization that offered to pay for habitat restoration — something many provinces were not in a position to do themselves.

In addition, DUC's effectiveness was also due to its strong grassroots support. Despite its blue-ribbon board of directors, it relied on donations from ordinary people in both the United States and Canada to fund its projects. Moreover, without the willingness of prairie farmers to negotiate easements on their land or to alter their séasonal round of stubble burning and haying, the organization's vision of "more game birds for America" would never have been realized.

More broadly, DUC succeeded because it worked within the existing regime of resource rights. Saving wetlands did not fundamentally challenge private property and the notion that ownership conferred broad powers of control exercised at the discretion of the individual property holder. If anything, it reinforced them: habitats were restored at private initiative, largely with private money, and where landowners were amenable. That which was saved was that which was or could be owned. DUC's approach to conservation also appealed because it was consistent with rural political culture, with the traditions of self-help that ran deep in the Canadian countryside. In response to charges that hunters could not really be conservationists, one of the organization's Alberta supporters shot back, noting the amount of money DUC spent on wetlands reclamation. "Not one dime of this was Government money," he remarked. "It was all donated by sportsmen – cash out of their pockets. What non-hunting group would come within a mile of this?"[28]

DUC also represented a way of seeing nature that was mainstream. A wetland was "a factory without a roof," a unit of production that could be managed scientifically to maximize outputs for the recreational benefit of urban hunters.[29] Like the scientists working for the CWS, DU's directorship saw the organization as "utilizing the tremendous natural reproductive forces available," increasing production by creating conditions that would boost the "biopower" of birds.[30] If DUC's views of what nature was – the nature of nature – were typical of the times, so too were its views regarding where nature was. It was a place separate, geographically distant, from that where DUC's members lived, a place that was the location of neither home nor work. These limits are ones that Tommy Walker and Andy Russell highlighted.

WILD LIVES: TOMMY WALKER, ANDY RUSSELL, AND THE MEANINGS OF HABITAT CONSERVATION

Tommy Walker (1904-89) and Andy Russell (1915-2005) were western Canadian guide-outfitters in the mid-twentieth century who became advocates for habitat conservation when they found the places they lived in threatened by industrial development. Both had hunted and trapped for their own pots and pleasure, and both made a good living and reputation introducing wealthy armed tourists to the rigorous joys of stalking trophy animals in the mountains of British Columbia and Alberta.

Yet neither man was in the business of saving habitat to save his job. There was more than simple economic interest behind Walker's efforts to save Spatsizi and Russell's efforts on behalf of "Grizzly Country." For both men, preserving these places was a way to promote a certain kind of relationship to nature. The wilderness areas they brought to the public's attention were not simply the breeding grounds of the game animals that provided them with an income, but places where they worked and played, where they lived and dreamed. Even more, British Columbia's mountains and Alberta's foothills had shaped and mediated their relationships with other people – family, neighbours, co-workers. In that sense natural history and human history intersected in the lives of Tommy Walker and Andy Russell in a way that even in their own lifetimes was becoming less common because of urbanization. When industrial development encroached in the 1950s, it did not just threaten the goats and bears of these regions: it threatened a way of life for the people who also lived in those habitats, people whose sense of who they were was powerfully tied to particular places.

The Republic of Spatsizi

English, middle class, and public-school-educated, Tommy Walker would be instantly recognizable to historians of British Columbia as a familiar "type." Although he was not a remittance man, his background qualified him as one of the many "gentlemen emigrants" who came to the province hoping to get a regular and respectable return on their status. Advised at Canada House to settle on the prairies, Walker would have none of it. His early career working for a London grain importer had given him an aversion to wheat, and he made his way instead to British Columbia from Gravesend in 1929.[31] Unlike many of his countrymen, Walker did not establish a private school, become a local JP, or try his hand at orcharding or ranching. Instead, his romantic tendencies – stoked by a reading of Bryan Williams' *Game Trails of British Columbia* – led him to seek his future where the wild things were: in the North.[32]

Settling first in the Bella Coola Valley, he tried his hand at farming before becoming a guide-outfitter, helping to build Stuie Lodge in the 1930s. He was involved in the creation of Tweedsmuir Provincial Park in 1937, and continued running the lodge (renamed after the park and governor general) until 1948, conducting his first extensive hunts for a wealthy international clientele after the war. Although his business was on a firm footing, Walker felt the valley was changing, becoming too developed. As civilization encroached, the wilderness retreated – and along with it a certain morality. When one neighbour reported returning to his cabin "to find no kindling, water left in buckets, dirty dishes and his sauce pans stolen," Walker knew it was time to leave. He sought a "sanctuary from progress," a place where "the unwritten laws of the frontier and ... a Christian code of ethics" still governed relationships.[33] He sold the lodge and travelled nine hundred miles north to the headwaters of the Stikine in Cassiar country, the culmination of a long-time fascination with the area. There he established a big game hunting business headquartered at Cold Fish Lake on the Spatsizi Plateau in the Eaglesnest Mountains, an operation he ran until 1968 and whose clients included British Columbia forestry magnate H.R. Macmillan and UBC president Norman Mackenzie, as well as a number of prominent and wealthy American industrialists.[34]

The mountains were where Tommy Walker felt he belonged. They were where his most meaningful relationships were forged, given shape, and sustained – with Marion Bullock-Webster, the woman he married; with the Aboriginal people who worked for him, and whom he considered his closest friends; and with the white men whom he called upon in his fight to save Spatsizi. Marion Bullock-Webster had come to Stuie Lodge in 1940 as one of Walker's clients.[35] A twisted ankle prolonged her stay, giving guide-outfitter and customer a chance to get to know each other and discover they had much in common. "We talked about my dream valley," he recalled. "We were both independent people. Our values were not of the city where wealth signified success, but we were well aware that we could not abandon the world like Thoreau; we had to face realities." Reality meant sharing their "mutual devotion to the wilderness" with others.[36] It was a compromise. Their years together in the Bella Coola Valley and the Cassiar were governed by a seasonal cycle as well as an economic one – something that was not entirely to Walker's liking.

"The need to make a living ... forced us to live part of our lives ... without that utter peace of living with nature," he reflected.[37]

Other than Marion, the principal people in Walker's life were the First Nations he employed as guides, cooks, and wranglers. His relationships with Aboriginal people were important ones, all the more so because he did not hold the local white population in high esteem, considering it boorish. The frontier did not, it seems, level Tommy Walker's middle-class sensibilities; nor did it disabuse him of the more positive stereotypes about Aboriginals. Perceiving them as noble savages, he considered them "part of the undisturbed ecology," living authentic lives close to nature – the kind of life he dreamed of.[38] As with his wife, life outdoors brought Walker and his Tahltan and Sekani neighbours together. Their knowledge of the mountains and the animals that lived there made them invaluable to his business. But he was also reliant on them for friendship – companionship of a kind he found only in remote places. "It was easy for settler and aboriginal to merge with little friction in a wide land where there was scope for all," he observed, where people were "free from a restrictive society."[39] For all the paternal and racial assumptions Walker carried, the fellowship of the trail allowed him to see the social possibilities of life in the mountains.

If Spatsizi created and mediated Tommy Walker's relationship with his family and friends, it was also the foundation of his association with a group of wealthy and educated men who would be instrumental allies in his fight to preserve the valley. Some clients were solely interested in bagging a trophy animal and saw Walker and his employees as tools to help them do that. For instance, when "two tall raw-boned Pendleton wheat farmers" showed up to hunt with Tommy and Marion, they were "quite definite regarding their needs. 'Don't show us any of your scenery,'" they declared. "'[W]e have plenty of that in Oregon. We have come to hunt and shoot.'"[40] But there were others who walked (and shot) among the mountains and came to see Spatsizi in much the same way Walker did. Robert Uihlein, a vice president with the Schlitz Brewing Company in Milwaukee, was one such person. He came year after year in the 1950s, bringing his children and grandchildren. Spatsizi was an integral part of his relationships with them. Although "the smell of bacon frying and other activities around camp all helped to bring back memories of past hunting expeditions," Uihlein was most pleased to see his grandson "acquit himself in the hunting field." The executive knew from first-hand experience that "there was no better place to learn self-reliance ... [and] the true value of the necessities of life."[41] Equally importantly, on the trail industrialists like Uihlein came to see the prospect of another way of being that stood in stark contrast to their southern urban existence. The fact that such men were willing to "spend money on a hunting trip that costs nearly three times as much as a hunt in other sections of our province" was, in Walker's view, "an indication of the value they place on these wilderness expeditions. They need peace of mind they knew they could find in a primitive wilderness."[42] Walker and Spatsizi embodied the alternative that Uihlein and others were looking for and they lent their support to the campaign to save it.

Walker had been attracted to the Cassiar because of its remoteness, but in the 1950s he felt the outside world encroaching, raising the possibility that Spatsizi's splendid isolation might end. His desire to live in pristine wilderness – to "live with nature" – ran counter to the development ethos of postwar Canada. After 1945, governments across the country devoted their energies to opening up the North. British Columbia was no exception to that trend and in many ways exemplified it most completely. For W.A.C. Bennett and his Social Credit government, exploiting the hydroelectric, mineral, and timber potential of the northern reaches of the province would drive industrial development and make British Columbia fully modern.

While Alcan's Kenney Dam on the Nechako River (1952) was worrying enough, Walker considered the government's plans for the Peace country, a region that bordered the Cassiar, deeply disturbing.[43] The sheer scale of Peace country development, the confident assertions of its backers, and the involvement of a mysterious and slightly shady foreign investor embodied the flamboyant and sometimes quixotic politics of achievement that was the hallmark of the Bennett regime. In partnership with Swedish vacuum cleaner magnate and alleged Nazi sympathizer Axel Wenner-Gren, the province created a development company and turned over control of forty thousand square miles of northern British Columbia – some 10 percent of the province's landmass – to it in 1956.[44] In all, such development would, in Bennett's opinion, amount to "rolling the frontier back 500 miles" to create a great "industrial empire north of Prince George" comparable, one resident opined, "to the German Ruhr."[45]

FROM WILDLIFE TO WILD PLACES

But it was the transformative potential of the region's waterways that was most dazzling. Although the grandiose plans for developing the entire district quickly faded, visions of the Peace as an electric river did not. Just nine months after signing the initial memorandum of intention with the Wenner-Gren group, W.A.C. Bennett made the "most momentous announcement of his career," publicizing his plans to build "the greatest hydro-electric power project in the world" in partnership with the Swedish millionaire.[46] At an estimated cost of between $400 and $600 million, harnessing the Peace would generate energy on the order of four million horsepower, the equivalent of the Grand Coulee and Hoover Dams combined.[47] Peace power would literally alter the face of the earth and fundamentally reorganize human economies and societies. Damming the river would convert part of the Rocky Mountain Trench into the largest artificial lake in the world, some 260 miles long and 10 to 15 miles wide – a body of water so substantial that commentators at the time recognized it would probably alter the climate of northern British Columbia.[48]

Walker worried about the impact of such development on Spatsizi's wildlife and the area's wildness, and as early as 1954 began talking about the need to preserve it. "Cold Fish Lake is one of the most remote places in Northern British Columbia and while I do not believe we are threatened in the *immediate* future," he warned his family, friends, and clients, "I am more than ever convinced that serious efforts should be made to preserve this primeval wilderness."[49] His concerns intensified in 1957. That year the future arrived on the Walkers' doorstep in three different forms, appearing first as fifty red gas drums dumped on the beach opposite their camp at Cold Fish Lake – souvenirs from a mineral exploration team.[50] Then in the summer it materialized as Axel Wenner-Gren and his survey party. "Consider Wenner a definite menace to this country," Walker confided to his diary after encountering him and his crew camped in their pastures.[51] Less than a week later, the future took the form of a surveyor for one of the province's resource companies. "Fat & unpleasant. Expressed my feelings regarding desecration of primeval wilderness … Hope weather clears so as they can get on with their work and get out of here."[52]

The Walkers' annual letter reflected their anxieties about the year's events and revealed that Tommy's worries about the impact of development on Spatsizi's wildlife were part of a larger unease with the speed and complexity of modern life. "Near the end of the season Sputnik had been launched and was rushing around the earth at breath-taking speed, which seemed unreal and horrible as we gazed into the heavens from such a wilderness of simplicity and peace," he wrote. "Civilization's mad rush is rapidly engulfing what little we have left of this last great wilderness and we are fast becoming an island refuge."[53]

The helicopter became Walker's favourite target, embodying for him modernity's worst aspect: the degrading intrusiveness of convenience. "To-day the new man of the north is dropped on a mountain summit by a helicopter, steaks and fresh fruit are flown in at regular intervals to ensure a well-balanced diet," he complained in 1963.[54] "At any moment ... [one] may come flup flup flupping over you to disturb the peace."[55] With the wilderness breached, he feared that he would have to become "a mass producer like the rest and do what we can to attract the crowds." Machines would reduce Marion and him to "operating a hot dog stand."[56]

Not content to simply let northern development engulf the landscape he loved, Walker organized to save Spatsizi, enlisting the help of some of his powerful clients to lobby the government. In 1956 he and Phil Connors, a wealthy Virginian who had hunted with the Walkers, proposed that Spatsizi be set aside as the Cassiar Primitive Research Area, an ecological reserve whose trustees would be drawn from "Education, Industry, Government, and the People." He quickly gained the support of Ian McTaggart-Cowan and Norman Mackenzie, who pledged university resources to the project, and H.R. Macmillan, who gave Walker an entrée into Vancouver's business community. Research and education were key components of Walker's vision. Arguing that "it was wrong to padlock a biological treasure chest," he hoped that research in Spatsizi, valuable of itself, would provide scientists with "bench-marks for comparing the effects of change on a natural environment," and in so doing teach British Columbians about the value of wilderness. Although the area would host university researchers, commercial operations and all mechanical travel would be prohibited to preserve its aesthetic qualities. The Walkers would close down their outfitting business and devote themselves instead to administering the project, to governing what their friends jokingly called the new "Republic of Spatsizi."[57]

Even with the help of his influential backers, Walker's fight to save Spatsizi was a long and bureaucratic one. Although functionaries in the Department of Recreation and Conservation as well as their counterparts in Lands expressed support for the idea, concrete action was lacking, and did not come until after Social Credit was defeated in 1972. The New Democratic Party created Spatsizi Plateau Wilderness Park in 1975, almost twenty years after Walker launched his idea. It was a bittersweet victory: the park was neither as large as Walker envisioned, nor did its designation come with the stringent protections he would have liked.[58] Moreover, the battle had given him a real distaste for politicians and bureaucrats. The "homburg indifference" of the former was as frustrating as the mindless rule-bound tendencies of the latter, who, from their "steam-heated offices" dictated "the correct and proper use of every acre" of the province's land.[59] In his view, the real defenders of wilderness were the industrialists. "How ironical," he recalled, "that the industrialists, whom so many condemned for their destruction of a natural landscape, were prepared to help perpetuate a primeval environment, while the politicians, elected by the people, were determined to wreak havoc."[60]

Walker's experience with government made him leery of leaving Spatsizi in the hands of the province's parks and fish and wildlife bureaucrats, particularly when there was so little scientific knowledge about the area's ecology. Since private enterprise had provided him with some of his strongest supporters, it was not surprising that it also gave him a model for managing the park. Walker established a private foundation in 1976 and proposed that for a ten- or twelve-year period it do the research and development work, as it were, that would inform wildlife management. Working with government, the Spatsizi Association for Biological Research (SABR), with its board of directors drawn from the upper ranks of scientific and wildlife management communities, set out the research directions for the park. It engaged scientists to carry out projects that would not only provide the kind of basic data necessary to formulate a management plan for Spatsizi, but which would also further an understanding of northern ecology – something of vital benefit to Canada and the United States.[61] This work was highly technical, and while much of it involved what Ian McTaggart-Cowan called "single-species research," other initiatives were more innovative "process-oriented" projects designed to explore "predation, territoriality, and the social interaction" among species.[62] Grounding their approach in the ecological science of the time,

SABR's scientists were committed to understanding the natural environment as a whole "so as to apply management at a systems level." Tommy Walker may have complained that "science [was] forcing tremendous changes in our way of living," but he also believed that in the "atomic age," it held out the prospect of redemption.[63]

As committed as he was to saving Spatsizi's wildlife, Walker was also driven by a desire to save a way of life he had carved out for himself amidst the mountains. Helicopters and roads made the North accessible to increasing numbers of people, threatening the survival of the region's wildlife as well as his own operations. As the North opened up, the Walkers faced more competition and found themselves in a paradoxical position: in order to continue living as and where they wanted to, they had to expand their operations, to commercialize more of Spatsizi. Doing so eroded the area's wildness and diminished the Walkers' own quality of life. Running "a business that stretched from Tatogga for over a hundred miles to the headwaters of the Finlay, where [they] had a fishing camp, and which included a ranch, a store and twenty-five outlying camps," Tommy and Marion no longer had time to ride together: each was too busy working and supervising a growing staff.[64] They also "grieved over the fading intimacies of a small camp, so soon overshadowed by the complexities of a large crew."[65] In addition, they had to put up with a new breed of hunter. Competition among outfitters was matched, it seemed, by a new, and in Walker's view, unhealthy competitiveness among sportsmen. The "status hunter" was a client whose only ambition was to see his name in the Boone and Crockett record book and "to hang a trophy on his office wall as an outward visible sign of his renown as a hunter." Those who hunted for prestige were "insensible to a wilderness environment," complained about the discomforts of camp, and were not above engaging in unethical practices like shooting out of season to get the trophy they wanted.[66]

From the time he arrived in British Columbia, Tommy Walker's relationships with people had been shaped by and given meaning through his relationship with nature. In that sense, he had, he wrote, "become part of Spatsizi."[67] As his association with it changed, so too did his connections with his wife, his employees, his clients. If he could end the commercialization of nature in one part of the North by establishing Spatsizi as an ecological reserve, there was a chance he might re-establish the close bonds he once had with the people who were important in his life. But preserving this part of the North had wider benefit: for Walker, the wild life was an ethical life: it was one where people connected across cultural lines, were tested and made aware of the impact of their actions on the world they lived in – and governed their behaviour accordingly. If living in Spatsizi had taught him how to be in the world, it could do the same for others. Preserving nature and attending to one's relationship with it was thus a way of cultivating better dealings with other people.

Grizzly Country

"Andy Russell was raised on a horse and has the legs to prove it," observed the *Winnipeg Free Press*. "Like two exclamation marks that decided to part company, they neatly balance his 6 foot 2 inch frame into a pair of well-worn cowboy boots."[68]

People would not have been surprised to learn that the Albertan in "tight blue jeans, leather jacket with fringe ... and large ... hat" was a keen hunter who wrote glowingly of "the elation of dropping that first big game," and coming home "covered with blood, hair, and exhaustion."[69] But they might have been a bit taken aback to learn the same man could also wax lyrical about the "energy" of a tree.[70] "I can take hold of a tree with both hands or put my arms around it and lean against it and feel the flow of energy," he explained to an interviewer. "Sometimes when I'm feeling very low, I can do this and it perks me up. It really makes me feel good."[71]

Just who was this man and how do we make sense of his commitment to habitat protection?

Born in 1915 near Lethbridge, Alberta, Andy Russell was a working cowboy. He grew up on a ranch beside the St. Mary River before moving with his family to the foothills of the Rockies, near Pincher Creek and the headwaters of Drywood Creek.[72] High school in Lethbridge made him feel like "a big horn in a zoo surrounded by the ... confusion of the city," so he quit at the age of fifteen or sixteen. It was the Depression, and not wanting to ride the rails, Russell did what many single young men in the '30s did: he became a trapper, running a line ninety miles long.[73] This was his introduction to living in the wilderness and it honed his skills to the point where Bert Riggall, one of southern Alberta's well-established guide-outfitters, hired him in 1936 to work as a "rough string rider, packer and guide."[74] Russell became his partner three years later and took over the business in 1946 when Riggall retired. The self-professed grade ten dropout made an already successful enterprise even more successful, expanding its operations into trail-riding in the 1950s. At its peak, Russell's business owned more than a hundred horses and had an exclusive contract with the Great Northern Railroad to handle all of its Canadian trail-riding tours.[75]

Russell's background may have been humble, but his clients were well-heeled, "very important people, highly educated people" from the northeast and Midwest of the United States. Many of them came year after year to explore and hunt the spectacular wild country surrounding the upper Oldman, Castle, and Waterton Rivers, as well as the watershed of British Columbia's Flathead.[76] Russell's Alberta territory had the highest diversity of plant and animal species in the province, and part of it, now known as the Castle Wilderness Area, is an important corridor for large carnivores travelling through the Rockies.[77] Jack O'Connor, the editor of the American magazine *Outdoor Life,* considered Russell's outfit the best on the continent.[78] Yet despite his success, Andy Russell quit the business in 1960 to begin a career as a full-time writer, filmmaker, and public speaker, one who would make his reputation as "a living icon of Canada's conservation movement."[79]

So who was Andy Russell? He was not Tommy Walker for one thing. Although he became a successful businessman, his rural working-class roots meant that he had none of the urban, middle-class Walker's anti-modern romanticism. There is very little in his writing about the purifying, simplifying benefits of a life outdoors and the possibilities of regeneration through an authentic encounter with the wild. While Walker was schooled at Marlborough, Russell was a Marlboro man. He described his own education as "short on the formal kind and long on the Rocky Mountain variety."[80] In the university of the outdoors, the son of a rancher's favourite subject was hunting. He kept a diary to record his deadly progress. "Today I brought home my new gun and scope," he wrote in October 1941. "It is beautiful and should prove very good on coyotes." It was. A few days later, he recorded a typical entry. "I took the shot that he offered," he wrote of his prey. "The bullet struck high on the right hip blowing up in his insides ... The fur is pretty poor – coyote being a little mangy."[81] Although his attitudes toward predators changed over time and he picked up a gun less and less, Russell remained a life-long defender of hunting, calling its opponents "bambi-types" and "cultists."[82] Sentiments and actions like the ones Russell recorded in his diary were commonplace and part of what made Tommy Walker despise his white neighbours. Yet he and Russell were friends, sharing more common ground than their social backgrounds might suggest.

Even more than those of Tommy Walker, Andy Russell's life and relationships were made by the habitat he shared with the animals he came to defend. His childhood on a ranch gave him an early introduction to the world of the four-leggeds, and his youthful foray into trapping taught him more about the creatures who lived beyond the fenceline. Under Bert Riggall's tutelage, Russell got an education in Rocky Mountain ecology, learning "the names of the wildflowers, the ... things they were good for, and what animals liked which ... [I]t was a very ... condensed, prolonged course in ... natural history and the environment."[83]

He also, as it turned out, got a set of in-laws. In 1938 Andy Russell married Kay, Bert Riggall's daughter, and like the Walkers the two spent much of their domestic life together outdoors. Like Marion Bullock-Webster, Kay Riggall played an active role in the family business. An expert shot, she worked as a camp cook and manager with her father and – after she and Andy spent their honeymoon riding in the mountains – alongside her new husband.[84] The couple's five children grew up in the foothills and mountains. Two of their sons worked closely with their father filming Dall sheep, bighorns, and grizzly, an experience that, as will be discussed, was instrumental in shaping Andy Russell's environmentalism.

Walker and Russell were also brought together by a common concern about the impact of development on the mountain habitats they called home. The discovery of oil at Leduc in 1947 signalled the start of postwar Alberta's resource development boom. Seemingly overnight, derricks sprung up. Fifty oil companies moved into Edmonton in the first six months of 1949, and by the end of the 1950s every major petroleum company in the world had representatives in the province that *Time* magazine dubbed the "Texas of the North."[85] In the "dynamic decade" after Leduc, oil transformed Alberta's economy from one rooted in agriculture to one fuelled by petroleum.[86] As cattle country was invaded by "Leduc livestock" and "oil donkeys" (local slang for oil-well pumps), the province got rich on money from royalties, leases, and sales of crown reserves. So did its citizens.[87] With the average per capita income increasing by 60 percent from 1946 to 1956, few people had patience for those who counselled caution.

While resource development merely surrounded Spatsizi, it made serious inroads into Grizzly Country – and Russell territory. In 1957, Shell discovered what turned out to be one of Canada's richest sour gas deposits beneath the mountains of southwestern Alberta, and began construction of its Waterton processing plant twenty miles from Pincher Creek, close to Russell's home. Roads and pipelines soon slashed through his guiding territory, surface scars that diverted attention from the deeper damage inflicted by hydrogen sulphide, the "sour" in sour gas. Toxic even in small amounts, H_2S can "rust fences, peel paint, and acidify water." In addition, it can cause nausea, memory loss, skin rashes, and asthma, among other things, and induce miscarriages. In larger quantities, it can kill instantly.[88]

As dead fish floated down Drywood Creek, Russell contemplated his future.[89] Section after section of land along the eastern slope of the Rockies was leased for exploration and development, with little regard for the impact. "The era of the fast buck was with us," Russell reflected, "and the buck wearing antlers ghosted away, dismayed and frightened by the snorting of the iron monsters."[90] He not only felt for the animals, he felt like them. "I found myself forting up with the grizzly in a rapidly shrinking range ... sharing a drastically changing environment," he wrote.[91] "I knew that outfitting was finished, at least the way I'd known it ... I'd seen some ... guys try to hang on, and it was just pitiable to see what happened."[92]

Not content to hang on and fade away, in the late 1950s Russell decided to do something about the assault on Alberta's wild places. Unlike Tommy Walker, however, he did not put his energies into protecting a particular place. While development had come to Tommy Walker's doorstep, it actually razed Andy Russell's home. Instead of trying to salvage his guiding territory and use it as a vehicle to change attitudes, as Walker did, Russell focused on changing attitudes first, hoping that would foster a commitment to preserving wildlife habitat. Although he had written sporadically for magazines since 1945, he began to contemplate the possibility of writing full time and making films to educate people about natural history and the cost of progress.

In the late 1950s, Russell went north to the Yukon to film Dall sheep with his sons, and then worked on bighorns with the Glenbow

Foundation before embarking on the project that would establish his reputation. Shot between 1961 and 1963, *Grizzly Country* was Russell's attempt to rehabilitate an animal that had been sorely "misjudged". by the public – including him. Convinced he was "ridding the country of a dangerous menace," the young Andy had no compunctions about killing the predators.[93] "I was inclined to pick up my rifle and go on the war path at the mere sight of grizzly tracks," he admitted. "Later ... as a professional guide and outfitter, I became more conservation minded, albeit selfishly, for the species meant money in my pocket."[94] But putting together the footage for the film had given him a new appreciation for the animal's intelligence and its role as "an important and highly desirable link in the ecological life chain." The health of the population was an indicator of the overall health of an ecosystem; in Russell's view, as the grizzly goes so goes the wilderness – and human society with it.[95] "Wilderness and the species of living things it supports can get along without man, but ... man cannot get along without them."[96]

While *Grizzly Country* was remarkable for capturing the bear in ways never before seen – the result of over two hundred close-range contacts – it was significant because it encouraged people to think in ecological terms.[97] That meant considering the interrelationships among different animals and their habitat. Despite its title, the film did not focus solely on the grizzly: instead, it dealt with bighorns, mountain goats, mule deer, moose, and caribou – other creatures that shared their range with the big bear. By implication, it also suggested that people needed to think differently about conservation: Effective measures would be achieved only by protecting a vast habitat – a biological unit – not small parcels of wild land broken up by areas of intensive development. Grizzly Country, an extensive area stretching from Alaska through Alberta and then southward into the United States, was a prime candidate for such an approach. In actuality, what Russell was asking people to do (albeit indirectly) was make biological values a part of the decision making about land use and allocation, in short, to make ecology part of politics.

The silent film, which Russell narrated live to audiences across the province, received good reviews and the book that followed in 1967 commanded an appreciative national and international readership that included both ordinary people and professional scientists.[98] To a great extent, the success of *Grizzly Country* spoke to Russell's skills as a storyteller. "Telling a story is like selling a horse," he confided to one interviewer. "Appreciation of the product will be higher if you do a bit of currying and brushing."[99]

But what made his message unusual and noteworthy was that it went beyond simply celebrating the diversity, interconnectedness, and complexity of the natural world to make a case for how people could – and should – live. The time in which Russell and his sons spent filming Dall sheep, bighorns, and grizzlies revealed that nature was not entirely "red in tooth and claw," a constant, bloody, Darwinian struggle for survival. Animals could and did coexist peacefully.[100] Russell's time outdoors taught him what he "would never have believed before – that so-called wild animals are not really wild at all." True, they fled at the sight of humans, but given humans' behaviour toward them, that was a rational response.[101] Indeed, in Andy's opinion, "the wildest thing at large in the wilderness today is man."[102]

As Russell and his sons discovered, the key to filming wild things – and to living with them – was to tame themselves. Once they had done that, they were accepted as "friends" by the sheep and bears and had no qualms about going into Grizzly Country unarmed.[103] What Russell did have misgivings about was picking up a gun again: it was hard for him to think about shooting his new friends. Seventeen months of living with the bighorns made the prospect of ever returning to guiding and hunting unappealing. His friendship with the animals he had previously hunted had given him a glimpse of a "new world" – one which if seen by more people would convince them of the need for wilderness.[104]

But that world would be rendered visible and salvageable only if people did what Andy and his boys did, namely, tame their wild natures. That meant acquiring a new set of attitudes, cultivating a different way of being in nature. People had to "learn something of humility."[105] They would have to dispense with the arrogance that lay behind the notion that they would have dominion over the earth – that they were and should be the dominant species. At the same time, people would also have to stop being fearful of nature. Being humble did not mean being afraid. As much as arrogance, fear contributed to seeing nature as an adversary and thus had been responsible for much of the havoc humans had wrought on the natural world. For Andy Russell, "learning to live" had required him to "mov[e] beyond the barriers of fear" – his own and those of the animals.[106] Doing so brought him serenity and, equally importantly, it allowed him to see the connections between himself and the creatures whose habitat he shared. "Many of us think of ourselves as divine beings far above other warm blooded creatures," he observed. "But in truth we are only a part of nature, a portion of a vast ecosystem."[107]

Andy Russell wanted people to cultivate the same sense of connectedness he had, believing that, as much as humility, it too was crucial to saving the wilderness. Much more than Tommy Walker, Russell emphasized the need for people to see themselves as part of a larger ecological whole, to appreciate the effects of their actions, and to see that all of them had an impact on the natural world. In response to readers' questions about why he spent so much time talking about people in his "Ecolog," a column he wrote for the *Lethbridge Herald* in the 1970s, Russell argued that it was because people were "the single greatest influence" on the environment. "Just because one happens to [sic] making his living at a desk in some huge monolithic pile of steel and stone in the heart of a big city does not separate him from nature," he wrote. "Every time that man walks into his home, turns a tap, eats, puts on his clothes or drives his car, he is calling on nature for the means to his way of life."[108] Ensuring a future for people meant "knowing it [was] tied to that of all other associated forms of life."[109]

The idea of nature that underlay Andy Russell's arguments about the importance of preserving habitat is remarkable, for it went against the grain of centuries of Western thinking about wilderness. As William Cronon argues, "the trouble with wilderness" is the manner in which it has been and continues to be conceptualized. People – including environmentalists – see it as a place separate from human settlement. By definition, wilderness is devoid of people and hence outside of history: while humans are rooted in time and space, nature transcends both. The problem – or trouble – with thinking about nature in that way is that it denies the interconnectedness of life; it denies the linkages Russell made between the countryside and the people labouring in the steel and stone monoliths of the city. In Cronon's view, perpetuating this sense of nature as separate is ultimately destructive of the very environments people wish to save. As long as wilderness is somewhere "out there," people will not have to take responsibility for the environments they do live in, much less acknowledge the impact their actions have on the distant places they purport to cherish.

In contrast, Andy Russell's wilderness was a place where people could – and should – live, for all the benefits that doing so brought. Living in nature required making use of it: Russell was not an advocate of preservation. For him, the issue was the kind and extent of use. Although he hunted less and less over the years, Russell defended the practice as good management and was highly critical of the anti-hunting lobby, whose arguments were overly reliant on emotion.[110] His support extended to defending the grizzly hunt. "I would never hunt grizzly again, but I'll defend others hunting them," he wrote in 1978. "Closing grizzly hunting is not the answer to perpetuating them. Ensuring they have room to roam is what will protect the grizzly."[111] Russell considered his brand of environmentalism practical. As he argued in *Nature Canada,* "good environmental policy is not contradictory to human and industrial welfare."[112] He was "realistic" about commercial and industrial development. "I can't really afford to be tough on the oil companies," he admitted. "After all, I own oil stock, and on top of that I own a vehicle that I use the product in every day."[113]

Russell's pragmatism is of the same kind that underlies current ideas about sustainable use, and reflects his class origins and experience. Grizzly Country was where he lived, worked, and played, where he was sustained materially, socially, and spiritually. There was no division between home and work in his life, no separation between nature and culture. It was this unity that underlay his passion for wild places and his commitment to saving them.

Ducks Unlimited Canada, Tommy Walker, and Andy Russell were at the forefront of habitat protection in Canada, making the case that saving wildlife could be achieved only by saving wild places. Their work underscores one of the main arguments of this book: some of the most important wildlife work was done outside the state, by ordinary people from Canada's countryside, the same rural people who were marginalized by game acts and whose knowledge of the natural world was not always taken seriously by those in the ranks of government.

That said, the differences among them are also revealing of the diversity of the conservation movement, of its unity and points of fracture. Ducks Unlimited's work, though dependent on the cooperation

of local farmers, was really an undertaking of well-heeled business-
men committed to scientific management, whose only connection to
the habitats they worked to save was through sports hunting.

In contrast, Tommy Walker and Andy Russell called the habitats
they lobbied for home. While both had spent much of their lives
in the mountains, their approaches to habitat preservation differed.
Walker preferred to work behind the scenes. He organized some of
his influential clients and friends, many of whom were scientists,
into a lobby group to pressure the provincial government to set aside
Spatsizi. Russell, on the other hand, took his case for conservation to
the public. In a tradition established by Jack Miner, Grey Owl, Farley
Mowat, and Bill Mason, Russell used a variety of media – newspa-
pers, magazines, books, film, and live performance – to call attention
to the plight of Grizzly Country, and to habitats threatened by industrial development generally.

For both men, the value of wild places went far beyond recreation
or aesthetics. Instead, Spatsizi and Grizzly Country were significant
for broader social reasons. Wilderness cultivated different ways of
being in people – fellowship, connection, humility – and for that reason was worth protecting. From their vantage point in the backcountry, Walker and Russell could see the link between environmental
integrity and social integrity. For them, protecting wild places was
the key to upholding a way of life – for people as well as for animals.

CONCLUSION

◆

THREE YEARS AFTER *Never Cry Wolf* was published, British Columbia reorganized its Department of Recreation and Conservation. After nearly sixty years, the government got out of the "game" business, replacing its "Fish and Game" division with one responsible for the province's "Fish and Wildlife." According to the man who headed it, this small semantic change altered more than the branch's letterhead, and the explanation for it was rooted in the same shift in attitudes that had made Farley Mowat's book a best-seller.

For branch director James Hatter, the name change reflected a deeper shift in the direction and aims of government conservation.[1] Not only would he and his staff be responsible for a wider variety of species, but they were also expected to frame policy in accordance with different principles. No longer were recreational values the only or even the most important ones governing management. Instead, "environmental" considerations began to shape the division's initiatives, a development that signalled the public's growing ecological consciousness.[2]

From the mid-1960s on, Canadians, and North Americans in general, became increasingly concerned about the impact of postwar industrial growth. Questions about effects of pesticides and the extent of air and water pollution manifested themselves in an awareness of the interconnectedness and interdependence of living things and a general concern about the state of the earth. "Environment," as Hatter put it, "became the 'in' thing."[3]

In the absence of government environmental agencies – which were not established until the 1970s – people turned to fish and wildlife departments for action. But, as Hatter ruefully recalled, the action they wanted handcuffed his staff. The same ecological consciousness that had made Rachel Carson's *Silent Spring* a best-seller in 1962 and Farley Mowat's book an international success the following year rendered the kind of intensive interventions into wildlife populations that, for instance, characterized caribou and bison conservation, much more difficult. For Carson, "'the control of nature' [was] a phrase conceived in arrogance, born of the Neanderthal age of biology and philosophy when it was supposed that nature exist[ed] for the convenience of mankind."[4]

The public equated human intervention with environmental destruction, and pushed for a much less intrusive approach to conservation. Hatter was frustrated. "It is not in the interest of all wildlife to simply advocate zero management and 'let nature take its often wasteful course,'" he fumed, echoing Jack and Manly Miner, as well as Aldo Leopold. Healthy populations depended on actively pursuing a policy of wise use – "sustainability" as he termed it. Substituting preservation for conservation would result only in dead animals.[5] But to the "misinformed" public, death by starvation and disease was preferable to death at the hands of the recreational hunter.

None of this made sense to Hatter, based as it was on emotional, rather than scientific, arguments. Writers like Farley Mowat and film-makers like Bill Mason were to blame. They had rehabilitated the wolf, but had demonized the government scientist and the hunter. In the late 1960s and early 1970s, a scientist-hunter like James Hatter felt like a wolf being pursued by an aerial hunter on the open tundra: exposed, and with no place to hide. Following a public controversy over the awarding of a guide-outfitting licence to a man who had been convicted of several violations of the Wildlife Act, Hatter was forced to step down, accused by his minister and the public of being too close to the province's pro-hunting lobby. He was, he reflected, a victim of "political correctness," a change in attitudes toward wild-life that had rendered his ideas objectionable. It was a bitter end to a long career. What he found especially galling was the judgement that because he hunted and enjoyed doing so, he was possessed of ideas about wildlife that belonged to another century and hence was unfit to direct an agency devoted to its conservation.

Such a harsh judgement must have been especially confusing to Hatter because for most of his career he had been accused of just the reverse, namely, of being a wet-behind-the-ears university man with no real or practical understanding of the outdoors. Hatter was among the first generation of people in Canada to be trained in the new science of game management. After doing an undergraduate honours thesis on predator-prey relations in the 1940s, he completed a doctorate on the ecology of moose at Washington State University in 1952, and taught zoology part-time at the University of British Columbia, all the while working as the province's first wildlife biologist.[6] In short, James Hatter represented the cutting edge of postwar conservation in Canada; he was part of a generation of wildlife workers who helped realize the Progressivist promise of wise use through scientific management.

Hatter's education and hiring represented the culmination of changes in wildlife conservation that had started at the beginning of the twentieth century. In the hundred years after Confederation, the focus of government wildlife management shifted from initiatives aimed at controlling the harvest to those aimed at actively managing populations and habitats to increase numbers. The interventionist impulse was strongest at some of the national parks in western Canada, where wardens poisoned wolves to keep them from taking their toll on the bison and then slaughtered the bison to keep their numbers within the carrying capacity of their range. With the shift in emphasis came a shift in the organization of conservation. In the postwar period, government wildlife work became more professional, scientific, and systematic; in the process, it also became less reliant on local knowledge. Different levels and branches of government worked together at joint conservation initiatives in recognition of the fugitive nature of the resource, but with a few exceptions – namely, co-management of beaver preserves – ordinary people did not play a significant role in shaping conservation policy. Instead, they found themselves like the wildlife itself: objects of policies they had no role in framing.

The changes that occurred in wildlife conservation over the twentieth century amounted to a rationalization of people's relationship to the natural world. The repercussions of this reconfiguration were far-reaching, bringing urban and rural Canada together in new ways that generated conflict, marginalizing the backcountry even as it provided some opportunities for a handful of its residents.

If the relationship between regions and among groups of people was transformed by the changes in the organization, substance, and aims of wildlife conservation, so too was wildlife itself. Over the twentieth century, wildlife was perceived in increasingly generalized terms, even as it became more regulated. Across jurisdictions defined politically rather than socially or ecologically, animals were cast as populations, or "factors" to be manipulated and controlled for recreational purposes. They went from being part of a local commons controlled informally by a community of users to being part of a provincial or national commons, subject to regulations framed by a distant centralized bureaucracy.

In the 1960s, people like Farley Mowat and Bill Mason challenged this view of wildlife. Rather than thinking of them as populations, or even more conceptually, as factors, they insisted – as Roberts, Seton, Miner, and Grey Owl had before them – that animals such as wolves be considered individuals. George, Angeline, and Uncle Albert. Charlie and Sparky. While their individualism made it impossible for them to be possessed as property – common or otherwise – this status also rendered wildlife an abstraction. Mowat's and particularly Mason's wolves transcended habitat and the bonds of ecological community, existing simply as wild things; they stood for wildness. Like Lewis Carroll's Cheshire cat, all that remained of these wolves was their howl, a powerful symbol of wildness.

But abstractions, whether legal or literary, are abstractions. And neither the one formulated by government conservation policy nor the one devised in opposition to it captured the range and variety of relationships – ecological, economic, social – in which wild animals were implicated. For people like Jack Miner and the Cree in northern Quebec, wildlife made it possible to survive in the backcountry and at the same time threatened their survival. As the lives of Tommy Walker and Andy Russell suggest, animals provided more than sustenance. They also forged powerful social bonds between people and places, and among people: fathers and sons, husbands and wives, Aboriginals and whites, employers and employees. None of this was captured in definitions of wildlife as a thing (property) or a spirit (wildness).

Miner's sanctuary, the HBC beaver preserves, Tommy Walker's campaign for Spatsizi, and Andy Russell's campaign for Grizzly Country were all effective. In part, they worked because, rather than imposing one role to the exclusion of others, they acknowledged, and to differing degrees addressed and tried to accommodate, the variety of roles that wildlife played in people's or groups of people's lives.

It was an accommodation that did not characterize government policies or the demands of preservationists. Both wanted to remove wildlife conservation as much as possible from its messy context of human interests. Bureaucrats, from Otto Schierbeck in Nova Scotia to James Hatter in British Columbia, justified their policies by appealing to the neutrality and authority of the science that underpinned them. Preservationists like Mowat and Mason took issue with the impartiality of science. In its place, they asserted the disinterested authority of nature, the idea that, left to its own devices, nature would balance itself. This was exactly the wrong approach. Wildlife policy, instead of being detached from human interests, should be grounded in them – as it is in many places outside North America, where conservation is part of local community development.

Politicizing conservation makes it possible to acknowledge what its history has revealed, namely, that policy decisions have been as much matters of sociology as they are of biology, of (though James Hatter would have objected) emotion as much as intellect. Human morals and values are as much "limiting factors" in wildlife conservation as are ground cover and pH. That being the case, why not embrace the political nature of conservation to talk openly about the social needs and values it should serve? Why not forge a balance that includes people and wildlife? Acknowledging and incorporating human needs and values in conservation, as was the case with the HBC's foray into beaver preserves, Tommy Walker's fight for Spatsizi, and Andy Russell's work on behalf of Grizzly Country, would clarify their choices and their implications. Moreover, acknowledging that conservation has and should serve human interests would highlight the extent to which culture and nature are interconnected, and diminish the alienation that is the cause of so much environmental destruction. The balance of nature might have outlived its usefulness as a concept, but the notion of balance has not.

NOTES

FOREWORD

1 These initial paragraphs are drawn in substantial part from Lillian Ford, "Coyote Goes Downriver: An Historical Geography of Coyote Migration into the Fraser Valley" (MA thesis, Geography, University of British Columbia, 2000), especially Chapter 7, 112-19. Quotes can be found here and in the *Vancouver Sun,* 12 September 1994, 15 January 1996; *Vancouver Courier,* 25 May 1994; *Province* (Vancouver), 10 May 1991, 22 September 1993. However, see also Kristine Webber, "Urban Coyotes (*Canis latrans,* Say 1823) in the Lower Mainland, British Columbia: Public Perceptions and Education" (MSc thesis, Department of Animal Science, University of British Columbia, 1997); Jennifer Wolch and Jody Emel, *Animal Geographies* (London and New York: Verso, 1998); and M.I. Grinder and P.R. Krausman, "Home Range, Habitat Use, and Nocturnal Activity of Coyotes in an Urban Environment," *Journal of Wildlife Management* 65, 4 (2001): 887-98.
2 Ian Hacking, *The Social Construction of What?* (Cambridge, MA: Harvard University Press, 1999) offers a useful primer and engagement with the issues relating to questions of "social constructionism" that are at the core of this paragraph.
3 The classic essay here is William Cronon, "The Trouble with Wilderness; or, Getting Back to the Wrong Nature," in *Uncommon Ground: Toward Reinventing Nature,* ed. W. Cronon (New York: W.W. Norton, 1995), 69-90. For the quote, see the commentary by Paul Wapner, "Leftist Criticism of 'Nature': Environmental Protection in a Postmodern Age," *Dissent* Magazine 50, 1 (Winter 2003): 71. This is also available at http://www.dissentmagazine.org/menutest/articles/wi03/wapner.htm.
4 David Quammen, *Monster of God: The Man-Eating Predator in the Jungles of History and the Mind* (New York: W.W. Norton, 2003), 3, and "Planet of Weeds," *Harper's Magazine,* October 1998, 57-69.
5 Or, as Raymond Williams had it many years ago, "The idea of nature contains, though often unnoticed, an extraordinary amount of human history." Raymond Williams, *Keywords: A Vocabulary of Culture and Society* (London: Fontana, Croom Helm, 1976), 184-89, quote on 184.
6 Richard W. Judd, *Common Lands, Common People: The Origins of Conservation in Northern New England* (Cambridge, MA: Harvard University Press, 1997); Samuel P. Hays, *Conservation and the Gospel of Efficiency: The Progressive Conservation Movement, 1890-1920* (Cambridge, MA: Harvard University Press, 1959); Robert H. Wiebe, *The Search for Order, 1877-1920* (New York: Hill and Wang, 1967); and, for a Canadian perspective somewhat akin to that adopted by Wiebe, see Robert Craig Brown

and Ramsay Cook, *Canada, 1896-1921: A Nation Transformed* (Toronto: McClelland and Stewart, 1974). Comparison with Thomas R. Dunlap, *Saving America's Wildlife: Ecology and the American Mind, 1850-1990* (Princeton: Princeton University Press, 1988) is also worthwhile.

7 Karl Jacoby, *Crimes against Nature: Squatters, Poachers, Thieves, and the Hidden History of American Conservation* (Berkeley: University of California Press, 2001); Louis S. Warren, *The Hunter's Game: Poachers and Conservationists in Twentieth-Century America* (New Haven, CT: Yale University Press, 1997); Mark David Spence, *Dispossessing the Wilderness: Indian Removal and the Making of the National Parks* (Oxford: Oxford University Press, 1999).

8 Janet Foster, *Working for Wildlife: The Beginning of Preservation in Canada* (Toronto: University of Toronto Press, 1978 and 1998), 13, 222.

9 Kurkpatrick Dorsey, *The Dawn of Conservation Diplomacy: U.S.-Canadian Wildlife Protection Treaties in the Progressive Era* (Seattle: University of Washington Press, 1998).

10 Roderick Nash, "Wilderness and Man in North America," in *The Canadian National Parks: Today and Tomorrow,* eds. J.G. Nelson and R.C. Scace. Proceedings of a conference organized by the National and Provincial Parks Association of Canada and the University of Calgary, 9-15 October 1968 (Calgary: University of Calgary Press, 1969), 1: 66-93.

11 Alan MacEachern, "Voices Crying in the Wilderness: Recent Works in Canadian Environmental History," *Acadiensis* 31, 2 (2002): 217-18. See also his *Natural Selections: National Parks in Atlantic Canada, 1935-1970* (Montreal: McGill-Queen's University Press, 2001), and for a useful discussion of some of the ambiguities in attitudes towards predators and national parks, his "Rationality and Rationalization in Canadian National Parks Predator Policy," in *Consuming Canada: Readings in Environmental History,* eds. Chad Gaffield and Pam Gaffield (Toronto: Copp, Clark, 1995), 197-212.

12 MacEachern, "Voices," 217.

13 Farley Mowat, *Never Cry Wolf* (Toronto: McClelland and Stewart, 1973), vi; see also this volume pp. 173, 202.

14 See this volume pp. 82, 90, 174.

15 Ralph H. Lutts, ed., *The Wild Animal Story* (Philadelphia: Temple University Press, 1998); Thomas R. Dunlap, "The Realistic Animal Story: Ernest Thompson Seton, Charles Roberts, and Darwinism," *Forest and Conservation History* 36 (1992): 56-62, reprinted in Lutts, ed., *The Wild Animal Story,* 237-47; James Polk, *Wilderness Writers: Ernest Thompson Seton, Charles G.D. Roberts, Grey Owl* (Toronto: Clarke, Irwin, 1972).

16 Donald B. Smith, *From the Land of Shadows: The Making of Grey Owl* (Saskatoon: Western Producer Prairie Books, 1990), 205; see also p. 113 below; Lovatt Dickson, *Wilderness Man: The Strange Story of Grey Owl* (Toronto: Macmillan of Canada, 1973); and Jane Billinghurst, *Grey Owl: The Many Faces of Archie Belaney* (Vancouver: Greystone Books, 1999).

17 Frank Zelko, "Making Greenpeace: The Development of Direct Action Environmentalism in British Columbia," in "On the Environment," ed.

Graeme Wynn, special issue, *BC Studies,* nos. 142-43 (Summer-Autumn 2004): 197-240, offers a rich summary of this context.

18 Joy Adamson, *Born Free: A Lioness of Two Worlds* (New York: Pantheon Books, 1960). *Born Free,* the film directed by James Hill, was released by Columbia Pictures in 1966; a sequel, *Living Free,* was released in 1972.

19 Mowat, *Never Cry Wolf,* 175; see also this volume p. 180.

20 Russell quote from this volume, p. 205. Ernest Thompson Seton, *Wild Animals I Have Known and 200 Drawings: Being the Personal Histories of Lobo, Silverspot, Raggylug, Bingo, the Springfield Fox, the Pacing Mustang, Wully, and Redruff* (Toronto: George N. Morang, 1898), and Ernest Thompson Seton, *Wild Animals at Home* (New York: Grosset and Dunlap, 1913), vi, vii.

21 Charles G.D. Roberts, *The Kindred of the Wild: A Book of Animal Life* (Toronto: Copp Clark, 1902; London: Thomas Nelson and Sons, n.d.), 19.

INTRODUCTION

1 Eric Kaufmann, "'Naturalizing the Nation': The Rise of Naturalistic Nationalism in Canada and the United States," *Comparative Studies in Society and History* 40 (1998): 666-95. Also see George Altmeyer, "Three Ideas of Nature in Canada, 1893-1914," in *Consuming Canada: Readings in Environmental History,* ed. Chad Gaffield and Pam Gaffield (Toronto: Copp Clark, 1995), 96-118.

2 Mary Louise Pratt, *Imperial Eyes: Travel Writing and Transculturation* (London: Routledge, 1992). On the colonialist nature of the Group of Seven's painting, see Jonathan Bordo, "Jack Pine – Wilderness Sublime or the Erasure of the Aboriginal Presence in the Landscape," *Journal of Canadian Studies* 27, 4 (1992): 98-128. First Nations surrealist Lawrence Paul Yuxweluptun considers his landscapes (paintings he calls "land claims") a direct response to the work of Emily Carr. See Charlotte Townsend-Gault, "The Salvation Art of Yuxweluptun," in *Lawrence Paul Yuxweluptun: Born to Live and Die on Your Colonialist Reservations,* ed. Lawrence Paul Yuxweluptun (Vancouver: Morris and Helen Belkin Art Gallery, 1995), 5.

3 Ramachandra Guha, "Radical American Environmentalism and Wilderness Preservation: A Third World Critique," *Environmental Ethics* 11, 1 (1989): 284-93.

4 William Cronon, "The Trouble with Wilderness, or Getting Back to the Wrong Nature," in *Uncommon Ground: Rethinking the Human Place in Nature,* ed. William Cronon (New York: W.W. Norton, 1996), 69-90.

5 Alec Lucas, "Nature Writing in English," in *The Oxford Companion to Canadian Literature,* 2nd ed., ed. E. Benson and W. Toye (Toronto: Oxford University Press, 1997), 789.

6 James Polk, "Lives of the Hunted," *Canadian Literature* 53 (1972): 58.

7 Margaret Atwood, "Animal Victims," in *The Wild Animal Story,* ed. R. Lutts (Philadelphia: Temple University Press, 1998), 215.

8 Ibid., 216.

9 Ibid., 216, 221.

10 Ibid., 220.

11 Some of the work that looks at wildlife conservation in a particular region of Canada includes George Colpitts, *Game in the Garden: A Human History of Wildlife in Western Canada to 1940* (Vancouver: UBC Press, 2002); Donald Dodds, *Challenge and Response: A History of Wildlife and Wildlife Management in Nova Scotia* (Halifax, NS: Department of Natural Resources, 1993); Robert G. McCandless, *Yukon Wildlife: A Social History* (Edmonton: University of Alberta Press, 1985); John Sandlos, "From the Outside Looking In: Aesthetics, Politics, and Wildlife Conservation in the Canadian North," *Environmental History* 6, 1 (2001): 6-31. The stories of individual conservationists are represented by Donald B. Smith, *From the Land of the Shadows: The Making of Grey Owl* (Saskatoon: Western Producer Prairie Books, 1990); Peter Unwin, "The Man Who Would Have Dominion," *Beaver,* October-November 2001; T.A. (Tommy) Walker, *Spatsizi* (Surrey, BC: Hunaga Publishing, 1976). George Colpitts deals with the work of Alberta's fish and game associations in "Fish and Game Associations in Southern Alberta, 1907-1928," *Alberta History* 42, 4 (1994): 16-26. Two books that deal with the federal government's work in wildlife conservation are Janet Foster, *Working for Wildlife: The Beginning of Preservation in Canada* (Toronto: University of Toronto Press, 1978); J. Alexander Burnett, *A Passion for Wildlife: The History of the Canadian Wildlife Service* (Vancouver: UBC Press, 2003). Much of the best work on the conservation of particular species has been produced in the technical reports of the Canadian Wildlife Service and the conference proceedings of the Federal-Provincial Wildlife Conference and the North American Wildlife Conference. But I have also drawn on the following: Karen Jones, *Wolf Mountains: A History of Wolves along the Great Divide* (Calgary: University of Calgary Press, 2002); Patricia A. McCormack, "The Political Economy of Bison Management in Wood Buffalo National Park," *Arctic* 45, 4 (1992): 367-80; John Sandlos, "Where the Scientists Roam: Ecology, Management and Bison in Northern Canada," *Journal of Canadian Studies* 37, 2 (2002): 93-129. Particular wildlife management policies are dealt with in Dan Gottesman, "Native Hunting and the Migratory Birds Convention Act: Historical, Political, and Ideological Perspectives," *Journal of Canadian Studies* 18, 3 (1983): 67-89; Brenda Ireland, "'Working a Great Hardship on Us': First Nations People, the State, and Fur Conservation in British Columbia before 1935" (master's thesis, University of British Columbia, 1995); Alan MacEachern, "Rationality and Rationalization in Canadian National Parks' Predator Policy," in *Consuming Canada: Readings in Environmental History,* ed. Chad Gaffield and Pam Gaffield (Toronto: Copp Clark, 1995), 197-212; François-Xavier Riborpy, "Histoire sociologique du droit de la chasse et de la pêche en Ontario," *Anthropologica* [Canada] 30, 2 (1988): 155-73; Kevin Wamsley, "'Good Clean Sport and a Deer Apiece': Game Legislation and State For-

mation in Nineteenth-Century Canada," *Canadian Journal of the History of Sport* 25, 2 (1994): 1-20.

12 See in particular two articles by Sean Cadigan, "Whose Fish? Science, Ecosystems and Ethics in Fisheries Management Literature since 1992," *Acadiensis* 31, 1 (2001): 171-95; "The Moral Economy of the Commons: Ecology and Equity in the Newfoundland Cod Fishery, 1815-1855," *Labour/Le Travail* 43 (1999): 9-42; Matthew Evenden, *Fish versus Power: An Environmental History of the Fraser River* (New York: Cambridge University Press, 2004); Douglas C. Harris, *Fish, Law, and Colonialism: The Legal Capture of Salmon in British Columbia* (Toronto: University of Toronto Press, 2001); Dianne Newell, *Tangled Webs of History: Indians and the Law in Canada's Pacific Coast Fisheries* (Toronto: University of Toronto Press, 1993); Bill Parenteau, "Care, Control, and Supervision: Native People in the Canadian Atlantic Salmon Fishery, 1867-1900," *Canadian Historical Review* 79, 1 (1998): 1-35; J. Michael Thoms, "A Place Called Pennask: Fly Fishing and Colonialism at a British Columbia Lake," *BC Studies*, no. 133 (2002): 69-98.

13 Key works on the history of wildlife conservation in the United States include the following: Thomas R. Dunlap, *Saving America's Wildlife* (Princeton, NJ: Princeton University Press, 1988); Andrew Isenberg, *The Destruction of the Bison: An Environmental History* (New York: Cambridge University Press, 2000); John Reiger, *American Sportsmen and the Origins of Conservation* (New York: Winchester, 1975); James Tober, *Who Owns Wildlife? The Political Economy of Conservation in Nineteenth-Century America* (Westport, CT: Greenwood Press, 1981); Louis S. Warren, *The Hunter's Game: Poachers and Conservationists in Twentieth-Century America* (New Haven: Yale University Press, 1997).

14 Robert D. Bullard, *Dumping in Dixie: Race, Class, and Environmental Quality* (Boulder: Westview, 1994); Karl Jacoby, *Crimes against Nature: Squatters, Poachers, Thieves and the Hidden History of American Conservation* (Berkeley: University of California Press, 2001); Mark David Spence, *Dispossessing the Wilderness: Indian Removal and the Making of the National Parks* (New York: Oxford University Press, 1999); Louis S. Warren, *The Hunter's Game: Poachers and Conservationists in Twentieth-Century America* (New Haven: Yale University Press, 1997); Richard West Sellers, *Preserving Nature in the National Parks: A History* (New Haven: Yale University Press, 1977).

15 Ramachandra Guha, *Environmentalism: A Global History* (New York: Longman, 2000), ch. 6. Also see his *The Unquiet Woods: Ecological Change and Peasant Resistance in the Himalaya* (Berkeley: University of California Press, 2000); *Ecology and Equity: The Use and Abuse of Nature in Contemporary India,* with Madhav Gadgil (London: Routledge, 1995); and "Radical American Environmentalism and Wilderness Preservation: A Third World Critique," *Environmental Ethics* 11, 1 (1989): 284-93.

CHAPTER 1: WILD BY LAW

1 The body of literature on the meanings of nature and wilderness is large. For a starting place, see Roderick Nash, *Wilderness and the American Mind,* 4th ed. (New Haven: Yale University Press, 2001); William Cronon, "The Trouble with Wilderness, or Getting Back to the Wrong Nature," in *Uncommon Ground: Rethinking the Human Place in Nature,* ed. William Cronon (New York: W.W. Norton, 1996), 69-90; for Canada, see George Altmeyer, "Three Ideas of Nature in Canada, 1893-1914," in *Consuming Canada: Readings in Environmental History,* ed. Chad Gaffield and Pam Gaffield (Toronto: Copp Clark, 1995), 96-118.

2 C. Gordon Hewitt, *The Conservation of the Wild Life of Canada* (New York: Charles Scribner's Sons, 1921), 1.

3 Louis S. Warren, *The Hunter's Game: Poachers and Conservationists in Twentieth-Century America* (New Haven: Yale University Press, 1997).

4 P.B. Munsche, *Gentlemen and Poachers: The English Game Laws, 1671-1831* (Cambridge: Cambridge University Press, 1981), 118.

5 William Blackstone, *Commentaries on the Laws of England,* vol. 2, ed. A.W.B. Simpson (Chicago: University of Chicago Press, 1979), 411.

6 Thomas A. Lund, *American Wildlife Law* (Berkeley: University of California Press, 1980), 21, 24; James A. Tober, *Who Owns Wildlife? The Political Economy of Conservation in Nineteenth-Century America* (Westport, CT: Greenwood Press, 1981), 146-47.

7 Ibid., 19.

8 George Colpitts, *Game in the Garden: A Human History of Wildlife in Western Canada to 1940* (Vancouver: UBC Press, 2002), 125-27, 131.

9 Donald Dodds, *Challenge and Response: A History of Wildlife and Wildlife Management in Nova Scotia* (Halifax, NS: Department of Natural Resources, 1993), 35-36. Also see the *Reports of the Game and Inland Fishery Protection Society of Nova Scotia,* Nova Scotia Archives and Records Management (NSARM), F 90 G14 R29.

10 R.S.N.S. 1884, c. 76.

11 Dodds, *Challenge and Response,* 178-80.

12 Statutes of Nova Scotia, 36 Geo 3, c. 12 (1796).

13 R.S.N.S. 1851, c. 92, s. 3, and c. 93, s. 1.

14 R.S.N.S. 1872, c. 73, s. 25.

15 Statutes of New Brunswick, 50 Geo 3, c. 22 (1810), s. 3.

16 Statutes of Quebec, 60 Vic, c. 27 (1897); Statutes of New Brunswick, 62 Vic, c. 8 (1899); Statutes of Manitoba, 63 and 64 Vic, c. 14 (1900); Statutes of Ontario, 63 Vic, c. 49 (1900); Ordinances of the Yukon Territory, No. 2 (1901); Statutes of Saskatchewan, 3 Edw 7, c. 29 (1903); Statutes of British Columbia, 5 Edw 7, c. 25 (1905); Statutes of Alberta, 7 Edw 7, c. 14 (1907); Statutes of Nova Scotia, 8 Edw 7, c. 17 (1908).

17 Robert J. Burns with Mike Schnitz, *Guardians of the Wild: A History of the Warden Service of Canada's National Parks* (Calgary: University of Calgary Press, 2000), 6. Also see C.J. Taylor, "Legislating Nature: The National

Parks Act of 1930," in *To See Ourselves/To Save Ourselves: Ecology and Culture in Canada,* ed. Rowland Lorimer, Michael M'Gonigle, Jean-Pierre Revéret, and Sally Ross (Montreal: Association for Canadian Studies, 1991), 125-38.

18 C. Gordon Hewitt, "The Conservation of Our Northern Mammals," in Canada, Commission of Conservation, *Report of the Seventh Annual Meeting, 1916* (Montreal: Federated Press), 32-40. Statutes of Canada, 7-8 Geo 5, c. 36 (1917).

19 Foster, *Working for Wildlife,* 161-64. The members of the Advisory Board on Wild Life Protection were James White, chair of the Commission of Conservation; R.M. Anderson, who worked in the mammals division of the National Museum; J.B. Harkin, dominion commissioner of parks; Duncan Campbell Scott, deputy superintendent-general of Indian Affairs; and C. Gordon Hewitt. See C. Gordon Hewitt, "The Conservation of Wild Life in Canada in 1919: A Review," in Canada, Commission of Conservation, *Report of the Ninth Annual Meeting, 1917* (Montreal: Federated Press, 1918), 121.

20 On the American conservation movement, see Samuel P. Hays, *Conservation and the Gospel of Efficiency: The Progressive Conservation Movement, 1890-1920* (Cambridge, MA: Harvard University Press, 1959). Michel F. Girard's study of the commission lists its various members and their occupations. Although the applied sciences were certainly represented in its membership (in the form of engineers, professional foresters, and agronomists), there was also a significant number of university academics (drawn from physics, mathematics, literature, and history), as well as politicians. The subcommittee dealing with forestry was distinct, as it counted several prominent lumber merchants in its ranks. See his *L'écologisme retrouvé: Essor et déclin de la Commission de la conservation du Canada* (Ottawa: Les Presses de l'Université d'Ottawa, 1994), 91-92, 112-15, 139-40, 152-54, 178-79, and 205-7.

21 Philip P. Wells, "Conservation of Natural Resources," cited in Hays, *Conservation and the Gospel of Efficiency,* 123.

22 Girard, *L'écologisme retrouvé,* 2.

23 Colpitts, *Game in the Garden,* 129.

24 Chris H. Lewis, "Charles Elton," in *Conservation and Environmentalism: An Encyclopedia,* ed. Robert Paehlke (New York: Garland Publishing, 1995), 209.

25 Charles Elton, *Animal Ecology* (London: Sidgwick and Jackson, 1927), viii.

26 Aldo Leopold, *Game Management* (1933; repr., Madison: University of Wisconsin Press, 1986), 3.

27 Ibid., xxxiii.

28 John L. Cranmer-Byng, "A Life with Birds: Percy A. Taverner, Canadian Ornithologist, 1875-1947," Special issue, *Canadian Field-Naturalist* 110, 1 (1996). Also see J. Alexander Burnett, *A Passion for Wildlife: The History of the Canadian Wildlife Service* (Vancouver: UBC Press, 2003), 9.

29 Sabean to Chief Game Warden, 26 September 1921, NSARM, RG 20, vol. 822, file 21.

30 Burns with Schnitz, *Guardians of the Wild,* 7-8.

31 For instance, the letters of recommendation for men applying for the position of deputy game warden in British Columbia almost invariably underscored the fact that the candidate was a "keen sportsman." One, for a Mr. Fall, noted "he is a keen sportsman, very strong and athletic, stands 6ft in his socks, has been up north in Atlin, La Touche Island etc for years. I have been out myself with him prospecting for months, and know him to be a very hard man to beat in the woods." J. Musgrave to A. Bryan Williams, 28 February 1908, British Columbia Archives (BCA), GR 446, box 16, file 1. Also see GR 446, box 12, file 1, which contains letters of application for the position of deputy game warden.

32 Statutes of New Brunswick, 11 Geo 5, c. 12 (1921), s. 68.

33 Colpitts, *Game in the Garden,* ch. 5.

34 Dominion Parks Commissioner's Report, Canada, Department of the Interior, *Annual Report, 1910,* in Foster, *Working for Wildlife,* 71. Also see W.F. Lothian, *A History of Canada's National Parks,* vol. 4 (Ottawa: Minister of Supply and Services, 1981), 23-39.

35 For instance, the government of Nova Scotia established a pheasant farm near Lawrencetown in Annapolis County in 1930 to, in the words of Chief Game Warden Otto Schierbeck, "increase our attractions for the sportsmen and tourists." Otto Schierbeck's notes for the annual report, 1931, NSARM, RG 20, vol. 751, file 13.

36 Beaver and red deer were introduced to the Queen Charlottes during the First World War, and moose to Newfoundland in 1878 and 1904. McMynn to James Dunning, 16 December 1918, BCA, GR 446, box 87, file 11; and "Introduction of Exotics into British Columbia, 1956," BCA, GR 961, Scrapbook 1 of 3, which lists all the exotics imported into the province. For moose in Newfoundland, see D.H. Pimlott, "Newfoundland Moose," *Transactions of the North American Wildlife Conference,* edited by J.B. Trefethen, 563-81 (Washington, DC: Wildlife Management Institute, 1953).

37 Canada's Commission of Conservation published a manual on fur farming that noted "the hunting and trapping of wild fur-bearing animals must be supplemented by their domestication if the demand for furs is to be satisfied." J. Walter Jones, *Fur Farming in Canada,* 2nd ed. (Ottawa: Mortimer, 1914), 10.

38 George Colpitts, "Conservation, Science, and Canada's Fur Farming Industry, 1913-45," *Histoire Sociale/Social History* 30, 59 (1997): 77-107.

39 Statutes of New Brunswick, 62 Vic, c. 8 (1899), s. 39; Statutes of Saskatchewan, 3 Edw 7, c. 29 (1903), s. 18; Statutes of Alberta, 7 Edw 7, c. 13 (1907), s. 15 and 26; and Statutes of Nova Scotia, 8 Edw 7, c. 17 (1908), s. 31 (1b and 1c).

40 Statutes of British Columbia, 3 Geo 5, c. 27 (1913), s. 9 amended the Game Act, making it illegal for any resident to hunt or to carry a firearm

of any kind without first taking out a licence. On the introduction and reception of this law, see British Columbia, *Game Commission Report for the Year 1913* (Victoria: Government Printer, 1914), N6-N7.

41 Patricia A. McCormack, "The Political Economy of Bison Management in Wood Buffalo National Park," *Arctic* 45, 4 (1992): 367-80.

42 Richard West Sellers, *Preserving Nature in the National Parks: A History* (New Haven: Yale University Press, 1977), 57.

43 Arthur J. Ray, *The Canadian Fur Trade in the Industrial Age* (Toronto: University of Toronto Press, 1995), 116-17. For British Columbia, see Brenda Ireland, "'Working a Great Hardship on Us': First Nations People, the State, and Fur Conservation in British Columbia before 1935" (master's thesis, University of British Columbia, 1995).

44 Statutes of Ontario, 63-64 Vic, c. 49 (1900), s. 8 (4) and 9 (1); Statutes of Nova Scotia, 8 Edw 7, c. 17 (1908), s. 6 and 12 (1); and Statutes of Saskatchewan, 3 Edw 7, c. 29 (1903), s. 8 and 9 (1).

45 See for instance, Statutes of British Columbia, 4 Geo 5, c. 33 (1914), s. 15, which made it unlawful to have a pump or repeating shotgun with a magazine capable of holding more than one cartridge, or an automatic shotgun of any kind.

46 W.T. Hornaday, "Rational Use of Game Animals," *National Conference on Conservation of Game, Fur-Bearing Animals and Other Wild Life, 1919* (Ottawa, 1919), 64.

47 Ibid., 69.

48 For instance, Statutes of Alberta, 7 Edw 7, c. 13 (1907), s. 16; and Statutes of Ontario, 63-64 Vic, c. 49 (1900), s. 15 (2) and 13 (3).

49 Statutes of Nova Scotia, 8 Edw 7, c. 17 (1908), s. 9.

50 For instance, Statutes of Saskatchewan, 6 Geo 5, c. 75 (1916), s. 14; and Statutes of British Columbia, 4 Geo 5, c. 33 (1914), s. 34 (1).

51 For instance, see Statutes of Manitoba, 63-64 Vic, c. 14 (1900), s. 31; Statutes of Ontario, 63-64 Vic, c. 49 (1900), s. 31 (2); Statutes of British Columbia, 5 Edw 7, c. 25 (1905), s. 6; and Statutes of Alberta, 7 Edw 7, c. 13 (1907), s. 28.

52 Robert G. McCandless, "Trophies or Meat: Yukon Game Management, 1896-1976," (unpublished report, 7 January 1976, 36).

53 Sportsman's creed or code of ethics was written by W.T. Hornaday in 1908 and reproduced in Hewitt, *The Conservation of the Wild Life of Canada,* 298-99; and in the Canadian Pacific Railway's (CPR) tourist brochure, *Fishing and Shooting along the Lines of the Canadian Pacific Railway* (Montreal: Canadian Pacific Railway Company, 1904).

54 Hewitt, *The Conservation of the Wild Life of Canada,* 298.

55 Ibid.

56 Ibid., 299.

57 "Report on Proposed Reserve on Vancouver Island, by A. Bryan Williams," in Williams to the Attorney General, 19 July 1907, BCA, GR 446, box 14, file 2.

58 Lothian, *A History of Canada's National Parks,* vol. 4, 17.

59 Ibid., 18.
60 Foster, *Working for Wildlife*, 56.
61 Lothian, *A History of Canada's National Parks*, vol. 4, 18-19.
62 Burns with Schnitz, *Guardians of the Wild*, 78.
63 Ibid., 78-79.
64 Much of what follows is drawn from Tina Loo, "Making a Modern Wilderness: Conserving Wildlife in Twentieth Century Canada," *Canadian Historical Review* 82, 1 (2001): 92-121. More generally, see Altmeyer, "Three Ideas of Nature in Canada, 1893-1914."
65 The Doctor, "The Look-em Deer Club at Play," *Rod and Gun in Canada*, January 1908, 711.
66 See T.J. Jackson Lears, *No Place of Grace: Antimodernism and the Transformation of American Culture, 1880-1920* (Chicago: University of Chicago Press, 1981); and Ian McKay, *The Quest of the Folk: Antimodernism and Cultural Selection in Twentieth-Century Nova Scotia* (Montreal and Kingston: McGill-Queen's University Press, 1994).
67 Patricia Jasen, *Wild Things: Nature, Culture, and Tourism in Ontario, 1790-1914* (Toronto: University of Toronto Press, 1995).
68 W.E. Playfair, "The 'Simple Life' on the Rideau," *Rod and Gun in Canada*, September 1905, 403. Also see Altmeyer, "Three Ideas of Nature in Canada, 1893-1914," 98-105.
69 L.O. Armstrong, "Boredom and One of Its Antidotes," *Rod and Gun in Canada*, October 1904, 241.
70 Wahnipitae, "A Woman on the Mississauga," *Rod and Gun in Canada*, October 1904, 221.
71 On the relationship between manliness and civilization, see Gail Bederman's book of the same name, *Manliness and Civilization: A Cultural History of Gender and Race in the United States, 1880-1917* (Chicago: University of Chicago Press, 1995); and E. Anthony Rotundo, *American Manhood: Transformations in Masculinity from the Revolution to the Modern Era* (New York: Basic Books, 1993), 227-32, 252-54.
72 Thomas Johnson, "Nature's Elixir – And It Is Not Work," *Rod and Gun in Canada*, January 1908, 736.
73 *The Saguenay Club, Fifth Season, 1915* (Quebec, 1915), 7. McLennan Library Rare Book Division, McGill University.
74 "The Haunts of Big Game," *Rod and Gun in Canada*, October 1905, 503.
75 *Prospectus of the Triton Fish and Game Club* (Quebec, 1894), 14. McLennan Library Rare Book Division, McGill University. For more on Triton Club members, see Paul-Louis Martin, *La chasse au Québec* (Montreal: Boréal, 1990), 106-14.
76 E.E., "Notes by E.E.," *Rod and Gun in Canada*, September 1900, 331.
77 A.L. Phelps, "In the Woods," *Rod and Gun in Canada*, February 1905, 492.
78 Emphasis in the original. Dr. Franklin Hawley, "Scientific Deer-Hunting," *Rod and Gun in Canada*, October 1906, 324.
79 Altmeyer, "Three Ideas of Nature," 100.

80 Ibid., 114n28.
81 On the role of the Canadian Pacific Railway (CPR) in creating a particular identity for Canada built around its scenery, see E.J. Hart, *The Selling of Canada* (Banff: Altitude Publishing, 1983).
82 Bill Parenteau, "Angling, Hunting and the Development of Tourism in Late Nineteenth Century Canada: A Glimpse at the Documentary Record," *Archivist* 117 (1998): 10-19.
83 Cited in Colpitts, *Game in the Garden,* 133.
84 Hewitt, *The Conservation of the Wild Life of Canada,* 15.
85 Ibid.
86 Ibid.
87 John Jervis argues that modernity is a "project" characterized by "an orientation to rational and purposive control of the environment, both natural and social." A key part of the modern project entails the reconstruction of humans "as appropriate subjects that can carry on this process." See his *Exploring the Modern: Patterns of Western Culture and Civilization* (London: Blackwell, 1998), 6.

CHAPTER 2: MAKE WAY FOR WILDLIFE

1 Wilson to Williams, 24 May 1913, British Columbia Archives (BCA), GR 446, box 41, file 5.
2 "Spring Shooting," *Rod and Gun in Canada,* November 1906, 461.
3 Saulnier to Knight, 1 August 1921, Nova Scotia Archives and Records Management (NSARM), RG 20, vol. 825, file 4.
4 Third Report of the Provincial Game and Forest Warden of the Province of British Columbia, 1907, BCA, GR 446, box 17, file 2.
5 "First Report of the Ontario Fish and Game Commission, 1892," in *Ontario Sessional Papers, 1893* (Toronto: Government Printer, 1893), 63-64.
6 Rourke to Commissioner of Forests and Game, 12 December 1925, NSARM, RG 20, vol. 830, file 34.
7 Foster to Bowser, 1 November 1913, BCA, GR 446, box 38, file 7.
8 Cross to Department of Lands and Forests, 12 September 1934, NSARM, RG 20, vol. 613, file 12.
9 Statutes of New Brunswick, 11 Geo 5, c. 12 (1921), s. 65.
10 Jackson to Department of Lands and Forests, 1 December 1930, NSARM, RG 20, vol. 732, file 13.
11 Williams to Bowser, 27 February 1908 and 3 February 1908, BCA, GR 446, box 16, file 3.
12 Ibid.; and Williams to Fulton, 7 September 1907, BCA, GR 446, box 14, file 2.
13 "Eighth Annual Report of the Game and Fisheries Department, 1914," in *Ontario Sessional Papers, 1915, No. 14* (Toronto: Government Printer), 27.
14 Harrison to Williams, 13 September 1905, BCA, GR 446, box 12, file 3.

15 Williams to Fulton, 23 October 1908, BCA, GR 446, box 17, file 3; Williams to Bowser, n.d. [1910], BCA, GR 446, box 25, file 2; and Junget to Harrison, 27 April 1934, NSARM, RG 20, vol. 612, file 29.

16 Petition of the Calgary Rod and Gun Club to the Minister of the Interior and the Superintendent-General of Indian Affairs, 3 February 1893, Library and Archives Canada (LAC), RG 10, vol. 6732, file 420-2. Similar petitions from the other rod and gun clubs are included with this one.

17 "Killing Off the Big Game," clipping included with letter from Inspector Markle dated 20 November 1905, which was included in Campbell to the Deputy Superintendent General, Memorandum, 1 December 1905, LAC, RG 10, vol. 3855, file 80,143. As George Colpitts points out, Brewster was being somewhat disingenuous. At the same time that he was pointing a finger at the Stoney for the decline in wildlife, Brewster himself and his family's trading company were doing their part in "cleaning the country." Not only was he credited with killing 150 grizzlies, but he also made a tidy profit helping his clients exact a toll on mountain wildlife. George Colpitts, *Game in the Garden: A Human History of Wildlife in Western Canada to 1940* (Vancouver: UBC Press, 2002), 153.

18 Moore to Oliver, 25 May 1905, LAC, RG 10, vol. 6732, file 420-2.

19 Canada, Commission of Conservation, *National Conference on Conservation of Game, Fur-Bearing Animals and Other Wildlife under the Direction of the Commission of Conservation with the Cooperation of the Advisory Board on Wild Life Protection, February 18 and 19, 1919* (Ottawa: J. de Labroquerie, 1919), 22-23.

20 Ibid., 29-30.

21 Colpitts, *Game in the Garden,* 153-55.

22 Petition to E. Bell (Agent), Lillooet, 19 September 1905, LAC, RG 10, vol. 6735, file 420-3.

23 Secretary of the Royal Commission on Indian Affairs for British Columbia to the Attorney General of British Columbia, 18 February 1914, LAC, RG 10, vol. 11020, file 516.

24 Lawton to Finley, 24 November 1908, LAC, RG 10, vol. 6732, file 420-2A.

25 Frank Tough, "Conservation and the Indian: Clifford Sifton's Commission of Conservation, 1910-1919," *Native Studies Review* 8, 1 (1992): 68.

26 Circular Letter to Various Indian Agents and Inspectors of Indian Agencies, 28 April 1914 from Bryan Williams, LAC, RG 10, vol. 11,020, file 516.

27 Petition of the Chiefs of Stuart Lake, Stony Creek, and Fraser Lake tribes to the Superintendent of Indian Affairs, 30 October 1905, LAC, RG 10, vol. 6735, file 420-3.

28 Robert G. McCandless, "Trophies or Meat: Yukon Game Management, 1896-1976," Report dated 7 January 1976, held by the Government of the Yukon, Department of Renewable Resources, 36-37.

29 McLean to Williams, 6 March 1917, and the correspondence that follows in the file, LAC, RG 10, vol. 6735, file 420-3.

30 J.F. Smith, Special Report, 2 November 1921, LAC, RG 10, vol. 6735, file 420-3A.

31 Mark David Spence, *Dispossessing the Wilderness: Indian Removal and the Making of the National Parks* (New York: Oxford University Press, 1999).

32 Memorandum, "Condition of Hunting Indians in Remote Districts," n.d., LAC, RG 10, vol. 6731, file 420-1.

33 On Aboriginals in Wood Buffalo, see Patricia A. McCormack, "The Political Economy of Bison Management in Wood Buffalo National Park," *Arctic* 45, 4 (1992): 367–80.

34 McDougal to Finnie, 3 July 1926, LAC, RG 10, vol. 6732, file 420-2B.

35 LaViolette to Chief of the Indian Department, 20 February 1927, LAC, RG 10, vol. 6732, file 420-2B.

36 Assistant Secretary of the Royal Commission on Indian Affairs for British Columbia to Williams, 29 July 1914, LAC, RG 10, vol. 11,020, file 516.

37 Carter to Bradbury, 16 January 1917, LAC, RG 10, vol. 6731, file 420-1.

38 Petition from Indians of Stuart Lake Agency, 1919, LAC, RG 10, vol. 6735, file 420-3A.

39 Petition of the Chiefs of Stuart Lake, Stony Creek, and Fraser Lake tribes to Superintendent of Indian Affairs, 30 October 1905, LAC, RG 10, vol. 6735, file 420-3.

40 C. Gordon Hewitt, *The Conservation of the Wild Life of Canada* (New York: Charles Scribner's Sons, 1921), 296.

41 Stiles to Chief Game Commissioner, 5 November 1929, NSARM, RG 20, vol. 727, file 27.

42 Brown to Schierbeck, 15 April 1929, and Schierbeck to Brown, 23 April 1929, NSARM, RG 20, vol. 727, file 27.

43 Clarke to Goucher, 2 March 1926, NSARM, RG 20, vol. 718, file 4.

44 Schierbeck to *Halifax Herald,* 27 February 1928, NSARM, RG 20, vol. 746, file 12.

45 "I have it on good authority that these boys shot their moose and then come up and got their licences (some joke ha)," reported Warden George Goudey in 1921. Goudey to Knight, 19 January 1921, NSARM, RG 20, vol. 822, file 12.

46 Adams to Chief Commissioner of Forests and Game, 4 November 1921, NSARM, RG 20, vol. 820, file 3.

47 "One who wishes the game protected" to Chief Commissioner, 1 October 1924, NSARM, RG 20, vol. 827, file 42.

48 Osborne to Knight, 2 September 1921, NSARM, RG 20, vol. 824, file 42.

49 Smith to Clarke, 8 April 1925, NSARM, RG 20, vol. 826, file 69.

50 Lockwood to Cushing, 7 December 1926, NSARM, RG 20, vol. 719, file 1.

51 Goudey to Knight, 22 February 1922, NSARM, RG 20, vol. 822, file 12.

52 L.O. Armstrong, passenger agent for the CPR and sportsman, told the North American Fish and Game Protective Association meeting at Saint John that "labour organizations have come out strongly against all preserves held by clubs or private individuals." See "How Best to Form Public Opinion as to the Need of Fish and Game Protective Laws," *Rod*

and Gun in Canada, March 1905, 543-44. Ontario's chief game warden, Edward Tinsley, told the League of American Sportsmen in Buffalo that he was "opposed to wealthy men being allowed to obtain possession of large portions of the public domain for game preserves to the exclusion of the general public. The hunting and fishing instinct is as strongly inherent in the men who constitute the backbone and sinew of our respective countries as it is in the millionaires." See "Spring Shooting," *Rod and Gun in Canada,* November 1906, 460. On local opposition to private preserves in British Columbia, see British Columbia, Legislative Assembly, Annual Reports of the Game Commissioner, British Columbia Sessional Papers (BCSP) 1928, J32; BCSP 1930, H28; BCSP 1931, D28-9; BCSP 1945, W9; and BCSP 1946, GG10. On one particular conflict over the creation of a private preserve in Nova Scotia, see "Medicine Bag," *Rod and Gun in Canada,* January 1908, 770. On another in New Brunswick, see "Hunting and Fishing in New Brunswick: The Attempt to Organize a Private Preserve, and the Government's Action Thereon," *Rod and Gun in Canada,* November 1906, 499-500.

53 Daniel Samson, ed., *Contested Countryside: Rural Workers and Modern Society in Atlantic Canada, 1800-1950* (Fredericton, NB: Acadiensis Press for the Gorsebrook Institute for Atlantic Canadian Studies, 1994), introduction.

54 Allan Swinton, "Business," *Maclean's Magazine,* 14 April 1928, 5.

55 These themes are explored at greater length in Tina Loo, "Of Moose and Men: Hunting for Masculinities in British Columbia, 1880-1939," *Western Historical Quarterly* 32, 3 (2001): 296-319.

56 Robert G. McCandless, *Yukon Wildlife: A Social History* (Edmonton: University of Alberta Press, 1985), 59-60.

57 Ibid., 60.

58 Johnnie Johns and Son, *Big Game Hunting in the Yukon,* ca. 1960. Pamphlet, Yukon Archives, PAM ND-0342.

59 Cited in Robert G. McCandless, *Yukon Wildlife: A Social History* (Edmonton: University of Alberta Press, 1985), 60.

60 Ibid.

61 Catharine McClellan, *My Old People Say: An Ethnographic Survey of Southern Yukon Territory, Part 1* (Ottawa: National Museum of Man Publications, 1975), 89-90.

62 Constitution and By-laws of the Nova Scotia Guides' Association, 1920. Cited in Mike Parker, *Guides of the North Woods: Hunting and Fishing Tales from Nova Scotia, 1860-1960* (Halifax: Nimbus Publishing, 1990), 165.

63 Creighton Balcomb interview, in Parker, *Guides of the North Woods,* 210.

64 Ibid.

65 Cited in Parker, *Guides of the North Woods,* 187.

66 Cited in Parker, *Guides of the North Woods,* 184.

67 Ibid., 194.

CHAPTER 3: THE DOMINION OF FATHER GOOSE

1 Janet Foster, *Working for Wildlife: The Beginning of Preservation in Canada* (Toronto: University of Toronto Press, 1978), 3-4.
2 http://www.jackminer.com.
3 Manly Forest Miner, preface to *Wild Goose Jack,* by Jack Miner, rev. ed. (1969; repr., Richmond Hill, ON: Simon and Schuster, 1971), 8.
4 Ibid., 7.
5 Ibid., 14.
6 Ibid., 8.
7 Fred Bodsworth, "Billy Sunday of the Birds," *Maclean's Magazine,* 1 May 1952, 12.
8 Manly Miner, preface to *Wild Goose Jack,* 9.
9 Ibid., 14.
10 H.R. Wade, "Jack Miner," *Wild Goose Jack,* 29.
11 John B. Kennedy, "Jack Miner," *Colliers,* 3 December 1927; and "Ancient Greek Doctrine Is Unconsciously Voiced by Sage of Kingsville," *Toronto Globe,* 14 June 1926, reprinted in *Wild Goose Jack,* 15 and 29.
12 Ibid., 30.
13 Ibid., 31.
14 Bodsworth, "Billy Sunday of the Birds," 12.
15 James M. Linton and Calvin W. Moore, foreword to *The Story of Wild Goose Jack: The Life and Work of Jack Miner* (Toronto: CBC Enterprises, 1984), 7.
16 Cited in Linton and Moore, *Story of Wild Goose Jack,* 153.
17 Genesis 1:26.
18 Jack Miner, *Jack Miner and the Birds and Some Things I Know about Nature* (1923; repr., Chicago: Reilly and Lee, 1925), 33.
19 Manly F. Miner, "The 'Experts' Are Getting in My Hair," *Forest and Outdoors,* November 1948, 30.
20 Jack Miner, *Wild Goose Jack,* 57.
21 Ibid., 59-60.
22 Ibid., 5.
23 "Report of the Commissions Appointed to Collect Information upon the Game and Fish of the Province of Ontario," in *Sessional Paper No. 79,* 55 Vic (1892), 192.
24 Jack Miner, *Jack Miner and the Birds,* 5.
25 Ibid.
26 Jack Miner, *Wild Goose Jack,* 88-96; Jack Miner, *Jack Miner and the Birds,* 174.
27 Richard White, "'Are You an Environmentalist or Do You Work for a Living?' Work and Nature," in *Uncommon Ground: Rethinking the Human Place in Nature,* ed. William Cronon (New York: W.W. Norton and Company, 1996), 174-78.
28 Norman S. Rankin, "Jack Miner, Philosopher and Bird-Lover," *Canadian Magazine,* October 1922, 480.

29 Jack Miner, *Wild Goose Jack*, 49.
30 Rankin, "Jack Miner, Philosopher and Bird-Lover," 480.
31 Jack Miner, "Some Original Sayings of Jack Miner," *Wild Goose Jack*, back cover.
32 Jack Miner, *Jack Miner and the Birds*, 95-96.
33 Margaret Wade, cited in Manly Forest Miner, preface to *Wild Goose Jack*, 13.
34 Jack Miner, *Jack Miner and the Birds*, 96-97.
35 Manly F. Miner, "We Must Control the Timber Wolf," *Canadian Forest and Outdoors*, November 1949, 16.
36 Jack Miner, *Jack Miner and the Birds*, 69. The directive was probably from Ecclesiastes 10:20, which, according to Margaret Wade, "was often quoted by Jack Miner as being specially apt for his banding work." The passage reads: "And the bird of the air shall carry the voice, and that which hath wings tell the matter." See Margaret Wade, "'No Man Starts Living Until He Starts Believing,'" *Forest and Outdoors*, April 1949, 12.
37 The cartoon is undated. Jack Miner Papers, Archives of Ontario (AO), MU 7678.
38 Taverner to Swales, 22 February 1919, cited in John L. Cranmer-Byng, "A Life with Birds: Percy A. Taverner, Canadian Ornithologist, 1875-1947," Special issue, *Canadian Field-Naturalist* 110, 1 (1996): 99.
39 Bodsworth, "Billy Sunday of the Birds," 56.
40 Manly F. Miner, "We Must Provide Safety Zones and Food for Our Game Birds," *Forest and Outdoors*, October 1948, 8.
41 For an introduction, see Douglas L. Medin and Scott Atran, introduction to *Folkbiology*, ed. Douglas L. Medin and Scott Atran (Cambridge, MA: MIT Press, 1999). Scholars of folk biology are interested in the relationship between folk and scientific taxonomies, and in whether folk taxonomies are culturally dependent or universal.
42 Jack Miner, *Jack Miner and the Birds*, 18, 45.
43 Ibid., 45.
44 Ibid., 46.
45 Ibid., 37.
46 Ibid., 62.
47 Ibid., 101-4.
48 Ibid., 127; see 124-27 for "The Career of Jack Johnson."
49 Ibid., 128.
50 Ibid., 62.
51 Ibid., 128.
52 Ibid., 113.
53 Paul A. Johnsgard, *Waterfowl of North America* (Bloomington and London: Indiana University Press, 1975), 232.
54 Ibid., 226.
55 Ibid., 138.
56 Ibid., 141.
57 Cited in ibid., 138.

58 Miner, *Jack Miner and the Birds,* 107.
59 Ibid., 22, 27.
60 Ibid., 28-29.
61 Ibid., 44.
62 Ibid., 28.
63 A.W. Schorger, *The Passenger Pigeon: Its Natural History and Extinction* (Norman: University of Oklahoma Press, 1973), 199-205.
64 Jack Miner, *Wild Goose Jack,* 218.
65 Ibid., 222-23.
66 Ibid., 159.
67 Ibid., 157.
68 Ibid., 163.
69 Ibid., 166.
70 Jack Miner, introduction to *Jack Miner and the Birds,* v.
71 Lisa Mighetto, *Wild Animals and American Environmental Ethics* (Tucson: University of Arizona Press, 1991), 16.
72 Jack Miner, *Jack Miner and the Birds,* ch. 26 and 114-15.
73 Ibid., 13-14, 20.
74 Robert H. MacDonald, "The Revolt against Instinct: The Animal Stories of Seton and Roberts," *Canadian Literature* 84 (1980): 18-29.
75 Jack Miner, *Jack Miner and the Birds,* 128.
76 Jack Miner, *Wild Goose Jack,* 156.
77 Ibid., ch. 8; and Jack Miner, *Jack Miner and the Birds,* 58.
78 Jack Miner, *Jack Miner and the Birds,* 53.
79 Cited in Linton and Moore, *Story of Wild Goose Jack,* 41.
80 Ralph H. Lutts, *The Nature Fakers: Wildlife, Science, and Sentiment* (Golden, CO: Fulcrum, 1990).
81 The exception is a popular piece by Peter Unwin. See "The Man Who Would Have Dominion," *Beaver,* October-November 2001, 28-35.
82 Cited in Cranmer-Byng, "Life with Birds," 193.
83 Manly F. Miner, "The 'Experts' Are Getting in My Hair," *Forest and Outdoors,* November 1948, 30.
84 R.O.M., "Review of *Jack Miner and the Birds,*" *Canadian Field-Naturalist* 38 (1924): 59.
85 "Editorial – Bird Sanctuaries," *Canadian Field-Naturalist* 37 (1923): 149.
86 Speck to Editor, 11 December 1923, *Canadian Field-Naturalist* 38 (1924): 34-35.
87 "Editorial – Bird Sanctuaries," 149.
88 Townsend to Editor, 14 January 1924, *Canadian Field-Naturalist* 38 (1924): 35.
89 The phrase was Speck's. See Speck to Editor, 11 December 1923, *Canadian Field-Naturalist* 38 (1924): 34.
90 "Editorial – Bird Sanctuaries," 150.
91 Manly Miner, "We Must Control the Timber Wolf," 17.
92 Manly Miner, "The 'Experts' Are Getting in My Hair," 12.
93 Margaret Wade, "Jack Miner's Philosophy," *Forest and Outdoors,* April 1948, 18.

94 Manly Miner, "The 'Experts' Are Getting in My Hair," 12; and Alan B. Baker, "Facts on the Balance of Nature," *Forest and Outdoors,* October 1955, 24.

95 Manly Miner, "We Must Control the Timber Wolf," 18.

96 Brooks to Editor, 25 January 1924, *Canadian Field-Naturalist* 38 (1924): 33.

97 Rowan to Editor, 19 January 1924, *Canadian Field-Naturalist* 38 (1924): 32-33.

98 Cranmer-Byng, "Life with Birds," 167. On ornithology as a particularly inclusive science and the reliance of professional ornithologists on amateurs, see Mark V. Barrow Jr., *A Passion for Birds: American Ornithology after Audubon* (Princeton, NJ: Princeton University Press, 1998), 5-6.

99 Taverner to Miner, 10 February 1926, Percy Taverner Papers, Canadian Museum of Nature (CMN), CMNAC/1991-021, box 13.

100 Taverner to Miner, 10 February 1926, Percy Taverner Papers, CMN, CMNAC/1991-021, box 13.

101 Cranmer-Byng, "Life with Birds," 168.

102 Taverner to Miner, 1 December 1926, Percy Taverner Papers, CMN, CMNAC/1991-021, box 13.

103 Taverner to Miner, 22 February 1926, Percy Taverner Papers, CMN, CMNAC/1991-021, box 13.

104 Taverner to Miner, 22 February 1926, Percy Taverner Papers, CMN, CMNAC/1991-021, box 13.

105 Taverner to Miner, 26 February 1926, Percy Taverner Papers, CMN, CMNAC/1991-021, box 13.

106 The Miners had taken pains to build Jack's reputation, and they were quite astute about managing public opinion to serve their own purposes. In this context, it is not surprising that they took Taverner's comments to heart. Writing in response to Taverner's request for specimens from Jack's traps, Manly noted that up to that point they had buried the dead birds to avoid "a big controversy ... over Jack Miner killing hawks and owls. You get my idea." Similarly, the Miners were careful not to let the public know the extent of their crow kill. "Had we told the press the exact number of thousands we killed there would sure have been a big yell," he confided to Taverner in 1926. "We killed enough last winter to fertilize a 5 acre field. They make great fertilizer." See Manly Miner to Taverner, 19 November 1926 and 13 April 1926, Percy Taverner Papers, CMN, CMNAC/1991-021, box 13.

107 Manly Miner to Taverner, 2 December 1926, Percy Taverner Papers, CMN, CMNAC/1991-021, box 13.

108 Manly F. Miner, "Jack Miner, His Philosophy and Reasoning" (1968), 16, Jack Miner Papers, AO, MU 7678.

109 Unwin, "The Man Who Would Have Dominion," 33.

110 "Bird Banding in Canada," *Forest and Outdoors,* April 1951, 22-24.

111 Linton and Moore, *Story of Wild Goose Jack,* 111-12.

112 Cited in Cranmer-Byng, "Life with Birds," 168.

113 Taverner to Miner, 12 December 1926, Percy Taverner Papers, CMN, CMNAC/1991-021, box 13.

114 Cited in Cranmer-Byng, "Life with Birds," 168.

115 Ibid.

116 Ibid.

117 "Bird Banding in Canada," 23.

118 Marianne Ainley, "The Contribution of the Amateur to North American Ornithology," *Living Bird* 18 (1979): 169.

CHAPTER 4: THE HUDSON'S BAY COMPANY AND SCIENTIFIC CONSERVATION

1 Charles S. Elton, *Voles, Mice and Lemmings: Problems in Population Dynamics* (Oxford: Clarendon Press, 1942).

2 See Stuart Houston, Tim Ball, and Mary Houston, *Eighteenth-Century Naturalists of Hudson Bay* (Montreal and Kingston: McGill-Queen's University Press, 2003); and Debra Lindsay, *Science and the Subarctic: Trappers, Traders, and the Smithsonian Institution* (Washington, DC: Smithsonian Institution Press, 1993).

3 Arthur J. Ray, "Some Conservation Schemes of the Hudson's Bay Company, 1821-50: An Examination of the Problems of Resource Management in the Fur Trade," *Journal of Historical Geography* 1, 1 (1975): 67.

4 For a discussion of some of the indigenous conservation measures, see Georgiana Ball, "The Monopoly System of Wildlife Management of the Indians and the Hudson's Bay Company in the Early History of British Columbia," *BC Studies,* no. 66 (1985): 37-58; and Charles Bishop and Toby Morantz, eds., "Who Owns the Beaver? Northern Algonquian Land Tenure Reconsidered," Special issue, *Anthropologica* 18, 1-2 (1986).

5 Ray, "Some Conservation Schemes of the Hudson's Bay Company," 50.

6 John S. Galbraith, "Sir George Simpson," *Dictionary of Canadian Biography Online,* http://www.biographi.ca.

7 Ray, "Some Conservation Schemes of the Hudson's Bay Company," 51.

8 Ibid., 51-54.

9 Daniel Francis and Toby Morantz, *Partners in Furs: A History of the Fur Trade in Eastern James Bay, 1600-1870* (Montreal and Kingston: McGill-Queen's University Press, 1983), 129.

10 "Beaver Chief," *Beaver,* September 1944, 44.

11 Glyndwr Williams, "Peter Skene Ogden," *Dictionary of Canadian Biography Online,* http://www.biographi.ca.

12 Cited in Lorne Hammond, "Marketing Wildlife: The Hudson's Bay Company and the Pacific Northwest, 1821-49," *Forest and Conservation History* 37 (1993): 17.

13 Cited in Ray, "Some Conservation Schemes of the Hudson's Bay Company," 53-54.

14 Houston, Ball, and Houston, *Eighteenth-Century Naturalists of Hudson Bay,* 97.

15 Hammond, "Marketing Wildlife," 18.

16 Cited in ibid.

17 Ibid.

18 Ibid.

19 *British Journal of Experimental Biology* 2 (1924): 119-63.

20 C. Gordon Hewitt, *The Conservation of the Wild Life of Canada* (New York: Charles Scribner's Sons, 1921), 213-34.

21 The Hudson's Bay Company's records remain the most complete information available on an animal population, second only to those for Baltic herring fisheries. See Houston, Ball, and Houston, *Eighteenth-Century Naturalists of Hudson Bay,* 182. Although the HBC records have been invaluable in the study of fur-bearer population dynamics, they are not without their shortcomings. See Lloyd B. Keith, *Wildlife's Ten-Year Cycle* (Madison: University of Wisconsin Press, 1963), 9-12.

22 Charles Elton, "Periodic Fluctuations in the Number of Animals: Their Causes and Effects," *British Journal of Experimental Biology* 2 (1924): 121.

23 Keith was quoting zoologist William Rowan. See *Wildlife's Ten-Year Cycle,* 116.

24 Ibid., 102-7.

25 Elton, "Periodic Fluctuations," 152.

26 Elton was not the first to use the HBC's fur returns to plot the periodicity of wildlife cycles. But he was the first to make the most systematic use of them, and, it appears, the first scientist to be supported financially by a grant from the company. See Houston, Ball, and Houston, *Eighteenth-Century Naturalists of Hudson Bay,* appendix D.

27 Lindsay, *Science and the Subarctic,* 42.

28 Houston, Ball, and Houston, *Eighteenth-Century Naturalists of Hudson Bay,* introduction.

29 Ibid., 12, and ch. 10.

30 Ibid., 177.

31 Peter Crowcroft, *Elton's Ecologists: A History of the Bureau of Animal Population* (Chicago: University of Chicago Press, 1991).

32 Sir Alister Hardy, "Charles Elton's Influence in Ecology," *Journal of Animal Ecology* 37 (1968): 3.

33 Ibid.

34 Charles Elton, *Animal Ecology* (London: Sidgwick and Jackson, 1927), 168.

35 Dennis Chitty, "The Canadian Arctic Wild Life Enquiry, 1938-39," *Journal of Animal Ecology* 9 (1939): 227.

36 For more details on these questionnaires, see Keith, *Wildlife's Ten-Year Cycle,* 13-18.

37 Ellsworth Huntington, ed., *Matamek Conference on Biological Cycles* (Labrador, 1932), 21.

38 Governor and Committee of the Hudson's Bay Company to Elton, 18 February 1931, Correspondence between C. Sale and C.S. Elton, Hudson's Bay Company Archives (HBCA), A.92/260/1.

39 Cited in Huntington, *Matamek Conference on Biological Cycles,* 21.

40 Huntington, *Matamek Conference on Biological Cycles,* 15.

41 Denmark to Parsons, 8 November 1939, Correspondence Files, Northern Stores Department – Fur Preserves, January 1933-November 1946, HBCA, RG 2/8/540.
42 J.W. Anderson, "Report on Beaver Conservation in James Bay District," March 1936, Fur Trade Conference Minutes, HBCA, RG 2/62/6.
43 Donald E. Denmark, "James Bay Beaver Conservation," *Beaver,* September 1948, 40.
44 Watt to Parsons, 17 August 1932, James Watt Papers, Archives of Ontario (AO), F 431 (MU 1385).
45 James Watt considered the advances paid out by the company to be its "contribution towards fur conservation – the Indian sure of his living did not hunt to capacity"; Ibid.
46 Cited in Toby Morantz, *The White Man's Gonna Getcha: The Colonial Challenge to the Crees in Quebec* (Montreal and Kingston: McGill-Queen's University Press, 2002), 158.
47 Opening Remarks – Letter from the Governor of the Hudson's Bay Company read by Ralph Parsons, Fur Trade Commissioner, November 1932, Fur Trade Conference Minutes, HBCA, RG 2/62/2.
48 Cited in Morantz, *White Man's Gonna Getcha,* 110.
49 The issue of what Cree land tenure was before and after contact is controversial. Many, like John Cooper, argued that the Cree had a system of "private" ownership that existed prior to European contact. Subsequently, anthropologists have made the case that private ownership was not "traditional," but rather came about as a result of contact. See Shepard Krech III, *The Ecological Indian: Myth and History* (New York: W.W. Norton, 1999) for an overview.
50 Rev. John M. Cooper, "Aboriginal Land Holding Systems," Appendix E, 1933, 2, Fur Trade Conference Minutes, HBCA, RG 2/62/3.
51 Ibid.
52 J.W. Anderson, "Beaver Sanctuary," *Beaver,* June 1937, 8-9
53 Ibid., 9.
54 Garrett Hardin, "The Tragedy of the Commons," *Science* 162 (December 1968), 1243-48.
55 Cooper, "Aboriginal Land Holding Systems," 7.
56 Watt to West, 17 August 1929, James Watt Papers, AO, F 431 (MU 1385).
57 Morantz, *White Man's Gonna Getcha,* 158-60. Also see Richard to Parsons, 17 March 1932, James Watt Papers, AO, F 431 (MU 1385).
58 J.W. Anderson, "7000 Square Miles of Beaver Sanctuary," *Beaver,* June 1934, 18.
59 Ibid.
60 Ibid.
61 D.E. Denmark, "James Bay Beaver Conservation," *Beaver,* September 1948, 39.
62 "Beaver Chief," *Beaver,* September 1944, 44.
63 Anderson, "Beaver Sanctuary," 11.
64 Information on the HBC's fur preserves is from Denmark to Parsons, 8

November 1939, Correspondence Files, Northern Stores Department – Fur Preserves, January 1933-November 1946, HBCA, RG 2/8/540; Denmark to Ryan, 24 September 1940, ibid.; and J.W. Anderson, "Report on Beaver Conservation in James Bay District," March 1936, Fur Trade Conference Minutes, HBCA, RG 2/62/6.

65 In setting family quotas, Donald Denmark, the supervisor of the company's preserves, asked the manager of Waswanipi Post for "the names of grown-up sons not counted as minors, the ages of all the trappers, ... widowers if there are any and give any other pertinent information which would be useful in deciding the number of beaver to be allowed each man." 15 November 1946, Beaver Sanctuaries, 1943-1962, Correspondence Files, HBCA, RG 7/1/1009.

66 Denmark to Parsons, 6 May 1940, Correspondence Files, Northern Stores Department – Fur Preserves, January 1933-November 1946, HBCA, RG 2/8/540.

67 Ibid. Also see R.H.G. Bonnycastle to the Governor and Committee, 17 August 1943, Northern Stores Department – Fur Preserves, January 1933-November 1946, Correspondence Files, HBCA, RG 2/8/540.

68 Annual Report, 13 February 1948, Manager's Reports, Annual Reports – Years Ending 31 January 1945-31 January 1950, HBCA, RG 3/67A/1, 5; Annual Report, 28 February 1949, Manager's Reports, Annual Reports – Years Ending 31 January 1945-31 January 1950, HBCA, RG 3/67A/1, 4; and Annual Report, 15 February 1950, Manager's Reports, Annual Reports – Years Ending 31 January 1945-31 January 1950, HBCA, RG 3/67A/1, 6.

69 "Experiment at Steeprock," *Beaver,* June 1939, 10-11; Donald Denmark, "Conservation at Cumberland," *Beaver,* March 1940, 47.

70 McKinnie to District Manager, 5 June 1939, Fur Conservation, 1938-64, Correspondence Files, HBCA, RG 7/1/990.

71 Robinson to the Hudson's Bay Company, 15 December 1949, Fur Conservation, 1938-64, Correspondence Files, HBCA, RG 7/1/987.

72 Hatter to Denmark, 1 February 1949, and Denmark to Hatter, n.d., Fur Conservation, 1938-64, Correspondence Files, HBCA, RG 7/1/987.

73 Ashbrook to Denmark, 29 September 1950, Fur Conservation, 1938-64, Correspondence Files, HBCA, RG 7/1/987; and Errington to Denmark, 3 January 1951, Fur Conservation, 1938-64, Correspondence Files, HBCA, RG 7/1/988.

74 Denmark, "James Bay Beaver Conservation," 40.

75 Lovat Dickson, *Wilderness Man: The Strange Story of Grey Owl* (Toronto: Macmillan, 1973), 203.

76 Ibid., 242.

77 Ibid.; and Jane Billinghurst, *Grey Owl: The Many Faces of Archie Belaney* (Vancouver: Greystone Books, 1999), 100.

78 Dickson, *Wilderness Man,* 242.

79 Ibid., 268.

80 Cited in Donald B. Smith, *From the Land of the Shadows: The Making of Grey Owl* (Saskatoon: Western Producer Prairie Books, 1990), 211.

81 Cited in ibid., 205.

82 Grey Owl, "King of the Beaver People," *Canadian Forest and Outdoors,* January 1931, 14.

83 Grey Owl, "Re-builder of the Wilderness, Part 2," *Canadian Forest and Outdoors,* September 1932, 337.

84 "Grey Owl Speaks His Mind," *Canadian Forest and Outdoors,* September 1936, 269-70.

85 Cited in Lovat Dickson, *The Green Leaf: A Tribute to Grey Owl* (London: Lovat Dickson, 1938), 84. Also see Billinghurst, *Grey Owl,* 100.

86 Cited in Dickson, *Wilderness Man,* 211 and 54.

87 Grey Owl, *Tales of an Empty Cabin* (London: Lovat Dickson, 1936), viii-ix.

88 Grey Owl, "Re-builder of the Wilderness, Part 1," *Canadian Forest and Outdoors,* August 1932, 289.

89 Billinghurst, *Grey Owl,* 154.

90 Smith, *From the Land of the Shadows,* 184.

91 Grey Owl, "Re-builder of the Wilderness, Part 1," *Canadian Forest and Outdoors,* August 1932, 291.

92 Grey Owl, "My Beavers," *Canadian Magazine,* January 1935, 27.

93 Grey Owl, "Re-builder of the Wilderness, Part 1," 289; and Grey Owl, "Who Will Repay?" *Canadian Forest and Outdoors,* March 1931, 121.

94 Grey Owl, "We Keep the Faith," *Canadian Magazine,* February 1935, 12.

95 Grey Owl, "Re-builder of the Wilderness, Part 1," 289-90.

96 Grey Owl, "King of the Beaver People," 15.

97 Shepard Krech III, *The Ecological Indian: Myth and History* (New York: W.W. Norton and Company, 1999), 15-28.

98 Dickson, *Wilderness Man,* 181 and 168-69.

99 Cited in Smith, *From the Land of the Shadows,* 120.

100 Grey Owl, "Who Will Repay?" 120.

101 "Grey Owl Speaks His Mind," 270.

102 Dickson, *Wilderness Man,* 241.

103 Cited in ibid., 233.

104 Ibid., 5; and Smith, *From the Land of the Shadows,* 124.

105 Cited in Billinghurst, *Grey Owl,* 126.

106 On the increasingly rocky relationship between the HBC and the province of Quebec over preserves, see Brief History of Beaver Preserves and Fur Marketing Arrangements in the Province of Quebec, November 1952, Northern Stores Department – Fur Preserves, HBCA, RG 2/8/541. That document also notes that the Quebec preserves were for beaver and were located at Grand Lac-Victoria (1948), Mistassini (1948), Bersimis (1951), Roberval (1951), and Manowan (1951).

107 Hugh R. Conn, "Federal Aid in Fur-Resources Management in Canada," in *Transactions of the Sixteenth North American Wildlife Conference,* ed. E.M. Quee (Washington, DC: Wildlife Management Institute, 1951), 438.

108 Ibid., 437.

109 Ian McTaggart-Cowan "Wildlife Conservation in Canada," *Journal of*

Wildlife Management 19 (1955): 171. The provincial–Indian Affairs preserves were as follows. Quebec: Nottaway (1938), Peribonca (1940), Old Factory (1941), and Abitibi (1942). Ontario: Albany (n.d.) and Kesagami (1946). Manitoba: Summerberry Game Preserve (1936) and the Dominion-Manitoba Joint Muskrat Rehabilitation Project (1938). Saskatchewan: Carrot River (1938), Porcupine Mountain (n.d.), and St. Walberg (n.d.). See Brief History of Beaver Preserves and Fur Marketing Arrangements in the Province of Quebec, November 1952, Northern Stores Department – Fur Preserves, HBCA, RG 2/8/541; Fur Conservation Projects, n.d., Correspondence Files, Northern Stores Department – Fur Preserves, January 1933-November 1946, HBCA, RG 2/8/540; D.E. Denmark, "James Bay Beaver Conservation," *Beaver,* September 1948, 41.

110 The information in this and the following paragraph is taken from Conn, "Federal Aid," 439-41.

111 Ibid., 441.

112 Ibid., 440 and 439.

CHAPTER 5: BUFFALO BURGERS AND REINDEER STEAK

1 Minister of Indian Affairs and National Resources News Release, 16 January 1962, Library and Archives Canada (LAC), RG 84, vol. 482, file E. 299, vol. 9, Slaughter of Animals (1961-64), cited in Graham A. MacDonald, *Science and History at Elk Island: Work in a Canadian National Park: 1906-1994.* Microfiche Report Series, 525 (Ottawa: Canadian Heritage Parks Canada, 1994), 40.

2 On the subject generally, see LAC, RG 84, Canadian Parks Service, Series A-2-a, vol. 2140, file U299, Universal – Slaughter of Parks Animals.

3 MacDonald, *Science and History,* 38.

4 C.B. Blyth and R.J. Hudson, *A Plan for the Management of Vegetation and Ungulates: Elk Island National Park* (Ottawa: Environment Canada, Parks, 1987), 194.

5 Lorne Lapp, interview by S. Dolan, cited in Diane Payment and Patrick Carroll, *Hay Camp: A Social and Land Use History – Part One: A Social History* (Winnipeg: Parks Canada Western Canada Service Centre, 2001), 40.

6 On the iconic status of the bison, see Valerius Geist, *Buffalo Nation: History and Legends of the North American Bison* (Saskatoon: Fifth House, 1996).

7 Geoffrey Wall, "Recreational Lands," *The Historical Atlas of Canada,* vol. 3 (Toronto: University of Toronto Press, 1990), plate 36.

8 David A. Munro, "Legislative and Administrative Limitations to Wildlife Management," in *Resources for Tomorrow: Conference Background Papers,* vol. 2 (Ottawa: Department of Northern Affairs and National Resources, July 1961), 869-70.

9 J. Alexander Burnett, *A Passion for Wildlife: The History of the Canadian Wildlife Service* (Vancouver: UBC Press, 2003), 22.

10 Ibid.

11 V.E.F. Solman, "Wildlife Research and the Role of the Canadian Wildlife Service," in *Wildlife Management Papers Delivered at the Twenty-First to Twenty-Fourth Federal-Provincial Wildlife Conferences* (Ottawa: National Parks Branch, Department of Northern Affairs and National Resources, 1961), 81.

12 Donald Dodds, *Challenge and Response: A History of Wildlife and Wildlife Management in Nova Scotia* (Halifax: Department of Natural Resources, 1993), 62, 64. On scientific personnel involved in wildlife management in the Atlantic provinces, see Harrison F. Lewis, "Wildlife as a Recreational Resource," in *Resources for Tomorrow*, 857-66. Ian McTaggart-Cowan lists the biological staff employed by provincial conservation authorities in "Wildlife Conservation in Canada," *Journal of Wildlife Management* 19, 2 (1955): 165.

13 Harrison F. Lewis, "Lively: A History of the Canadian Wildlife Service" (unpublished manuscript, 1975, Canadian Wildlife Service Archives, file number CWSC 2018), 266, cited in Burnett, *Passion for Wildlife*, 24.

14 Burnett, *Passion for Wildlife*, 24.

15 Ian McTaggart-Cowan, "A Review of Wildlife Research in Canada," in *Resources for Tomorrow*, 893.

16 Stuart S. Peters, "Newfoundland Game Management," in *Wildlife Management Papers Delivered at the Twenty-First to Twenty-Fourth Federal-Provincial Wildlife Conferences*, 35-44.

17 Jean Dugay, "Wildlife Management in Quebec," in ibid., 54-55; E.S. Huestis, "The Pheasants of Alberta," in ibid., 32.

18 Dodds, *Challenge and Response*, 61.

19 J.R. Dymond, "The Organization of Wildlife and Fisheries Research in Canada," in *Resources for Tomorrow*, 903.

20 Burnett, *Passion for Wildlife*, 25.

21 Robert J. Burns with Mike Schnitz, *Guardians of the Wild: A History of the Warden Service of Canada's National Parks* (Calgary: University of Calgary Press, 2000), 202.

22 Ibid., 204.

23 W.J.K. Harkness, "Training Programme for Fish and Wildlife Personnel in Ontario," in *Wildlife Management Papers Delivered at the Twenty-First to Twenty-Fourth Federal-Provincial Wildlife Conferences*, 25. Also see W.W. Mair, "Elements of a Wildlife Policy," in *Resources for Tomorrow*, 934.

24 Harkness, "Training Programme," 27.

25 Ibid., 28.

26 Ibid., 29.

27 These developments are covered in the following overviews of the history of the Canadian North: Kenneth Coates, *Canada's Colonies: A History of the Yukon and Northwest Territories* (Toronto: James Lorimer, 1985), especially chs. 6 and 7; William R. Morrison, *True North: The Yukon and Northwest Territories* (Toronto: Oxford University Press, 1998), especially chs. 8 and 9; Morris Zaslow, *The Northward Expansion of Canada, 1914-1967* (Toronto: McClelland and Stewart, 1988), chs. 11 and 12.

28 John G. Diefenbaker, "A New Vision," a speech given at the Civic Auditorium, Winnipeg, 12 February 1958, http://northernblue.ca/canchan/cantext/speech2/1958dfnv.html.

29 Denis Smith, *Rogue Tory: The Life and Legend of John G. Diefenbaker* (Toronto: Macfarlane, Walter, and Ross, 1995), 279.

30 John G. Diefenbaker, "A Northern Vision," a speech given at the Civic Auditorium, Winnipeg, Manitoba, 12 February 1958, http://www.canadahistory.com/sections/documents/diefenbaker_-_the_northern_vision.htm.

31 Zaslow, *Northward Expansion,* 312-14, 334-35.

32 Caribou are particularly important in Inuit and Aboriginal cultures. See George W. Calef, *Caribou and the Barren-Lands* (Ottawa: Canadian Arctic Resources Committee, 1981); H. John Russell, *The Nature of Caribou: Spirit of the North* (Vancouver: Greystone, 1998); Erin Sherry and Vuntut Gwitchin First Nation, *The Land Still Speaks: Gwitchin Words about Life in Dempster Country* (Old Crow: Vuntut Gwitchin First Nation, 1999), ch. 5; and Natasha Thorpe, Naikak Hankongak, and Sandra Eyegetok, *Thunder on the Tundra Inuit Qaujimajatuqangit of the Bathurst Caribou* (Ikaluktuuthak, NUN: Tuktu and Nogak Project, 2001).

33 Cited in John P. Kelsall, *The Migratory Barren-Ground Caribou of Canada* (Ottawa: Queen's Printer, 1968), 143.

34 Ibid., 17.

35 Gerald T. Conaty with Lloyd Binder, *The Reindeer Herders of the Mackenzie Delta* (Toronto: Key Porter Books in Association with the Glenbow Museum, 2003), 8.

36 Dodds, *Challenge and Response,* 54.

37 C.S. MacKinnon, "A History of the Thelon Game Sanctuary," *Musk-Ox* 32 (1983): 44-61.

38 They did, however, seem to have a positive effect on the musk-ox. See William Barr, *Back from the Brink: The Road to Musk-Ox Conservation in the Northwest Territories* (Calgary: Arctic Institute of North America of the University of Calgary, 1991), 45-48.

39 Kelsall, *Migratory Barren-Ground Caribou,* 290.

40 Elisa J. Hart, *Reindeer Days Remembered* (Inuvik: Inuvialuit Cultural Resource Centre, 2001), 16.

41 George W. Scotter, "Reindeer Ranching in Canada," *Journal of Range Management* 25, 3 (1972): 170. The reserve was expanded to eighteen thousand square miles in 1952.

42 Kelsall, *Migratory Barren-Ground Caribou,* 291. On "sociological" reasons for the failure of the Canadian reindeer experiment, see M. Lantis, "Problems of Human Ecology in the North American Arctic," *Arctic* 7 (1954): 307-20.

43 Scotter, "Reindeer Ranching," 173.

44 A.W.F. Banfield, "The Caribou Crisis," *Beaver,* Spring 1956, 4.

45 Ibid., 5.

46 Kelsall, *Migratory Barren-Ground Caribou,* 148-50.

47 Resumé of the First Caribou Conservation Meeting, at Saskatoon, 13 October 1955, LAC, RG 10, vol. 8573, file 1/1-2-2-10, pt. 1.
48 Ibid.
49 Caribou Slaughter – Duck Lake, Manitoba Game Branch Officer's Report, 26 September 1955, cited in Kelsall, *Migratory Barren-Ground Caribou,* 219.
50 Kelsall, *Migratory Barren-Ground Caribou,* 219.
51 Ibid., 259.
52 Ibid., 289.
53 Ibid., 228.
54 Office of the·Commissioner, NWT, Circular, Ottawa, 1 November 1950, LAC, RG 109, vol. 440, file WLU 300-37, pt. 1.
55 Resumé of the First Caribou Conservation Meeting, at Saskatoon, 13 October 1955, LAC, RG 10, vol. 8573, file 1/1-2-2-10, pt. 1.
56 Minutes of the First Meeting of the Administrative Caribou Conservation Committee, 4 June 1956, LAC, RG 10, vol. 8573, file 1/1-2-2-10, pt. 1. Indian Affairs offered to purchase surplus .303 rifles from the Canadian Army and distribute them to their wards if the provincial game branches would supply confiscated .303s to Metis. Indian Affairs also said it would talk to the Hudson's Bay Company about keeping the costs of ammunition for these rifles to a minimum to encourage their use. Also see Jones to Battle and Regan, 21 August 1956, LAC, RG 10, vol. 8573, file 1/1-2-2-10, pt. 1.
57 Kelsall, *Migratory Barren-Ground Caribou,* 203.
58 See, for instance, "Organized Caribou Hunts," a report of the Superintendent of the Yellowknife Agency, 23 January [1956], LAC, RG 10, vol. 8573, file 1/1-2-2-10, pt. 1.
59 Kelsall, *Migratory Barren-Ground Caribou,* 203.
60 Excerpt from a letter to Deputy Minister Northern Affairs and National Resources from Northern Administration Branch, n.d. [1960], LAC, RG 10, vol. 8574, file 1/1-2-2-10, pt. 5. Kelsall estimated that 30 to 60 percent of the caribou kill went to feeding dogs. See Kelsall, *Migratory Barren-Ground Caribou,* 223.
61 Ibid., 224; Bell to Regan, 2 September 1958, and Warden to Superintendents – Meadow Lake and Carlton Agencies, 10 September 1958, LAC, RG 10, vol. 8573, file 1/1-2-2-10, pt. 3.
62 Kelsall, *Migratory Barren-Ground Caribou,* 203.
63 Annual Meeting Technical Committee Caribou Preservation, 6 December 1960, LAC, RG 10, vol. 8574, file 1/1-2-2-10, pt. 5.
64 "The Current Barren-Ground Caribou Situation," n.d., in *Sessional Paper No. 7, 1961 (First Session),* LAC, RG 10, vol. 8574, file 1/1-2-2-10, pt. 5; and Minutes of the Annual Meeting of the Technical Committee for Caribou Preservation, Edmonton, 1-2 December 1960, LAC, RG 10, vol. 8574, file 1/1-2-2-10, pt. 5. Finding someone to sit on the Administrative Committee was not easy. While Manitoba's regional supervisor of Indian Affairs, J.G. McGilp, managed to identify a potential candidate

who possessed "the qualifications of living in the caribou range and speaking English," he informed his superiors that it would be no simple or inexpensive task to get him to Saskatoon, where the committee was meeting. He would first have to find Pierre Toussaint, who was probably out on the land, and then convince him to leave his family for two or three weeks. Provided that he agreed, Indian Affairs would have to pay for a chartered flight from Fond du Lac to Fort Smith and back, at a cost of no less than $1,000. The costs would not end once Toussaint was in Fort Smith, for "we would have to outfit [him] in city clothes and pay his expenses until his return here. (Conservative estimate $300)." Under the circumstances, McGilp did not think he could fulfill the committee's request. McGilp to Indian Affairs Branch, 16 November 1961, LAC, RG 10, vol. 8574, file 1/1-2-2-10, pt. 5.

65 Leslie to Indian Affairs Branch, 8 September 1961, LAC, RG 10, vol. 8574, file 1/1-2-2-10, pt. 5.

66 Kelsall, *Migratory Barren-Ground Caribou,* 148-50.

67 Ibid., 203.

68 McGilp to Battle, 29 April 1959, LAC, RG 10, vol. 8573, file 1/1-2-2-10, pt. 3.

69 Kelsall, *Migratory Barren-Ground Caribou,* 203.

70 Ibid., emphasis added.

71 Virginia Petch, "The Relocation of the Sayisi Dene of Tadoule Lake," in *For Seven Generations: The Information Legacy of the Royal Commission on Aboriginal Peoples* (Ottawa: Libraxus, 1997), 16-20, suggests that the Sayisi Dene might have been moved to conserve the barren ground caribou. Also see Ila Bussidor and Üstün Bilgen-Reinart, *Night Spirits: The Story of the Relocation of the Sayisi Dene* (Winnipeg: University of Manitoba Press, 1997).

72 Discussion and comments during the Technical Barren Ground Caribou Committee Meeting, held in Winnipeg, 13-14 November 1959, LAC, RG 10, vol. 8574, file 1/1-2-2-10, pt. 4.

73 Kelsall, *Migratory Barren-Ground Caribou,* 288.

74 Jones to Warden, 22 September 1958, LAC, RG 10, vol. 8573, file 1/1-2-2-10, pt. 3.

75 McTaggart-Cowan, "A Review of Wildlife Research in Canada," 891-92.

76 Resumé of the First Caribou Conservation Meeting, at Saskatoon, 13 October 1955, LAC, RG 10, vol. 8573, file 1/1-2-2-10, pt. 1.

77 Kelsall, *Migratory Barren-Ground Caribou,* 281.

78 Ibid., 281; in general, see 279-81.

79 Scotter, "Reindeer Ranching in Canada," 172-73.

80 Kelsall, *Migratory Barren-Ground Caribou,* 280.

81 Blyth and Hudson, *Plan for the Management,* 187.

82 Janet Foster, *Working for Wildlife: The Beginning of Preservation in Canada* (Toronto: University of Toronto Press, 1978), 66-72 and 104-16; John Sandlos, "Where the Scientists Roam: Ecology, Management and Bison in Northern Canada," *Journal of Canadian Studies* 37, 2 (2002): 98-106.

83 Hume to Soper, n.d., LAC, RG 85, vol. 1200, file 400-15-1/1, cited in Barry Potyondi, *Dual Allegiance: The History of Wood Buffalo National Park, 1929-1965* (Ottawa: Parks Canada, 1981), 14.
84 Blyth and Hudson, *Plan for the Management,* 183-85.
85 Sandlos, "Where the Scientists Roam," 111.
86 W.A. Fuller, "The Biology and Management of the Bison of Wood Buffalo National Park" (PhD dissertation, University of Wisconsin, 1957), 4-5.
87 Ibid., 56.
88 Ibid., 59.
89 Potyondi, *Dual Allegiance,* 322.
90 David Hems, *Hay Camp: A Social and Land Use History – Part Two: Cultural Resource Assessment: An Archaeological Inventory* (Winnipeg: Parks Canada Western Canada Service Centre, 2001), 108-9.
91 Figures derived from Patricia A. McCormack, "The Political Economy of Bison Management in Wood Buffalo National Park," *Arctic* 45, 4 (1992): 372.
92 "Buffalo Slaughter, 1952," LAC, RG 85, vol. 320, file 472-3/9, cited in Potyondi, *Dual Allegiance,* 123.
93 Payment and Carroll, *Hay Camp,* 41.
94 Ibid.
95 Payment and Carroll, *Hay Camp,* 42; and Hems, *Hay Camp,* 110-11.
96 Memorandum for the Director, 18 November 1954, LAC, RG 85, vol. 1255, file 472-1/1, cited in Potyondi, *Dual Allegiance,* 132; Appendix A: Outline of Future Operating Procedures in Connection with the Slaughtering of Buffalo in Wood Buffalo Park, 22 August 1951, LAC, RG 85, vol. 157, file 472-3 [3], cited in Payment and Carroll, *Hay Camp,* 40n139; Payment and Carroll, *Hay Camp,* 41.
97 Payment and Carroll, *Hay Camp,* 40-41.
98 Potyondi, *Dual Allegiance,* 125. For a government price list of different cuts of bison meat, see LAC, RG 85, vol. 320, file 472-3/9.
99 McCormack, "Political Economy," 372.
100 "Promotion Plans for Sweetgrass Buffalo," 7 November 1961, LAC, RG 22, vol. 467, file 32-2-9A, cited in Potyondi, *Dual Allegiance,* 173.
101 Appendix A: Outline of Future Operating Procedures in Connection with the Slaughtering of Buffalo in Wood Buffalo Park, 22 August 1951, LAC RG 85, vol. 157, file 472-3 [3], cited in Payment and Carroll, *Hay Camp,* 40, and 40n139.
102 Lloyd Brooks to R.T. Flanagan, 9 May 1968, LAC, RG 84, vol. 1011, file E. 42, "Farming Operations – General," cited in MacDonald, *Science and History,* 38.
103 Donald Worster, *Nature's Economy: A History of Ecological Ideas,* 2nd ed. (New York: Cambridge University Press, 1994), 291-315.
104 Ibid., 304-11.
105 Ibid., 313.
106 Ibid., 312.
107 Christian C. Young makes the point that though the idea of carrying

capacity was developed by resource managers in the 1920s and '30s, it did not become a part of ecological science until the 1950s. See his "Defining the Range: The Development of Carrying Capacity in Management Practice," *Journal of the History of Biology* 31 (1998): 61-83.

108 R.Y. Edwards and C. David Fowle, "The Concept of Carrying Capacity," *Twentieth North American Wildlife Conference,* ed. J.B. Trefethen (Washington, DC: Wildlife Management Institute, 1955), 589-602.

109 Robert Paehlke, ed., *Conservation and Environmentalism: An Encyclopedia* (New York: Garland Publishing, 1995), 110-11.

110 W. Dasmann, "A Method for Estimating the Carrying Capacity of Range Lands," *Journal of Forestry* 43 (1945): 401-2, cited in Edwards and Fowle, "Concept of Carrying Capacity," 591.

111 Edwards and Fowle, "Concept of Carrying Capacity," 591.

112 Aldo Leopold, *Game Management* (1933; repr., Madison: University of Wisconsin Press, 1986), xxxii.

113 Ibid., 20.

114 Ibid., 46.

115 Ibid., 339.

116 For an examination of this in the context of industrial agriculture, see William Boyd, "Making Meat: Science, Technology, and American Poultry Production," *Technology and Culture* 42, 4 (2001): 631-64.

117 Potyondi, *Dual Allegiance,* 122 and 126.

118 Cited in Potyondi, *Dual Allegiance,* 122.

119 Sandlos, "Where the Scientists Roam," 112.

120 B.E. Olson to C.L. Merrill, 28 October 1962, LAC, RG 84, vol. 2239, file WB299, cited in Sandlos, "Where the Scientists Roam," 112.

121 Blyth and Hudson, *Plan for the Management,* 198.

122 Ibid., 196-98.

123 Ibid., 198.

124 Ibid., 200-1.

125 McCormack, "Political Economy," 372.

CHAPTER 6: PREDATORS AND POSTWAR CONSERVATION

1 "Values for varmints" from Donald Worster, *Nature's Economy: A History of Ecological Ideas,* 2nd ed. (New York: Cambridge University Press, 1994), 258.

2 Thomas R. Dunlap, *Saving America's Wildlife* (Princeton, NJ: Princeton University Press, 1988), ch. 4.

3 Ibid.

4 Christian C. Young, *In the Absence of Predators: Conservation and Controversy on the Kaibab Plateau* (Lincoln: University of Nebraska Press, 2002).

5 Manly F. Miner, "Predator Control," *Fish, Fur and Game,* October 1951, Jack Miner Papers, Archives of Ontario (AO), MU 7678.

6 Ibid.

7 Aldo Leopold, "Thinking Like a Mountain," in *A Sand County Almanac,*

with *Essays on Conservation from Round River* (1949; repr., New York: Ballantine Books, 1970), 138.

8   Roderick Nash, "Aldo Leopold's Intellectual Heritage," in *Companion to "A Sand County Almanac": Interpretive and Critical Essays,* ed. J. Baird Callicott (Madison: University of Wisconsin Press, 1987), 77.

9   Ibid., 78-79.

10 Susan L. Flader, *Thinking Like a Mountain: Aldo Leopold and the Evolution of an Ecological Attitude toward Deer, Wolves, and Forests* (Columbia: University of Missouri Press, 1974), 24; and Nash, "Aldo Leopold's Intellectual Heritage," 78.

11 Aldo Leopold, *Game Management* (1933; repr., Madison: University of Wisconsin Press, 1986), xxxi, emphasis in original.

12 Ibid., 21.

13 Ibid., 3.

14 Leopold, *Sand County Almanac,* 246.

15 Ibid., xviii.

16 Ibid., 246.

17 Ibid., 239.

18 Thomas R. Dunlap, "Wildlife, Science, and the National Parks, 1920-1940," *Pacific Historical Review* 59, 2 (1990): 188.

19 Ibid., 192 and 197.

20 Cited in Robert J. Burns with Mike Schnitz, *Guardians of the Wild: A History of the Warden Service in Canada's National Parks* (Calgary: University of Calgary Press, 2000), 88.

21 Cited in Thomas R. Dunlap, "Ecology, Nature, and Canadian National Park Policy: Wolves, Elk, and Bison as a Case Study," in *To See Ourselves/ To Save Ourselves: Ecology and Culture in Canada,* ed. Rowland Lorimer, Michael M'Gonigle, Jean-Pierre Revéret, and Sally Ross (Montreal: Association for Canadian Studies, 1991), 142.

22 Stevens to Chief, Department of Northern Affairs and National Resources, 3 May 1965, Library and Archives Canada (LAC), RG 109, vol. 30, file WLT 200-7.

23 For instance, even after the wolf population in the Northwest Territories had been significantly reduced and caribou numbers stabilized, the Technical Committee for Caribou Preservation recommended that the kill continue because of its scientific value. "Because the biological study of wolves is yielding important information," it noted, "wolf control operations should be continued on a scale which will provide specimens for study." See Minutes of the Administrative Committee for Caribou Preservation, Saskatoon, Saskatchewan, 1 December 1961, LAC, RG 10, vol. 8574, file 1/1-2-2-10, pt. 6.

24 For instance, in 1955 two Inuit men, David Chocolate and Charlie Apple, from Fort Rae, came upon a large chunk of meat sitting on a frozen lake. They had never heard of the poisoning program and could not read the warning signs that had been posted, so took the meat, intending to eat it themselves. Fortunately for them, they fed some to their six sled dogs first.

All died almost immediately. When Chocolate and Apple got back to their settlement, they reported the incident and learned that the meat was wolf bait. Their demands for compensation were met with threats of arrest for theft. See Joe Sangris, Jimmie Bearlake, Suzi Abel, Michael Sikeye, Paul Drybone (Chiefs and Subchiefs of the Yellowknife and Rae Indians) to CWS, 29 December 1955, LAC, RG 109, vol. 29, file WLT 200, pt. 2.

25 Burns with Schnitz, *Guardians of the Wild,* 205.
26 Ibid., 200.
27 Douglas H. Pimlott, "Wolf Control in Canada," *Canadian Audubon,* November-December 1961, 147.
28 Karen Jones, *Wolf Mountains: A History of Wolves along the Great Divide* (Calgary: University of Calgary Press, 2002), 135.
29 Ibid.
30 Barry Lopez, *Of Wolves and Men* (New York: Scribner's, 1978), 195.
31 John P. Kelsall, *The Migratory Barren-Ground Caribou of Canada* (Ottawa: Queen's Printer, 1968), 254-55.
32 See, for instance, D'Astous to Chief, Economic Development Division, 24 April 1964, LAC, RG 10, vol. 8574, file 1/1-2-2-10, pt. 8.
33 Kelsall says the toll was 11,000, Lopez 17,500. See Kelsall, *Migratory Barren-Ground Caribou,* 259; and Lopez, *Of Wolves and Men,* 194. Kelsall cites C.H.D. Clarke's 1940 population estimate of 36,000 wolves, but notes that this is a "generous" figure. Thus, the 1950s wolf kill might have resulted in an even greater decline. See Kelsall, *Migratory Barren-Ground Caribou,* 251.
34 Cited in Eric Cameron, "Is the Timber Wolf a Gangster?" *Forest and Outdoors,* August 1951, 22.
35 E. Kuyt, *Food Habits and Ecology of Wolves on Barren-Ground Caribou Range in the Northwest Territories* (Ottawa: Information Canada, 1972), 8.
36 Stevens to Chief, Department of Northern Affairs and National Resources, 15 April 1965, LAC, RG 109, vol. 30, file WLT 200-7.
37 Kelsall, *Migratory Barren-Ground Caribou,* 259.
38 Kelsall to McKay, 23 October 1967, LAC, RG 109, vol. 30, file WLT 200-8.
39 Kelsall, *Migratory Barren-Ground Caribou,* 254.
40 Pimlott, "Wolf Control in Canada," 150.
41 D'Astous to Chief, Economic Development Division, 24 April 1964, LAC, RG 10, vol. 8574, file 1/1-2-2-10, pt. 8.
42 Pimlott, "Wolf Control in Canada," 150.
43 Burns with Schnitz, *Guardians of the Wild,* 89.
44 Cited in ibid., 93.
45 Burns with Schnitz, *Guardians of the Wild,* 94.
46 Cited in MacEachern, "Rationality and Rationalization," 200; and cited in Jones, *Wolf Mountains,* 167.
47 Cited in MacEachern, "Rationality and Rationalization," 203.
48 Ibid.
49 Cited in Burns with Schnitz, *Guardians of the Wild,* 97.

50 Cited in MacEachern, "Rationality and Rationalization," 210n37.

51 Cited in ibid., 203.

52 Loughery to Lewis, 24 January 1952, LAC, RG 109, vol. 29, file WLT 200, pt. 1.

53 Pimlott, "Wolf Control in Canada," 146.

54 D.N. Omand, "The Bounty System in Ontario," *Journal of Wildlife Management* 14, 4 (1950): 426.

55 Anton Swanson, "They Kill for Joy," *Canadian Forest and Outdoors,* November 1963, 18.

56 I.P. Callison, "Blood-Thirsty Trail," *Canadian Forest and Outdoors,* November 1953, 6.

57 Lopez, *Of Wolves and Men,* section 3.

58 Ian McTaggart-Cowan, "Predation," in Province of British Columbia Game Department, *Report of Proceedings, Game Convention, 1947* (Victoria: King's Printer, 1947), 43.

59 Cited in ibid.

60 James Hatter, "A Summarized Interim Report on a Study of the Moose of Central British Columbia, 1946," in British Columbia Legislative Assembly, *Sessional Papers, 1946* (Victoria: King's Printer, 1946), DD 48.

61 Cited in Cameron, "Is the Timber Wolf a Gangster?" 23.

62 W.E. Stevens, "Caribou Program," 15 June 1964, LAC, RG 10, vol. 8574, file 1/1-2-2-10, pt. 8.

63 Omand, "Bounty System," 434.

64 Kelsall, *Migratory Barren-Ground Caribou,* 242.

65 Cited in ibid., 243.

66 Ibid.

67 Kerry Wood, "Again We're Crying Wolf!" *Canadian Forest and Outdoors,* August 1949, 28. Also see A.J. Mitchener, "Let's Leave the Wolf Alone," *Canadian Forest and Outdoors,* November 1953, 18.

68 Tony Lascelles, "Why Exterminate the Cougar?" *Forest and Outdoors,* August 1937, 245.

69 Pimlott, "Wolf Control in Canada," 146 and 148.

70 Omand, "Bounty System," 433.

71 Burton to Wright, 11 August 1952, LAC, RG 109, vol. 29, file WLT 200, pt. 1.

72 Lopez, *Of Wolves and Men,* 186.

73 Richard Mackie, "Cougars, Colonists, and the Rural Settlement of Vancouver Island," in *Beyond City Limits: Rural History in British Columbia,* ed. R.W. Sandwell (Vancouver: UBC Press, 1999), 125.

74 Gwen Cash, *I Like British Columbia* (Toronto: Macmillan, 1938), 127. Cougar hunters were the subject of naturalist Roderick Haig-Brown's first novel, which discussed the exploits of a Vancouver Island cougar and the man and dogs who hunted it. See *Panther* (London: William Collins and Sons, 1946).

75 Del Hall, *Island Gold: A History of Cougar Hunting on Vancouver Island* (Victoria: Cougar Press, 1990), 7.

76 Mackie, "Cougars," 126.

77 Ibid., 125.

78 Hall, *Island Gold,* 8.

79 Manly Miner, "Manly Miner Says 'We Must Control the Timber Wolf,'" *Forest and Outdoors,* November 1949, 25.

80 Manly F. Miner, "Jack Miner, His Philosophy, His Reasoning" (1968), 28, Jack Miner Papers, AO, MU 7678.

81 "Report of the Provincial Game Commission, 1947," in British Columbia Legislative Assembly, *Sessional Papers, 1947* (Victoria: King's Printer, 1947), L 9-10.

82 Province of British Columbia, Game Department, *Report of Proceedings: Game Convention, 1947* (Victoria: King's Printer, 1947), 153.

83 Ibid., L 10.

84 "Report of the Provincial Game Commission, 1950," in British Columbia Legislative Assembly, *Sessional Papers, 1950* (Victoria: King's Printer, 1950), T 38.

85 Ibid., T 39.

86 John B. Theberge, "Wolf Management in Canada through a Decade of Change," *Nature Canada* 2, 1 (January-March 1973): 9.

87 Ibid., 9.

88 Theberge, "Wolf Management," 6; also see Pimlott, "Wolf Control in Canada," 149.

89 Farley Mowat, *Never Cry Wolf* (Toronto: McClelland and Stewart, 1973), vi.

90 Ibid., 76-77.

91 Ibid., 62, 65.

92 William French, "To the Rescue of the Wolf," *The Globe and Mail Magazine,* 9 November 1963, 17.

93 R.M. Saunders, "Nature," *Queen's Quarterly,* Summer 1964, 439-40.

94 W.A Fuller, "It Is Fiction from End to End," *Edmonton Journal,* 21 January 1964, 23; and Douglas H. Pimlott, typescript review of *Never Cry Wolf* for the *Toronto Telegram,* 18 January [1964], Canadian Wildlife Service, LAC, RG 109, vol. 30, file WLT 200-7.

95 Douglas H. Pimlott, "Review of *Never Cry Wolf,*" *Canadian Audubon,* January-February 1964, 27.

96 A.W.F. Banfield, "Review of *Never Cry Wolf,*" *Canadian Field-Naturalist* 78, 1 (1964): 52-53.

97 Adolph Murie, *The Wolves of Mount McKinley* (Washington, DC: US Government Printing Office, 1944).

98 Banfield, "Review of *Never Cry Wolf,*" 54.

99 Ibid., 53; also see Pimlott's *Canadian Audubon* review.

100 Cited in Karen Jones, "*Never Cry Wolf:* Science, Sentiment, and the Literary Rehabilitation of *Canis lupus,*" *Canadian Historical Review* 84, 1 (2003): 77.

101 Banfield, "Review of *Never Cry Wolf,*" 54.

102 Eaton McKay, "Biologists, Get off Those Pedestals!" *Edmonton Journal,* 14 January 1964, 19.

103 Jenney to CWS, 6 April 1967, LAC, RG 109, vol. 384, file WLU 200, pt. 3.

104 Munro to Bacher, 10 December 1965, LAC, RG 109, vol. 30, file WLT 200-7.

105 [Shawn to the CWS], n.d., but stamped "received" 26 November 1969, RG 109, vol. 384, file WLU 200, pt. 4.

106 Weaver to the Jack Miner Migratory Bird Foundation, 3 April 1969, LAC, RG 109, vol. 384, file WLU 200, pt. 4.

107 Memo from David A. Munro, Director, Canadian Wildlife Service, Department of Indian Affairs and Northern Development, 15 December 1967, LAC, RG 84, A-2-a, vol. 2134, file U266, pt. 4.

108 James Raffan, *Fire in the Bones: Bill Mason and the Canadian Canoeing Tradition* (Toronto: Harper Collins, 1996), 161-63.

109 Ibid., 173.

110 Ibid., 287-88.

111 Ibid., 184. In his 1996 book, Raffan noted it was *the* most successful feature-length documentary to date.

112 Mason to Eagles, 22 November 1967, LAC, RG 84, A-2-a, vol. 2134, file U266, pt. 4.

113 Cited in Raffan, *Fire in the Bones,* 188.

114 Ibid.

115 Ibid.

116 *Cry of the Wild* (Ottawa: National Film Board of Canada in Cooperation with the Canadian Wildlife Service, 1972).

117 Ibid.

118 Ibid.

119 This is the line with which Mowat ended his book; it concludes his report of a poisoning campaign that had targeted the Wolf House Bay pack. Mowat, *Never Cry Wolf,* 176.

120 *Cry of the Wild,* emphasis added.

121 Mowat, *Never Cry Wolf,* 175.

122 Leopold, *Game Management,* 19.

CHAPTER 7: FROM WILDLIFE TO WILD PLACES

1 J. Alexander Burnett, *A Passion for Wildlife: The History of the Canadian Wildlife Service* (Vancouver: UBC Press, 2003), 149-61.

2 http://www.ducks.ca/aboutduc/progress/index.html.

3 Cited in S. Kip Farrington Jr., *The Ducks Came Back: The Story of Ducks Unlimited* (New York: Coward-McCann, 1945), 13-14.

4 More Game Birds in America, A Foundation, *More Waterfowl by Assisting Nature* (New York: More Game Birds in America, A Foundation, 1931), 10-11, emphasis in original.

5 W.G. Leitch, *Ducks and Men: 40 Years of Cooperation in Conservation* (Winnipeg: Ducks Unlimited Canada, 1978), 13-14.

6 More Game Birds in America, *More Waterfowl,* 12-19.

7 Ibid., 18-19.

8 Leitch, *Ducks and Men,* 16.

9 Compiled from ibid., 18. The breakdown was as follows: Alberta 16.4

million; Saskatchewan 12 million; Manitoba 7.5 million; portion of the Mackenzie District 4.6 million; North Dakota 1.2 million; South Dakota 350,000; and Minnesota 650,000.

10 More Game Birds in America, *More Waterfowl,* 19.

11 On Richardson and Ross, see *The Canadian Who's Who, 1939* (Toronto: Trans-Canada Press, 1940), 570 and 588; on Leigh Spencer, see *The Canadian Who's Who, 1948* (Toronto: Trans-Canada Press, 1949), 547.

12 "The Founders are appalled at the economic waste which has resulted from the depletion of one of our greatest natural resources," they wrote. "They believe that by applying sound business methods to this problem ... that a substantial and permanent increase in game birds in this country can be obtained." More Game Birds in America, *More Waterfowl,* 107.

13 Leitch, *Ducks and Men,* 141.

14 Ibid., 39.

15 For a list of DUC's projects, see Farrington, *Ducks Came Back,* 26-27.

16 Leitch, *Ducks and Men,* 42.

17 Ibid., 110-11 and 141.

18 Farrington, *Ducks Came Back,* 33-35.

19 Leitch, *Ducks and Men,* 100-1.

20 "Jake the Drake and Mary the Mallard," cited in Farrington, *Ducks Came Back,* 36-37.

21 Leitch, *Ducks and Men,* 23.

22 Speeches by E.B. Pitblado (Chairman), John C. Hutchinson, and Judge W.G. Ross at the Annual Banquet of the Manitoba Fish and Game Association, 25 March 1937, cited in Leitch, *Ducks and Men,* 220.

23 Ibid., 43. The plaintiffs lost.

24 Ibid., 143.

25 Ibid., 51.

26 Ibid., 52.

27 Ibid., 57-58.

28 Russell to Klassen, 25 March 1974, Andy Russell Fonds, Whyte Museum of the Canadian Rockies, M153, file 208.

29 The phrase is Richard Rajala's, coined to describe the west coast forests. See his "The Forest as Factory: Technological Change and Worker Control in the West Coast Logging Industry, 1880-1930," *Labour/Le Travail* 32 (1993): 73-104.

30 More Game Birds in America, *More Waterfowl,* 10.

31 T.A. (Tommy) Walker, *Spatsizi* (Surrey, BC: Hunaga Publishing, 1976), 19.

32 Ibid., 21.

33 Ibid., 67 and 69.

34 The latter included "men like Elisha Gray, President of the largest washing machine manufacturing company in the United States, Ross Siragusa, President of the Admiral Corporation, Spence Olin of Olin Industries, an industrial empire in itself." Form letter from Philip Connors and Tommy Walker to prospective donors, 10 November 1956, T.A. (Tommy) Walker Papers, British Columbia Archives (BCA), MS-2784, box 23, file 6.

35 Walker, *Spatsizi,* 55.

36 Ibid., 58.

37 Diary entry, 15 September 1968, T.A. (Tommy) Walker Papers, BCA, MS-2784, box 3, file 3.

38 Walker, *Spatsizi,* 52.

39 Ibid., 53.

40 Ibid., 66.

41 Tommy Walker Annual Letter, 1957, T.A. (Tommy) Walker Papers, BCA, MS-2784, box 9, file 5.

42 Form letter from Philip Connors and Tommy Walker to prospective donors, 10 November 1956, T.A. (Tommy) Walker Papers, BCA, MS-2784, box 23, file 6.

43 Walker, *Spatsizi,* 226.

44 "Big Plan Foreseen to Develop North," *Vancouver Sun,* 15 February 1957, 1. Also see "Is BC Fanfare for Wenner-Gren Another False Alarm?" *Maclean's Magazine,* 13 April 1957, 17.

45 British Thomson-Houston Export Company, *Report on the Feasibility of Building Dams on the Peace River* (London: Wenner-Gren British Columbia Development Company, 1958), 1; "Wenner-Gren Plan Will Take 'a Life-time,'" *Vancouver Province,* 13 February 1957, 3; and "Who was the Guide?" *Vancouver Province,* 14 February 1957, 3.

46 "Huge Power Plan for Peace River," *Vancouver Sun,* 9 October 1957, 1.

47 "Vast Power Plant for BC," *Vancouver Province,* 9 October 1957, 1.

48 "Huge Power Plan for Peace River," 1. Although hydroelectricity is often advertised as clean energy because it does not burn fossil fuels, research suggests that the reservoirs created for hydro generation, particularly in tropical areas, can be significant sources of carbon dioxide and methane, the greenhouse gases that contribute to global warming. Indeed, some Canadian research indicates that, for every kilowatt-hour of electricity it generates, the Grand Rapids Dam in northern Manitoba contributes as much to global warming as does a gas-fired generator. See Patrick McCully, *Silenced Rivers: The Ecology and Politics of Large Dams* (London: Zed Books, 1996), 141-44; and World Commission on Dams, *Dams and Development: A New Framework for Decision-Making* (London: Earthscan, 2000), 75-77, and ch. 3 generally.

49 Tommy Walker Annual Letter, 1954, T.A. (Tommy) Walker Papers, BCA, MS-2784, box 9, file 5.

50 Walker, *Spatsizi,* 226.

51 Diary entry, 13 July 1957, T.A. (Tommy) Walker Papers, BCA, MS-2784, box 2, file 5.

52 Diary entry, 18 July 1957, T.A. (Tommy) Walker Papers, BCA, MS-2784, box 2, file 5.

53 Annual Letter, 1957, T.A. (Tommy) Walker Papers, BCA, MS-2784, box 9, file 5.

54 Annual Letter, 1963, T.A. (Tommy) Walker Papers, BCA, MS-2784, box 9, file 6.

55 Diary entry, 4 July 1968, T.A. (Tommy) Walker Papers, BCA, MS-2784, box 3, file 3.

56 Annual Letter, 1966, T.A. (Tommy) Walker Papers, BCA, MS-2784, box 9, file 6.
57 Walker, *Spatsizi,* 224-25 and 243.
58 Ibid., 264.
59 Ibid., 230; and Annual Letter, 1963, T.A. (Tommy) Walker Papers, BCA, MS-2784, box 9, file 6.
60 Walker, *Spatsizi,* 232.
61 Most of the material in this paragraph is drawn from *The Spatsizi: Conservation of Its Wildlife Resources* (n.d.), a pamphlet published by the Spatsizi Association for Biological Research, designed for circulation to prospective donors. T.A. (Tommy) Walker Papers, BCA, MS-2784, box 23, file 6. The pamphlet listed SABR's directors as W. Winston Mair, president, formerly director of the Canadian Wildlife Service and Parks Canada, and deputy minister of Natural Resources for Manitoba; Dr. Ian McTaggart-Cowan, vice president, dean emeritus, University of British Columbia and chancellor, University of Victoria; T.A. Walker, treasurer, former big game guide in the Spatsizi Plateau area; Dr. Richard Stace-Smith, secretary, research scientist, Agriculture Canada in Vancouver; Mr. Irving Fox, professor, School of Community and Regional Planning and Westwater Research Centre, University of British Columbia; Robert D. Harris, formerly of the Canadian Wildlife Service; Dr. Vladimir Krajina, honorary professor of botany, University of British Columbia; Dr. Barry Leach, director, Environmental Studies, Douglas College; and Dr. James Pojar, biologist, Smithers, formerly assistant coordinator, Ecological Reserve Unit, British Columbia. SABR commissioned a research plan for the park from two University of British Columbia zoologists, who in turn consulted with government biologists to set out eight projects. See G.G.E. Scudder and A.R.E. Sinclair, "A Research Plan for Spatsizi Plateau Wilderness Park and Gladys Lake Ecological Reserve," December 1976, T.A. (Tommy) Walker Papers, BCA, MS-2784, box 24, file 6.
62 Spatsizi Association for Biological Research, "Proposed Wildlife Research Program for the Spatsizi Area of British Columbia," 14 September 1979, T.A. (Tommy) Walker Papers, BCA, MS-2784, box 23, file 8.
63 Form letter from Walker to prospective supporters of preserving the Cassiar, 10 November 1956, T.A. (Tommy) Walker Papers, BCA, MS-2784, box 23, file 6.
64 Walker, *Spatsizi,* 245.
65 Ibid., 243.
66 Ibid., 245-46.
67 Ibid., 233.
68 "Grizzly Bear Is Fast Disappearing," *Winnipeg Free Press,* n.d., Andy Russell Fonds, Whyte Museum of the Canadian Rockies, M153, file 304. This file contains a number of clippings regarding Russell's career.
69 "The Life of Andy Russell – 1: Famous Waterton Guide Leads Exciting, Action-Packed Life," 1954, Whyte Museum, Andy Russell Fonds, M153, file 304; and Andy Russell, "I Work for My Bucks," *Outdoor Life,* October 1962, Andy Russell Fonds, Whyte Museum, M153, file 399.

70 Andy Russell, interview by R. Bruce Morrison, April 1988, Andy Russell Fonds, Whyte Museum, M153, file 553, 46.

71 Ibid.

72 Kevin Van Tighem, "Still Rarin' Up: Andy Russell Has Been Fighting to Save Our Wild Places and Wild Animals for More Than Half a Century," *Outdoor Canada,* Summer 2000, 15.

73 "News Release," n.d., Andy Russell Fonds, Whyte Museum, M153, file 371.

74 "Business History Outline," n.d., Andy Russell Fonds, Whyte Museum, M153, file 371.

75 Ibid.

76 Transcript of an interview with Russell conducted by Dreamland Picture Company for a docudrama that was never produced, n.d., Andy Russell Fonds, Whyte Museum, M153, file 554, 5; and Van Tighem, "Still Rarin' Up," 14.

77 http://www.castlewilderness.ca.

78 "Business History Outline," n.d., Andy Russell Fonds, Whyte Museum, M153, file 371.

79 Van Tighem, "Still Rarin' Up," 12.

80 "A Personal History," Andy Russell Fonds, Whyte Museum, M153, file 368, 1.

81 Diary entries, 29 October and 5 November 1941, Hunting Diary, 1941-42, Andy Russell Fonds, Whyte Museum, M153, file 2.

82 "Andy Russell Reminisces: 'Free as the Wind,'" *Lethbridge Herald,* 1 April 1977, Andy Russell Fonds, Whyte Museum, M153, file 306; and Andy Russell, "What of Bear Hunting?" (1974), 4, Andy Russell Fonds, Whyte Museum, M153, file 375.

83 Transcript of an interview with Russell conducted by Dreamland Picture Company for a docudrama that was never produced, n.d., Andy Russell Fonds, Whyte Muscum, M153, file 554, 4.

84 Van Tighem, "Still Rarin' Up," 15.

85 Cited in Ted Byfield, ed., *Leduc, Manning, and the Age of Prosperity* (Edmonton: United Western Communications, 2001), 23-24.

86 Eric Hanson, *Dynamic Decade* (Toronto: McClelland and Stewart, 1959).

87 Byfield, *Leduc, Manning,* 36-37, 39.

88 Matt Price and John Bennett, *America's Gas Tank: The High Cost of Canada's Oil and Gas Export Strategy* (New York: National Resources Defense Council and the Sierra Club of Canada, 2002), 14. Recently it has been linked to multiple sclerosis. Alberta has the highest incidence of MS in North America; the Turner Valley, location of its oldest sour gas field, has the highest rate in the world.

89 Van Tighem, "Still Rarin' Up," 16.

90 Andy Russell, *Bighorns for Teachers,* ch. 6, 1, Andy Russell Fonds, Whyte Museum, M153, file 432.

91 Andy Russell, "Early Recollections of Grizzly Country," 2, Andy Russell Fonds, Whyte Museum, M153, file 367.

92 Van Tighem, "Still Rarin' Up," 15.

93 Andy Russell, "A Grizzly Hunted Me," *Outdoor Life,* September 1960, 106, Andy Russell Fonds, Whyte Museum, M153, file 395.
94 Andy Russell, "Early Recollections of Grizzly Country," 2.
95 Andy Russell, "The Way of the Grizzly," *BC Outdoors,* December 1971, 21 and 20, Andy Russell Fonds, Whyte Museum, M153, file 406.
96 Andy Russell, "Why Man Needs Wilderness," *BC Outdoors,* February 1971, 35, Andy Russell Fonds, Whyte Museum, M153, file 405.
97 "News Release: Grizzly Country – A Film of Adventure and Action without Bloodshed," 1, Andy Russell Fonds, Whyte Museum, M153, file 369.
98 For instance, Russell's book was cited by scientist Stephen Herrero in an article for *Science.* See his "Human Injury Inflicted by Grizzly Bears," *Science* 170 (6 November 1970): 593-98, in Andy Russell Fonds, Whyte Museum, M153, file 231.
99 Robert Collins, "The Wild Free Life of Andy Russell," *Reader's Digest,* April 1975, 75, Andy Russell Fonds, Whyte Museum, M153, file 311.
100 "News Release: Grizzly Country – A Film of Adventure and Action without Bloodshed," 1.
101 Andy Russell, "Are Wild Animals Really Wild?" *Reader's Digest,* May 1960, 152, Andy Russell Fonds, Whyte Museum, M153, file 393.
102 Andy Russell, "Wilderness and the Environment of Man," 1, Andy Russell Fonds, Whyte Museum, M153, file 369.
103 Andy Russell, "Supplement to 'A Photographer among Bighorns,'" 3, Andy Russell Fonds, Whyte Museum, M153, file 365.
104 Ibid.
105 Andy Russell, "What Good Is Wilderness?" 6, Andy Russell Fonds, Whyte Museum, M153, file 352.
106 Russell, "Supplement to 'A Photographer among Bighorns,'" 3.
107 Andy Russell, "Andy Russell's Ecolog: What Is the Wildest Animal?" 1, Andy Russell Fonds, Whyte Museum, M153, file 504, item 12.
108 Andy Russell, "Andy Russell's Ecolog: A Way of Life," 1, Andy Russell Fonds, M153, file 504, item 14.
109 Andy Russell, "What Is Wildlife Management?" 1, Andy Russell Fonds, Whyte Museum, M153, file 232.
110 Andy Russell, "The Anti-Hunting Movement," 1, Andy Russell Fonds, Whyte Museum, M153, file 505, item 94.
111 "Andy Russell: Man to Match the Mountains," *BC Outdoors,* April 1978, 34, Andy Russell Fonds, Whyte Museum, M153, file 311.
112 Andy Russell, "Grizzly Country a Vanishing Heritage," *Nature Canada,* April-June 1975, 13, Andy Russell Fonds, Whyte Museum, M153, file 407.
113 "A Mountain Man," *Environment Views,* September 1986, 31, Andy Russell Fonds, Whyte Museum, M153, file 517.

CONCLUSION

1 James Hatter, *Politically Incorrect: The Life and Times of British Columbia's First Game Biologist* (Victoria: O and J Enterprises, 1997), 72-73.
2 Ibid., 81.
3 Ibid.
4 Cited in Alex MacGillivray, *Rachel Carson's "Silent Spring"* (Lewes: Ivy Press for Barron's, 2004), 59.
5 Hatter, *Politically Incorrect*, 82.
6 Ibid., 50-65.

SELECTED BIBLIOGRAPHY

◆

ARCHIVAL COLLECTIONS

Archives of Ontario (AO)
Jack Miner Papers, MU 7678.
James Watt Papers, F 431 (MU 1385).
Neil MacNaughtan Papers, F 4330.

British Columbia Archives (BCA)
Ball Family Papers, MS-2185.
Fish and Wildlife Records, 1922-77. GR-1027.
Provincial Game Warden Records, 1905-22. GR 446.
T.A. (Tommy) Walker Papers, MS-2784.

Canadian Museum of Nature (CMN)
Percy Taverner Papers, CMNAC/1991-021.

Hudson's Bay Company Archives (HBCA)
Correspondence between C. Sale and C.S. Elton, A.92/260/1.
Correspondence Files.
    Northern Stores Department – Fur Preserves, January 1933-November
        1946. RG 2/8/540.
    Northern Stores Department – Fur Preserves, RG 2/8/541.
Correspondence Files, RG 7/1/1009.
Fur Trade Conference Minutes, RG 2/62/2-6.
Fur Conservation, 1938-64. Correspondence Files, RG 7/1/987-990.
Manager's Reports, Annual Reports – Years Ending 31 January 1945-
    31 January 1950. RG 3/67A/1.

Library and Archives Canada (LAC)
Canadian Parks Service, RG 84.
Canadian Wildlife Service, RG 109.
Department of Indian Affairs Records, RG 10.
Northern Affairs Program, RG 85.

Nova Scotia Archives and Records Management (NSARM)
Department of Lands and Forests Fonds, 1738-1989. RG 20.
Reports of the Game and Inland Fishery Protection Society of Nova Scotia, F 90 G14
    R29.

Whyte Museum of the Canadian Rockies
Andy Russell Fonds, M153/304.

GOVERNMENT DOCUMENTS

British Columbia. Legislative Assembly. *Sessional Papers.*
Canada. Commission of Conservation. *National Conference on Conservation of Game, Fur-Bearing Animals and Other Wildlife under the Direction of the Commission of Conservation with the Cooperation of the Advisory Board on Wild Life Protection, February 18 and 19, 1919.* Ottawa: J. de Labroquerie, 1919.
–. *Report of the Annual Meeting.* Ottawa: Mortimer, 1910-19.
Canada. *Report of the Royal Commission upon the Possibilities of the Reindeer and Musk-Ox Industries in the Arctic and Sub-Arctic Regions.* Ottawa: F.A. Acland, 1922.
Manitoba. Legislative Assembly. *Sessional Papers.*
Nova Scotia. *Journals and Proceedings of the House of Assembly of the Province of Nova Scotia.*
Ontario. Legislative Assembly. *Sessional Papers.*
Saskatchewan. Legislative Assembly. *Sessional Papers.*
Statutes of Alberta, British Columbia, Manitoba, New Brunswick, Newfoundland, Northwest Territories, Nova Scotia, Ontario, Prince Edward Island, Quebec, Saskatchewan, and Yukon.

SERIALS

The Beaver
Canadian Field-Naturalist
Canadian Forest and Outdoors
Canadian Who's Who
Dictionary of Canadian Biography
Edmonton Journal
Forest and Outdoors
Maclean's Magazine
Rod and Gun in Canada
Toronto Globe and Mail
Vancouver Province
Vancouver Sun

SECONDARY SOURCES

Ainley, Marianne. "The Contribution of the Amateur to North American Ornithology." *Living Bird* 18 (1979): 161-77.
Altmeyer, George. "Three Ideas of Nature in Canada, 1893-1914." In *Consuming Canada: Readings in Environmental History,* edited by Chad Gaffield and Pam Gaffield, 98-105. Toronto: Copp Clark, 1995.
Anderson, J.W. "Beaver Sanctuary." *Beaver,* June 1937, 6-11.
–. "7000 Square Miles of Beaver Sanctuary." *Beaver,* June 1934, 16-18.
Armstrong, L.O. "How Best to Form Public Opinion as to the Need of Fish and Game Protective Laws." *Rod and Gun in Canada,* March 1905, 543-45.

–. "Boredom and One of Its Antidotes." *Rod and Gun in Canada,* October 1904, 241-43.

Atwood, Margaret. "Animal Victims." In *The Wild Animal Story,* edited by R. Lutts, 215-24. Philadelphia: Temple University Press, 1998.

Baker, Alan B. "Facts on the Balance of Nature." *Forest and Outdoors,* October 1955, 23-24.

Ball, Georgiana. "The Monopoly System of Wildlife Management of the Indians and the Hudson's Bay Company in the Early History of British Columbia." *BC Studies* 66 (1985): 37-58.

–. "History of Wildlife Management Practices in British Columbia to 1918." MA thesis, University of Victoria, 1981.

Banfield, A.W.F. "Review of *Never Cry Wolf.*" *Canadian Field-Naturalist* 78, 1 (1964): 52-54.

–. "The Caribou Crisis." *Beaver,* Spring 1956, 3-7.

Barr, William. *Back from the Brink: The Road to Musk-Ox Conservation in the Northwest Territories.* Calgary: Arctic Institute of North America of the University of Calgary, 1991.

Barrow, Mark V. Jr. *A Passion for Birds: American Ornithology after Audubon.* Princeton, NJ: Princeton University Press, 1998.

"Beaver Chief." *Beaver,* September 1944, 44.

Bederman, Gail. *Manliness and Civilization: A Cultural History of Gender and Race in the United States, 1880-1917.* Chicago: University of Chicago Press, 1995.

Billinghurst, Jane. *Grey Owl: The Many Faces of Archie Belaney.* Vancouver: Greystone Books, 1999.

"Bird Banding in Canada." *Forest and Outdoors,* April 1951, 22-24.

Bishop, Charles, and Toby Morantz, eds. "Who Owns the Beaver? Northern Algonquian Land Tenure Reconsidered." Special issue, *Anthropologica* 18, 1-2 (1986).

Blackstone, William. *Commentaries on the Laws of England.* Vol. 2. Edited by A.W.B. Simpson. Chicago: University of Chicago Press, 1979.

Blyth, C.B., and R.J. Hudson. *A Plan for the Management of Vegetation and Ungulates: Elk Island National Park.* Ottawa: Environment Canada, Parks, 1987.

Bodsworth, Fred. "Billy Sunday of the Birds." *Maclean's Magazine,* 1 May 1952.

Bordo, Jonathan. "Jack Pine – Wilderness Sublime or the Erasure of the Aboriginal Presence in the Landscape." *Journal of Canadian Studies* 27, 4 (1992): 98-128.

Boyd, William. "Making Meat: Science, Technology, and American Poultry Production." *Technology and Culture* 42, 4 (2001): 631-64.

British Columbia. *Game Commission Report for the Year 1913.* Victoria: Government Printer, 1914, N6-N7.

Bullard, Robert D. *Dumping in Dixie: Race, Class, and Environmental Quality.* Boulder, CO: Westview, 1994.

Burnett, J. Alexander. *A Passion for Wildlife: The History of the Canadian Wildlife Service.* Vancouver: UBC Press, 2003.

Burns, Robert J., with Mike Schnitz. *Guardians of the Wild: A History of the Warden Service of Canada's National Parks.* Calgary: University of Calgary Press, 2000.

Bussidor, Ila, and Üstün Bilgen-Reinart. *Night Spirits: The Story of the Relocation of the Sayisi Dene.* Winnipeg: University of Manitoba Press, 1997.

Byfield, Ted, ed. *Leduc, Manning, and the Age of Prosperity.* Edmonton: United Western Communications, 2001.

Cadigan, Sean. "Whose Fish? Science, Ecosystems and Ethics in Fisheries Management Literature since 1992." *Acadiensis* 31, 1 (2001): 171-95.

–. "The Moral Economy of the Commons: Ecology and Equity in the Newfoundland Cod Fishery, 1815-1855." *Labour/Le Travail* 43 (1999): 9-42.

Calef, George W. *Caribou and the Barren-Lands.* Ottawa: Canadian Arctic Resources Committee, 1981.

Callicott, J. Baird. *Companion to "A Sand County Almanac": Interpretive and Critical Essays.* Madison: University of Wisconsin Press, 1987.

Callison, I.P. "Blood-Thirsty Trail." *Canadian Forest and Outdoors,* November 1953, 6.

Cameron, J. Eric. "Is the Timber Wolf a Gangster?" *Forest and Outdoors,* August 1951, 22-25.

Canadian Pacific Railway. *Fishing and Shooting along the Lines of the Canadian Pacific Railway.* Montreal: Canadian Pacific Railway Company, 1904.

Cardinal, Harold. *The Unjust Society.* Edmonton: M.G. Hurtig, 1969.

Cash, Gwen. *I Like British Columbia.* Toronto: Macmillan, 1938.

Chitty, Dennis. "The Canadian Arctic Wild Life Enquiry, 1938-39." *Journal of Animal Ecology* 9 (1939): 227-42.

Choquette, Mgr. "Conservation of Our National Traditions, in Canada, Commission of Conservation." In *Report of the Seventh Annual Meeting, 1916,* 24-31. Montreal: Federated Press, 1916.

Coates, Kenneth. *Canada's Colonies: A History of the Yukon and Northwest Territories.* Toronto: James Lorimer, 1985.

Colpitts, George. *Game in the Garden: A Human History of Wildlife in Western Canada to 1940.* Vancouver: UBC Press, 2002.

–. "Conservation, Science, and Canada's Fur Farming Industry, 1913-45." *Histoire Sociale/Social History* 30, 59 (1997): 77-107.

–. "Fish and Game Associations in Southern Alberta, 1907-1928." *Alberta History* 42, 4 (1994): 16-26.

Conaty, Gerald T., with Lloyd Binder. *The Reindeer Herders of the Mackenzie Delta.* Toronto: Key Porter Books in Association with the Glenbow Museum, 2003.

Conn, Hugh R. "Federal Aid in Fur-Resources Management in Canada." *Transactions of the Sixteenth North American Wildlife Conference,* edited by E.M. Quee, 437-45. Washington, DC: Wildlife Management Institute, 1951.

Cranmer-Byng, John L. "A Life with Birds: Percy A. Taverner, Canadian Ornithologist, 1875-1947." Special issue, *Canadian Field-Naturalist* 110, 1 (1996).

Cronon, William. "The Trouble with Wilderness, or Getting Back to the Wrong Nature." In *Uncommon Ground: Rethinking the Human Place in Nature,* edited by W. Cronon, 69-90. New York: W.W. Norton, 1996.

Crowcroft, Peter. *Elton's Ecologists: A History of the Bureau of Animal Population.* Chicago: University of Chicago Press, 1991.

Denmark, Donald E. "James Bay Beaver Conservation." *Beaver,* September 1948, 38-43.

–. "Conservation at Cumberland." *Beaver,* March 1940, 47-49.

Dickson, Lovat. *Wilderness Man: The Strange Story of Grey Owl.* Toronto: Macmillan, 1973.

–. *The Green Leaf: A Tribute to Grey Owl.* London: Lovat Dickson, 1938.

Doctor, The. "The Look-em Deer Club at Play." *Rod and Gun in Canada,* January 1908, 711-17.

Dodds, Donald. *Challenge and Response: A History of Wildlife and Wildlife Management in Nova Scotia.* Halifax, NS: Department of Natural Resources, 1993.

Dorsey, Kurkpatrick. *The Dawn of Conservation Diplomacy: US-Canadian Wildlife Protection Treaties in the Progressive Era.* Seattle: University of Washington Press, 1998.

Dugay, Jean. "Wildlife Management in Quebec." In *Wildlife Management Papers Delivered at the Twenty-First to Twenty-Fourth Federal-Provincial Wildlife Conferences,* 54-57. Ottawa: National Parks Branch, Department of Northern Affairs and National Resources, 1961.

Dunlap, Thomas R. "Ecology, Nature, and Canadian National Park Policy: Wolves, Elk, and Bison as a Case Study." In *To See Ourselves/To Save Ourselves: Ecology and Culture in Canada,* edited by Rowland Lorimer, Michael M'Gonigle, Jean-Pierre Revéret, and Sally Ross, 139-49. Montreal: Association for Canadian Studies, 1991.

–. "Wildlife, Science, and the National Parks, 1920-1940." *Pacific Historical Review* 59, 2 (1990): 187-202.

–. *Saving America's Wildlife.* Princeton, NJ: Princeton University Press, 1988.

Dymond, J.R. "The Organization of Wildlife and Fisheries Research in Canada." In *Resources for Tomorrow: Conference Background Papers.* Vol. 2, 901-8. Ottawa: Department of Northern Affairs and National Resources, July 1961.

"Editorial – Bird Sanctuaries." *Canadian Field-Naturalist* 37 (1923): 149.

Edwards, R.Y., and C. David Fowle. "The Concept of Carrying Capacity." *Twentieth North American Wildlife Conference,* edited by J.B. Trefethen, 589-602. Washington, DC: Wildlife Management Institute, 1955.

E.E. "Notes by E.E." *Rod and Gun in Canada,* September 1900, 331.

Elton, Charles. *Voles, Mice and Lemmings: Problems in Population Dynamics.* Oxford: Clarendon Press, 1942.

–. *Animal Ecology.* London: Sidgwick and Jackson, 1927.

–. "Periodic Fluctuations in the Number of Animals: Their Causes and Effects." *British Journal of Experimental Biology* 2 (1924): 119-63.

Evenden, Matthew. *Fish versus Power: An Environmental History of the Fraser River.* New York: Cambridge University Press, 2004.

"Experiment at Steeprock." *Beaver,* June 1939, 10-11.

Farrington, S. Kip Jr. *The Ducks Came Back: The Story of Ducks Unlimited.* New York: Coward-McCann, 1945.

Flader, Susan L. *Thinking Like a Mountain: Aldo Leopold and the Evolution of an Ecological Attitude toward Deer, Wolves, and Forests.* Columbia: University of Missouri Press, 1974.

Foster, Janet. *Working for Wildlife: The Beginning of Preservation in Canada.* Toronto: University of Toronto Press, 1978.

Francis, Daniel, and Toby Morantz. *Partners in Furs: A History of the Fur Trade in Eastern James Bay, 1600-1870.* Montreal and Kingston: McGill-Queen's University Press, 1983.

Fuller, W.A. "The Biology and Management of the Bison of Wood Buffalo National Park." PhD diss., University of Wisconsin, 1957.

Gaffield, Chad, and Pam Gaffield, eds. *Consuming Canada: Readings in Environmental History.* Toronto: Copp Clark, 1995.

Geist, Valerius. *Buffalo Nation: History and Legends of the North American Bison.* Saskatoon: Fifth House, 1996.

Girard, Michel F. *L'écologisme retrouvé: Essor et déclin de la Commission de la conservation du Canada.* Ottawa: Les Presses de l'Université d'Ottawa, 1994.

Gottesman, Dan. "Native Hunting and the Migratory Birds Convention Act: Historical, Political, and Ideological Perspectives." *Journal of Canadian Studies* 18, 3 (1983): 67-89.

Grey Owl. *Tales of an Empty Cabin.* London: Lovat Dickson, 1936.

–. "We Keep the Faith." *Canadian Magazine,* February 1935, 12, 41.

–. "My Beavers." *Canadian Magazine,* January 1935, 14, 26-27.

–. "Re-builder of the Wilderness, Part 2." *Canadian Forest and Outdoors,* September 1932, 335-38, 349.

–. "Re-builder of the Wilderness, Part 1." *Canadian Forest and Outdoors,* August 1932, 289-92, 304.

–. "King of the Beaver People." *Canadian Forest and Outdoors,* January 1931, 13-15.

–. "Who Will Repay?" *Canadian Forest and Outdoors,* March 1931, 119-22.

"Grey Owl Speaks His Mind." *Canadian Forest and Outdoors,* September 1936, 269-70.

Guha, Ramachandra. *Environmentalism: A Global History.* New York: Longman, 2000.

–. *The Unquiet Woods: Ecological Change and Peasant Resistance in the Himalaya.* Berkeley: University of California Press, 2000.

–. "Radical American Environmentalism and Wilderness Preservation: A Third World Critique." *Environmental Ethics* 11, 1 (1989): 284-93.

–, with Madhav Gadgil. *Ecology and Equity: The Use and Abuse of Nature in Contemporary India.* London: Routledge, 1995.

Haig-Brown, Roderick. *Panther.* London: William Collins and Sons, 1946.

Hall, Dell. *Island Gold: A History of Cougar Hunting on Vancouver Island.* Victoria: Cougar Press, 1990.

Hammond, Lorne. "Marketing Wildlife: The Hudson's Bay Company and the Pacific Northwest, 1821-49." *Forest and Conservation History* 37 (1993): 14-25.

Hanson, Eric. *Dynamic Decade.* Toronto: McClelland and Stewart, 1959.

Hardin, Garret. "The Tragedy of the Commons." *Science* 162 (1968): 1243-48.

Hardy, Sir Alister. "Charles Elton's Influence in Ecology." *Journal of Animal Ecology* 37 (1968): 3-8.

Harkness, W.J.K. "Training Programme for Fish and Wildlife Personnel in Ontario." In *Wildlife Management Papers Delivered at the Twenty-First to Twenty-Fourth Federal-Provincial Wildlife Conferences,* 25-29. Ottawa: National Parks Branch, Department of Northern Affairs and National Resources, 1961.

Harris, Douglas C. *Fish, Law, and Colonialism: The Legal Capture of Salmon in British Columbia.* Toronto: University of Toronto Press, 2001.

Hart, E.J. *The Selling of Canada.* Banff: Altitude Publishing, 1983.

Hart, Elisa J. *Reindeer Days Remembered.* Inuvik: Inuvialuit Cultural Resource Centre, 2001.

Hatter, James. *Politically Incorrect: The Life and Times of British Columbia's First Game Biologist.* Victoria: O and J Enterprises, 1997.

"The Haunts of Big Game." *Rod and Gun in Canada,* October 1905, 503.

Hawley, Dr. Franklin. "Scientific Deer-Hunting." *Rod and Gun in Canada,* October 1906, 318-24.

Hay, Douglas. *Albion's Fatal Tree: Crime and Society in Eighteenth-Century England.* London: Allen Lane, 1975.

Hays, Samuel P. *Conservation and the Gospel of Efficiency: The Progressive Conservation Movement, 1890-1920.* Cambridge, MA: Harvard University Press, 1959.

Hems, David. *Hay Camp: A Social and Land Use History, Part Two – Cultural Resource Assessment: An Archaeological Inventory.* Winnipeg: Parks Canada Western Canada Service Centre, 2001.

Hewitt, C. Gordon. *The Conservation of the Wild Life of Canada.* New York: Charles Scribner's Sons, 1921.

–. "The Conservation of Wild Life in Canada in 1919: A Review." In *Report of the Ninth Annual Meeting, 1917,* edited by Canada, Commission of Conservation, 118-39. Montreal: Federated Press, 1918.

–. "The Conservation of Our Northern Mammals." Canada. Commission of Conservation. *Report of the Seventh Annual Meeting, 1916.* Montreal: Federated Press, 1917.

Hornaday, W.T. "Rational Use of Game Animals." *National Conference on Conservation of Game, Fur-Bearing Animals and Other Wild Life, 1919,* 60-68. Ottawa, 1919.

Houston, Stuart, Tim Ball, and Mary Houston. *Eighteenth-Century Naturalists of Hudson Bay.* Montreal and Kingston: McGill-Queen's University Press, 2003.

Huestis, E.S. "The Pheasants of Alberta." In *Wildlife Management Papers Delivered at the Twenty-First to Twenty-Fourth Federal-Provincial Wildlife Conferences,* 30-34. Ottawa: National Parks Branch, Department of Northern Affairs and National Resources, 1961.

"Hunting and Fishing in New Brunswick: The Attempt to Organize a Private Preserve, and the Government's Action Thereon." *Rod and Gun in Canada,* November 1906, 499-500.

Huntington, Ellsworth, ed. *Matamek Conference on Biological Cycles.* Matamek Factory, Labrador, 1932.

Ireland, Brenda. "'Working a Great Hardship on Us': First Nations People, the State, and Fur Conservation in British Columbia before 1935." MA thesis, University of British Columbia, 1995.

Isenberg, Andrew. *The Destruction of the Bison: An Environmental History.* New York: Cambridge University Press, 2000.

Jacoby, Karl. *Crimes against Nature: Squatters, Poachers, Thieves and the Hidden History of American Conservation.* Berkeley: University of California Press, 2001.

Jasen, Patricia. *Wild Things: Nature, Culture, and Tourism in Ontario, 1790-1914.* Toronto: University of Toronto Press, 1995.

Jervis, John. *Exploring the Modern: Patterns of Western Culture and Civilization.* London: Blackwell, 1998.

Johns, Johnnie, and Son. *Big Game Hunting in the Yukon.* Yukon Archives pamphlet PAM ND-0342, ca. 1960.

Johnsgard, Paul A. *Waterfowl of North America.* Bloomington and London: Indiana University Press, 1975.

Johnson, Thomas. "Nature's Elixir – And It Is Not Work." *Rod and Gun in Canada,* January 1908, 734-36.

Jones, J. Walter. *Fur Farming in Canada.* 2nd ed. Ottawa: Mortimer, 1914.

Jones, Karen. "*Never Cry Wolf:* Science, Sentiment, and the Literary Rehabilitation of *Canis lupus.*" *Canadian Historical Review* 84, 1 (2003): 65-93.

–. *Wolf Mountains: A History of Wolves along the Great Divide.* Calgary: University of Calgary Press, 2002.

Kaufmann, Eric. "'Naturalizing the Nation': The Rise of Naturalistic Nationalism in Canada and the United States." *Comparative Studies in Society and History* 40 (1998): 666-95.

Keith, Lloyd B. *Wildlife's Ten-Year Cycle.* Madison: University of Wisconsin Press, 1963.

Kelsall, John P. *The Migratory Barren-Ground Caribou of Canada.* Ottawa: Queen's Printer, 1968.

Kerr, Donald, Deryk Holdsworth, and Susan Laskin, eds. *The Historical Atlas of Canada.* Vol. 3. Toronto: University of Toronto Press, 1990.

Krech, Shepard, III. *The Ecological Indian: Myth and History.* New York: W.W. Norton, 1999.

Kuyt, E. *Food Habits and Ecology of Wolves on Barren-Ground Caribou Range in the Northwest Territories.* Ottawa: Information Canada, 1972.

Lantis, M. "Problems of Human Ecology in the North American Arctic." *Arctic* 7 (1954): 307-20.

Lascelles, Tony. "Why Exterminate the Cougar?" *Forest and Outdoors,* August 1937.

Lears, T.J. Jackson. *No Place of Grace: Antimodernism and the Transformation of American Culture, 1880-1920.* Chicago: University of Chicago Press, 1981.

Leitch, W.G. *Ducks and Men: 40 Years of Cooperation in Conservation.* Winnipeg: Ducks Unlimited Canada, 1978.

Leopold, Aldo. *A Sand County Almanac, with Essays on Conservation from Round River.* New York: Ballantine Books, 1970. First published in 1949.

–. *Game Management.* 1933. Reprint, Madison: University of Wisconsin Press, 1986.

Lewis, Harrison F. "Wildlife as a Recreational Resource." In *Resources for Tomorrow: Conference Background Papers.* Vol. 2, 857-66. Ottawa: Department of Northern Affairs and National Resources, July 1961.

Lindsay, Debra. *Science and the Subarctic: Trappers, Traders, and the Smithsonian Institution.* Washington, DC: Smithsonian Institution Press, 1993.

Linton, James M., and Calvin W. Moore. *The Story of Wild Goose Jack: The Life and Work of Jack Miner.* Toronto: CBC Enterprises, 1984.

Loo, Tina. "Making a Modern Wilderness: Conserving Wildlife in Twentieth Century Canada." *Canadian Historical Review* 82, 1 (2001): 92-121.

–. "Of Moose and Men: Hunting for Masculinities in British Columbia, 1880-1939." *Western Historical Quarterly* 32, 3 (2001): 296-319.

Lopez, Barry. *Of Wolves and Men.* New York: Scribner's, 1978.

Lothian, W.F. *A Brief History of Canada's National Parks.* Vol. 4. Ottawa: Minister of Supply and Services, 1987.

–. *A History of Canada's National Parks.* Ottawa: Minister of Supply and Services, 1981.

Lucas, Alec. "Nature Writing in English." In *The Oxford Companion to Canadian Literature,* edited by E. Benson and W. Toye, 786-92. 2nd ed. Toronto: Oxford University Press, 1997.

Lund, Thomas A. *American Wildlife Law.* Berkeley: University of California Press, 1980.

Lutts, Ralph H. *The Nature Fakers: Wildlife, Science, and Sentiment.* Golden, CO: Fulcrum, 1990.

Martin, Paul-Louis. *La chasse au Québec.* Montreal: Boréal, 1990.

McCandless, Robert G. *Yukon Wildlife: A Social History.* Edmonton: University of Alberta Press, 1985.

–. "Trophies or Meat: Yukon Game Management, 1896-1976." Report dated 7 January 1976, held by the Government of the Yukon, Department of Renewable Resources.

McClellan, Catharine. *My Old People Say: An Ethnographic Survey of Southern Yukon Territory, Part 1.* Ottawa: National Museum of Man Publications, 1975.

McCormack, Patricia A. "The Political Economy of Bison Management in Wood Buffalo National Park." *Arctic* 45, 4 (1992): 367-80.

McCully, Patrick. *Silenced Rivers: The Ecology and Politics of Large Dams.* London: Zed Books, 1996.

MacDonald, Graham A. *Science and History at Elk Island: Work in a Canadian National Park: 1906-1994.* Microfiche Report Series, 525. Ottawa: Canadian Heritage Parks Canada, 1994.

MacDonald, Robert H. "The Revolt against Instinct: The Animal Stories of Seton and Roberts." *Canadian Literature* 84 (1980): 18-29.

MacEachern, Alan. "Rationality and Rationalization in Canadian National Parks' Predator Policy." In *Consuming Canada: Readings in Environmental History,* edited by Chad Gaffield and Pam Gaffield, 197-212. Toronto: Copp Clark, 1995.

MacGillivray, Alex. *Rachel Carson's "Silent Spring."* Lewes: Ivy Press for Barron's, 2004.

McKay, Ian. *The Quest of the Folk: Antimodernism and Cultural Selection in Twentieth-Century Nova Scotia.* Montreal and Kingston: McGill-Queen's University Press, 1994.

Mackie, Richard. "Cougars, Colonists, and the Rural Settlement of Vancouver Island." In *Beyond City Limits: Rural History in British Columbia,* edited by R.W. Sandwell, 120-41. Vancouver: UBC Press, 1999.

MacKinnon, C.S. "A History of the Thelon Game Sanctuary." *Musk-Ox* 32 (1983): 44-61.

McTaggart-Cowan, Ian. "A Review of Wildlife Research in Canada." In *Resources for Tomorrow: Conference Background Papers.* Vol. 2, 889-900. Ottawa: Department of Northern Affairs and National Resources, July 1961.

—. "Wildlife Conservation in Canada." *Journal of Wildlife Management* 19, 2 (1955): 161-76.

—. "Predation." In *Report of Proceedings, Game Convention, 1947,* 43-44. Victoria: Province of British Columbia Game Department, King's Printer, 1947.

Mair, W.W. "Elements of a Wildlife Policy." In *Resources for Tomorrow: Conference Background Papers.* Vol. 2, 931-36. Ottawa: Department of Northern Affairs and National Resources, July 1961.

Martin, Paul-Louis. *La chasse au Québec.* Montreal: Boréal, 1990.

"Medicine Bag." *Rod and Gun in Canada,* January 1908, 789-99.

Medin, Douglas L., and Scott Atran, eds. *Folkbiology.* Cambridge, MA: MIT Press, 1999.

Meine, Curt, and Richard L. Knight, eds. *The Essential Aldo Leopold Quotations and Commentaries.* Madison: University of Wisconsin Press, 1999.

Mighetto, Lisa. *Wild Animals and American Environmental Ethics.* Tucson: University of Arizona Press, 1991.

Miner, Jack. *Wild Goose Jack.* Richmond Hill, ON: Simon and Schuster, 1971. First published in 1969 by the Jack Miner Migratory Bird Foundation.

—. *Jack Miner and the Birds and Some Things I Know about Nature.* Chicago: Reilly and Lee, 1925. First published in 1923 by Ryerson Press.

Miner, Manly F. "Predator Control." *Fish, Fur and Game,* October 1951.

—. "Manly Miner Says 'We Must Control the Timber Wolf.'" *Forest and Outdoors,* November 1949, 16-18, 25.

—. "We Must Provide Safety Zones and Food for Our Game Birds." *Forest and Outdoors,* October 1948, 8-9, 33.

—. "The 'Experts' Are Getting in My Hair." *Forest and Outdoors,* November 1948, 12, 30-31.

Mitchener, A.J. "Let's Leave the Wolf Alone." *Canadian Forest and Outdoors,* November 1953, 18, 23.

Morantz, Toby. *The White Man's Gonna Getcha: The Colonial Challenge to the*

Crees in Quebec. Montreal and Kingston: McGill-Queen's University Press, 2002.

More Game Birds in America, A Foundation. *More Waterfowl by Assisting Nature.* New York: More Game Birds in America, A Foundation, 1931.

Morrison, William R. *True North: The Yukon and Northwest Territories.* Toronto: Oxford University Press, 1998.

Mowat, Farley. *Never Cry Wolf.* Toronto: McClelland and Stewart, 1963.

Munro, David A. "Legislative and Administrative Limitations to Wildlife Management." In *Resources for Tomorrow: Conference Background Papers.* Vol. 2, 867-80. Ottawa: Department of Northern Affairs and National Resources, July 1961.

Munsche, P.B. *Gentlemen and Poachers: The English Game Laws, 1671-1831.* Cambridge: Cambridge University Press, 1981.

Nash, Roderick. "Aldo Leopold's Intellectual Heritage." In *Companion to "A Sand County Almanac": Interpretive and Critical Essays,* edited by J. Baird Callicott, 63-88. Madison: University of Wisconsin Press, 1987.

–. *Wilderness and the American Mind.* 4th ed. New Haven: Yale University Press, 2001.

Newell, Dianne. *Tangled Webs of History: Indians and the Law in Canada's Pacific Coast Fisheries.* Toronto: University of Toronto Press, 1993.

Omand, D.N. "The Bounty System in Ontario." *Journal of Wildlife Management* 14, 4 (1950): 425-34.

Paehlke, Robert, ed. *Conservation and Environmentalism: An Encyclopedia.* New York: Garland Publishing, 1995.

Parenteau, Bill. "Angling, Hunting and the Development of Tourism in Late Nineteenth Century Canada: A Glimpse at the Documentary Record." *Archivist 117* (1998): 10-19.

–. "Care, Control, and Supervision: Native People in the Canadian Atlantic Salmon Fishery, 1867-1900." *Canadian Historical Review* 79, 1 (1998): 1-35.

Parker, Mike. *Guides of the North Woods: Hunting and Fishing Tales from Nova Scotia, 1860-1960.* Halifax: Nimbus Publishing, 1990.

Payment, Diane, and Patrick Carroll. *Hay Camp: A Social and Land Use History – Part One: A Social History.* Winnipeg: Parks Canada Western Canada Service Centre, 2001.

Petch, Virginia. "The Relocation of the Sayisi Dene of Tadoule Lake." In *For Seven Generations: The Information Legacy of the Royal Commission on Aboriginal Peoples.* Ottawa: Libraxus, 1997.

Peters, Stuart S. "Newfoundland Game Management." In *Wildlife Management Papers Delivered at the Twenty-First to Twenty-Fourth Federal-Provincial Wildlife Conferences,* 35-44. Ottawa: National Parks Branch, Department of Northern Affairs and National Resources, 1961.

Phelps, A.L. "In the Woods." *Rod and Gun in Canada,* February 1905, 492.

Pimlott, Douglas H. "Review of *Never Cry Wolf.*" *Canadian Audubon,* January-February 1964.

–. "Wolf Control in Canada." *Canadian Audubon,* November-December 1961.

–. "Newfoundland Moose." *Transactions of the North American Wildlife Con-*

ference 18, edited by J.B. Trefethen, 563-81. Washington, DC: Wildlife Management Institute, 1953.

Playfair, W.E. "The 'Simple Life' on the Rideau." *Rod and Gun in Canada,* September 1905, 402-4.

Polk, James. "Lives of the Hunted." *Canadian Literature* 53 (1972): 51-59.

Potyondi, Barry. *Dual Allegiance: The History of Wood Buffalo National Park, 1929-1965.* Ottawa: Parks Canada, 1981.

Pratt, Mary Louise. *Imperial Eyes: Travel Writing and Transculturation.* London: Routledge, 1992.

Price, Matt, and John Bennett. *America's Gas Tank: The High Cost of Canada's Oil and Gas Export Strategy.* New York: National Resources Defense Council and the Sierra Club of Canada, 2002.

Prospectus of the Triton Fish and Game Club. Quebec, 1894. McLennan Library Rare Book Division, McGill University.

Raffan, James. *Fire in the Bones: Bill Mason and the Canadian Canoeing Tradition.* Toronto: Harper Collins, 1996.

Rajala, Richard. "The Forest as Factory: Technological Change and Worker Control in the West Coast Logging Industry, 1880-1930." *Labour/Le Travail* 32 (1993): 73-104.

Rankin, Norman S. "Jack Miner, Philosopher and Bird-Lover." *Canadian Magazine,* October 1922.

Ray, Arthur J. *The Canadian Fur Trade in the Industrial Age.* Toronto: University of Toronto Press, 1995.

–. "Some Conservation Schemes of the Hudson's Bay Company, 1821-50: An Examination of the Problems of Resource Management in the Fur Trade." *Journal of Historical Geography* 1, 1 (1975): 49-68.

Reiger, John. *American Sportsmen and the Origins of Conservation.* New York: Winchester, 1975.

Ribordy, François-Xavier. "Histoire sociologique du droit de la chasse et de la pêche en Ontario." *Anthropologica* [Canada] 30, 2 (1988): 155-73.

R.O.M. "Review of *Jack Miner and the Birds.*" *Canadian Field-Naturalist* 38 (1924): 59-60.

Rotundo, E. Anthony. *American Manhood: Transformations in Masculinity from the Revolution to the Modern Era.* New York: Basic Books, 1993.

Russell, Andy. *Grizzly Country.* New York: Knopf, 1967.

Russell, H. John. *The Nature of Caribou: Spirit of the North.* Vancouver: Greystone, 1998.

The Saguenay Club, Fifth Season 1915. Quebec, 1915. McLennan Library Rare Book Division, McGill University.

Samson, Daniel, ed. *Contested Countryside: Rural Workers and Modern Society in Atlantic Canada, 1800-1950.* Fredericton, NB: Acadiensis Press for the Gorsebrook Institute for Atlantic Canadian Studies, 1994.

Sandlos, John. "Where the Scientists Roam: Ecology, Management and Bison in Northern Canada." *Journal of Canadian Studies* 37, 2 (2002): 93-129.

–. "From the Outside Looking In: Aesthetics, Politics, and Wildlife Conservation in the Canadian North." *Environmental History* 6, 1 (2001): 6-31.

Saunders, R.M. "Nature." *Queen's Quarterly,* Summer 1964, 439-40.

Schorger, A.W. *The Passenger Pigeon: Its Natural History and Extinction.* Norman: University of Oklahoma Press, 1973.

Scotter, George W. "Reindeer Ranching in Canada." *Journal of Range Management* 25, 3 (1972): 167-73.

Sellers, Richard West. *Preserving Nature in the National Parks: A History.* New Haven: Yale University Press, 1977.

Sherry, Erin, and Vuntut Gwitchin First Nation. *The Land Still Speaks: Gwitchin Words about Life in Dempster Country.* Old Crow: Vuntut Gwitchin First Nation, 1999.

Smith, Denis. *Rogue Tory: The Life and Legend of John G. Diefenbaker.* Toronto: Macfarlane, Walter, and Ross, 1995.

Smith, Donald B. *From the Land of the Shadows: The Making of Grey Owl.* Saskatoon: Western Producer Prairie Books, 1990.

Solman, V.E.F. "Wildlife Research and the Role of the Canadian Wildlife Service." In *Wildlife Management Papers Delivered at the Twenty-First to Twenty-Fourth Federal-Provincial Wildlife Conferences,* 77-83. Ottawa: National Parks Branch, Department of Northern Affairs and National Resources, 1961.

Spence, Mark David. *Dispossessing the Wilderness: Indian Removal and the Making of the National Parks.* New York: Oxford University Press, 1999.

Swanson, Anton. "They Kill for Joy." *Canadian Forest and Outdoors,* November 1963, 6, 18.

Swinton, Allan. "Business." *Maclean's Magazine,* 14 April 1928, 3-6, 51-54, 57-58.

Taylor, C.J. "Legislating Nature: The National Parks Act of 1930." In *To See Ourselves/To Save Ourselves: Ecology and Culture in Canada,* edited by Rowland Lorimer, Michael M'Gonigle, Jean-Pierre Revéret, and Sally Ross, 125-38. Montreal: Association for Canadian Studies, 1991.

Theberge, John B. "Wolf Management in Canada through a Decade of Change." *Nature Canada* 2, 1 (January-March 1973).

Thoms, J. Michael. "A Place Called Pennask: Fly Fishing and Colonialism at a British Columbia Lake." *BC Studies,* no. 133 (2002): 69-98.

Thorpe, Natasha, Naikak Hankongak, and Sandra Eyegetok. *Thunder on the Tundra Inuit Qaujimajatuqangit of the Bathurst Caribou.* Ikaluktuuthak, NUN: Tuktu and Nogak Project, 2001.

Tighem, Kevin Van. "Still Rarin' Up: Andy Russell Has Been Fighting to Save Our Wild Places and Wild Animals for More Than Half a Century." *Outdoor Canada,* Summer 2000, 12-17, 72, 74.

Tinsley, Edward. "Spring Shooting." *Rod and Gun in Canada,* November 1906, 460.

Tober, James A. *Who Owns Wildlife? The Political Economy of Conservation in Nineteenth-Century America.* Westport, CT: Greenwood Press, 1981.

Tough, Frank. "Conservation and the Indian: Clifford Sifton's Commission of Conservation, 1910-1919." *Native Studies Review* 8, 1 (1992): 61-73.

Townsend-Gault, Charlotte. "The Salvation Art of Yuxweluptun." In *Lawrence Paul Yuxweluptun: Born to Live and Die on Your Colonialist Reservations,* edited by Lawrence Paul Yuxweluptun, 7-19. Vancouver: Morris and Helen Belkin Art Gallery, 1995.

Unwin, Peter. "The Man Who Would Have Dominion." *Beaver,* October-November 2001, 28-35.

Wade, Margaret. "'No Man Starts Living Until He Starts Believing.'" *Forest and Outdoors,* April 1949, 10-12.

–. "Jack Miner's Philosophy." *Forest and Outdoors,* April 1948, 18-21.

Wahnipitae. "A Woman on the Mississauga." *Rod and Gun in Canada,* October 1904, 217-28.

Walker, T.A. (Tommy). *Spatsizi.* Surrey, BC: Hunaga Publishing, 1976.

Wamsley, Kevin. "'Good Clean Sport and a Deer Apiece': Game Legislation and State Formation in Nineteenth-Century Canada." *Canadian Journal of the History of Sport* 25, 2 (1994): 1-20.

Warren, Louis S. *The Hunter's Game: Poachers and Conservationists in Twentieth-Century America.* New Haven, CT: Yale University Press, 1997.

White, Richard. *The Organic Machine: The Remaking of the Columbia River.* New York: Hill and Wang, 1995.

Wood, Kerry. "Again We're Crying Wolf!" *Canadian Forest and Outdoors,* August 1949, 13, 28.

World Commission on Dams. *Dams and Development: A New Framework for Decision-Making.* London: Earthscan, 2000.

Worster, Donald. *Nature's Economy: A History of Ecological Ideas.* 2nd ed. New York: Cambridge University Press, 1994.

Young, Christian C. *In the Absence of Predators: Conservation and Controversy on the Kaibab Plateau.* Lincoln: University of Nebraska Press, 2002.

–. "Defining the Range: The Development of Carrying Capacity in Management Practice." *Journal of the History of Biology* 31 (1998): 61-83.

Zaslow, Morris. *The Northward Expansion of Canada, 1914-1967.* Toronto: McClelland and Stewart, 1988.

INDEX

Note: Page numbers in **bold** type refer to illustrations.

abattoirs, 141
Aboriginal peoples: absence of, from
    national narratives, 2; and barren
    ground caribou management, 129-30,
    134-37; commercial activities of,
    restrictions on, 47; conservation
    practices of, 49; criticism of, 44-45;
    displacement of, by parks and preserves,
    48; environmental beliefs and practices
    of, 5; federal responsibility toward,
    23-24, 117-19; as guides, 55-58, **56**;
    HBC and, 95-98, 102-11, **107, 109**;
    involvement of in government conser-
    vation efforts, 135, 241n64; licensing
    exemptions for, 23-24; penalties given,
    for game law violations, 47; relationship
    of, to nature, 116; relocation of, 136;
    and resource depletion, 95; and wage
    labour, 135-36; Walker and, 195; wild-
    life cycles and, 102; wildlife regulations
    and, xvi, 23-24, 40, 44-50; wolf control
    and, 161
Achow, George, 47
Adams, Charles C., 157
Adams, John, 52
Adams, Noah, 43
Adamson, Joy, xix
Administrative and Technical Barren
    Ground Caribou Preservation Com-
    mittees, 132, 134, 137, 160-61
Advisory Board on Wild Life Protection,
    18, 221n19
agricultural model of conservation, 121,
    139, 147. *See also* production model of
    conservation
Agricultural Rehabilitation and Develop-
    ment Act (ARDA) (1962), 183
Ainley, Marianne, 90
aircraft, 103, **182**, 198
airplanes, 103
Alberta, 46, 124, 202-3
Alberta Fish and Game League, 191
Alcan, 196

Algonquin Park, 176
American Bird Banding Association, 88
American Fur Company, 98
Amory, Copley, 102
Anderson, J.W., 103-5
Anderson, R.M., 221n19
Angeline (wolf), xviii, 174, 179, 213
animal ecology, 19
Animal Ecology (Elton), 19
animals, Aboriginal beliefs about, 58. *See
    also* wildlife
anthropocentrism, 83, 91, 114
anthropomorphism, 114
anti-modernism, 29-35; Grey Owl and,
    111-17; hunting and, 33; and idealiza-
    tion of rural life, 54-55; Progressivism
    vs, 29, 34, 35; promotion of, 34; and
    therapeutic value of wildlife, 29-32,
    34-35; Walker and, 193-201
appreciation of wildlife, 27-29
Aristotle, 66
arms manufacturers, 34
Armstrong, L.O., 227n52
Arthur, "Cougar" Annie Rae, 167-68
Asians, 41
Atwood, Margaret, 2-3
Auk (journal), 90
Auston, A.R. "Shorty," 56
authenticity, 30-31

Bacher, Mrs. F.J. Jr., 175
Baden-Powell, Robert Stephenson Smyth,
    34
balance of nature, 84, 144, 154, 169
Balcomb, Creighton, 60
Ball, Tim, 100
Banff Crag and Canyon (newspaper), 163
Banff National Park, xx, 159
Banfield, A.W.F., 125, 132-34, 137, 159-60,
    175
barren ground caribou management,
    128-38; carrying capacity and, 146; eco-
    nomic perspective on, 137-38; predator

21-22, 36-37, 50-54, 172; fish and
game associations' influence on, 21; in
medieval England, 13; predator control
in, 152-53
local knowledge: bounty system and, 169;
fur conservation and, 119-20; government conservation practices vs, 50-54;
and HBC conservation strategy, 105-11;
of predators, 152-53, 163-64; transformation of, 54-62
Lockwood, J.D., 53
logging, and wildlife regulations, 43
Lomen Reindeer Company, 130
Lopez, Barry, 160
Louisiana Lakes, 190
Luxton, Norman, 45
lynx, 98

McCandless, Robert, 47
McClellan, Catharine, 58
Macdonald, John A., 127
MacEachern, Alan, xvii
McGinnis (beaver), 113
McGinty (beaver), 113
McIntosh, Alex, 53
McKay, Eaton, 175
Mackenzie, Norman, 194, 198
Mackenzie Reindeer Grazing Reserve, 130
Mackie, Richard, 167
MacLoughlin, John, 97
Macmillan, H.R., 194
McNab, Campbell, **32**
McTaggart-Cowan, Ian, 124, 163, 165, 198,
199, 252n61
magazines, 34
Main, Tom, 184-86, 186
Mair, W.W., 149, 171, 252n61
Maloney, Stephen, 44
management. See federal conservation and
management practices; game manage-
ment; local conservation and manage-
ment practices; scientific management;
wildlife management
Manitoba, 119
Manitoba Fish and Game Association, 190
Many Island Lake (AB), 187
marginalization, through conservation
laws, 41-54
Martindale, Thomas, 55
Mary the Mallard, 189
Mason, Bill, xix-xx, 9, 152, 176-81, 211, 213

Mason, Clarence, 129
Matamek Conference on Biological Cycles,
20, 102, 155
meat. See wild meat
Migratory Birds Convention Act (1916), 18,
20, 23, 45, 64, 85, 88, 126, 227n31
Miles, Robert Seaborn, 95
Miner, Jack, xvii-xviii, 63-91, 178; bird
research by, 63-64, 70-72, 75-77, 85-89,
230n36; comic strip on, **65, 67**; as
controversial, 82; early life of, 63, 68-
70; elite support of, 64; on evolution,
79-81; on extinction, 78-79; as father
of conservation movement, 64, 66;
as Father Goose, 71; as guide, 70; on
human-nature relationship, 66, 68, 72-
73, 84, 91; and hunting, 69-70, 81-82;
moral view of wildlife held by, 74-82,
84, 213; official attitude toward, 85-90,
232n106; practical approach to nature
of, 72-73; on predators, 82-85; public
image of, protection of, 87, 232n106; as
public speaker, 71-72; and religion, 68,
72, 74, 79, 81, 230n36; vision of, 66, 68
Miner, Manly, 73, 82, 84-90, 154, 169, 176,
232n106
Miner, Ted, 69, 75
mining, and wildlife regulations, 43
Ministry of Northern Affairs and National
Resources. See Department of Northern Affairs and National Resources
modernism/modernity: conservation as,
36; and environmental control, 225n87.
See also anti-modernism
Moore, Philip, 44
moose, 80, 130, 172, 205
morality: hunting restrictions and, 26-27;
nature writing and, 180-81
More Game Birds in America Foundation,
185
mountain goats, 205
Mowat, Farley, xviii-xx, 2, 9, 152, 173-76,
179-81, 210-11, 213
Muir, John, xvii
mule deer, 205
multiple sclerosis, 253n88
Murie, Adolph, 175
musk-ox, 129
muskrat: DUC and, 188; government
preserves of 1930s to '50s, 117-19; HBC
and, 94, 96-98, 108, 110-11

West Pictou Rod and Gun Club, 50-51
Western Canadian Sportsman (magazine), 34
westward expansion, effect on wildlife of, 16-17
Wetland Inventory Program, 187
wetlands, 183-92
White, James, 221n19
White, Richard, 70
white-tailed deer, 130
wild animal stories, 80-82, 174
Wild Animals at Home (Seton), xx
Wild Life Division, National Park Service (US), 157
wild meat: consumption of, 26-27, 42-47, 135, 141-43, 147-48; sale of, 25-26, 43-44, 47, 121
wild places. *See* wilderness
wilderness: accessibility of, **182**, 200; concept of, xix, xx, 12, 207; preservation movement for, 2; Russell and, 201-8; Walker and, 193-201. *See also* habitat preservation
wildlife: in Canadian literature, xix, 2-3, 180-81; concept of, xix-xx, 4, 212-13; declining populations of, 16-17, 25; demography, 97-101, 146; and ethic of existence, 180-81; human relationship to (*see* human relationship to nature); Mowat's and Mason's view of, 180-81; observation cards for, 125; pedagogical use of, 27-29; postwar pressures on, 123; research on, 124; restocking of, 22; tameness of, 206; tourist feeding, **30**; in urban areas, xi-xiii. *See also* habitat preservation; wildlife management
wildlife conservation. *See* conservation

wildlife cycles, 79, 98-102
wildlife management: emergence of, as discipline, 19; Miner on, 66; practical vs expert emphasis in, 20. *See also* conservation; game management
Williams, Bryan, 39, 41, 43, 193
Williams, Francis, 191
Wilson, Albert J., 39
Wilson Bulletin (journal), 90
Winnipeg Free Press (newspaper), 201
wise use, 19, 25, 35, 45, 211
wolfers, 167
wolf-howling nights, 176
wolves: bounty system and, 164-66; diet of, 174; eradication program for, 133-34; in film, 176-80; Mason and, xix, 176-80; Mowat and, xviii-xix, 173-76, 179-80; poisoning of, 159-61, 245n24. *See also* predators
women, in guides' meets, 60
wood buffalo, 139
Wood Buffalo National Park, 23, 48, 121, 139-41, 147-48, 158, 172
woodcraft, 55-61
Woodcraft Indians, 34
Worster, Donald, 144

XY Company, 95

yaks, **29**
Yellowknife Agency, 136
Yellowstone National Park (US), xx
Yukon, 26, 55-58
Yukon Game Ordinance (1900), 25

zoos, 28